Broadway Musical MVPs 1960–2010

Also by Peter Filichia

Broadway Musicals:
The Biggest Hit and the Biggest Flop of the Season, 1959–2009

Let's Put on a Musical

Broadway Musical MVPs 1960–2010

The Most Valuable Players of the Past Fifty Seasons

Peter Filichia

APPLAUSE
THEATRE & CINEMA BOOKS

An Imprint of Hal Leonard Corporation

Published in 2011 by Applause Theatre & Cinema Books
An Imprint of Hal Leonard Corporation
7777 West Bluemound Road
Milwaukee, WI 53213

Trade Book Division Editorial Offices
33 Plymouth St., Montclair, NJ 07042

All photos courtesy of Photofest

Printed in the United States of America
Book design by Kristina Rolander

Library of Congress Cataloging-in-Publication Data

Filichia, Peter.
Broadway musical MVPs, 1960--2010 : the most valuable players of the past 50 seasons / Peter Filichia.
p. cm.
Includes bibliographical references and index.
ISBN 978-1-61774-086-2 (pbk.)
1. Musicals--New York (State)--New York--History and criticism. 2. Musicals--New York (State)--New York--Chronology. I. Title.
ML1711.8.N3F54 2011
792.609747'1--dc23
2011028492

www.applausebooks.com

Contents

Preface

July 26, 1961. The curtain has just come down on the Wednesday matinee of *My Fair Lady.* It's the show's 2,229th record performance, but it's also my first Broadway experience.

The production is surely tired after five-plus years, but to my fifteen-year-old eyes, it's the greatest entertainment I've ever seen. There may not have been genuine stars on the stage—who are Michael Allinson and Margot Moser, anyway?—but there are certainly stars in my eyes.

Outside the Mark Hellinger Theatre, my father is waiting for me. Now we'll head to the Bronx to see most of a twilight double-header between the Yankees and the White Sox. After the long ride on the D-train, we enter the House That Ruth Built. We soon learn from our seatmates that Roger Maris, who this year is threatening Babe Ruth's record of sixty homeruns in a single season, has already thwacked two round-trippers this afternoon. Before the night is over, we'll see him hit two others, leading to the record-breaking sixty-one he'll amass that season.

It's as close to a perfect day as I'll ever experience: seeing great musical theater and great baseball. The former is a brand-new experience, while the latter is a nicely familiar one.

I'll grant you that all musical-theater fans don't share a love of baseball, and that many who follow what's happening on the diamond don't know much about what's occurring on the musical stage. But I see many commonalities between the two art forms—and not just because musicals and baseball games both have runs, hits, and errors.

True, the scores both have are very different. But both baseball and musicals require teamwork. Both have well-paid stars. Each has a season that results in the thrill of victory for some and the agony of defeat for others. Both strive for happy endings, but each finds that that's simply not always possible.

Fans find that each sells cheap seats that aren't so cheap and overpriced concessions. That's all to provide handsome salaries to its stars, drawing cards, and legends.

There's some cross-pollination, too. Major-league baseball is often nicknamed "The Big Show"—a term that could easily apply to what's currently playing at the New Amsterdam, the Majestic, or the Lunt-Fontanne.

An actor who succeeds in a role is often said to have "hit it out of the park." A baseball player who hits a home run, returns to the dugout, and then comes out to acknowledge the fans and tips his cap to them is "taking a curtain call." Better still, when that player thwacks that homer, he's often said to have hit it "right down Broadway." 'Nuff said.

Damn Yankees, Falsettos, and *Ragtime* have had baseball-themed songs. Baseball often embraces songs from musicals between innings as the teams switch from offense to defense and back again. Sometimes these songs even comment on the action. During one game I attended in Houston, as the coach for the Astros approached the mound to talk to his pitcher, the organist atypically but appropriately played "There's a Coach Comin' In" from *Paint Your Wagon.* That's a loftier choice than what usually happens these days when an opposing team's pitching coach and manager go to the mound to consult with their hurler; many a major-league and minor-league organist seizes the occasion to mockingly play "Send in the Clowns."

Finally, both art forms give out awards at the end of each season. Not the same awards, mind you. Baseball doesn't have a Best Actor, let alone—for obvious reasons—a Best Actress. But baseball does have what the Tonys, Drama Desk, and Theatre World awards don't offer: an annual Most Valuable Player award given to the single individual who made the most impact either for his team or on the season.

What if musical theater did choose an MVP? Considering that theater has taken no steps to embrace this award, I've taken the liberty of doing it. Here are my own selections—or guesses—for which individuals would have been named MVPs in the fifty-year time span between the 1960–1961 and 2009–2010 seasons.

Who was eligible? Anyone who worked on a musical that made it to Broadway—or maybe even someone behind the scenes. I was tempted to name David Edward Byrd the 1970–1971 MVP for his dynamic and unforgettable logo for *Follies.* But Stephen Sondheim deserved it more, don't you think, for the same show?

There are other baseball awards that intrigue me: Reliever of the Year, Rookie of the Year, Manager of the Year, and Comeback Player of the Year. I've sprinkled in a few of those in the seasons where I found them relevant. Manager of the Year—meaning producer—is harder to define as on through the seasons we sail, for the days of the single producer have long passed. How to glean which of the dozens that produce a single show is the most important?

I've chosen some people more than once, but never as many times as the Baseball Writers of America chose Barry Bonds as MVP (seven). Some of the people I've selected for more than one award in the same season. That's happened in baseball, too; Fred Lynn of the Boston Red Sox was both MVP and Rookie of the Year in 1975. Ditto Ichiro Suzuki of the Seattle Mariners in 2001. (That's Ichiro Suzuki—not Pat.)

True, theater almost offers a Rookie of the Year prize: the Clarence Derwent Award and the Theatre World Awards. But the former prize committee chooses one man and one woman, while the latter dispenses twelve prizes, six to each sex. I've done away with the gender distinction and have simply given one prize to the most deserving individual.

Just what is a rookie, anyway? In baseball, minor leaguers often come to their parent clubs in the major leagues a month before the season comes to an end; this practice is meant to break them in gently. The following season is almost always considered their rookie season—as long as they haven't accumulated more than forty-five at-bats in any or all previous seasons.

I did not, however, decide that an individual whose previous show exceeded forty-five performances would be disqualified. Instead, I used the standard that the Derwent and Theatre World committees use, by recognizing an individual's first significant assignment to represent his rookie season. So if, say, an actor came into *The Lion King* in the umpteenth year of its run and played a giraffe, and then the following season got a new show and a great role that brought him his first notice, he was still eligible for the Rookie of the Year honors. And considering that this is a book about musicals, we'll deem a performer's first foray into musicals his rookie experience, even if he's done a straight play (or even a gay play) or two.

Comebacks will center more on individuals who have had a stage career than those who haven't. But anyone who had been out of the public eye for some time—and wasn't necessarily expected to return—was eligible.

Relievers were culled from two different categories. First, there were the performers who took over roles from original or subsequent performers who played them. And then of course I had to recognize the classic story of the understudy who went out there a youngster and came back a star.

All clear? Then let's play ball!

Peter Filichia
March 2011

Broadway Musical MVPs 1960–2010

David Merrick In 1972, *TV Guide* conducted a poll that asked, "Which sportscaster do you hate the most?" Howard Cosell received the most votes. But for the question, "Which sportscaster do you like the most?" Howard Cosell also received the most votes. If the word *sportscaster* had been changed to *producer* and the questions were asked about Broadway from the 1950s through the 1980s, the answer to both might well have been "David Merrick."

Pearl Bailey as Dolly Broadway hadn't been good to Pearl Bailey. She'd done four musicals, and none of them could even crack the six-month mark. But a dozen years after *House of Flowers* folded, Bailey took over an ailing *Hello, Dolly!* from Betty Grable and made it the hottest ticket in town.

1960–1970

Larry Kert in *Company* In the seven decades of the Tony Awards, only once has a performer who wasn't with the show on opening night been nominated. Larry Kert, who took over for Dean Jones only a few weeks after *Company* opened, got the nomination for playing not-so-confirmed bachelor Bobby.

Molly Picon in *Milk and Honey* She was the star of Second Avenue's Yiddish theater scene in the 1920s. But in 1961, Molly Picon moved up six avenues to Eighth Avenue and Forty-fifth Street to portray an endearing but determined widow who sought a second husband, in *Milk and Honey*.

1960–1961

MVP: Tammy Grimes

The Unsinkable Molly Brown

And to think that had Tammy Grimes trusted her own instincts, she wouldn't have even auditioned for *The Unsinkable Molly Brown.*

Grimes had read the libretto that Richard Morris had written based on the life of Margaret "Molly" Tobin (1867–1932). It told of an unschooled girl from Hannibal, Missouri, who was determined to better herself, become educated, marry rich, and–perhaps most important of all—be accepted by high society.

Molly and her father decided to try their luck in gold-rich Leadville, Colorado. There Molly met Johnny Brown, a just-starting-out prospector. He was immediately smitten with her, but because he didn't have money, Molly ruled him out.

But Johnny had persistence–and that, as well as his offering to provide for her father—made Molly fall in love with him. As it turned out, Johnny did strike gold and became wildly wealthy, but he had no interest in Molly's mania for social climbing. That was a constant wedge between them, and it led to their separation. But in true musical-comedy fashion, both learned that there would be no happiness without each other—especially after Molly had a near-death experience as a passenger on the *Titanic.*

The best musicals are based on big characters and big events, and *The Unsinkable Molly Brown* had both. What's more, the show was much anticipated because the score was by Meredith Willson, his first since his triumph three years earlier with *The Music Man.* That show was so successful that it even beat *West Side Story* for the Best Musical Tony. *The Music Man* ran also almost twice as long, too.

So *The Unsinkable Molly Brown* would have seemed to be a golden opportunity. But when Grimes's agent told her to go to the Winter Garden and audition with two songs, she said, "I read the script, and I don't want to do it. This girl is too dumb."

Grimes had a point, at least in one scene. When Johnny gives Molly hundreds of thousands of dollars, she decides to store the bills in a wood-burning stove. Later during the night, Johnny lights the stove—proving that his wife was the unthinking Molly Brown.

But Grimes's agent wouldn't take no for an answer. As the actress recalls, "He grabbed me by my shoulders and said, 'Do you want to be a star or not?' I told him I did, and he said, 'Then you've got to take this part! This character is only offstage seven minutes! She sings nine songs! Anyone with a role like that has the chance to become famous.'"

At this point, Grimes had had all of seven weeks of Broadway experience: three weeks in *The Littlest Revue* (1956) and a month in Noël Coward's *Look After Lulu* (1959). She had come to acting a little late in life, for she had been a serious swimmer and came close to making the 1952 freestyle swimming Olympic team.

Now, in 1960, Grimes wasn't getting any younger. She was born in Lynn, Massachusetts, on January 30, 1934, and grew up in nearby Brookline. "But it was really in New Hampshire, at our summer place, where I think I decided I wanted to be an actress," she says. "We had this big attic full of grandmothers' and great-grandmothers' clothes, and I loved putting them on. Then I'd put on shows in the hayloft, where I'd love jumping into the hay below." That was probably good training for her 1964 role as Elvira in *High Spirits,* where she had to fly over the stage.

But first, Grimes had to go to her Molly Brown audition and meet Dore Schary, the show's co-producer and director. He was well known to the American public not only as head of production at MGM from 1948 to 1956, but also from being a prominent character in a 1955 episode of *I Love Lucy* (in which he was supposed to play himself but withdrew at the last minute).

Schary was surprised when he heard what Grimes had decided to sing: "Melancholy Baby," a song not suited to Molly, who never sits still and waits for things to happen. Grimes recalls, "He and everyone else there laughed when I told them that's what I was going to sing. They thought I was kidding." (Indeed, the song title itself has become a cliché over the decades: "Hey, play "Melancholy Baby!"")

Despite Grimes choosing the wrong song, she impressed with her distinctive sound. The word "unique" has often been devalued to simply mean "special," but Grimes's voice does deserve that adjective. It seems to be the love child of a foghorn's mating with a flute.

So Schary asked Grimes to perform another song. Here she came out with a more Molly Brown–worthy "I Got Rhythm." That prompted Schary to have her read a soliloquy. Immediately afterward, he was asking if the blond actress would mind dyeing her hair Molly-Brown red.

The two got along well during the rehearsal period. Says Grimes, "Dore gave me trust, which is what a fine director gives a performer. He never told me to do anything, but let me do what I felt was right for the character. But when I got stuck, I felt free to tell him, 'I just can't find it here.' He'd talk to me, and somehow it'd all get worked out."

But during the Philadelphia tryout, Grimes lost her voice and a bit of her confidence. As she recalls, "Everyone wanted me fired but Dore and our choreographer, Peter Gennaro."

Everyone but Schary and Gennaro were apparently wrong. Her reviews were all raves. Then came one of the Tony Awards' great ironies: Grimes wasn't placed in category of the Best Leading Actress in a Musical. Never mind that she rarely left the stage, or even that artist Tom Morrow featured her face in the logo. In that era of Tony history, billing determined the category in which a performer would be placed. Because Grimes wasn't yet an established star, she had been billed under the title. The rules stated that only those performers billed above the title would be placed in the leading-actor categories.

So Grimes was deemed one of the season's Best Featured Musical Actresses (Chita Rivera in *Bye Bye Birdie,* in another starring role, and true featured actress Nancy Dussault in *Do Re Mi* were the two others). Grimes won.

Grimes is also 1960–1961's MVP because she not only played the entire Broadway run from November 3, 1960, through February 10, 1962, but also then took the show on a national tour. "It was a complete era in my life," she says. "When we started rehearsals, my daughter Amanda was about three years old and had a problem pronouncing the title; she called it *The* Unthinkable *Molly Brown.* By the time I finished doing it three years later, Amanda could pronounce it perfectly."

"Amanda" is Amanda Plummer, born during Grimes's 1956-1960 marriage to Christopher Plummer. He, too, has won two Tony Awards (for *Cyrano* in 1974 and *Barrymore* in 1997). Because Amanda Plummer won for *Agnes of God* in 1982, the three represent the only mother–father–daughter team to have won Tonys. So Tammy Grimes is an MVP in the theatrical history books, too.

Rookie of the Year: Elizabeth Seal
Irma La Douce

Some may say, "What? Robert Goulet as Lancelot in *Camelot* wasn't the Rookie of the Year?"

To be sure, Goulet would get many deserved votes in this category. He brought to Lancelot good looks and sexual charisma (although the legendary Lancelot was said to be hideous). Goulet's crisp voice helped "If Ever I Would Leave You" become a standard.

But, as many may be surprised to hear, Robert Goulet didn't even get a Tony nomination as Best Featured Actor in a Musical.

Elizabeth Seal, on the other hand, won the Best Actress in a Musical Tony over Julie Andrews (*Camelot*), Carol Channing (*Show Girl*), and Nancy Walker (*Do Re Mi*). All three of them had been nominated once before, but newcomer Seal sent each of them to a second straight defeat.

Irma La Douce was the story of a working girl. But there was such an innocence about Irma that Seal provided. Such incendiary words as *prostitute, whore,* or even *tart* would not seem accurate; the euphemism employed for the employed Irma was "poule."

At one point in the show, Irma's so happy that she celebrates with the rollicking, piano-barreling "Dis-Donc, Dis-Donc." Here Seal gave us a hint of what a good love-maker Irma must have been. She verbally went up the entire scale with a melisma on "Dis" that lasted a full seven seconds. If she could do that to a word, imagine what she could do to a man.

Alas, it was the only appearance Seal ever made in a Broadway musical. Although Michael Bennett originally hired her to play Cassie in the original London cast of *A Chorus Line,* he found her wanting and fired her during rehearsals. Seal did return to Broadway with a small role in a short-lived revival of *The Corn Is Green,* but that was all. She may have been a one-hit wonder, but Elizabeth Seal was a wonder nonetheless.

Manager of the Year: David Merrick
Carnival, Do Re Mi, Irma La Douce, Vintage '60

We'll encounter the name David Merrick more than once, and here he is, right at the start.

The four musicals he produced this season racked up 1,651 performances. The other eleven new musicals by other producers combined totaled 2,127—only 476 performances higher.

Three of Merrick's—*Carnival, Do Re Mi,* and *Irma La Douce*—ran more than a year. The other—a revue called *Vintage '60*—couldn't last more than a week.

But that flop gave a young Fred Ebb the chance to have one of his songs heard on Broadway. Also represented by a song were William Link and Richard Levinson, who two years later had an out-of-town closer called *Prescription: Murder* about a detective named Columbo. They later sold the idea to TV.

Bonnie Scott, the first Rosemary in *How to Succeed in Business Without Really Trying,* made her Broadway debut in it. So did Michele Lee—the second Rosemary in *How to Succeed.* They both appeared in the same number, each portraying a "G.O.P. Chorus Member" and "G.O.P. Dancer."

So who knows how much these young people and others learned from getting their feet wet in a Broadway flop? Merrick was a famous megalomaniac who was certainly out for himself first and foremost, but that doesn't mean that he didn't wind up helping Broadway neophytes in the process.

1961–1962

MVP and Co-Reliever of the Year: Abe Burrows
How to Succeed in Business Without Really Trying

It started out as a play, not a musical, of Shepherd Mead's 1952 satirical instruction book *How to Succeed in Business Without Really Trying.* The playwrights were Jack Weinstock and Willie Gilbert, whose claim to fame was writing all seven episodes of the *Tom Corbett, Space Cadet* series in 1955.

No producer liked their script enough to bring it to Broadway, but Feuer and Martin, who'd had five musical hits in six tries—*Guys and Dolls* among them—thought it had musical potential. So they went to the man who had doctored their *Silk Stockings* in 1955 and, more importantly, had given *Guys and Dolls* a new book when it needed it: Abe Burrows.

"When Abe came in and rescued *Guys and Dolls* from the absolutely unworkable script that Jo Swerling had given us, not one word of what Swerling wrote remained," said Feuer hyperbolically.

Burrows, however, wasn't immediately convinced that *How to Succeed* could succeed. He'd actually read Mead's pseudo-how-to book years earlier when an agent thought it would make a good musical, too. But because Cy Feuer and Ernest Martin were offering him the chance to write and direct the show, he was interested. What's more, his recent involvement as the executive producer of the 1959 TV series *The Big Party* (which partied for all of three episodes) had him in constant contact with executive s from Revlon Cosmetics. He saw the revolving-door policy of managers who were here-today, gone-this-afternoon. That could be an important component of his *How to Succeed.*

What got Burrows to sign on was Feuer and Martin's suggestion that Robert Morse play J. Pierrepont Finch, the window washer who becomes the head of World Wide Wickets in no time at all. Burrows had cast Morse in *Say, Darling,* the comedy that he'd co-written about the making of *The Pajama Game.* Morse was ever so adorable as Ted Snow (read: Harold Prince), the young producer determined to—well, succeed.

Burrows had written for Rudy Vallee's radio show, so he's responsible for getting that crooner of yore to portray as J. B. Biggley, the lecherous president of World Wide Wickets. Far more importantly, Burrows was the one to convince Frank Loesser, his *Guys and Dolls* composer-lyricist, to do the new show. He felt that Loesser, a sharp businessman (his Frank Music Corporation was a leading publisher of Broadway music), would have an affinity for the material.

Loesser said no, but Burrows kept pushing. Still, Loesser was concerned about the lack of love story. He did envision a secretary in love with Finch and wrote a song for her to sing: "I Believe in You." Burrows, however, was the one to suggest that Finch sing it to himself—which became one of the show's highlights.

So many times, a tragedy leads to comedy. Burrows said that the CIA's unsuccessful invasion of the Bay of Pigs to overthrow Cuban leader Fidel Castro in April 1961 inadvertently helped *How to Succeed.* When he saw President Kennedy say that he was ultimately responsible, he made certain that Biggley would claim he was not remotely responsible for his company's big mistake. (And of course he was.)

Charles Nelson Reilly remembered that during the Philadelphia tryout, Burrows agonized over a word. He'd written it for Hedy LaRue, Biggley's well-kept—and well-endowed—mistress (in the old-world sense of the word). When Hedy and her glorious figure arrived for her first day on the job, all the other executives ogled her—"and the first word out of the mouth of Virginia Martin," Reilly said, citing the actress who played her, "was 'Screw.' Poor Abe put it in, then took it out, and back again. We had the screw version and the unscrew version. Finally he told her to keep it in, because it was getting an enormous laugh."

As is the case with any other director of a musical, Burrows had to be ruthless. "Bonnie Scott," said Reilly of Finch's love interest Rosemary Pilkington, "had a second-act number called 'I Worry about Him.' It stopped the show, but it wasn't good for the book, so Abe knew that he had to take it out. That's the type of thing a good director has to do."

How to Succeed won the Pulitzer Prize. Abe Burrows was the primary reason why.

Comeback Player of the Year: Molly Picon
Milk and Honey

Although she had been for decades "The Queen of Second Avenue"—referring to the home of Yiddish-speaking theater—Molly Picon (1898–1992) had made only three Broadway appearances in her first fifty years.

In 1940, she had a dramatic role in *Morning Star,* in which she played a mother whose daughter died in the notorious Triangle Shirtwaist Factory fire. Two years later, she made her musical debut in *Oy Is Dus a Leben!* (*What a Hard Life!*), in which she told her own story of rising from a bit player to a Second Avenue star. It lasted less than three months, but it still gets credit as the first Yiddish musical to move from downtown to Broadway.

After appearing in the comedy *For Heaven's Sake, Mother* for all of seven performances in 1948, Picon went back to Second Avenue, apparently for good. But once producer Gerard Oestreicher commissioned bookwriter Don Appell and composer-lyricist Jerry Herman to write a musical about Israel, Picon would soon have her second chance. "Gerard sent us to Israel to soak up the atmosphere," says Herman. "Once we saw this group of little-old-lady tourists, we knew that they had to be in our show."

Good thing for Picon that the authors wrote in six widows who came to Israel primarily to find new mates. Picon would play Clara Weiss, who wears dark sunglasses, space shoes, and a bolero hat—and is the most interested in landing a new husband. And yet another widow, the much more demure Ruth Stein (Mimi Benzell), has already met Phil Arkin. Clara is impressed. As Picon said with her trademark shrug, "She wins the sweepstakes and she didn't even buy a ticket."

Eventually Clara finds her mate. Appell originally called him Albert, but after Picon was signed, he changed his name to the more Semitic Hymie.

Picon stayed with the show for a year (and was succeeded by a most unlikely choice: Hermione Gingold). No one could say she left because she was too tuckered to continue; during her curtain calls, she would often do her trademark cartwheel. Indeed, she'd still be doing them fifteen years later when performing the title role in *Hello, Dolly!* in stock.

Co-Reliever of the Year: Jerome Robbins
A Funny Thing Happened on the Way to the Forum

Considering the sterling reputation George Abbott had as a great director of comedy and show doctor, one would think that he'd be able to see the fundamental problem that was sinking *A Funny Thing Happened on the Way to the Forum* in New Haven and Washington.

But Jerome Robbins was the director who came to Washington, saw this musical farce, and said that the opening number needed to be replaced. Both songs that Stephen Sondheim had written for this spot were gentle affairs that didn't set the table for the boisterously low comedy that would follow. Robbins told Sondheim to write a song that would inform theatergoers of exactly what they were about to see.

Sondheim returned to his Washington hotel room, used "Cakewalk Your Lady" from the 1946 flop *St. Louis Woman* as his model, and came up with one of Broadway's greatest opening numbers: "Comedy Tonight." Robbins staged it—and if anyone had any doubts that he did, it was proved in 1988, when *Jerome Robbins' Broadway*, a collection of his greatest hits, debuted—with "Comedy Tonight" in there along with his *West Side Story* and *Fiddler* dances.

Interesting, isn't it, that man who insisted on being called "Mister Abbott" should be the weak sister on this project?

Rookie of the Year: Barbra Streisand
I Can Get It for You Wholesale

How fitting that the first notes sung in *I Can Get It for You Wholesale* should be sung by the person who will always first and foremost be remembered for it.

"He's not a well man," Miss Marmelstein sang of her boss Mr. Pulvermacher, who was enduring a strike that opportunist Harry Bogen was able to settle.

She, of course, was played by Barbra Streisand, while Bogen was portrayed by Elliott Gould, also known as Mr. Barbra Streisand soon after they were married, when his career was stalled and hers was soaring.

Streisand had appeared in all of one off-Broadway show: *Another Evening with Harry Stoones,* a revue about a fictional entertainer. It opened on October 21, 1961, and closed on—yes—October 21, 1961, despite also having Diana Sands, who'd already done *A Raisin in the Sun,* and Dom DeLuise in the cast.

The closing freed up Streisand to audition, but her strange features and longer nose did not give her the looks that, as the *Saturday Evening Post* later reported, "would launch a thousand ships." When a girl isn't pretty like a Miss Atlantic City, she often turns to comedy as a sometime schlemiel, sometime schlimazel.

That was Streisand's persona in those days, and the reason she was right for the harried, pencil-in-hair, Girl Friday-Saturday-and-Sunday in *Wholesale.* Director Arthur Laurents endured that she'd been late to the audition (because, she explained, she'd been window shopping). He'd already cast Miss Marmelstein with Marilyn Cooper, whom he'd known from her small roles in his *West Side Story* and *Gypsy.* But once he saw Streisand, he knew he had to have her in the role. He offered Cooper quite a nice consolation prize: he promoted her from this small role to the show's romantic lead.

Streisand wasn't just a comic. The lady had a voice. She'd been making a few fans by appearing in *boîtes* such as the Bon Soir and the Blue Angel. Thanks to arranger Mort Lindsey (who'd become Judy Garland's conductor), Streisand delivered a completely new take on the barrelhouse rave-up "Happy Days Are Here Again." She did it slowly, as if to suggest she was the survivor of a long struggle, and that happiness came only after a long battle and a steep price. But she also conveyed the joy of emerging victorious over a formidable foe.

And yet, she was a funny girl at heart. With pinpoint comic timing, Streisand beautifully conveyed the very overworked and quite underappreciated Yetta Tessye Marmelstein. Once audiences kvelled to "Miss Marmelstein," the comic masterpiece Harold Rome had written, they dove into their *Playbills* to learn more about this young woman. How exotic she sounded from her bio, which said that she was "born in Madagascar and reared in Rangoon."

Actually, Barbra Joan Streisand was born in Brooklyn, as might have been inferred from the bio's next sentence, which admitted that she'd been graduated from Erasmus Hall High School. In the past, a few actors had played fast and loose with *Playbill* bios, but Streisand's fiction opened the floodgates for similar bios. *Theatre Arts* magazine did an article on her fictional claims and titled it "Playbull."

By the time Goddard Lieberson, the president of Columbia Records, produced the original cast album of *I Can Get It for You Wholesale,* he'd seen the show a number of times and was impressed by Streisand's comic and singing abilities. He signed her to a contract, and by the time she was slated to play Fanny Brice in *Funny Girl* in the summer of 1963, she'd already had two best-selling albums for Columbia: the generically named *The Barbra Streisand Album* and *The Second Barbra Streisand Album.*

Lieberson made his biggest mistake in his decades of shepherding original cast albums by letting rival Capitol Records have the rights to record Streisand in *Funny Girl.* There were weeks in 1964 when it was Capitol's best-selling album—even though Capitol was also releasing quite a few albums by the Beatles that year.

As for *Funny Girl,* Walter Kerr said it best in the opening line of his March 27, 1964, *Herald-Tribune* review: "Everybody knew that Barbra Streisand would be a star and she is."

Someone begged to differ: Streisand herself. As she was quoted in the soundtrack album of *Funny Girl,* "For me, being a star is being a movie star."

And so, Barbra Streisand's Broadway career, which she saw as the smallest of stepping stones to launch the rest of her far more important career, consisted of *Wholesale*'s March 21–December 8, 1962, stint to her run in *Funny Girl* from March 10 to December 26, 1965. After that total of 1,198 days, she never for an instant considered doing another Broadway show. The only time she ever again stepped on a Broadway stage was on April 19, 1970, at the Mark Hellinger Theatre to pick up her Special Tony Award as "Star of the Decade." That was worth a trip to a place she now viewed as remote as Madagascar and Rangoon.

Manager of the Year: David Merrick

Subways Are for Sleeping

A new Jule Styne–Betty Comden and Adolph Green musical? Even Frank Sinatra was impressed enough to buy the screen rights to *Subways Are for Sleeping* in advance. In August 1961, four months before it would open on

Broadway, Sinatra spent $300,000 (with a clause saying the price could balloon to $1 million), all so he and Dean Martin could star in a film version.

Why not? Styne had provided Sinatra with the music to thirty songs that ranged from hits ("Five Minutes More") to smash hits ("Three Coins in the Fountain") to novelties ("I Got a Gal I Love in North and South Dakota"). Meanwhile, Martin had already starred in film versions of two Styne musicals: *Bells Are Ringing* and *Living It Up,* the renamed and reworked *Hazel Flagg.*

If Sinatra saw the full-page ad in the *New York Herald-Tribune*'s early edition on December 28, 1961, he would have congratulated himself on his wise investment. Walter Kerr insisted that *Subways Are for Sleeping* was "a triumph." "One of the few great musical comedies of the last thirty years, one of the best of our time," Howard Taubman stated with certainty. Norman Nadel said it was "a whopping hit," while John Chapman went all out and said that "*Subways Are for Sleeping* is the best musical of the century."

Such sentiments aren't commensurate with what would turn out to be a six-month flop. But the men who gave those above-stated raves weren't Walter Kerr of the *Herald-Tribune,* Howard Taubman of the *Times,* Norman Nadel of the *World-Telegram and Sun,* or John Chapman of the *News.* They were simply four civilians that producer David Merrick had invited to see the show—men who shared the same exact names with the aisle-sitters who'd review the Comden, Green, and Styne musical at the St. James Theatre on December 27, 1961.

The notorious producer had his press agent Harvey Sabinson also find three more identically named would-be drama critics: a John McClain to ape the *Journal-American* reviewer, Richard Watts to stand in for the *Post* aisle-sitter, and Robert Coleman to mirror the *Mirror* critic. All of them would get their pictures in the paper, too, right beside the bogus quotes that they wouldn't even be troubled to write; Sabinson would provide the copy.

Merrick, then in the seventh year of his reign as Broadway's most prolific, successful—and audacious—producer, had thought of the ruse years before. But as long as Brooks Atkinson remained the *Times* critic (and he'd been on the job since 1925), Merrick couldn't put his plan into motion; Sabinson could never find anyone else with this unique name. So Merrick breathed a sigh of relief when the hardly uniquely named Howard Taubman succeeded him. (The irony is that Atkinson's first name was actually Justin. If he had chosen to use that instead of his middle name Brooks, would Merrick have been able to find a Justin Atkinson long before *Subways* began stalling?)

After Atkinson retired following the 1959–1960 semester, Merrick could have used his idea on the revue *Vintage '60,* but he knew it was too low-profile a show on which to waste it. Then he found he didn't need to use it most of on his subsequent 1960–1961 shows, because *Irma La Douce, A Taste of Honey, Becket, Do Re Mi,* and *Carnival* had all received strong notices. Even Merrick's productions of *Sunday in New York* and Terence Rattigan's *Ross* didn't fare all that poorly with the New York press. And besides, you don't use such a clever ruse on a mere low-budget play; you save it for a great big Broadway musical.

Subways, however, seemed a logical property for the scam, for the musical had not fared well during its Philadelphia and Boston tryouts. After Sabinson submitted the full-page ad, the *Times* caught on and didn't run it, but the *Herald-Tribune* was tripped up at least long enough for its first edition on December 28, 1961.

"7 out of 7 are ecstatically unanimous about *Subways Are for Sleeping.*" Not "7 out of 7 critics," mind you–simply "7 out of 7." And Merrick rates a perfect 10 for thinking of it–although Comden and Green were incensed and humiliated by the gambit. They never worked with Merrick again. Comden also felt that if *Subways* hadn't had the stigma of the ad, Sinatra and Martin might well have made the film.

1962–1963

MVP: Anthony Newley
Stop the World—I Want to Get Off

Sunday, April 28, 1963. Anthony Newley enters the Hotel Americana's Imperial Ballroom to see if he can win one, two, three, or four Tony Awards for his musical *Stop the World—I Want to Get Off.* In the seventeen-year history of the awards, no person has ever been eligible for so many different Tonys in a single season.

Not bad for a simple show about an Everyman whom Newley and his co-writer Leslie Bricusse called Littlechap. The character was born lower middle class, becomes at least semi-educated, gets his first job, marries the boss's daughter, cheats on the boss's daughter, has a couple of children, gets ahead in the world, enters politics, wins—and dies. Life's like that.

Soon after the 1962–1963 Tony ceremony begins, the prize for Best Book is announced. Newley and Bricusse get ready to stand and speak, just in case. But they must remain seated, for the winners are a different team: Burt Shevelove and Larry Gelbart for their script to *A Funny Thing Happened on the Way to the Forum.*

All right, *Forum*'s book is one of Broadway's all-time bests, so Newley and Bricusse didn't really didn't expect to win it. But there's always Best Score. Newley and Bricusse may have an edge here. In the last six months, three of *Stop the World*'s songs have become very well known thanks to recordings as well as several airings by singers on TV's many variety shows. "Once in a Lifetime" is Littlechap's rumination on his lucky stroke of fate; "Gonna Build a Mountain" is his gospel-infused celebration in which he shows his ambition; and finally, there was the biggest hit of them all, the eleven-o'clock number "What Kind of Fool Am I?" It's Littlechap's look back at his life in which he calculates the many mistakes he made.

Newley himself has had a hit single with it. He's becoming so well known that his mannered singing and plummy vowel tones are being parodied on those same TV variety shows that have been promoting his songs.

And the Best Score Tony goes to ... Lionel Bart for *Oliver!* Granted, three of Bart's songs—"As Long As He Needs Me," "Who Will Buy?" and "Where Is Love?"—have had a few recordings, too. But they can't compare to *Stop the World*'s three. Still, the rest of *Oliver*'s score is admittedly solid.

Years later, there would be questions on whether Bart composed the entire score; in 2009, composer Jack Grossman told *The Independent,* a London newspaper, that he wrote the music for "Be Back Soon" and "Boy for Sale." And the verse of "Who Will Buy?" was actually a British folk song, as is proved by its appearing in the films of *Gaslight* in 1944 and *Witness for the Prosecution* in 1957. But on this April night, Bart stops *Stop the World.*

Even before the ceremony, Newley knew he wouldn't be named Best Director of a Musical, for he wasn't even nominated. Perhaps the nominating committee didn't feel Newley had much to do as director. *Stop the World* was set on a bunch of bleachers, which meant that its performers got up, came to the lip of the stage, sang or spoke, and then returned to their seats. They apparently missed that the simple nature of the musical demanded a simple approach. That he only had to direct twelve performers besides himself might have had something to do with it, too.

Instead, the committee nominated *Funny Thing* director George Abbott, Peter Coe (*Oliver!*), Cy Feuer and Bob Fosse (*Little Me*), and—here was a surprise—John Fearnley for a revival of *Brigadoon* at City Center. The show played a two-week limited engagement at a theater that usually isn't considered a Broadway house. Compounded with the fact that Fearnley had merely restaged a revival, shouldn't Newley have gotten the nod?

To make matters less sensible, Abbott would wind up winning, although everyone on Broadway knew that he had had help from Jerome Robbins on *Forum*.

Finally, *Stop the World* wins something. But it's only a partial victory for Newley. Charles Nelson Reilly announces that the Best Featured Actress in a Musical is Anna Quayle. Certainly she benefitted from Newley and Bricusse's concept that one actress would play all four women in Littlechap's life: the British-born Evie, his wife; as well as Ginnie, his American girlfriend; Ilse, his German *freundin;* and Anya, his Russian *podruga.*

One melody served all four characters; perhaps that's why *Stop the World* doesn't win Best Score; some voters may have felt that this recycling of a melody meant lazy writing (instead of its saying that women all over the world have quite a bit in common). Nevertheless, Quayle came through with enticing and distinctive accents for each character and is now being rewarded.

Time for Best Actor in a Musical. Diahann Carroll reads the nominees and then announces Zero Mostel as the winner for *Funny Thing.* Soon after, co-hosts Abe Burrows and Robert Morse—victors last season for *How to Succeed in Business Without Really Trying*—announce the Best Musical winner. Once again, *Funny Thing* is named and *Stop the World* is not.

While the Tonys didn't recognize Anthony Newley as the 1962–1963 season's MVP, we must. How many other artists have had a hand in the writing of the book and score of a Broadway musical, then starred in and directed it, too? The immediate answer is, of course, George M. Cohan; between 1901 (with *The Governor's Son*) and 1927 (via *The Merry Malones*), he turned the trick nine times. Noël Coward took on all four jobs in 1928 for *This Year of Grace.* But the only one to make it to Broadway after that was Anthony Newley in 1962–1963. No one's done it since.

The closest *Stop the World* has had to a Broadway revival came via a touring production that played the State Theatre in Lincoln Center in August 1978. It lasted thirty performances, despite having as Littlechap Sammy Davis Jr., who'd previously had hit recordings of *Stop the World*'s three notable songs.

In 1996, Peter Scolari headed a TV version in which he was defeated by the material. Call him Littlechap of Horrors.

But both Davis and Scolari can't be totally blamed. Nineteen-sixty-two might well have been one of the last years that the musical could have succeeded, given that one of its plots involved Littlechap's disenchantment that his two children were girls. Much of the story had Littlechap loudly complaining that he had no son—a sentiment that wouldn't endear him to an audience even by the end of the 1960s.

Actually, Littlechap and Evie did have a son, but one who died soon after he was born. This sad incident comes from Newley's own life and his first marriage to actress Ann Lynn.

Still, Newley and Bricusse's title lives on as a virtual idiom. As late as 2001, Leo Bloom in the stage version of *The Producers* yelled out in frustration, "Stop the world—I want to get on!" (Never mind that *The Producers* takes place in 1959, three years before Bloom would have heard the expression.) In the 1992 film *Boris and Natasha*—about those Russian spies surnamed Badenov and Fatale—the Narrator described the action at one point as "Faster than you can say 'Stop the world—I want to get off.'" What a nice tribute to one of the film's supporting players, Anthony Newley, who played a villain named Sal Manelli.

Comeback Player of the Year: Vivien Leigh
Tovarich

In most any other season, Leigh would have been the MVP for *Tovarich* (a Russian word that means "comrade"). Without her, the musical with a score by Broadway newcomers (Lee Pockriss and Anne Croswell) wouldn't have happened.

True, its bookwriter David Shaw was one of the authors of the Tony-winning *Redhead,* but he was the last billed of the four bookwriters. Most people assumed that the heavy lifting in *Redhead* was accomplished by Herbert and Dorothy Fields, who had originated the project. (And who was *Redhead*'s other bookwriter? Sidney Sheldon. Yes, that Sidney Sheldon, who wrote *The Other Side of Midnight* and other best sellers.)

At the top of *Tovarich,* Leigh came on as Tatiana, a waif of a woman who strolled through the streets of Paris—shoplifting. She stole a baguette from a bakery, and when she saw a passerby with a bigger baguette sticking out of her grocery bag, she replaced it with her smaller one.

And why were Leigh's poised and elegant-looking fingers sticky ones? Because, as Tatiana and husband Mikail (Jean Pierre Aumont) sang in their first song, "Her Highness and Her Husband," they were once Russian royalty but became penniless émigrés thanks to the Communist Revolution that had displaced them a couple of years before. Now they were forced to seek employment, and find it courtesy of the Davises—Charles (George S. Irving) and Grace (Louise Kirtland), two wealthy Americans who were seeking a butler and a maid.

The Davises had two teenaged kids, George (Byron Mitchell) and Helen (Margery Grey), and they soon respectively fell in love with Tatiana and Mikail. That turn of events resulted in Tovarich's most celebrated dance number, "Wilkes-Barre, P.A." in which George taught Tatiana to Charleston.

The audience that had fallen in love with Leigh as Scarlett O'Hara twenty-four years earlier was even more enraptured at her working so hard to sing and dance to the peppy tune (even though she finessed much of the dancing). And despite her modest voice, Leigh did lovely work on the many very nice ballads.

Tovarich opened on March 18, 1963, at the Broadway Theatre without the prospect of an original cast album, because no record company had believed in it enough to invest. Only after Leigh won the Tony as Best Actress in a Musical did Capitol Records take a chance. By then, the better-situated Majestic Theatre was available because of *Hot Spot*'s abrupt closing; lead producers Abel Farbman and Sylvia Harris moved the show there in July hopes for improved business. That happened, but *Tovarich* had to vacate the Majestic less than four months later to make way for the expected smash hit *Jennie* with Mary Martin.

On October 7, *Tovarich* reopened at the Winter Garden. "And as odd as this sounds," says Leigh's understudy Joan Copeland, "I sometimes think that Vivien became disoriented when the show moved there. It may well have been part of the reason she had a breakdown."

Irving sadly remembers the night it happened. He recalls seeing that Leigh stayed in her dressing room and that the door was open throughout the entire performance. The star changed into each costume she would have been wearing onstage at that moment.

Eva Gabor took over two weeks later on October 21, but the public believed the reason to see the show was Leigh. Nineteen days later, *Tovarich* closed after 263 performances and a loss of its entire $400,000 investment.

Reliever of the Year: David Jones
Oliver!

He's one of the very few actors to open a hit musical on Broadway and yet not appear on the original cast album.

But David Jones wasn't with *Oliver!* when the British hit had its American premiere in Los Angeles in August 1962. Michael Goodman was then playing the Artful Dodger in this musical version of *Oliver Twist*. Goodman continued in the role through stops in San Francisco, Detroit, and Toronto, too. Because the album was recorded in Hollywood during the first leg of the tryout, Goodman was heard on the disc singing "Consider Yourself" and "I'd Do Anything."

"[Producer David] Merrick wasn't happy with the kid," Jones says. "Merrick said he couldn't understand what the kid was saying. So he came over to London, saw me in the part, and felt he could understand me better. He had me fly back with him, and put me in the show a week before Broadway." (It was the same week Jones celebrated his seventeenth birthday.) Jones reports that Merrick also had his stars Clive Revill (Fagin) and Georgia Brown (Nancy) "take elocution lessons, too."

Jones well remembers the night that he and the cast of *Oliver!* appeared on *The Ed Sullivan Show*. "I thought all that commotion was for us," he says of the famous February 9, 1964, broadcast. "I didn't know it was really for the Beatles."

He admits that what he saw that night opened his eyes. "I hadn't thought about doing pop, because I'd been a theater kid all my life. In those days, you didn't cross over. When I saw the Beatles that night, I said 'Why not?'"

His manager Ward Sylvester had the idea for a TV show about a pop group. The result was the Monkees, Jones's biggest success. It even got him on a legendary (!) *Brady Bunch* episode where he played himself. All because David Merrick didn't like the way Michael Goodman spoke.

Rookie of the Year: Neil Simon
Little Me

In 1955, still under the tutelage of his brother Danny, Neil Simon contributed a few sketches to a revue called *Catch a Star*. It did not catch on and played only twenty-three performances at the Plymouth Theatre. Little did Simon know at the time that he'd later have four plays ensconced at that playhouse, including *The Odd Couple* and *Plaza Suite.* (For that matter, little did he know there'd eventually be a Broadway theater named after him.)

After Simon contributed one sketch to *New Faces of 1956,* he sat down to write his autobiographical comedy *Come Blow Your Horn.* It was a 1961–1962 Broadway hit that made a good deal of money for its investors, which included future U.S. president George H. Bush.

Producers Cy Feuer and Ernest Martin, who'd had six hits in seven tries (only *Whoop-Up* failed them), had enjoyed *Come Blow Your Horn.* They sought Simon to musicalize *Little Me,* Patrick Dennis's 1961 faux autobiography of an untalented sleep-around would-be star named Belle Poitrine. (Yes, that translates to "Beautiful Breasts" in French.) The book started with "A Star Is Born" in 1900 and went to "Frankly Forty" in 1960. (Belle never was much good at math and was one to believe that her readers wouldn't notice petty details.)

Simon liked the book, but he had a wild notion. He was once one of Sid Caesar's writers on the early 1950s television smash *Your Show of Shows.* How about hiring Caesar to play all seven men in Belle's life? Mr. Pinchley, the skinflint whose heart she opened; Fred Poitrine, the doughboy she married; lovers Otto Schnitzler, Prince Cherney, and Val du Val; and not only Noble Eggleston, the upper-crust young man whom she really loved, but Noble Eggleston Jr., too.

Frankly, the show would be more of an opportunity for Caesar. Since he had finished the 114th and final episode of *Your Show of Shows* in 1954, his television appearances had been sporadic. There were whispers that that he wasn't mentally well, but Simon insisted that if Caesar had the right vehicle, he'd be fine.

Simon thought he could provide it for him. His offhand remark to composer Cy Coleman and lyricist Carolyn Leigh—that Caesar needed to clear his throat from time to time—gave them the impetus to incorporate the lyric "and cleat his throat" in their song "Boom-Boom." Caesar got his breather.

Aside from the *New York Times,* the reviews were good for Simon and the show. Had Caesar not had health problems and begun missing performances, *Little Me* would have run substantially longer than its 257 performances.

Although Simon spent most of the next four decades writing comedies and dramas, he interspersed four other books for musicals among his twenty-five plays (twenty-six, if you care to view the male and female *Odd Couples* as two different shows). Although Cy Feuer said in public and in his memoir that Simon and Bob Fosse "were barely getting along" during *Little Me,* Fosse asked Simon to take over from him as bookwriter on *Sweet Charity.* It's that old line about never using a person ever again unless he's needed.

Sweet Charity—"The Adventures of a Girl Who Wanted to Be Loved," as it was officially subtitled—was a modest hit, delivering about 10 percent profit. Simon came up with a fast and funny book but could never solve the ending. After Oscar, Charity's presumed last chance, dumped her, Simon had a good fairy show up. Not really; when she turned around, she was wearing a sandwich sign that stated, "Watch *The Good Fairy* Tonight at 8 on CBS." We'd come to care about Charity and wanted more for her than a joke's-on-her finish. The film (with a screenplay by Peter Stone) tried three different endings, and as late at 2005, Simon was trying yet another one for the upcoming Broadway revival. This show has seemingly had more new endings than the number of deadly virtues that Mordred can name in *Camelot.*

In 1968, Simon had much more success with *Promises, Promises,* the musical version of the 1960 Oscar winner *The Apartment.* He looked at the screenplay, in which Chuck Baxter, the shy office worker, is in love with elevator operator Fran Kubelik, who doesn't know he's alive. She's instead in love with his boss, Mr. Sheldrake, who uses Chuck's apartment for their liaisons—unknown to Chuck.

Simon's smallest change: By 1968, elevator operators were either gone or an endangered species; Fran became a cafeteria worker. Simon's biggest change—and a masterstroke it was: he had Chuck break through the fourth wall and take us into his confidence. Even better: during scenes where Fran said how much she cared for Chuck, he then turned to us and admitted that she didn't say anything of the kind, but that he was engaging in some wishful thinking.

Simon also changed a salient ingredient. In the original film, Chuck's boss Sheldrake is on the phone and lying to his wife that he must take a client that night to a Broadway show. (*The Music Man,* in fact.) But he's really planning to meet Fran, so he gives the tickets to Chuck, who unknowingly asks Fran to go with him, for he's unaware of her relationship with Sheldrake. When Fran accepts, Chuck is thrilled.

That's a spot for a song, but Simon thought the idea of Chuck's being thrilled that she likes musicals would be too insular and self-serving to the musical theater. He suggested that Chuck ask Fran to a basketball game, and when she agreed, he'd sing one of Broadway's quirkiest waltzes, "She Likes Basketball."

One musical that Simon planned led to a very different one. He wanted to adapt his less-than-well-received *The Gingerbread Lady* (1970) and talked to composer Marvin Hamlisch about doing it. "But," says Hamlisch, "whenever we'd meet, I'd spend so much time complaining about my girlfriend, the songwriter Carol Bayer Sager. And after a few times of doing that, I showed up for a meeting, and Neil handed me a sheaf of papers. It was his take on a relationship between two songwriters that wasn't going well." The show turned out to be *They're Playing Our Song,* a 1979 Broadway hit.

Like every career, Simon's has had decline and fall. His 1993 musical version of *The Goodbye Girl,* based on his own hit screenplay, failed to amuse the way his old shows did. Despite a Marvin Hamlisch–David Zippel score and no less than Bernadette Peters and Martin Short starring, it had many empty seats.

Throughout his career, Simon became one of the musical's best show doctors. Sometimes he'd simply provide a few good jokes, as he did for *A Chorus Line.* Sometimes he'd suggest songs. He told Cy Coleman and Dorothy Fields, his *Sweet Charity* collaborators, that in *Seesaw* they should write Gittel Mosca a song about her tendency to ruin relationships. They took his advice and wrote "Nobody Does It Like Me." Said Coleman, "At one point, Dorothy and I wondered if we landed on that title because when it came to show-doctoring, nobody does it like him."

1963–1964

Most Valuable Player: Jule Styne

Arturo Ui, Funny Girl, and Fade Out—Fade In

There was a time, of course, when a Broadway composer could have three shows in a single season. For that matter, in 1917–1918, Jerome Kern had *five.*

But those days were long gone by the time that the 1963–1964 season rolled around. And yet, in fewer than 200 days, Jule Styne did have his music in three shows.

Not musicals. Shows. Styne's first 1963–1964 representation was for a play: Bertolt Brecht's *Arturo Ui.* David Merrick, one of two producers who sponsored Styne's *Gypsy,* hired him to write incidental music. The show lasted only ten days in November, but Styne's score wasn't faulted for the failure.

Arturo Ui's quick closing allowed Roger DeKoven, who'd played "The Actor" in it, to join Styne's next show: *Funny Girl.* DeKoven played Florenz Ziegfeld, the impresario who would become infuriated with Fanny Brice (Barbra Streisand). He'd selected her as the centerpiece in a salute to weddings—which she sabotaged by pretending to be at least 260 days pregnant.

Why Ziegfeld would choose to star the ungainly Brice in a sincere number about beauty has never been satisfactorily explained. Nevertheless, "His Love Makes Me Beautiful" was one of the few moments in *Funny Girl* that worked splendidly during its first Boston preview on January 11, 1964.

In the years that followed, Styne never tired of telling of that infamous night. Barbra Streisand was wearing a body mic, for as odd as it may sound, director Garson Kanin felt she couldn't be heard without one. But this was early in the history of infrared electronic amplification, so several times when Streisand was singing Bob Merrill's lyrics or reciting Isobel Lennart's dialogue, her radio signal picked up interfering bulletins from the Boston Police Department. There was a surreal parallel to hearing Fanny Brice and Nicki Arnstein (Sydney Chaplin) dealing with their marital problems only to be interrupted by dispatchers who were ordering policemen to get to Shawmut Avenue to break up an incident of domestic violence.

Styne often talked about what happened to Chaplin that night, too. During the song "Sleep Now, Baby Bunting," Chaplin was holding a little basket in which his "daughter" Frances was asleep. But Chaplin, trying to milk the situation that he was home caring for the baby while Brice was singin' and dancin' in the Follies, over-emoted when singing "Mommy is a big star!" He dropped the "baby," which bounced around on the stage a couple of times.

Those two catastrophes were easily remedied, but the rest of *Funny Girl* wasn't. So Styne immediately went to work. By the following Thursday's performance, a piece of paper was in the *Playbill,* showing that *Funny Girl* had already dropped five songs—in addition to "Sleep Now, Baby Bunting," "A Temporary Arrangement," "A Helluva Group," and "It's Home"—and added "Larceny In His Heart and "What a Helluva Day." The clever middle section of "You Are Woman" ("Isn't this the height of nonchalance?") wasn't yet in place but would come before the show moved to the Forrest in Philadelphia. Styne said that by the time the show got to Broadway, twenty-two songs came and went during tryouts.

Of course, Bob Merrill worked arguably harder; lyricists always do. But Styne alone made the move that would immeasurably benefit *Funny Girl.* After he saw that Kanin had no new ideas, he called Jerome Robbins, the directorial superstar of the day who, as we saw in *A Funny Thing Happened on the Way to the Forum,* was also the premier show doctor of his day.

Robbins took the call. After all, he and Styne had had a long professional relationship, starting with *High Button Shoes* in 1947 and continuing with *Bells Are Ringing* in 1956 and *Gypsy* in 1959. Most importantly, in 1954, when Robbins's production of *Peter Pan* was in San Francisco and desperately needed new songs, he called Styne—and Betty Comden and Adolph Green—to write them. They did by providing "Wendy," "Ugg-a-Wugg," "Distant Melody," and "Mysterious Lady," not to mention one of Broadway's most beautiful ballads: "Neverland."

Now, Styne reasoned, Robbins should repay the favor. What's more, Robbins had long ago expressed interest in directing *Funny Girl.* Now he'd have his chance.

Robbins's suggestions meant that the show needed additional time to implement them. Staying in Philadelphia was the obvious solution, but in those days, theaters in tryout cities had so many bookings that *Funny Girl* couldn't stay at the Forrest for a two-week extension; *Anyone Can Whistle* was set to come in the Monday after *Funny Girl*'s Saturday-night closing. So producer Ray Stark made a decision that tryouts seldom if ever saw during the last half of the twentieth century: he moved *Funny Girl* to another house in the same town: the Erlanger Theatre.

Despite the chaos, Styne was "lovable, likeable and very jovial" according to the show's rehearsal pianist, Marvin Hamlisch, who was enjoying his first-ever Broadway job. Hamlisch verifies the long-held opinion that Styne was capable of coming up with a new melody at a moment's notice. "I remember particularly one song that was not in originally," he said on the *Merv Griffin Show* the following decade. Hamlisch said everyone knew the show needed a nice start to the second act, and in precious little time, Styne came up with "Sadie, Sadie."

The big controversy was whether or not Fanny Brice should sing "My Man," her signature song. Styne was adamant that she should not, but must sing an original song in the style of "My Man." What he and Merrill wrote was a stunner: "The Music That Makes Me Dance."

Said Milton Rosenstock, the show's conductor, "Everyone was pressuring Jule, even Fanny's daughter Frances—and she was the wife of the producer Ray Stark. Jule was fuming. We left the theater together, got into a taxicab and the cabbie said, 'You with the show?' When we said we were, he asked, 'What kind of show is it about Fanny Brice without "My Man?"'" But Styne held his ground, and "The Music That Makes Me Dance" is one of *Funny Girl's* strongest songs.

(Today, "My Man" would undoubtedly be used, as it was in the 1968 film. Now originality is worth less than familiarity.)

With all the changes, the planned Broadway opening on Thursday, February 27, 1964, had to be postponed. *Funny Girl* didn't officially meet the press at the Winter Garden until Thursday, March 26. Many a musical has been known to have that long a delay—and more—but the added work was a bigger problem than usual for Jule Styne.

For the week that *Funny Girl* opened, Styne already had another musical in rehearsal. Ironically, it was a show that was supposed to have preceded *Funny Girl* to Broadway. *A Girl to Remember,* starring Carol Burnett, had been set to open in November 1963. But Burnett's pregnancy caused a postponement of this story of an ungainly young woman who went to Hollywood to become a star. For a scene in which she fantasized winning an Academy Award, Styne loaned the production the Oscar he won for *Three Coins in the Fountain.*

Now, after the authors briefly flirted with the title *The Idol of Millions,* the show was called *Fade Out—Fade In,* after the jaunty song that Styne, Comden, and Green had penned. But how jaunty could the fifty-eight-year-old Styne be after the grueling *Funny Girl* tryout? And if that wasn't enough, Styne was one of *Fade Out—Fade In's* two producers, so he had to be on hand to mind the store, too.

Unlike *Funny Girl, Fade Out—Fade In* does not possess one of Styne's most sterling scores. But it's decent enough. It might have been more highly regarded if the show had run, but Burnett claimed that she was injured and dropped in and out of the show before quitting. The show closed, but the producers sued and won—so Burnett returned to the reopened show. But too many theatergoers didn't trust that the performance for which they bought tickets would be one that Burnett would make.

Fade Out—Fade In actually received better reviews that *Funny Girl.* And while Streisand has never made a secret that she became easily bored with stage work (and walked through many performances to prove just that), at least she honored her contract. Burnett tried to move heaven and earth to break hers, and *Fade Out—Fade In* ran only a fifth as long as *Funny Girl.*

Still, a Brecht, Brice, and Burnett trifecta hasn't been matched.

Coda: On March 2, 1987, a tribute to Styne was held at Lincoln Center's Avery Fisher Hall. Barbra Streisand sent to the composer who'd provided her with the vehicle that elevated her to stardom a prerecorded speech. She began by talk-singing: "People, people who know Jule, are the luckiest—Oh God, I can't sing when I'm not being paid. I did want to be there tonight—even though I couldn't be with you in person—just to say that you've always been a wonderful friend to me and a wonderful composer—and I wanted to say 'thank you' and I hope this night is very special to you as you are very special to me. I love you, Jule."

Streisand had actually been scheduled to appear but sent this taped message at the eleventh hour. It wasn't aired at the show because of, as the announcement said, "technical difficulties." After the event, stagehands and crew went on record saying that everything had been in order for it to be played.

What had happened was that Styne had demanded it not be played. That's what Streisand got for raining on his parade.

Rookie of the Year: Steve Lawrence
What Makes Sammy Run?

Steve Lawrence had had a successful recording career, whether he was paired with his wife Eydie Gormé or singing solo. Often he'd record standards, and other times he do teen-oriented hits–such as his 1962 smash "Go Away, Little Girl." (Considering that the former Sidney Liebowitz was born on July 8, 1935, his discouraging the "little girl" was appropriate for a twenty-seven-year-old man.)

But could he do *What Makes Sammy Run?,* the musical version of Budd Schulberg's famous 1941 debut novel? It wouldn't be an easy role. The notorious Sammy Glick starts out as a lowly copy boy in a newspaper office but soon makes shady deals, blames others, betrays lovers, and causes a friend to commit suicide—all to get to the top in Hollywood.

Sammy Glick is far more antihero than hero than Joey Evans ever was in *Pal Joey.* For the latter, Brooks Atkinson's famous *New York Times* review stressed, "Can you draw sweet water from a foul well?" Would critics in 1964 think even worse about a musical-comedy Sammy Glick?

The actor portraying him would have to be extraordinary to keep an audience's interest. So who was around who could do it?

"Steve Lawrence wasn't our first choice. Bobby Darin was," says Ervin Drake, the show's composer-lyricist. "He told us that he really wanted to do movies so he'd be recognized when he walked down the streets of Calcutta."

So Steve Lawrence got the assignment–and quite a workload. He sang in virtually all the songs. The twenty-nine-year-old Lawrence started out as the sixteen-year-old Glick, who had to grow and age. Lawrence did it all very impressively. He made Sammy go from a lovable young rogue when he explained how he sneakily got "A New Pair of Shoes" before becoming a vulture during "You Help Me," an admirable quodlibet he shared with co-star Robert Alda, who played his wary mentor Al Manheim. "My Hometown" allowed Lawrence to put Sammy in a rare sincere mood—although his deep feelings were for Hollywood and not a human being.

With people, he could be smarmy, as was witnessed in "You Can Trust Me," a sexual pitch to writer Kit Sargent (Sally Ann Howes) and "I See Something," his flirting with Laurette (Bernice Massi), the studio boss's daughter. Add to these "I Feel Humble," Sammy's show of false modesty on the night his new picture opens, and a snarling and effective eleven-o'clock number, "Some Days Everything Goes Wrong."

Best of all was "A Room Without Windows," which would be a quasi-pop hit for Lawrence. (How much of a hit? Forty-four years later, in *Will and Grace*'s pilot, Jack McFarland was heard singing it.) So there was quite a bit on Lawrence's musical and dramatic plates.

During the Philadelphia tryout, the show itself wasn't impressing theatergoers or critics. Producer Joseph Cates fired director Arthur Storch and replaced him with Abe Burrows. That seemed to be a good idea, for Burrows had just had a smash with *How to Succeed in Business Without Really Trying,* which also had an antihero in J. Pierrepont Finch. But Finch wasn't as unlikeable as Sammy Glick, so Burrows endeavored to tenderize the show.

Says Drake, "We were deprived of staging a tougher show by Cates, who felt it would not appeal to the audience of that time. Both the script and the songs were softened, and Steve Lawrence's Sammy was played fetchingly. The audiences loved him, but I felt the novel had been betrayed. Budd and [his brother, co-librettist] Stuart Schulberg thought so, too."

Burrows also lightened Lawrence's workload. In a song called "Two-Cent Encyclopedia"—a derisive term for a newspaper—Lawrence was running around the office as a copy boy. Doubles for Sammy would be used to show the chaos, but choreographer Matt Mattox couldn't make it work, so it was dropped.

"Don't Bite the Hand That Feeds You," about the need to play ball with your bosses, originally had Sammy singing that observation to Al, but that went, too.

Though *What Makes Sammy Run?* was originally was to open in late January 1964, it was delayed. As chance had it, another show was having terrible trouble in Philadelphia: *Funny Girl,* which decided it couldn't be ready for its already announced February 27, 1964, date. So *What Makes Sammy Run?* took it instead.

Critics and audiences were impressed at how Lawrence breathed fire and brimstone en route to becoming the won't-be-denied and utterly ruthless Sammy. A pop singer can't necessarily be expected to act well in a Broadway musical—especially when he's never previously done any serious acting in film, television, or theater. But Lawrence got a Tony nomination as Best Actor in a Musical, while the also-eligible David Burns, Stephen Douglas, José Ferrer, Harry Guardino, Robert Horton, Daniel Massey, Craig Stevens, and Edward Woodward did not.

What Makes Sammy Run's reviews were decidedly mixed, but the star power of Lawrence helped to sell the show. It amassed 540 performances in the days when that was a very impressive run. This was even more remarkable given that Lawrence had made his name as a fresh-faced, engaging young entertainer, one who oozed wholesomeness, especially when paired with Gormé. None of Lawrence's fans wanted to believe he was anything like Sammy Glick. "Oh, he was a little," says Drake.

While we have to judge Glick as the outstanding rookie of the 1963–1964 season, he hardly turned out to be the MVP of the 1964–1965 semester. For Lawrence soon tired of *What Makes Sammy Run?* In July 1964, he prematurely took a week's vacation. Replacing him was another pop singer: Paul Anka. Says Drake, "Sally Ann Howes later told me that she saw Steve sitting in the audience watching him. Steve didn't have to worry, though; the grosses went way down that week. By then, people were really coming to see him. We ran 16 months—

and could have run longer—but Steve had contracted to do a TV variety series for CBS and lost interest in us. I'd say he missed 36 performances in the last six weeks of the run, which his understudy Richard France had to play."

Anka was asked to take over but didn't want to, and no one could be found with enough star power to succeed Lawrence. During the final weeks of the run, Lawrence took to ad-libbing, but producer Joseph Cates didn't want to fight him. For everyone knew that without Lawrence, *What Makes Sammy Run?* wouldn't have run.

Comeback Player of the Year: Carol Channing
Hello, Dolly!

It was early 1963, and Carol Channing was starting to believe that she'd be only a one-hit wonder.

"I was aware that for fifteen years, every time I entered a room at a function where a band was engaged, they'd start playing 'Diamonds Are a Girl's Best Friend,'" says the actress, citing her signature song from *Gentlemen Prefer Blondes.* She'd scored quite a personal success as gold digger Lorelei Lee—in 1949. Adds Channing, "I wondered if I'd ever enter a room and hear the band play a new song to acknowledge me."

Channing had a point. After *Gentlemen Prefer Blondes* closed in 1951, the decade was not a kind one. She was not asked to repeat Lorelei Lee on film, for Marilyn Monroe was Hollywood's choice. Says Channing, "At least Marilyn she came to see me do it onstage and afterward told me she thought I was very good."

Channing succeeded Rosalind Russell in *Wonderful Town* and saw the show close in four months' time. In 1955, she got the starring role in *Delilah,* a spoof of the silent-movie era; but when out-of-town theatergoers assumed the show was biblical in nature, the title was changed to *The Vamp.* Success still eluded the show, which ran sixty performances and even failed to get an original cast album. (It's also the one show about which Channing will not speak; she'll coldly change the subject if it's broached.)

So Channing tried Hollywood and joined Ginger Rogers in the 1956 film *The First Traveling Saleslady.* Channing's willing to discuss this one: "Wasn't it awful?" she rhetorically asks. No one knew it at the time, but the picture starred the first two actresses who would play the leads in Broadway's *Hello, Dolly!*

There were a few (but not many) appearances on various TV series before her next Broadway appearance in 1961. It was an especially Channing-centric musical called *Show Girl,* in which Jules Munshin and a few chorus boys provided some support. Much of the show reprised material from *Lend an Ear,* the 1948 revue that brought Channing to Broadway's attention.

So, as Carlotta Campion would later sing in *Follies,* "Top billing Monday, Tuesday you're touring in stock"—for in 1963, Channing was doing George Bernard Shaw's *The Millionairess* on Long Island. But one night in her audience was director-choreographer Gower Champion. David Merrick had entrusted him to stage *Dolly: A Damned Exasperating Woman,* the musical version of *The Matchmaker.* Ethel Merman, Mary Martin, and Lucille Ball had already said no, so Champion was semi-desperate–until *The Millionairess* began. He came away more convinced than he expected that he'd found his Dolly Gallagher Levi.

During the Detroit tryout, Channing made a comeback in another way—by coming back at the end of act 1 to sing "Before the Parade Passes By," a march that has poignancy and expresses resiliency. Originally, David Burns finished the act with "Penny in My Pocket," in which half-a-millionaire Horace Vandergelder told how he built his fortune. "But no one wanted to know those facts about him," said composer-lyricist Jerry Herman. "They wanted to know more about Dolly."

It was the biggest component of the show's turnaround from the "blue baby," as a leading Detroit critic called it. When *Hello, Dolly!* opened on Broadway at the St. James on January 16, 1964, two critics liked it and four absolutely adored it. Walter Kerr wrote many a wonderful and quotable rave in his time, but his most memorable one may well have been the one with which he concluded his *Hello, Dolly!* review: "Don't bother holding onto your hats. You'll only be throwing them in the air, anyway." Channing hasn't forgotten that Gower Champion, approaching her after the opening with Dolly's unanimous approvals, asked, "Isn't this better than sex?"—to which she answered in her trademark contralto voice, "Well, I wouldn't know."

The next day, in the pre–credit card and Internet era, the ticket lines were long and dense. "It was such a cold day," recalls Channing, "that I came down and gave free coffee to those good people in line."

Channing suddenly found herself on the cover of *Life* magazine and had the number-one album in the land (shared, of course, with co-stars David Burns, Charles Nelson Reilly, Eileen Brennan, and a host of waiters). Although

Barbra Streisand was far better regarded as a vocalist (to say the least), her *Funny Girl* original cast album could do no better than reach number two and never overtook the original cast album of *Hello, Dolly!* When the Grammy Awards were passed out, *Hello, Dolly!* even beat *Funny Girl* as Best Original Cast Album. Since then, it's never been out of print for even a day.

Hello, Dolly! was the start of a renaissance for Channing. In 1967, she got a featured role in the film *Thoroughly Modern Millie* and received an Oscar nomination. Today's Super Bowl offers such entertainers as Prince, P. Diddy, and Kid Rock, but the 1970 choice for halftime at Super Bowl IV was Carol Channing. What tickled the lifelong Democrat most, however, was being named to President Richard M. Nixon's enemies list.

Carol Channing kept her promise that "Dolly'll never go away again." In 1979, she did a production for Houston Grand Opera that traveled to Broadway. Playing Cornelius, the hapless Vandergelder employee, was Lee Roy Reams. He later directed her in the revival that began in July 1994 in Denver and played for fifteen months across the country.

"No one can play the road like Carol," says Tommy Tune. "She's the one who taught me that you have to get out there, for if you don't, the people in the rest of the country won't know who you are."

Many felt their eyes glazing over when Channing announced she'd do Dolly again. She rebutted by quoting John Gielgud: "When we were playing it in London, he said, 'You Americans forget your classic characters. I do Hamlet every 15 years or so. You should continue to do *Hello, Dolly!*' I realized that he was right. It's a classic character."

Although Channing had already received a honorary Tony in 1968, she received a Lifetime Achievement Tony in 1995 as *Hello, Dolly!* was wending its way across the country. "Isn't it wonderful?" she said with that standard-issue Channing astonishment in her voice. "The Tonys don't give Lifetime Achievements very often. The Oscars give them all over the place."

Channing opened on Broadway at the Lunt-Fontanne Theatre on October 19, 1995, and remained there until January 28, 1996. For both this and the previous revival, an Al Hirschfeld drawing of her in her second-act dress and headdress served as the production's logo. Wasn't she the real symbol of the show?

Even more than thirty-two years after she first played Dolly, Carol Channing was still barreling through it with sheer star power. She didn't lose a step, literally or figuratively. She shoved her fingers in her mouth and gave a loud, shrill whistle that was as superb as any a street urchin could give. And when a Yonkers yokel tried to peek into her purse, she still gave that insulted do-you-mind accusing stare.

But could Herman have ever known that when he wrote the title song for *Hello, Dolly!* that he was writing Carol Channing's future biography? So many lyrics applied to her doing both revivals: "It's so nice to have you back where you belong; you're looking swell ... you're still going, you're still crowing, you're still going strong."

Theatergoers felt the room swaying while the band was playing one of their old favorite songs from way back when. Few could resist, for when the waiters and Channing sang of "those good ol' days," wow, wow, wow, fellas, those good old days were suddenly here again. And Channing wasn't a whit slower when whisking around the stage. She took charge, and didn't just put her hand in here; she put her heart and soul in, too.

When asked if she changed anything about her performance from 1964 to 1995, she answered, "Change anything? We wouldn't dare. The show won 10 Tonys." Then she admitted, "Well, I have changed one thing. In 1964, when I sang 'So Long, Dearie' to Horace, I gave him a sideways bump. Now I do it straightforward."

This 1995 revival provided Channing with the chance to record a new cast album—and set a record: for spanning the most years in recording the same role on a cast album. Yul Brynner had recorded *The King and I* for Decca in 1951 and then for RCA Victor twenty-six years later. But Channing, thirty-one years after her Broadway debut as Dolly, recorded a new cast album for Varese Sarabande. (Long before that, she'd recorded another type of encore album when waxing *Lorelei* in 1973, twenty-four years after recording the show that inspired it: *Gentlemen Prefer Blondes.*

Channing never did another original musical on Broadway. There was talk of many, including one by Herman: *Vicki for President,* in which Channing would play nineteenth-century suffragette and firebrand Victoria Woodhull. So she'll be most remembered for providing *Hello, Dolly!* with a centerpiece star that was an important component in its initial success. As Herman has said, "There is never a day of the year when a woman in a red dress does not walk down a staircase to enter the Harmonia Gardens restaurant." For many of those days, it was Carol Channing.

"And," as Channing said in late 1964, "it was so wonderful to hear a new song played whenever I entered a room at a function where a band was engaged." *Hello, Dolly!* allowed Channing to become a two-hit wonder.

1964–1965

MVP: Jerome Robbins
Fiddler on the Roof

Actually, the person who expected to be this season's MVP was Zero Mostel, who originated the role of Tevye the milkman in *Fiddler on the Roof.*

Mostel was notorious for improvising and corrupting any role once he became bored with it. The most egregious crime of all came in *Fiddler*'s second act, when the Russians were driving the residents of Anatevka from their homes. Tevye was saying goodbye to his daughter Tzeitel, son-in-law Motel, and their baby.

Tevye had every reason to believe that he'd never see them again. The stage direction stated, "Tevye takes one last look at the baby," but as the run continued, that one last look wasn't enough for Mostel. He pretended that the infant had relieved himself, and then he vigorously waved his hand as if to shake off the urine.

"I was not sorry to see him go," says Sheldon Harnick, the show's lyricist. "But at the party we had after his last performance, I decided to tell him, 'We're going to miss you.' And Zero said, 'What you're going to miss are the high grosses.' He was completely convinced that the show wouldn't survive without him, and I know he was disappointed when it continued to thrive after he left."

Indeed, even with Harry Goz and Paul Lipson—names totally unknown to the theatergoing public–*Fiddler* continued to a then-record-breaking run, being the first show to surpass *Life with Father*'s 3,224 performances, which had stayed in place for nearly a quarter century.

And director-choreographer Jerome Robbins was one of the main reasons why. He was the one who asked Harnick, bookwriter Joseph Stein, and composer Jerry Bock, "But what is this show about?" which spurred the songwriting team to write "Tradition," still considered one of Broadway's best opening numbers.

Producer Fred Coe, who had this new musical called *Tevye* under option, was the one to suggest Robbins for the project. Bock and Harnick were interested—and concerned. Anyone who'd worked with Robbins could tell you that you'd get great work from a not-so-great human being. The harsh words he gave performers who weren't living up to his very high expectations weren't along the lines of "It's getting there. It's coming along." Carol Channing calls Gower Champion, her *Hello, Dolly!* director, a "benevolent despot." Robbins is usually afforded the noun but not the adjective.

Robbins, however, was invaluable to *Fiddler,* not simply because he came up with a directorial concept that made audience feel as if they were in nineteenth-century Russia, or because his dances so beautifully evoked the period. Said Bock, "When we opened in Detroit during a newspaper strike, our only review was from *Variety,* and it was terrible. I don't know why we all believed it, but we did—except for Jerry. I don't even know if he ever saw it. He just kept working, which is what you want from the person in charge of your show. People talk about people having 'poker faces,' and Jerry was one of those guys. We never really knew what he was thinking, but he obviously was."

Many of those thoughts were ruthless but necessary. According to Richard Altman, Robbins's assistant who authored *The Making of a Musical,* Robbins saw the scene in which Golde persuades Tevye to talk to butcher Lazar Wolf about marrying their daughter Tzeitel. It was followed by Tzeitel's telling Motel, the man she loved, that he had to take action now to make certain it didn't happen. Robbins decided to play both scenes on different sides of the stage simultaneously.

Altman wrote that Robbins also cut much of Gino Conforti's role as the Fiddler. Originally he was Tevye's virtual imaginary friend to whom he confided, but Robbins wisely cut that concept and used him at the beginning and end of the show. At least Conforti retained his job; Charles Durning, still years away from the stardom he'd acquire, would lose his when Robbins cut the character of the priest.

In a sense, Robbins had a hand in the songwriting. Says Harnick, "When I had the idea to have Tevye and Golde proclaim their feelings in 'Do You Love Me?' I had a very hard time with the lyric. I brought in a lot of words and lines, and Jerry was the one who really helped me to shape it and make it work."

Robbins was once a Most Valuable Player for a very different team. Eleven years before *Fiddler,* he testified as a friendly witness for the House Un-American Activities Committee, naming names of people whom he knew or suspected were Communists. This broke his friendship with Zero Mostel, who never considered forgiving him.

And yet, as we've seen, when *Funny Thing* needed help, star Mostel didn't veto Robbins coming in to save it. He knew that the ever-resourceful Robbins was their best chance.

That time, however, meant only a few days where Mostel would have to be in the same room with the man he detested. Now, for *Fiddler,* Mostel would be with Robbins through many weeks of rehearsals as well as Detroit and Washington tryouts.

And yet he didn't say no. Perhaps, in his own way, Zero Mostel was the season's MVP for approving Jerome Robbins as his director in *Fiddler on the Roof.*

Rookie of the Year: Tommy Steele

Half a Sixpence

During much of 1965 and 1966, those obsessed with Broadway musicals would come right home after seeing *Half a Sixpence* and call their friends to rave about Tommy Steele.

Those who were phoned and had already seen Steele would spend much of the time vigorously nodding or verbally agreeing with the caller. Steele, the possessor of a winning smile, was wonderfully engaging as Arthur Kipps, a Cockney clerk in Mr. Shalford's Emporium. How well he showed his affection for the lovely Ann, another Cockney who made her living as a servant.

But once Kipps came into an unexpected fortune, he became smitten with the much more high-born Helen, which devastated Ann. But, as many who phoned told the people they called, Steele was able to make the betrayal seem a foolish youthful mistake—the type we all made at one time (or more) in our lives.

As song-and-dance man, both phoners and callers agreed, Steele was sensational. He had a terrific theater voice, one that didn't suggest he'd been a rock-and-roll sensation in his native England. In fact, when composer David Heneker auditioned the score for him, it was in the club called the Cavern, where John, Paul, George, and Pete Best had been discovered by

Brian Epstein. Steele agreed to do the show, which ran into a setback when the management of the desired Savoy Theatre didn't want to book a show that starred a rock-and-roller, for he would "bring in the wrong crowd."

Many phoners and callers probably didn't know that when Steele commandeered *Half a Sixpence* to a 677-performance in London, he didn't do much dancing; during production numbers, he'd shyly and slyly saunter into the wings. However, after Onna White was signed to choreograph the Broadway edition, she insisted that Steele be a vital part of the dances. And dance he did, to excellent advantage.

After many phoners made the statement that "The guy can do anything!" perhaps both they and their callers simultaneously cried out, "He can even play the banjo!"—which Steele strummed expertly in the show's first rouser, "Money to Burn."

And then perhaps either the phoner or caller said, "And listen to what happened the night I was there! During 'If the Rain's Got to Fall,' when all the chorus boys were dancing in a circle, one guy's boater hat fell off his head, and a few seconds later, when Steele was dancing near it, he bent over, picked it up, and Frisbeed it over to the guy."

Then came a stunned silence from the person who'd been listening. Finally he'd croak, "That happened at my performance, too."

At every one, for that matter. It was a carefully worked-out routine to gild the theatrical lily. Once audience members saw Steele rescue the dancer and the number, they'd just have to look at their companions and say in an awed voice, "Is there anything this guy can't do?"

But perhaps this phony and calculated moment is at least one reason why Steele never again reached the popularity he had in the London and stage versions of *Half a Sixpence.*

Steele tried for a Hollywood career, reprising his Kipps on film, but the picture was one of those late-1960s extravaganzas that brought about the long-term death of the film musical. *The Happiest Millionaire,* released on Pearl Harbor Day, 1967, was just as big a disaster, as was *Finian's Rainbow* in 1968. Suddenly Steele's smile that once seemed so warm and inviting now appeared to be just a little too large to be real. What's more, instead of seeming joyous, he came across more as noisy. He appeared in only two more feature films, and, as of this writing, hasn't made one since 1979.

Steele never again appeared on Broadway, either. He starred in some London musicals, including *Singin' in the Rain* and *Some Like It Hot,* but never where he erased the memory of the original stars that played his roles.

Still, the memory of Steele in *Half a Sixpence* lingers in many theatergoers' minds.

"I know this is sacrilege," says lyricist Joe Bravaco, "but Steele carried a very slight show on his shoulders, and made it an evening of exhilarating musical comedy. He should have won the Best Actor in a Musical Tony over Zero Mostel." Former Broadway press agent Joshua Ellis (*42nd Street*) agrees. "Time has proven that nearly every fine actor can play Tevye, but when there's talk about a revival of *Half a Sixpence,* people say, 'But who these days can play the Tommy Steele role?' It was the most exciting Broadway star debut performance until Hugh Jackman did *The Boy from Oz.*"

Manager of the Year: Alexander H. Cohen
Baker Street

What is now the Camelot apartment building at 301 West Forty-fifth Street was, in 1962, an empty lot.

One of the two exposed brick walls from the abutting buildings sported logos for two upcoming musicals that Alexander H. Cohen would produce: the left side trumpeted *Barnum,* the right *Baker Street.*

The latter's logo was inspired by the famous two-headed Janus of Roman mythology. In this case, however, the faces—one green, one blue—that were facing in opposite directions were silhouettes of Sherlock Holmes. Each had his trademark deerstalker hat atop it, and that famous meerschaum pipe jutted from each mouth.

Both *Barnum* and *Baker Street* would have scores written by newcomers Marian Grudeff and Raymond Jessel. A *Barnum* musical wouldn't surface until 1980, and from a completely different team and management. But Cohen, the last of the great Broadway razzmatazz showmen whose shows seldom returned their investments, made sure that *Baker Street* would.

Cohen deserves credit for giving two Broadway newcomers their big chance. Other producers wouldn't have proceeded without blue-chip writers. But Cohen liked what he'd heard from Grudeff and Jessel, and that was enough for him. He also gave one of his biggest (and more successful) rivals, Harold Prince, the chance to direct a musical from scratch without having to worry about producing it. That Prince had only had two flops as a director (and had turned down *Hello, Dolly!*) didn't dissuade him.

Baker Street wouldn't happen for nearly three more years after that Forty-fifth Street display. In the interim, Cohen produced *Hamlet* with Richard Burton—which caused one of his better brainstorms. Jessel and Grudeff had written a song called "A Married Man," sung near the end of the first act by Dr. Watson. He and Holmes had been captured by Professor Moriarty, who'd tied them to chairs next to a time bomb. Watson, minutes before death, mused about his wife. He sang that he was glad to have been "a happy man, contented man—a married man."

Because Richard Burton had married his superstar wife Elizabeth Taylor in March 1964 (after their then-scandalous and adulterous affair), Cohen had him record "A Married Man." He also had Taylor singing "Finding Words for Spring," another song from the score, but she couldn't handle it well enough for the record to be released. And while Burton spoke much more than he sang, the record was deemed to pass muster. It was released as a single, but also printed on cardboard and bound into an issue of *Show* magazine.

Cohen bought a *Baker Street* ad in *Playbill,* but not just an ordinary one. It was a two-page centerfold—in color, no less, at a time when little if anything else in *Playbill* was in color. The actual *Playbill* for *Baker Street* would have a color cover, and although a 1958 José Ferrer vehicle, *Edwin Booth,* was the first to hold that distinction, *Baker Street* was the first musical to go color. What's more, it didn't merely settle for the show's logo the way that shows routinely do today. Instead, the cover offered a handsome photo of Fritz Weaver as Sherlock Holmes, observed by both Inga Swenson as actress Irene Adler and Martin Gabel as Professor Moriarty.

Outside the Broadway Theater, Cohen installed a lavish $30,000 display over the marquee that was more than twice as wide. "Sherlock Holmes of Baker Street taught James Bond everything he knows," it said. (*Goldfinger,* the most esteemed Bond movie of all, had opened only a few weeks earlier.) The three-story exhibition had an action-figure ne'er-do-well climbing a ladder until he was shot—at which point he fell to the bottom and tried again. That didn't quite happen in the musical, but it made for a good display. To the left was a four-story-high representation of the logo, and to the right, a large ad for the cast album, which was produced by MGM records.

Baker Street wound up costing $630,000 at a time when $350,000 was the norm for a musical. One could certainly see where the money went as soon as the curtain went up. Oliver Smith created classy representations of Holmes's cluttered apartment, the Theatre Royal Stage, Irene's posh house, the inside of

Moriarty's yacht, and the cliffs of Dover. Bil Baird of marionette fame created a marching set of soldiers to celebrate Queen Victoria's Diamond Jubilee, which we saw as if we were peering down from a roof.

Cohen decided that the show would be such an event that men would not be admitted unless they were clad in jackets and ties, and women would be allowed in only if they wore dresses. That, though, was his pronouncement before the show opened at the Broadway Theatre—then the Great White Way's largest. Alas, then came a most mixed set of reviews, with the better ones not coming from the more important press outlets. As time wore on and *Baker Street* was not the smash Cohen had expected, patrons in T-shirts and flip-flops were gladly admitted as long as they'd bought tickets.

Set designer Smith won the Tony, and while the medal said he was being rewarded for three shows—*Baker Street, Luv,* and *The Odd Couple*—the latter two were one-set affairs that certainly didn't tax Smith the way *Baker Street* did.

Tony nominations went to Swenson as Best Actress; the single-named Motley, for her gorgeous Victorian-era costumes; and Jerome Coopersmith for his book. But that was all.

The real irony and disgrace is that back then a Tony award was given for Best Producer of a Musical—and Cohen wasn't even nominated. The winner was *Baker Street*'s director, Harold Prince, for producing *Fiddler on the Roof.* But for all the ballyhoo Alexander H. Cohen gave *Baker Street,* he certainly deserved the award.

Until he died in 2000, Cohen had a large blow-up of *Baker Street*'s *Playbill* cover behind his desk, suggesting that despite the musical's less-than-smash status, he still considered it a favorite memory. Tony or no Tony, he knew how well he'd produced it.

1965–1966

MVP: Mary Martin
Hello, Dolly!

One could effectively argue that the MVP this season was Richard Kiley for his Don Quixote in *Man of La Mancha.* But we must choose someone who, while not playing Broadway this season, certainly made a Broadway musical one of the most significant moments in many people's lives.

President Lyndon B. Johnson thought that the troops in Vietnam would be heartened by some good ol'-fashioned American entertainment and had the idea of sending *Hello, Dolly!* to the war-torn land. *Dolly!* producer David Merrick, a lifelong Democrat, readily agreed.

One would assume that Carol Channing would, too. After all, she, too, was a staunch Democrat and helped popularize "Hello, Lyndon" as the campaign song for the president's 1964 reelection. But as the syndicated gossip columnist Sheilah Graham reported on December 21, 1965, Channing rejected the offer.

(Goodbye, Lyndon.)

Mary Martin did not. She'd been doing the show in London and was scheduled to take it to "nearby" Japan and Korea. She'd now add Vietnam to the itinerary. "No one deserves to be entertained more than our troops overseas," said Martin.

On October 6, 1965, Martin and a seventy-one-member cast arrived to ninety-degree heat outside of Saigon. They began rehearsing as armed guards made certain that no enemy soldiers could come near.

Martin, in a February 7, 1966, TV special dedicated to her bringing *Hello, Dolly! Round-the-World,* used the words "grave, grim" and "a shock of reality" to describe what she saw in Vietnam. "We went through the danger zone but only after the area had been cleared on mines and booby traps. Above us was a noisy guardian angel," she said, using a euphemism for a helicopter. "This was the real theater of war."

Holding performances at night was considered too dangerous, so Martin and the cast would literally play matinees, some as early as 10:00 a.m. and none any later than 1:00 p.m. After 4:00 p.m., the cast would be confined to quarters. There would be eleven performances, and twelve thousand soldiers would see the show.

Martin was impressed that U.S. General William Westmoreland and Air Marshal Nguyen Cao Ky of South Vietnam would attend, too. But she may well have been more moved when she saw that soldiers came "by plane, jeep or on foot and sat on sandbags" to see a show on what had been an airplane hangar only hours earlier. "These boys were fitting us in between engagements," she said. In the audience were many soldiers from parts of the United States that were far from any a legitimate theater; they had never seen anything resembling a stage musical in their lives.

In those days, standing ovations didn't occur, but many in the crowd gave one to the *Dolly!* cast at performance's end. Martin then sang, "Hello, fellas, well, hello, fellas. It's so nice that we could come to where you are." The remaining lyrics stayed pretty much the same, but she changed the "I went away from the lights of 14th Street" line to "You went away from your homes in the USA," cramming in the last three syllables. She did again when singing, "But when you get back to your homes in the USA" before adding the much-appreciated "That day will be brighter than any other day."

Here Martin surreptitiously (and understandably) wiped a bead of sweat from her brow. She had a fan in her hand, but she used it for a different purpose. On it were the names of many soldiers, and her encore of the "Hello, Dolly!" song mentioned many of their names in place of the usual waiters at the Harmonia Gardens. "Dolly'll be yours forever and a day," she concluded.

Life magazine noted that "Often as Dolly sashayed her feathers and plumes around the sweltering, make-believe, crimson-and-gold interior of the Harmonia Gardens restaurant, she could watch real MEDEVAC rescue helicopters land their wounded and swiftly take off again right behind her audience's heads." So in off-hours, Martin and the cast visited the wounded. "It was a devastating experience for all of us," she said. But for the men, whether they knew Martin from seeing her as TV's *Peter Pan* in their youth or didn't know her at all, it must have been an exhilarating experience.

Comeback Player of the Year: Angela Lansbury
Mame

April 8, 1995. Carnegie Hall, New York City, 8:07 p.m. Angela Lansbury walks onto the stage of Carnegie Hall to a packed audience that applauds and cheers. She's there to introduce a concert presentation of *Anyone Can Whistle,* the 1964 Arthur Laurents–Stephen Sondheim nine-performance failure that was set in a town "so impoverished that only a miracle—real or manufactured—could save it." Recalls Lansbury, "I was a mayoress of such a town . . . for a very short term."

Yes, for a week and a day. Few on Broadway were surprised, for Lansbury was best known as a film actress who played callous-to-evil individuals since 1945, when she portrayed the supercilious maid in *Gaslight.*

Not long before she agreed to do *Anyone Can Whistle,* she'd appeared in *Blue Hawaii* and *The Manchurian Candidate.* In the former, she was Elvis

Presley's difficult mother (although she was fewer than ten years older than he); in the latter, Lansbury was Laurence Harvey's genuinely monstrous mother (although he was only three years younger than she).

So after *Whistle,* Broadway thought, musical theater had seen the last of Angela Lansbury. Imagine, then, everyone's shock when she was chosen to play the free-spirited Auntie Mame in the upcoming Jerry Herman–Lawrence and Lee musical.

This would be her biggest challenge, a true star turn: she'd sing seven songs, dance in four, and would have to carry the show. Even making the costume changes would prove demanding, as Mame is seen in everything from lounging pajamas to a fireman's outfit, an evening gown, fox-hunting duds, a turban, a fur-trimmed cape, a hoop-skirt dress, a hostess gown, and many others—including her costume for her role as the woman in the moon.

From the moment that Lansbury entered at the top of a staircase, blew a bugle, and slid down the banister, she put her audience at ease. Lansbury sent Gwen Verdon (of *Sweet Charity*) to her first-ever Tony defeat. Who else could have made a total transformation from a respected character actress to a grand leading lady?

Reliever of the Year: Mimi Hines
Funny Girl

A few weeks after *Funny Girl* opened, it was nominated for eight Tony Awards, including Best Musical. It would lose every one of them—including the one for Best Actress. Even Barbra Streisand's Fanny Brice Arnstein succumbed to Carol Channing's Dolly Gallagher Levi.

Still, good as Jule Styne and Bob Merrill's score was, Streisand was thought to be the reason that *Funny Girl* was drawing significant crowds. So what would happen after Streisand left the show (the minute her contract ran out) on December 26, 1965, after nearly seven hundred performances?

Even if an apt singer-comedienne could be found, would any theatergoer be interested in seeing her? She'd have to be someone special, along the lines of Mary Martin or Anne Bancroft—both of whom were originally mentioned and sought after for Fanny before Streisand burst on the scene. No one less would now seem to suffice.

All of Broadway was shocked when Mimi Hines got the job—and learned that her husband Phil Ford would tag along in the smaller role of Eddie Ryan,

Fanny's first champion. While the comedy team Ford and Hines were well known from appearances on *The Ed Sullivan Show, The Tonight Show,* and other variety programs, neither Hines nor Ford had had any Broadway experience.

Of course, Hines really *was* a funny girl, although some of her routines, written by Ford, wouldn't be tolerated today. At times, she took on the persona of a buck-toothed Japanese woman who said "rotsa ruck" because she couldn't correctly pronounce "lots of luck." And if the animal kingdom knew how Hines pretended to be a chipmunk, it might have been offended, too.

Still, the funny part of the equation was in place. But a sincere and powerful voice was needed to sing the vocally demanding "The Music That Makes Me Dance" and the stirring "Don't Rain on My Parade." And then there was "People," now staunchly associated with Streisand, who brought it as high as number four on the charts at the time when the Beatles were at their white-hottest.

But Hines did have a solid and dramatic singing voice. Those watching Jack Paar's *Tonight Show* on August 28, 1958, were convinced of that after she stirringly sang *The Music Man*'s "Till There Was You." However, in the ensuing years, TV viewers rarely got their chance to hear her sing because she spent so much on-air time clowning.

So in actuality, Hines was a good fit for *Funny Girl.* Audiences obviously thought so, too, for they kept her in it from December 28, 1965, through its closing after 1,348 performances on July 1, 1967, through its moves from its original home (the Winter Garden) to the Majestic and the Broadway theaters. Hines's appearance in the show spurred Decca to give her a recording contract. She did "The Music That Makes Me Dance" on her first album (*Mimi Hines Sings*) and then "I'm the Greatest Star" and, yes, "People" on her second (*Mimi Hines Is a Happening!*).

Styne was certainly grateful. He wrote the second album's liner notes, which he titled "A Love Letter to Mimi Hines." As he wrote, "I've watched you grow in stature as a performer, comedienne and vocalist, and you are 'something else.'" And while Styne didn't quite write that she was the *greatest* star, he did state, "You are a great star."

Hines's eighteen-month stint was three months shorter than Streisand's, but needless to say, replacements in long-running Broadway musicals have two strikes against them before they step on a stage: first, interest wanes when a far less famous person takes over a Broadway role, and second, the tens of thousands of people who have already seen the show are usually canceled out as potential customers. Hines deserves immense credit for running *Funny Girl* during a span when it had such competition as *Man of La Mancha,*

Sweet Charity, Mame, Cabaret, and *I Do! I Do!* What's more, Hines achieved over six hundred performances with *Funny Girl* at a time when only about two dozen Broadway musicals had ever run that long. No question that she was the Reliever of the Year.

Rookie of the Year: Frankie Michaels
Mame

Kid actors are often atrocious. They're utterly self-conscious, indicate like crazy, and over-enunciate in a most artificial way. Even if they do none of the above, they're often terribly precious. Think about Jan Handzlik, who played Patrick Dennis to Rosalind Russell's Auntie Mame onstage and in the movie. Remember Kirby Furlong, the lad that Lucille Ball trotted around in the movie version of *Mame?* Putrid.

That wasn't the case with Frankie Michaels, despite his being a mere ten when he played *Mame*'s Philadelphia and Boston tryouts. (He reached eleven just a few weeks before the show debuted at the Winter Garden.) This remarkable performer was the youngest to win a (well-deserved) Tony in the twenty-year history of the awards. He sent John McMartin (of *Sweet Charity*) to the first of his five consecutive defeats.

Michaels had sincerity in his soul. After Mame ruined Vera Charles's "terribly modern operetta," Michaels gingerly approached his aunt and, without a hint of grandiosity, tenderly sang to Mame that she would always be his "best girl." No wonder that Mame sincerely responded with "And if some day, another beau comes along determined to take your place, I hope he's resigned to fall in behind my best beau."

Actually, another beau literally did come along: Beau(regard) Jackson Pickett Burnside. Once Mame had charmed his friends, relatives, and Beau himself, they all just had to sing that big celebratory title song. We, too, were swept away into celebrating with all of them.

And then suddenly Michaels came on and repeated Mame's earlier words to him: "And if some day, another beau comes along determined to take my place . . ." And suddenly, as the first-act curtain fell, we were all ashamed for having forgotten the little boy. What made us all the more embarrassed was that Michaels was just so brave about the situation.

Moments into act 2, Michael had a more upbeat reprise of the title song in which he was typing a letter to his aunt. But then, as the stage directions stated, "Like figures in a Swiss clock, the small boy, small desk and small typewriter rotate out of sight, to be replaced by a larger desk, a larger typewriter and a considerably larger Patrick." Nothing against Jerry Lanning, who was perfectly fine as Patrick ages nineteen to twenty-nine, but our hearts sank as we knew we'd seen the last of Michaels until the curtain calls.

In fact, it was the last we've ever seen of Michaels on Broadway. The boy became fodder for one of those "Whatever Happened to . . ." books that make us mourn for former celebrities who eventually had to work in jobs as unglamorous as our own. Although Michaels played Tommy Hughes (and then Tom Hughes) on *As the World Turns* before and after his *Mame* triumph, he eventually became a lounge entertainer in Verona, New York, for a number of years. Might we yet see him in a revival as Mame's enemy, the imperious Mr. Babcock?

1966–1967

MVP: Alexander H. Cohen
The Tony Awards

Naming Harold Prince as the season's MVP would seem to be a lock. After all, Prince had not only produced the groundbreaking *Cabaret,* but he'd directed it, too. He'd receive a Tony Award to honor each achievement.

Prince deserved even more acclaim because he was the one who told bookwriter Joe Masteroff, composer John Kander, and lyricist Fred Ebb that they should use that Emcee they'd created to comment on the action. He also had the idea that what happened in the Kit Kat Club should mirror what was going on outside in the streets of increasingly Nazi Germany.

When Prince accepted his Best Direction trophy, he told a nationwide TV audience, "I'd like to thank so many people, but I'll confine myself to thanking my two producers, because I don't know who else would have hired me." The joke was that Prince himself was one of those two producers, and the lead one.

But after four straight flops–*A Family Affair, She Loves Me, Baker Street,* and *"It's a Bird . . . It's a Plane . . . It's Superman!"*—the word on the street was that Prince could certainly produce, but he couldn't direct. Now he'd proved otherwise with one of the most exciting stagings in years.

Nevertheless, viewers of ABC Television Network wouldn't have seen or heard Harold Prince say these words if it weren't for Alexander H. Cohen. He's the one who convinced the network brass that the Tony Awards, although New York–centric, would give the nation a free look at the biggest production numbers then on Broadway.

It worked, and Cohen would produce the Tonys for the first twenty years—when ratings and reviews were much better than they have been in the last quarter century.

Cohen liked to say, "I was born at 16—at a matinee." The show was *Hellzapoppin'*, and Cohen notes that the 50 cents he spent to see it eventually escalated into a $2 million loss on two editions of the show that he produced, first at Montreal's Expo '67, then ten years later in a highly touted Broadway-bound production that shuttered in Boston in 1977.

Not long after the teen Cohen attended *Hellzapoppin'*, he began "producing." He turned his high school gym into a carnival cruise ship and offered all the amenities of a luxury liner by calling and getting people and companies to donate their services and goods. "I got Monty Wooley to come, and Jane Wyatt, Maxine Sullivan and Louis Armstrong, too. I netted $1,150—which was a lot of money in those days."

He wasn't just good at making calls; he was exemplary in receiving them, too. "I've answered every phone call I've ever received," he'd say. "My secretary has been instructed never to say who-are-you, what-do-you-do, why-do-you-want-him, what's-this-in-reference-to. They just say that Mr. Finkleheim is on line four, and I pick up."

Cohen's pre-broadcast palaver for the Tonys was a show in itself. On April 20, 1969, Cohen welcomed the crowd at the Mark Hellinger Theatre by saying, "Welcome to the final preview of *Dear World*." Actually, Cohen's *Dear World* had opened thirteen weeks earlier, but only after playing an inordinately high forty-five previews. But Cohen could laugh at himself, and let the Tony audience that night laugh with him.

Most entertaining at the awards was his taking attendance to ensure that every nominee was in the correct seat—so that the cameras could show the right nominee (and winner) at the right time. For the 1977 broadcast, for example, Cohen called out "Julie Harris?" and that famous cracked-reed voice responded, "Here!" "Raul Julia?" was followed by a Spanish-accented "Here!" and "Barry Bostwick?" yielded the inevitable "Present." Of all the times any audience member had heard attendance called in grammar school, high school, and college, this was by far the most entertaining and the—well, toniest.

The first year of the national broadcast, Cohen would win a 1966–1967 Tony for producing *The Homecoming,* which was judged Best Play. He had a 50 percent chance of winning that category, for his production of *Black Comedy* was also one of the four nominees. As the years went on, he'd acquire three other Best Play nominees (*Home,* 1971; *Ulysses in Nighttown,* 1974; *Play Memory,* 1984) as well as one for Best Revival (*Ah, Wilderness!,* 1989) and one for Best Musical (*A Day in Hollywood/A Night in the Ukraine,* 1980).

There was never any secret that Cohen coveted a Best Musical Tony most of all. The irony is that the expansive showman who believed "bigger was better" produced more than a half dozen other musicals that were enormous in scope, but the modest, two-set *Hollywood/Ukraine* was his only shot at the prize. (It lost to *Evita.*)

In the corner of Cohen's apartment was a table that sported that one Tony along with two Emmys—one for the Tony broadcast in 1980, the other for the *Night of 100 Stars* in 1982. Also on the table was an Oscar.

"You don't know about my Oscar-winning triumph?" he'd asked a visitor in a mock-hurt voice, before giving a big smile and launching into the story. "In 1946, I was the director of advertising for Bulova Watches. At the time, there was a radio show called *Jimmy Fiddler's Hollywood,* and one night, Jimmy announced that the Academy of Motion Picture Arts and Sciences—at 9038 Melrose Avenue, I've never forgotten the address—was in terrible trouble and was losing its building because it couldn't pay its $250,000 mortgage.

"Now, Artie Bulova was one of the last of the big-time spenders, so I saw an opportunity. I told him to give me the $250,000 to pay the mortgage—in return for which we'd get the right to put Oscar on the face of a wristwatch, and the hands could be Oscar's arms—and we'll get an option to sponsor the Academy Awards broadcast on radio. I wound up making the deal, saving their building, and selling $14 million of watches in the first year. So they awarded me what was then the only Oscar given to someone outside the motion picture industry."

Amazing that Alexander H. Cohen didn't find the time and energy to get himself a Grammy, too.

Comeback Player of the Year: Ethel Merman
Annie Get Your Gun

Record producer Ben Bagley was never one to be taken seriously. After all, on the back cover of his records, he'd sign his liner notes "By Ben Bagley (who is incurably insane)." So when he referred to Ethel Merman as "that lovable has-been" on his *Irving Berlin Revisited,* his readers took it with a shakerful of salt.

When Ethel Merman had finished her national tour of *Gypsy* in 1961, Merman had retired on her own terms. She could have starred in *Hello, Dolly!* David Merrick first thought of her for the title role and actively courted her for it. But she turned it down.

Some may suggest that the reason was that she'd worked for Merrick as Rose in *Gypsy* and once was enough with this most difficult and parsimonious of producers. Perhaps. But chances are Merman was 100 percent sincere when she said that she no longer cared to do eight shows a week. She would have been right for such musicals as *A Family Affair, All-American, I Can Get It for You Wholesale, Mr. President, Little Me, Sophie, Jennie,* and *Anyone Can Whistle.* If she'd expressed any interest in any of them, their creative staffs would have been extraordinarily interested and incredibly grateful.

But in 1965, Music Theater of Lincoln Center president Richard Rodgers, who'd originally co-produced Merman in *Annie Get Your Gun* in 1946, decided to revive it. He enticed Merman to recreate her second-greatest triumph in her longest-running, 1,147-performance show.

Wasn't she worried that she'd be too old for the role? Some say Merman was born in 1912, some 1906, but most agree January 16, 1908, was the official date. Giving her the benefit of the doubt, she was somewhere between fifty-four and sixty.

But, as Merman wrote in her 1955 autobiography, "I can't remember ever being afraid of an audience, so I can see no reason to be afraid of you." (How do you like them egg rolls, Mr. Goldstone?)

Even when Ethel Merman originally played Annie Oakley—when she was between thirty-four and forty—she was technically too old; at the start of the musical, Annie isn't supposed to be all that much older than Annie Warbucks. In reality, Annie met Frank Butler when she was twenty-one.

So needless to say, in 1966 Merman was old enough for Broadway wags to call the production *Granny Get Your Gun.* Staff members feared for the scenes in which Merman would embrace Butler—played by Bruce Yarnell, who was thirty-one (which was, incidentally, exactly Frank's actual age when he met Annie).

Director Jack Sydow wisely had Merman and Yarnell hug affectionately rather than kiss lustily. (In one of musical theater's most tragic ironies, in 1973, the thirty-seven-year-old Yarnell died in a plane crash, eleven full years before Merman passed away anywhere between age seventy-two and seventy-eight.)

But audiences—especially those who'd never seen Merman live—were glad and grateful to have the chance to see her. Great stars often get great entrances, but only the greatest stars get matter-of-fact entrances, underplaying that they've happened to come on. Here in *Annie Get Your Gun,* audiences heard a gunshot, then saw a bird fly off a character's hat, followed by an ever-so-lazily-sauntering-on Ethel Merman. She'd make a lot of noise later.

Although Merman didn't look youthful any more, her singing ability wasn't much worse for wear. Take "Anything You Can Do (I Can Do Better)," in which Annie and Frank each claim to be the better singer in holding a note. This isn't an area in which two gunslingers would ever think to compete, but ever since Merman debuted in *Girl Crazy* in 1930 and became famous for holding a note for sixteen bars in "I Got Rhythm," she welcomed any opportunity to show she could still do it.

Actually, if the 1946 original cast album replicated what happened onstage, Merman's holding "Yes, I cannnnnnnnnnn!" was ten seconds long. Of course, records in the 78 rpm era couldn't contain as much music as later LPs and CDs would, so Merman may have been asked to keep it short for the recording (although any of us wouldn't have relished being the executive who'd have to tell her to abridge her note holding). On the other hand, even with more grooves at her disposal for the 1966 cast album, Merman seems to have lost only a little, giving a nine-second hold.

Composer-lyricist Irving Berlin made a nice comeback, too. After the lackluster reception that his perfunctory score to *Mr. President* had received in 1962, not much was expected from the seventy-eight-year-old Berlin. To be sure, one of the new songs he wrote for the show—"Who Needs the Birds and the Bees?" for Dolly Tate—wasn't impressive enough to stay in the lineup. But Berlin came up with "An Old-Fashioned Wedding," his last great quodlibet—the type of song where one character sings one melody, another character sings another, and then they sing each of their parts together. Merman and Yarnell often had to give five or six encores. Talk about a showstopper.

It would be Merman's penultimate Broadway run. She'd take over *Hello, Dolly!* for its last nine months. However, on May 15, 1977, both Merman and Mary Martin, her only First-Lady-of-the-American-Theater rival, appeared in the one-night benefit *Together on Broadway.* Act 2 began with both legends fully costumed as Dolly, each descending her own staircase, with Merman stage right, Martin stage left. As they reached the floor, Martin began the proceedings with, "Well, hello, Ethel!" and Merman countered with, "Well, hello, Mary!" Among the men paying the waiters in the famous Harmonia Gardens number was Jule Styne. At one point, he took a wrong turn onstage and Merman turned director: "This way, Jule"—echoing "This way, Louise" in *Gypsy.* We'll never know if it was as phony as Tommy Steele's picking up the dropped hat in *Half a Sixpence.*

Reliever of the Year: Clive Revill
Sherry!

Bookwriter-lyricist James Lipton—who decades later would become famous for hosting Bravo's *Inside the Actors Studio*—was first represented on Broadway in 1962 for providing all the words to *Nowhere to Go but Up,* a musical about bootleggers. Indeed, after it opened and closed on successive Saturdays, he did have nowhere to go but up.

That was an original musical, which is harder to write than an adaptation. So this time Lipton acquired the rights to George S. Kaufman and Moss Hart's classic *The Man Who Came to Dinner.* He adapted it into *Dinner with Sherry* with Laurence Rosenthal, a composer with whom he had worked in 1956; they wrote a musical version of Molière's *The Doctor in Spite of Himself,* called *The Genius,* in which Hal Holbrook, Betsy Palmer, and Jules Munshin starred. It played Westport, Connecticut, but didn't make it to Manhattan.

Rosenthal later wrote ballet music for *The Music Man, Goldilocks, Take Me Along,* and *Donnybrook!* But *Dinner with Sherry*—soon to be renamed *Sherry!* thanks to its Jerry Herman-ish title tune—would be his first assignment as a composer of a Broadway musical.

Who could play the irascible and dry Sheridan Whiteside, the radio commentator who creates chaos in Ernest W. Stanley's suburban Ohio home after he slips on the front steps? Lipton knew the perfect performer: George Sanders, the actor who had portrayed the irascible and dry theater critic Addison DeWitt in *All about Eve* (and had won an Oscar for it). If any more proof was needed that Sanders was right for Whiteside, one only had to look at his 1960 autobiography, which he called *Memoirs of a Professional Cad.*

"George Sanders was the perfect choice for Sheridan Whiteside," said Lipton. "But as we were about to open in Boston [in January 1967], he learned that his beloved wife Benita Hume, a mere 60, had only a few months to live." (She was Sanders's wife from 1959 until her death in November 1967, in between his marriages to two Gabor sisters: Zsa Zsa from 1949 to 1954 and Magda from 1970 to 1971.)

"It was our bad luck that George understandably wanted to spend every waking moment with his wife," said Lipton. "We tried cutting as much of his material as we could, so he wouldn't have too much to manage. That, however, made the show not quite what we wanted it to be."

To be sure, during the show's tryout at the Colonial Theatre, Sanders seemed at sea. From his first entrance from an airplane as he arrived in Mesalia, Ohio, Sanders was not the riveting presence required of Sheridan Whiteside. He came down the airplane staircase in most timid fashion and matter-of-factly delivered his opening song, "Why Does the Whole Damn World Adore Me?" Later, he seemed grateful to have the chance to sit in a wheelchair for most of the night. One could see in his performance the roots of the suicide note that he would write in five years: "I am bored. I feel I have lived enough."

And so it went on to Sanders's curtain call. As the chorus merrily sang "Sherry!"—already bit of a pop hit due to a recording by Marilyn Maye (presumably referring to someone of an opposite gender)—Sanders lumbered on. The audience, which ideally augments its applause to honor the lead performance they just saw, did not, but politely clapped in perfunctory fashion.

"We got killed in Boston," said Lipton, who was barely exaggerating: Kevin Kelly of the *Boston Globe* famously said the show was "so awful it makes *Holly Golightly* look like a nostalgic work of art and no, I'm not kidding." *Holly* would later change its name to *Breakfast at Tiffany's* and while it would come to New York, it would never open to the critics.

Sherry! appeared to have a worse fate in store: a death in Boston. But then Clive Revill agreed to take over as Sheridan Whiteside. "Clive couldn't be ready for the rest of the Boston run," said Lipton. "He said he'd join us in Philadelphia but that he wanted his own director and choreographer—Joe Layton, whom he knew. They came in as a pair, so our director Morton Da Costa and choreographer Ronald Field left. And Clive made an enormous difference."

The New Zealand–born Revill began his Broadway career by portraying Sam Weller in the play *Mr. Pickwick* in 1952. He segued into musicals as the narrator in *Irma La Douce* in 1960 and reached his apex with his Fagin in *Oliver!* in 1963. Both of those roles got him Tony nominations. But he had never played an American on Broadway.

Revill proved he could. Suddenly *Sherry!* caught fire with this Sherry, who zoomed around in his wheelchair with the speed of a kid with a bumper car and with a mischievous if not diabolical grin on his face. Revill ripped into his songs and dialogue with equal relish.

Alas, Revill couldn't make *Sherry!* a hit. Rosenthal's music wasn't strong enough (although Lipton's work was). Dolores Gray was a bad choice to portray the vamp Lorraine Sheldon, for the now heavy-set actress was well past her femme-fatale days. The show lasted but seventy-two performances—but that's seventy-two more than it would have had if Clive Revill hadn't come to *The Man Who Came to Dinner.*

Rookie of the Year: Michael Bennett
A Joyful Noise

He'd performed in three Broadway flops: *Subways Are for Sleeping, Here's Love,* and *Bajour.* At least each of them ran for more than two hundred performances; the first musical on which he was assistant choreographer was the aforementioned nine-performance flop *Nowhere to Go but Up.*

And yet, just around the time that many young people are getting out of college, twenty-two-year-old Michael Bennett, who never bothered to attend, got the job of choreographing his first Broadway musical.

To be sure, *A Joyful Noise* was not anticipated to be a highlight of the season. Oscar Brand, its co-composer-lyricist, had never been represented on Broadway. His partner Paul Nassau had, if only contributing two songs to *New Faces of 1956* and some additional material to *Happy Town,* a three-performance failure in 1959.

A Joyful Noise's producer was Edward Padula, who will always be known as the producer of *Bye Bye Birdie.* But *All-American* and *Bajour* followed. What would happen with this show, based on Borden Deal's novel *The Insolent Breed,* which concerned three generations of itinerant country musicians? (One makes it big, only to return to his roots.)

Padula wanted John Raitt to star. Once Raitt agreed, that set the stage for Bennett to get the job as choreographer. For Raitt had recently reprised his Sid in *The Pajama Game* in Phoenix in a production that Bennett had choreographed and directed. Recalled Raitt, "Michael was really clever. He'd staged 'Once a Year Day' with people on swings that swung out over the audience. I was so impressed with him that I told him I was doing a new Broadway musical and I thought he'd be great for it."

The former Michael DiFiglia apparently was. Through summer-stock tryouts that went from Framingham, Massachusetts, to Valley Forge, Pennsylvania, *A Joyful Noise* received lukewarm reviews, but many were taken with the choreography, which featured fresh-faced dancers Donna McKechnie and Tom [*sic*] Tune, who played Beanpole. Bennett devised a clog dance, a revival meeting, and even a ballet for settings as diverse as a sawmill, a town square, a state fair, and the Grand Ole Opry.

"But," says dancer Baayork Lee, "giving Michael what he wanted was very hard. Every step he ever saw was in that show. He had us do so much clog dancing that we got shin splints, and we couldn't move our thighs because he was having us dance so close to the ground."

Dory Schary was supposed to work on the book and direction but clashed with Padula. Ditto the next director, Ben Shaktman. So Padula took over the direction.

A Joyful Noise would play only twelve performances on Broadway after it opened on December 15, 1966. And yet Bennett received a Tony nomination for Best Choreography. While many assume that no choreographer had ever secured a nomination with a show that had run such a short time, one had: in 1960, when Lee Scott was nominated for the aforementioned *Happy Town,* which ran three days.

But Scott never again worked on Broadway. Bennett certainly did, doing nine more Broadway musicals and getting a Best Choreography Tony nomination for each and every one.

"Michael could have got a lot more votes for *A Joyful Noise* if more people had seen the show," said Raitt. "But crazy Edward Padula closed it before

Christmas week–the best week in show business. Afterward, I asked him why, and he said he needed $3,000 to keep it open and he didn't have it. I told him, 'I would have given you that $3,000!'"

As wondrous as Bennett's work might have been, he wouldn't have won, anyway; Ronald Field's work on *Cabaret* was too astonishing. But other Tony Awards were in store for Michael Bennett.

Manager of the Year: Harold Prince
Cabaret

In 1965, Harold Prince followed his smash production of *Fiddler on the Roof* with a musical that got smashed by critics: *Flora, the Red Menace.*

The score was written by a new team who'd had only a modicum of Broadway experience. The composer, John Kander, had provided dance music for *Gypsy* and *Irma La Douce* and the music for a quick flop called *A Family Affair.* The lyricist, Fred Ebb, had contributed to two Broadway revues that had averaged fewer than fifteen performances.

Prince hired his mentor George Abbott to co-adapt George Atwell's novel *Love Is Just Around the Corner* and direct the resulting musical, too. It told of young Flora Meszaros (Liza Minnelli), who was graduated from high school during the depths of the Depression and was now filling out employment applications "for no job," as she dourly noted. After she gave her name and address (307 West Fourth—which was Kander's address at the time) and listed her previous experience ("None"), she got to "reason for applying for this position." That led to a strong song called "All I Need Is One Good Break."

Flora meets Harry Toukarian (Bob Dishy), who doesn't just complain about current conditions; he's joined the Communist Party, and because Flora is infatuated with him, she joins, too. So when Flora does miraculously get her first job at a big company, the Communists want her to picket and protest.

Some of the songs that Kander and Ebb provided for *Flora* were inordinately quirky. One had Harry, a stutterer, try to sing after he'd literally put some marbles in his mouth, *à la* Demosthenes. Another song simply consisted simply of "knock-knock" jokes. Yet another was a loping country-western song about a man's love for his horse. A Communist activist had a song that detailed her terrorist activities, before she decided that she was honor-bound to do more of them.

To be sure, there was pure gold in "A Quiet Thing," Flora's lovely ballad that expressed her surprise at how happy moments need not be loud. What's more, Kander and Ebb had proved that while under pressure on the road, they could write a dynamic eleven-o'clock number for their star via "Sing Happy."

But the oddities were there. And even after *Flora* flopped in nine weeks and lost 95 percent of its investment, Harold Prince again signed these songwriters with the well-off-the-wall sense of humor for his next musical. Perhaps if he were going to do a slam-bang commercial musical comedy they'd be right, but Prince was planning a musical version of *I Am a Camera,* about a pair of mismatched lovers who meet in Germany at the start of Nazism.

Prince had already produced shows by Stephen Sondheim and the team of Jerry Bock and Sheldon Harnick; wouldn't any of them have been better equipped to write this terribly demanding show? But somehow, Prince believed that Kander and Ebb were the best team to do the job. It was a most courageous move.

When time came for the Tony Awards, Kander and Ebb's score was judged better than the one Bock and Harnick furnished for that same season's *The Apple Tree. Cabaret* won eight Tonys and became a musical-theater classic, and suddenly Harold Prince looked very smart.

1967–1968

MVP, Comeback Player of the Year, and Reliever of the Year: Pearl Bailey
Hello, Dolly!

And to think that the original plan was to simply send out a new touring company.

David Merrick decided to initiate an all-black troupe of *Hello, Dolly!* and start it at the National Theatre in Washington, D.C. He chose Pearl Bailey as his Dolly Levi, although she hadn't been on Broadway in more than a dozen years, ever since *House of Flowers*—her fourth straight flop—closed.

As Horace Vandergelder, Merrick selected Cab Calloway, who didn't have much Broadway pedigree; he'd only played Sportin' Life in a 1953 revival of *Porgy and Bess.* But Calloway, like Bailey, was an entertainer well known from records, radio, film, and TV. Many audience members still remembered his trademark "Hi-De-Hi-De-Hi-De" from his 1931 hit recording of "Minnie the Moocher."

National Theatre audiences swooned and cheered as Calloway's Vandergelder did battle with another moocher: Bailey's Dolly. Merrick was astonished at the response, which was far greater than he'd expected.

Meanwhile, back on Broadway, one could see signs that boasted "3rd Smash Year! Betty Grable Is Dolly!" But suddenly, Betty Grable wasn't. Since she'd joined the company on June 12, 1967, the grosses had been steadily dropping. What had happened to the hit that Merrick expected would beat *My Fair Lady* as the longest-running musical of all time? He started thinking that if he kept Grable at the St. James, *Hello, Dolly!* might not make it into its fourth year.

So Merrick immediately put Grable and the rest of her cast on unemployment and sent Bailey, Calloway, and everyone else to the St. James Theatre. But Bailey was the most important component and the one who once again made *Dolly!* the talk of the town. She stayed on Broadway for more than two years (although she soon began skipping Wednesday matinees and then Saturday afternoons, too) and then undertook the tour that had been originally planned.

RCA Victor, which had profited splendidly from *Hello, Dolly!*'s 1964 original cast album (it had been on the charts for more than a year), decided to record another with the Bailey-Calloway cast. Orchestrator Glenn Osser even created an overture that slyly and insouciantly delivered the now-famous title tune in a way that said, "You know this one, don't you? You've been expecting it, haven't you?"

Life magazine gave its second *Dolly!* cover to Bailey. Both she and Merrick would get Special Tonys that spring. That Bailey also performed for up to twenty minutes after the curtain calls—which unofficially became known as "*Hello, Dolly*'s third act"—added to the mystique and box office.

Composer-lyricist Jerry Herman today readily admits, "Without Pearl Bailey the show would have closed after four years. But even after Bailey left,

Dolly! [with Phyllis Diller and then Ethel Merman] had been reestablished enough in theatergoers' consciousness to propel the show past *My Fair Lady's* seemingly unbreakable record of 2,717 performances. However, even at 2,844 performances, *Dolly!* would hold the title for only eight months, at which point *Fiddler on the Roof* surpassed it.

Now all three of these "long-run" shows have been eclipsed by literally more than a dozen others.

Rookies of the Year: Galt MacDermot, James Rado, Gerome Ragni, and Tom O'Horgan *Hair*

"Red-black. Blue-Brown. Yellow-Crimson. Green-Orange. Purple-pink. Violet-White. White-White. White-White."

Those weren't typical Broadway lyrics circa 1968. Once could also say the same of "Gliddy glup gloopy, Nibby nabby noopy, La la la lo lo, Sabba sibby sabba, Nooby aba naba, Le le lo lo, Tooby ooby wala, Nooby aba naba."

But in time, thousands upon thousands came to know the former set of lyrics while arguably millions learned the latter group when "Good Morning, Starshine" became a number-three hit.

They're both from *Hair*, a musical look at the hippie and anti–Vietnam War movement. The household-name international smash had a cast album that stayed on the *Billboard* charts for years, and at number one for thirteen weeks. No matter that these lyrics bore no resemblance to the witty words that Lorenz Hart and E. Y. Harburg had given theater music during the years, or the poetic ones that Oscar Hammerstein II provided. Fewer than four years after Tevye in *Fiddler on the Roof* had told his wife Golde, "It's a new world," Broadway was experiencing one.

These lyrics sounded as if they'd been scribbled on scraps of paper, and some of them were, as Gerome Ragni and James Rado traveled on subways or ate in restaurants. In their eventual *Playbill* bio, they happily referred to what they'd written as "non-book and lyrics." The lyrics don't read particularly well, but they sang once Galt MacDermot got involved.

MacDermot, the theater's first genuine rock composer, wasn't a theater person. "I like to write theatrical music, so I guess that's the reason I wound up in the theater," he says in his John Wayne–like voice, before adding a shrug as to explain that there is no explanation. And for all the celebration of youth that this new musical *Hair* would be, MacDermot was already forty when the show opened.

Actors Ragni and Rado met after they were cast in a revue that would run 1/1750th as long as Hair's 1,750 performances: *Hang Down Your Head and Die* closed after its opening off-Broadway on October 18, 1964. More serendipity was in store for the pair after Ragni happened to run into producer Joseph Papp on the subway. Once he green-lit the project, they wanted Tom O'Horgan to direct. He was busy, so Gerald Freeman landed the job. *Hair* became an intriguing new experience as soon as it began previews at Papp's new New York Shakespeare Festival Public Theatre—exactly three years to the day after *Hang Down Your Head* died.

Hair moved to and misfired at a discotheque. But O'Horgan decided that he could make time to direct, after all. He also had a wild notion for the show. What if at the end of the second act, the cast shed its clothes—all its clothes—to make the statement "Look at these lovely young bodies. Do you really want to see them mutilated or killed in a war?"

The audacity of it greatly appealed to all three authors. It was just one more atypical move for a show that didn't seem at all like a Broadway musical. But if the creative team didn't seem quite to consist of Broadway Babies, they worked like old-timers.

"What I'm most proud of," says Rado, "is that in a very short period of time—from October to April—we came up with 13 new songs. We felt we could still go further with the show, and the outpouring of new songs proved it. You know, we wrote the show very specifically for Broadway. Going to the Public Theater was kind of a compromise, because we couldn't get any Broadway producers to touch it."

What was expected to be a *Hair*-today-gone-tomorrow experience has been nothing of the kind. Scott Miller, in his book *Let the Sun Shine In,* wrote, "Performing in this show is an experience unlike any other. Not only does it bond each member of the tribe to every other member (and this includes actors, director, designers, musicians, tech people), but it also bonds each tribe to all other tribes around the world."

Ragni and Rado's original *Playbill* bio ended with the notation that they and MacDermot "recently formed a love-rock singing group called Hair just to confuse heads." Nothing happened with that. Plenty happened with *Hair.*

Manager of the Year: Joseph Papp and Michael Butler
Hair

Here we have an anomaly. We have two producers who were partners on the same show, but not during either its off-Broadway or Broadway runs.

First, Joseph Papp decided to produce *Hair* as the inaugural attraction at his Public Theatre on Lafayette Street in October 1967. This was surprising, given that the producer was best known for spearheading Shakespearean productions in Central Park. If he'd had any penchant for musicals, he'd never made it known.

Gerald Freeman's production had been a success, although it wasn't a runaway one. Nevertheless, it picked up a fan in Michael Butler, a wealthy real-estate man whose big credits were president of the Illinois Sports Council and commissioner of the Chicago Regional Port. But he had the money to help move *Hair* to a nightclub called Cheetah, a few steps from the West Fifty-second Street post office.

It didn't do well there, so Papp felt, unlike Butler, that it couldn't possibly succeed on Broadway. Papp settled for a one-half of 1 percent of the Broadway gross, which did eventually garner his theater nearly $2 million. But that was chump change compared to the millions that Butler made.

To be fair, Papp didn't foresee Butler hiring O'Horgan, who would add nudity to the show. While *Hair* didn't have any stars per se, naked bodies at the end of act 1 became Hair's main drawing card. Excellent music, fun lyrics, and an energetic cast provided the rest.

1968–1969

MVP: William Daniels
1776

In scene 2 of *1776,* John Adams is trying to spur Benjamin Franklin into helping him achieve American independence. While Franklin is sympathetic to the cause, he doesn't have much faith that Adams can convince delegates from the colonies to agree with him. "Nobody listens to you," he tells Adams. "You're obnoxious and disliked."

The way that William Daniels takes the jest shows that he's been similarly scarred many times but has never felt a wound. Lesser men would get insulted or rebut the charge; Adams is interested only in taking care of business.

And so the steely-eyed Daniels says, "I'm not promoting John Adams. I'm promoting independence."

Although Daniels had opened the show with a short monologue and had then been the centerpiece of a series of songs that lasted almost seven minutes, this was the moment where audiences truly saw his seriousness of purpose. For the rest of the Tony-winning musical, Daniels's Adams would be single-minded and unswerving. No matter how difficult the odds are against Adams—and they are, for seven of the thirteen colonies are very hard sells—Adams soldiers on. He gets discouraged from time to time, but he will not be defeated. And yet, when he emerges victorious, he's a gracious winner in acknowledging the worth of his opponent John Dickinson of Pennsylvania—for Adams knows the man was simply being staunchly true to his own personal beliefs and principles.

That Daniels gave one of the strongest performances in recent musical-theater history is not the only reason why he was the season's MVP. One could argue that Peter Stone deserves the honor for the difficult task of poring over congressional transcripts, letters, journals, and biographies, and then crafting them into the best book ever written for a musical. But Daniels was ultimately more valuable to Broadway for the contribution he made after the Tony nominations were announced.

As we saw with Tammy Grimes, back then billing over or above the title determined the category in which a performer would be placed. Because Daniels didn't have any box-office clout or name recognition, producer Stuart Ostrow had matter-of-factly put him under the title. As a result, the Tony committee, in a knee-jerk reaction, nominated him for Best Featured or Supporting Actor in a Musical. Never mind that Clive Barnes, in his rave review of the show in the *New York Times,* specifically said that Daniels was giving a "star performance." The Tony committee went by the rule book.

Daniels became as incensed at the decision as Adams was with King George III. He declined the nomination and demanded that his name be taken off the ballot. Indeed, check the Tony website today; it sports the name of one winner and two other nominees, but Daniels' defection is not mentioned in any way.

Daniels's abdication paved the way for his castmate Ron Holgate to win the prize for his portrayal of the vainglorious Richard Henry Lee. (Now, *there* was a supporting performance: nineteen sentences, eight phrases, one song, and one encore before calling it a night after scene 3.)

Jerry Orbach had to breathe a big sigh of relief, too, at the Tony committee's ruling. He won in the Best Actor in a Musical category, but would not have if he'd been in competition with Daniels.

Daniels's removal of his name from the ballot was a very brave action. The actor could have kept his mouth shut and won the Tony in a walk. While winning (and spinning) a Tony doesn't guarantee future career success—just ask any Tony winner who's gone to Hollywood—it doesn't hurt one's résumé.

The sad irony is that the *1776* nomination was the only time in Daniels's Broadway career that he received any kind of award recognition. While he had more success off-Broadway—he won a 1960 Obie and Clarence Derwent Award for originating the role of Peter in Edward Albee's *The Zoo Story*—Daniels came up empty for the seven Broadway productions in which he originated a role.

Strangely enough, Daniels's Adams was even snubbed by the Drama Desk Awards. Its nominating committee that season simply decided to name twenty Best Performances and give each a prize. Marian Mercer got one for her (admittedly terrific) ten-minute stint in *Promises, Promises,* but Daniels got nothing. He wouldn't be appreciated by any award committee until he began playing Dr. Mark Craig on TV's *St. Elsewhere.* There he received five consecutive Emmy nominations as Outstanding Lead Actor in a Drama Series from 1983 to 1987, winning back-to-back prizes in 1985 and 1986. And he was fine in the series—but not as galvanic as in his should-have-won-a-Tony performance in *1776.*

Manager of the Year: Stuart Ostrow
1776

By 1969, Stuart Ostrow certainly had taken his lumps as a producer. His first effort was *We Take the Town,* a 1962 musical in which Robert Preston portrayed Pancho Villa. The score had music by Harold Karr and lyrics by Matt Dubey, who'd previously done the 1956 Ethel Merman flop *Happy Hunting.*

Ostrow had convinced Goddard Lieberson of Columbia Records to put up nearly all the needed $400,000. And $10,000 came from Frank Loesser, who, in the early 1950s, had made Ostrow his protégé.

Columbia and Loesser lost every dime, for Ostrow couldn't even get *We Take the Town* to town. At least Karr and Dubey got a semi-hit song out of the show; Barbra Streisand made room for their "How Does the Wine Taste?" on her fourth album. But that didn't do Ostrow much good. (Ostrow also claims that he wanted to cast Streisand in the show but that Preston didn't want her.)

A year later, Ostrow went back to Lieberson to ask for financing for *Here's Love,* a musical version of *Miracle on 34th Street.* He got it. Lieberson and Columbia had to be cheered that the score was by Meredith Willson, who'd had two hits in a row: *The Music Man* in 1957 and *The Unsinkable Molly Brown* in 1960.

Ostrow took a chance on TV variety show director Norman Jewison to stage the work. Jewison would later have a substantial Hollywood career as a director (*In the Heat of the Night*) and even had a musical movie hit with *Fiddler on the Roof.* But Ostrow didn't like the results Jewison was getting from *Here's Love,* so he fired him and hired himself as director. The problem really was Willson's excruciating score. The show ran for nine months but lost most of its money.

The Apple Tree, three one-act musicals from 1966 to 1967, was not only produced by Ostrow, but inspired by him, too. He'd noted what so many had seen before him: musicals almost always have second-act trouble. But what if they had no second acts, he reasoned. Once again, Lieberson had Columbia do all the bankrolling and this time got most of the money back in a show that ran more than a year. But still, Columbia's three forays into Ostrow musicals had cost them hundreds of thousands.

And now Ostrow went to Lieberson asking him to finance a musical about the signing of the Declaration of Independence? How could anyone be so foolhardy? And the director, Peter Hunt, had even less of a track record than Jewison had had in his youth. Lieberson would only take 20 percent of the action this time—and would later regret it.

Most of Broadway assumed that Ostrow would close the show after its terribly rocky New Haven start. Ostrow's working for Loesser on the six-years-in-the-making *The Most Happy Fella* and *How to Succeed,* which needed an Abe Burrows reimagining, allowed him to see that great shows don't necessarily come together quickly.

By the time the Washington tryout was over, *1776* looked secure. In New York, aside from Martin Gottfried in *Women's Wear Daily,* the other five daily reviewers all raved.

Ostrow wasn't merely one of the corporate moneymen who came in the decades ahead—the type that didn't know *The Man Who Came to Dinner* from *The Girl Who Came to Supper.* Ostrow was a creative producer with artistic ideas. Peter Stone, in the commentary of the DVD of *1776*'s 1972 film, says that he even gave him one of the script's best punch lines.

Stone had John Dickinson and Benjamin Franklin, two of the Pennsylvania delegates, at odds about possible independence. Franklin notes that he wouldn't mind being called an Englishman if he were given all the rights of one here in America. "But to call me one without those rights is like calling an ox a bull. He's grateful for the honor, but he'd rather have restored what's rightfully his."

Stone left it at that—but Ostrow suggested that Dickinson retort with, "When did you notice they were missing?" Everyone in Congress, no matter what side he was on, uproariously laughed—with Franklin perhaps laughing the hardest.

The line was in keeping, too, with Stone's inherent fairness to all the characters. This wasn't a script where the so-called good guys (i.e., the ones promoting the American independence that we want) are intelligent and the so-called bad guys (who want to stay true to England) are not. Stone made everyone intelligent and capable of wit. Ostrow caught that, and the line he suggested was very much in that spirit.

Finally, when conservative president Richard M. Nixon wanted to bring *1776* to the White House, he asked that the number "Cool, Cool Considerate Men" be dropped because it painted conservatives in a less-than-flattering light. Ostrow, to paraphrase Lillian Hellman's famous retort to the House Un-American Activities Committee, would not cut his show "to suit this year's fashions." All of *1776* was performed. Producing *1776* was courageous enough, but refusing to accommodate the nation's chief executive was much braver.

Rookie of the Year: Burt Bacharach
Promises, Promises

Even before *Promises, Promises* opened on December 1, 1968, at the Shubert, its composer had done very well for himself in the pop music world.

Since Marty Robbins had reached number fifteen on the charts with Burt Bacharach's "The Story of My Life" on November 11, 1957, the composer had seen thirty-eight of his songs make the Top 40. Two even made the list by virtue of two different recordings—"Alfie" by Cher and Dionne Warwick, and "I Say a Little Prayer" by Dionne Warwick and Aretha Franklin.

Miraculously, Bacharach had reached the Top 10 a sweet sixteen times, reaching every position except for number nine. To be dramatic and in keeping with the way in which top tens are usually revealed, we'll list them in reverse order:

Number 10: "Do You Know the Way to San Jose?" (Dionne Warwick, 1968); "I Say a Little Prayer" (Aretha Franklin, 1968)

Number 8: "Baby, It's You" (The Shirelles, 1961); "Anyone Who Had a Heart" (Dionne Warwick, 1963); "A Message to Michael" (Dionne Warwick, 1966)

Number 7: "What the World Needs Now Is Love" (Jackie DeShannon, 1965)

Number 6: "Walk on By" (Dionne Warwick, 1964); "Wishin' and Hopin'" (Dusty Springfield, 1964)

Number 5: "Tower of Strength" (Gene McDaniels, 1961)

Number 4: "Magic Moments" (Perry Como; 1958); "Liberty Valance" (Gene Pitney, 1962); "I Say a Little Prayer" (Dionne Warwick, 1967); "The Look of Love" (Sergio Mendes and Brasil '66, 1968)

Number 3: "Blue on Blue" (Bobby Vinton, 1963); "What's New, Pussycat?" (Tom Jones, 1965)

Number 2: "Only Love Can Break a Heart" (Gene Pitney, 1962)

Number 1: "This Guy's in Love with You" (Herb Alpert, 1968)

What a shame that no one connected with *Promises, Promises* noticed or suggested that that number-one hit—released only five months before the show went into rehearsal—could have fit the musical very well. For *Promises* was the musical version of the 1960 Oscar-winning film *The Apartment.* It was the story of Chuck Baxter, who loves his co-worker Fran Kubelik from afar. This guy was indeed in love with her.

He does, however, find that staying in love with her is more difficult once he discovers that she's having an affair with his boss Mr. Sheldrake, who's using his apartment for the liaison.

Most of Bacharach's pop songs had lyrics by Hal David, often thought of as a good and competent professional. He didn't, however, possess the genuine genius that Bacharach had. The composer had a distinct voice; the lyricist didn't. Bacharach was even able to do the seemingly impossible with a song he wrote between *Promises, Promises* rehearsals: "Raindrops Keep Fallin' on My Head" for the 1969 film *Butch Cassidy and the Sundance Kid.* While most songs are structured in thirty-two measures of eight bars each, "Raindrops" had thirty-six measures of nine bars each.

To be fair, writing to Bacharach's quirky rhythms and seemingly scattershot notes couldn't be easy. When Bacharach wrote the frenetic theme to *Casino Royale,* one can only imagine David saying to him, "Burt, that one's an instrumental." But to his credit, David even found a way to put lyrics to that one.

David would join Bacharach in writing *Promises, Promises* and would do a serviceable job. Because the music was strong, arresting, and unique, David's not finding the right spots for songs didn't much matter. When Chuck gets his first, long-lusted-for promotion from Sheldrake, David didn't have him sing. When Chuck must juggle the schedules of the many executives using his apartment, David didn't give him a comedy song. Chuck didn't break out in delighted song when he got the chance to cook for Fran. For that matter, when Chuck realized that he'd given up his integrity to Sheldrake along with his apartment in order to get his next promotion, there was no mournful song acknowledging the hollow victory.

Most interesting of all: After Fran had a suicide attempt over Sheldrake, she told Chuck, "I think I'm going to give it all up"—meaning love. That's certainly a song cue, and while Bacharach and David did write "I'll Never Fall in Love Again" for both Fran and Chuck, the idea didn't come to them until late in the Boston tryout.

The song, later covered by Dionne Warwick, reached number nine, in fact, allowing Bacharach a clean sweep of having at least one of his songs place in the Top Ten.

But Bacharach found writing a musical much too demanding. Although *Promises* ran 1,281 performances and closed as the thirteenth-longest-running musical in Broadway history, Bacharach was never enticed to return to the theater. No other composer who has ever had a show run as long as he did has so cavalierly walked on by.

David, meanwhile, returned to the theater in 1974, writing lyrics to Michel Legrand's music for a show called *Brainchild.* It closed in Philadelphia.

1969–1970

MVP: Katharine Hepburn
Coco

When the original cast album of *Coco* was released in early 1970, most people who chose to buy it selected the still-dominant medium of the long-playing record rather than a cassette or eight-track tape. But soon word spread among Broadway fans that the record was the best medium for this album.

For if *Coco* weren't played at the usual 33⅓ rpm speed, but at 45 rpm, Katharine Hepburn's frog voice would sound a little better. What's more, the fifty-two-minute record would also finish a few minutes faster.

Nice joke, but Katharine Hepburn proved she was the season's MVP. Without her, this not-so-hot bio-musical about the famed fashion designer Coco Chanel (1883–1971) might not have even made it to the stage.

Producer Frederick Brisson originally got involved so that his wife Rosalind Russell could play Coco. But Russell, already sixty-two, was not up to the challenge of eight a week. Indeed, after *Coco* debuted on December 18, 1969, Russell made only two more films before officially retiring.

Bookwriter-lyricist Alan Jay Lerner and composer André Previn turned to Hepburn, who provided the staunch characterization of a woman determined to succeed in the dress business by really trying. She'd sing eight songs and didn't leave the stage very often. Although Hepburn came from the era when ladies were ladies, she wasn't above opening the second act by saying "Shit"—because the big act 1 finale in which she was preparing to debut her new collection hadn't worked out. That's how committed she was to the project.

Not incidentally, Hepburn was a Wednesday matinee lady's MVP, too. She noticed during her first week that terrible noises were heard across the street from the Mark Hellinger Theatre. The cause was the construction of Paramount Plaza and the Uris Theatre. Hepburn actually went across the street and asked the laborers not to work during Wednesday afternoons. And they stopped until Hepburn left the show on August 1, 1970.

Danielle Darrieux replaced her. Many might say, "Who?" and for good reason: while Darrieux had made more than ninety movies (to Hepburn's three dozen), most of them were in her native France. Although art houses picked up her *La Ronde* (1950) and *The Earrings of Madame de…* (1953)—and despite the wider distribution for *The Young Girls of Rochefort* (1967)—she wasn't well known.

Darrieux did, however, have a regal bearing (fitting for a woman who counted "Marie Antoinette" as two of her three middle names) and a much more pleasant voice than Hepburn. Maybe she'd surprise everyone the way Mimi Hines did with *Funny Girl.*

No such luck. While Hepburn played eight months at capacity or close to it, Darrieux could manage only two months at embarrassingly low grosses. *Coco* closed at a loss, although Hepburn promised to tour with it.

Of course, many stars say they'll tour, but after a few days (let alone months) of freedom, they start thinking of their musical as their past and not their future. Hepburn, however, kept her word to Brisson and took *Coco* on a five-month national tour. Virtually every audience in Cleveland, Chicago, Rochester, Hartford, Baltimore, Toronto, Dallas, and Los Angeles was at capacity. Investors saw a return on their investment—which wouldn't have happened if Hepburn hadn't agreed to go on the road.

Hepburn also gets credit for recognizing a talent on the *Coco* staff and developing it. Not long into rehearsals, director Michael Benthall didn't seem to have enough vision to stage the show, but Hepburn noticed that this short, bearded choreographer named Michael Bennett did. Whatever Hepburn wanted, Hepburn got, and because she trusted Bennett, most everyone else started taking his suggestions and direction. It was an important building block in Bennett's career, and he never looked back. He never had to.

Comeback Player of the Year: Stephen Sondheim
Company

As the 1960s were turning into the 1970s, many a Broadway savant thought that Stephen Sondheim was all washed up.

Sondheim had started off with three household-name hits that everyone still knows: *West Side Story, Gypsy,* and *A Funny Thing Happened on the Way to the Forum.* But that first show was never known as "Stephen Sondheim's *West Side Story.*" Sometimes it was composer "Leonard Bernstein's *West Side Story,*" or, more often than not, director-choreographer "Jerome Robbins's *West Side Story.*"

Similarly, it was never "Stephen Sondheim's *Gypsy.*" Sometimes "Jule Styne's *Gypsy,*" "Arthur Laurents's *Gypsy,*" or "Jerome Robbins's *Gypsy.*" But never Sondheim's.

Compare this to Richard Rodgers, who throughout his forty-year career had been top-billed over his lyricists: It was always Rodgers and (Lorenz) Hart, Rodgers and (Oscar) Hammerstein.

In 1962, when Sondheim made the leap to composer-lyricist with *Funny Thing,* the show was said to have succeeded in spite of him. *Funny Thing* has arguably the greatest number of genuine laughs of any Broadway musical (even without the "improvements" that many of its leading men have sadly brought to it). It received Tonys for Best Book and Best Musical in 1963. But Sondheim didn't win for Best Score, and for good reason: He wasn't even nominated.

No one begrudges the Tony to Lionel Bart's *Oliver!* or nominations for Coleman and Leigh's *Little Me* or Newley and Bricusse's *Stop the World.* But now try to find someone who'll support a Tony nomination for Milton Schafer and Ronny Graham's *Bravo, Giovanni* over Sondheim's score. Today many agree that Sondheim wrote one of musical theater's best opening numbers ("Comedy Tonight"), one of its best showstopping vaudeville turns ("Everybody Ought to Have a Maid"), and hilarious lyrics for all his songs. (Note "Today, I woke too weak to walk." The English language contains five vowel sounds, and Sondheim matched three of them to the same consonant in one line.)

In the same five-year span, Rodgers had had three hits, too. For *Flower Drum Song* in 1958 and *The Sound of Music* in 1959, Hammerstein provided the lyrics. For the former show, Hammerstein atypically chose to have a collaborator on the book, and for the latter, he chose not to write the book at all—because he was dying. And because Hammerstein was Sondheim's mentor, he'd asked Rodgers to write with him.

But after Hammerstein died in 1960, Rodgers showed he was in no hurry to make Sondheim his partner. Instead, he worked with bookwriter Samuel Taylor on an original musical called *No Strings.* It was a 1962 hit—not a smash, true, but a hit in the era when 580 performances was a nice run and everybody made money.

It was, however, a triumph for Rodgers. For the first time in his career, he'd provided an entire set of lyrics as well as music. And those lyrics were very good. He set them to fine—and surprisingly jazzy—music, the kind he used to write during his twenty-four-year partnership with Hart. Rodgers, who was then pushing sixty, hadn't sounded this youthful in nearly thirty years.

What's more, Rodgers had been nominated for a Best Score Tony. He was pitted against Jerry Herman (*Milk and Honey*), Richard Adler (*Kwamina*), and Frank Loesser and his enormous hit *How to Succeed in Business Without Really Trying.* But Rodgers won the prize in 1962 for which Sondheim couldn't even get nominated in 1963.

So now, instead of working with Sondheim, Rodgers chose Alan Jay Lerner, whose last three projects had been *My Fair Lady, Gigi,* and *Camelot.* They worked on an original musical called *I Picked a Daisy*—but Rodgers abandoned it because he felt Lerner wasn't working quickly enough. That's how young he felt.

Then, in 1964, *Anyone Can Whistle,* for which Sondheim had written music and lyrics, closed after nine performances, one-thirty-fifth as long a run as *No Strings* had had. Still, Rodgers had invested in *Whistle* and did agree to meet with Sondheim to discuss projects.

Most every other wordsmith in the business would have been thrilled and honored to be even considered by the one, the only Richard Rodgers. By the time Sondheim was born in 1930, Rodgers had already provided music for eighteen Broadway productions and three London shows. Before Foxy and Herbert Sondheim had become little Stephen's parents, Rodgers had already had household-name hit songs with "Manhattan," "Mountain Greenery," "My Heart Stood Still," "Thou Swell," "You Took Advantage of Me," "With a Song in My Heart," "Dancing on the Ceiling," and "Ten Cents a Dance."

And while Sondheim was still hoping that some producer would want him to write both music and lyrics on a new show, none did. He must have felt terrible at even considering a lyrics-only position. He'd almost walked away from *Gypsy* because he wanted to do both music and lyrics but star Ethel Merman insisted that Jule Styne do the music. Now returning to lyrics-only had to feel like a big step backward. But Hammerstein did want him to work with Rodgers, and that mattered, too.

So Sondheim accepted Rodgers's offer to write lyrics. He knew that Broadway would say that *No Strings* proved Rodgers didn't need Sondheim, but *Forum* and *Whistle* proved that Sondheim needed Rodgers. What's more, Rodgers was in the position to do the hiring; since 1949, he'd been one of the producers on each of his seven shows. One can even picture Sondheim entering Rodgers's office only to hear The Man curtly tell him, "Hey, you—wipe your feet before you come in here."

Still, they were soon working with Arthur Laurents on *Do I Hear a Waltz?* a musical based on Laurents's play *The Time of the Cuckoo.* Early on the disagreements started: Rodgers versus Sondheim and Laurents. Perhaps Rodgers didn't abandon it because he'd already had one aborted project and didn't want the stigma of discarding another. But Rodgers the producer treated Laurents and Sondheim as hired hands.

So how did Sondheim feel on September 25, 1965, when *Waltz* closed at a substantial loss after only 220 performances? That Tony nomination for his part of Best Score was little consolation, for he considered it his least impressive work in five Broadway tries.

And Rodgers? Even with this failure, he was flying high because the film version of *The Sound of Music* was en route to becoming the highest-grossing film ever. Rodgers had reportedly written two new songs for the smash—music *and* lyrics. Now was there any doubt that he was the master and that Sondheim boy had been just a little overrated?

In 1966, Sondheim was relegated to writing *Evening Primrose,* a one-hour TV special that was poorly received. Then came absolutely nothing in 1967, 1968, or 1969. Oh, he was said to be "working on two musicals," but that didn't mean they'd ever get on. Not with the six solid years of failure.

But Sondheim knew he could show the world a thing or two. "If you can find me, I'm here," he wrote for his dropout hero in *Evening Primrose*—lines that could then apply to him, too.

Broadway was lucky that it did eventually find him and his subsequent eleven musicals. *Company* opened on April 26, 1970, too late for the 1969–1970 Tony Awards. But its being a year old on March 28, 1971—at the twenty-fifth annual Tony Awards—didn't impede Sondheim from winning not only one Tony for Best Score, but two: for that year (and that year alone), the Tonys gave a prize for Best Music and Best Lyrics.

Follies came in 1971 and *A Little Night Music* in 1973—and so did Best Score Tonys for those. Four Tonys in little more than a thousand days. Sondheim was the reigning king—nay, god—of the American musical theater.

One other point: on March 11, 1973, at the Shubert Theater, when *Sondheim: A Musical Tribute* took place, attendees must have been astonished when they took their seats, opened their programs, and found that one of the songs would be "We're Gonna Be All Right" from *Do I Hear a Waltz?* Why was that little throwaway of a nothing number included?

Because the version audiences got in the 1965 production and on the original cast album was not the entire lyric that Sondheim had written. It included far more wit and bite that had been lost on Rodgers, who insisted on dropping many verses and choruses on which Sondheim had meticulously worked. It was good a metaphor as any for the old guard giving way to the new.

Reliever of the Year: Larry Kert
Company

March 23, 1970. Shubert Theatre, Boston. The first preview and world premiere of *Company.* Dean Jones is playing Bobby, the uncommitted but not-so-confirmed bachelor. During the evening we've seen him with his good and crazy married friends, his on-again/off-again girlfriends, and his one-night stands.

Now it's time for the eleven-o'clock number. Jones takes center stage and, after a perky vamp, starts singing Stephen Sondheim's "Happily Ever After"—which concludes that being married means living "happily ever after in hell."

The theatergoing audience in Boston will change in a few years, but right now it's still the province of Boston brahmins and middle-class theatergoers, most of whom have been married for some time. They either don't believe or don't want to be reminded of what day-to-day married life can be. From his vantage point, Jones sees a great many scowling faces and arms folded across chests. Many audience members might well catch that his eyes widen to what seem to be twice their usual size. He just might very well be thinking, "I've got to get out of this show."

Not long after, Jones does indeed part company with *Company.* Was "Happily Ever After" the moment that made him want to abdicate the role of one of Broadway's landmark musicals?

Thirty-two years later, when Jones is inducted into his home state's Alabama Stage and Screen Hall of Fame, he reminisces about *Company* at a press conference. "I went out there in Boston and sang this song 'Happily Ever After,' and I could feel them asking me, 'Why do you hate us?' I saw their eyes widen, and it was, 'Why do you hate us?' I just can't do anything too nihilistic."

Sondheim, bookwriter George Furth, and director Hal Prince all had to face the reality that "Happily Ever After" was too hard-hitting a moment for the average theatergoer. So Sondheim softened the moment (and, some say, the show's message) by indicating that romantic commitment, which may or may not mean marriage, also means "being alive."

But even this shift of focus wasn't enough for Jones. Take a look at the D. A. Pennebaker documentary of *Company: Original Cast Album* and watch him when he finishes "Being Alive" One can feel him say, "Okay. That's it. I'm done with it. I'll never have to do that again and I never will."

Jones's leaving allowed an old Sondheim–Prince colleague to get his first significant role and run in a decade. Larry Kert, the original Tony in *West Side Story,* had originated leads in *A Family Affair* (1961), *Breakfast at Tiffany's* (1966), and *La Strada* (1969)—three shows that had averaged twenty-two performances. In between he took over as Cliff in Prince's *Cabaret* for the last year of the run.

Bobby was a nice return showcase for Kert and yielded him an unexpected bonus: A Tony nomination. Almost always, a person who assumes a role from the person who originates it isn't eligible for a Tony. In Kert's case, he got a break. Because *Company* opened on April 26, 1970—less than a dozen days after the April 15 cutoff—he had almost a full year to play the role and establish himself in it.

While Kert didn't make the original Broadway cast album, he did make the original London cast album—in a manner of speaking (and singing). Because the original Broadway company picked up en masse and moved to the West End, Kert simply recorded his tracks to the existing Broadway ones. Both his voice and a different recording technique make him sound stronger than Jones did in the role.

Jones did return to play Bobby in 1993 for a *Company* reunion concert in California and then New York. But would management have asked Kert had he not died two years earlier?

Manager of the Year: Philip Rose
Purlie

Philip Rose was born on the Fourth of July (in 1921), which is fitting, for he's All-American in the best sense of the term: a truly unprejudiced man.

He came to know African-Americans when he was a bill collector for a District of Columbia department store. Along with tendering the bills, he offered some advice: "Don't shop at this store. You're being cheated." He was outraged when he discovered that in the late 1930s, no black person was allowed to take a government test, because none would be employed by the government.

Rose didn't expect to be a producer, but a singer; he made appearances as rarefied as the St. Louis Opera Company and as mundane as a Boston burlesque house. Yet to make a few extra bucks, Rose sold "race records," as rhythm and blues discs were then known. That led to his becoming a distributor for Atlantic Records, the first successful post-war black label. It inspired him to start Glory Records. His first album was a spoken-word disc of Sidney Poitier reading "Poetry of the Negro," for which a young woman named Lorraine Hansberry provided the liner notes.

Hansberry and Rose had met at a desegregated summer camp. She fueled Rose's interest in theater by taking him to plays by Shakespeare and Chekhov. One night they went to a play about a black family. Neither she nor he liked it. When Hansberry said, "Well, if I were going to write about a black family, I could do better than that," Rose said, "Well, why don't you try it?"

Indeed she did, but now she had to find a producer for *A Raisin in the Sun,* in which Walter Lee Younger and his mother, Lena, disagree on how to spend a $10,000 insurance windfall. Rose was interested in producing, but where would he get the necessary $100,000? Who'd attend, given that blacks weren't theatergoers, and whites preferred musicals? *Anna Lucasta,* a 1944 black melodrama, ran 957 performances and closed on Broadway as its ninth-longest-running play, but many considered that success an anomaly.

Rose had hoped the play would interest such established producing pros as Roger L. Stevens or David Susskind. The former turned it down, while the latter, who Rose hoped would make a significant investment, gave him $500 and told him to produce it off-Broadway. Rose called William (*Two for the Seesaw*) Gibson out of the blue just to have him read the script, and Gibson wound up investing. So did David Cogan, Rose's accountant—to the tune of $30,000.

Glory Records put up the front money. Playing Ruth at the first reading was Ruby Dee, who did so well that no one else was ever considered for Ruth, the young wife and mother who's desperate to move to a nicer apartment, while her husband Walter Lee is just as desperate to quit as a chauffeur and open his own business.

Playing the lead was Poitier, who'd recently filmed *Porgy and Bess* and *The Defiant Ones.* He helped the play to have a higher profile. But *A Raisin in the*

Sun was the real star. Ruth brought tears to theatergoers' eyes when she said, "I'll work twenty hours a day in all the kitchens in Chicago ... I'll strap my baby on my back if I have to and scrub all the floors in America and wash all the sheets in America if I have to—but we've got to move." Suddenly even the hardest of white hearts melted and the idea of a black family living next door didn't seem a fate to be avoided.

When Poitier left the cast, Dee's husband Ossie Davis took over. He was in the process of writing a play called *Purlie Victorious,* in which he planned to play the title character, a preacher who is determined to break the economic stranglehold that a plantation owner has over his people. Purlie triumphs, and gets the girl, as well, one Lutiebelle Gussie May Jenkins, whom Davis planned for Dee to play.

Rose produced *Purlie Victorious* with Davis and Dee in the leads. It managed to run most of the 1961–1962 season and gave important early career roles to Godfrey Cambridge and Alan Alda. It didn't quite pay back its costs, but Rose's selling the property to Hollywood almost got investors their money back.

Now after five failures (including *Bravo, Giovanni* and *Café Crown*) and only one hit (*The Owl and the Pussycat*), Rose and Davis started thinking about *Purlie Victorious* as a musical. They wrote the book for *Purlie,* which Rose would direct.

Once again, Rose would give neophytes a chance. His songwriters, Gary Geld and Peter Udell, had no Broadway experience, just a few pop hits (including "Sealed with a Kiss"). As Purlie and Lutiebelle, he chose two young performers who had only one Broadway credit: Cleavon Little and Melba Moore, each of whom would win a Tony for *Purlie.* He also hired future TV star Sherman (*The Jeffersons*) Hemsley, who made his Broadway debut in a supporting role.

At a time when musicals were budgeted at near $1 million, Rose brought in *Purlie* for less than half that amount, forgoing an out-of-town tryout when they were still closer to the rule than the exception. And while *Purlie* didn't pay back its investment, it ran 657 performances and brought a new black audience to the theater.

In the decade before *Purlie*, seven musicals opened that had inherent black appeal, only three of which—*Golden Boy, Hallelujah, Baby!* and the retooled *Hello, Dolly!*—ran for any length of time.

In the decade after *Purlie,* twenty musicals with black appeal opened, including such long-running Tony winners as *Raisin, The Wiz,* and *Ain't*

Misbehavin'. Don't Bother Me, I Can't Cope, Me and Bessie, and *Bubbling Brown Sugar* may not have won any big prizes, but they each lasted over a year. Black musical theater was here to stay, and *Purlie* was one of the reasons why.

Rookie of the Year: Lewis J. Stadlen
Minnie's Boys

It's Claire Bloom's job to announce the winner of the 1969–1970 Tony for Best Featured Actor in a Musical. "And the nominees are," she says, "René Auberjonois for *Coco;* Brandon Maggart for *Applause;* and George Rose for *Coco.*"

What? No Lewis J. Stadlen for his funny yet poignant and believable young Groucho Marx in *Minnie's Boys*?

Stadlen had to be disappointed, even insulted. The nominating committee had selected only three entries, while four or even five had been the usual number. So if the group had selected, say, Sherman Hemsley for his role in *Purlie,* Stadlen could have at least consoled himself that the Tonys didn't necessarily admire him less, but admired those four actors more. But when there's a blank space where a nominee should be, the implication is that the Tony committee simply didn't think that Lewis J. Stadlen was good enough.

Much of Broadway was startled, including the cast of *Minnie's Boys,* who even paid for an ad in *Variety* to officially show their disapproval. Most every person with the show signed it. Not that that did any good.

Perhaps the Tony committee was too heavily influenced by Clive Barnes—then the critic for the *New York Times.* "Stadlen is remarkably good," Barnes wrote, before adding: "Whether he has any skills other than playing Groucho Marx, I hesitate to say." That comment may well have put the idea in people's heads that the young actor might be limited.

He proved otherwise. Thus far, Stadlen is still continuing a solid theatrical career. Later in the 1970s, he originated the role of the harried nephew-agent in *The Sunshine Boys* and then played Pangloss and Voltaire in the revisal of *Candide* that rejuvenated the previously troubled show. That latter outing yielded him his first Tony nomination.

It should have been his second.

Nevertheless, the actors playing his brothers would in the years to come have gladly traded places with him. Daniel Fortus (Harpo), Alvin Kupperman

(Zeppo), and Irwin Pearl (Chico) played Broadway only one more time, while Gary Raucher (Gummo) never appeared there again. A one-in-five success rate is about right for Broadway.

Or is it even much too high?

Andrea McArdle as Annie The sun wouldn't have come out tomorrow if there hadn't been a girl with the strength, charisma, timing, and sensitivity to play Little Orphan Annie. Some performances at the Goodspeed Opera House with another Annie had to pass before lyricist-director Martin Charnin noticed that the kid playing Pepper had enough pepper in her to play the role. That's when Andrea McArdle went to work—and made it work.

Liza Minelli with Bob Fosse *Phone rings.*
She: Hello?
He: Minnelli? Fosse. You busy?
She: No.
He: Good—you'd better not be, not for the next few weeks.
She: What's going on?
He: You are—on Friday night as Roxie Hart in *Chicago.* Gwen's sick and out of the show.
She: But Bob—it's Monday already.
He: See you tomorrow.

1970–1980

ɔe Papp It's one of the greatest ironies in theater history: Joseph Papp, off-Broadway's perennial hero who had little use for "the Main ꞇem," green-lit a project that became Broadway's longest-running production: *A Chorus Line.*

anie Sell and the Andrews Sisters in *Over Here!* Any fan of 1940s music will be able to identify the two women on the right: atty and Maxene Andrews, two members of the sister-act trio that sold millions of records. But who's that woman on the left? Why, Janie ell, who stood in for Laverne Andrews (who'd died in 1967) for the 1974 musical *Over Here!*

1970–1971

MVP: Stephen Sondheim
Follies

For four decades now, theatergoers have been arguing over the worth of *Follies*, one of the most celebrated of all modern musicals—and one that initially lost an inordinate fortune: $665,000.

Some find James Goldman's original book about Phyllis and Sally, two former showgirls, their respective husbands Ben and Buddy—and their unsuccessful marriages—an utter bore. Others see the two couples' plight as a fascinating metaphor for a once-promising but ultimately declining America.

Many playgoers were intrigued by the use of ghosts and younger actors to represent the now much-older characters in their prime; others were simply confused by it.

That the show was set at a reunion was certainly one of its strengths, but as playwright Jane Milmore says, "I would have liked to have learned more about the fascinating entertainers that Stephen Sondheim and Goldman created—Carlotta Campion, Stella Deems, Solange LaFitte, and Hattie Walker—rather than center on the miseries of Phyllis, Ben, Sally, and Buddy."

However, both the many who love *Follies* and those who hate it seem to agree that Stephen Sondheim wrote an extraordinary score. Certainly the production was lavish, down to Boris Aronson's purposely distressed set, Florence Klotz's exquisite costumes, and Tharon Musser's moody lighting. It was such an immense undertaking that producer-director Harold Prince not only had Michael Bennett choreograph it, but also asked him to co-direct.

And as valuable as all of the above personnel and the extraordinary cast were, Stephen Sondheim emerged as the season's MVP for his score, which became an immediate classic.

He channeled Irving Berlin's "A Pretty Girl Is Like a Melody" in his stunning and sweeping opening number, "Beautiful Girls," in which we met yesteryear's Follies "girls." They sang such gems as "Broadway Baby," modeled after the good-time sound of DeSylva, Brown, and Henderson, and

"One More Kiss," which reminded us that in the midst of all those operettas, Rudolf Friml also wrote for the *Ziegfeld Follies of 1921*. And who else could be represented by a ditty called "Ah, Paree" but the songwriter who celebrated Paris most of all: Cole Porter.

As for our four main characters, Jerome Kern was homaged through the quodlibet "You're Gonna Love Tomorrow" and "Love Will See Us Through," in which the younger versions of Phyllis, Ben, Sally, and Buddy compared notes.

Sondheim has often been criticized for not writing "a tune you can hum," but he provided plenty here. He did use his trademark dissonance for such songs as Ben's "The Road You Didn't Take," which is an entire middle-age crisis succinctly expressed in less than three minutes' time.

Lyrically, he shone once again. That Sondheim had won two Tonys for Best Music and Best Lyrics for *Company* the year before was certainly deserved. But too bad that the Tony powers-that-be decided this year to conflate the two categories into Best Score. For if there were ever a year that a songwriter deserved two awards for one score, this was the one.

While Sondheim had always written tricky rhymes that brought on smiles of admiration, here he reached his apotheosis. In "Beautiful Girls" he cited two historic female icons from completely different worlds and eras and got a felicitous rhyme for each: "Faced with these Loreleis / What man can moralize?" "Each in her style a / Delilah reborn." Add to these a heavenly "Beauty celestial / The best, you'll agree."

Ted Chapin, who worked on the original production, reported in his book *Everything Was Possible* that the spot where we're now accustomed to hearing Buddy sing "Buddy Blues" was originally conceived by Goldman as a songless array of vaudeville-like jokes that Buddy would tell. It reached nine full pages before Sondheim decided to musicalize the moment. This approach allowed him to have both of Buddy's women—wife Sally and girlfriend Margie—echo what Buddy had just said. So when Buddy claimed that Margie deems him to be "perfect, she swears," Margie followed it with "You're perfect, goddammit." When he spoke of Sally and alluded that Ben was "a fella she prefers," Sally took the opportunity to point out that she also liked "Furs! Furs!" And when he happened to mention the word "Anybody," Sally come out with "Buddy? Bleah!" and mimed vomiting. (Sondheim swears that he didn't name the character Buddy just to get in this joke.) And the "Thank-you-for-the- present-but-what's-wrong-with-it" stuff? Lord only knows how many times wives and husbands have had that exchange.

In "Love Will See Us Through," Young Sally cautions Young Ben "And though I'll do my utmost / To see you never frown / And though I'll try to cut most / Of our expenses down / I've some traits, I warn you / To which you'll have objections / I too have a cornu- / Copia of imperfections."

That's dazzling wordplay, to be sure, but what's equally effective is the subtext. Young Buddy is willing, nay eager, to swat away Young Sally's warnings about how she burns the toast and has the tendency to interrupt his jokes. But after all we've seen of the middle-aged Buddy and Sally, we know that he doesn't find such "imperfections" as adorable as he once did.

Cleverness in rhyme is not all that makes Sondheim's lyrics extraordinary. Phyllis's "Could I Leave You?" has her musing about splitting from Ben, but the word "leave" soon took on a new meaning: "Well, you could leave me the house"—and that was just the start of the litany. Notice, too, that in just six lines, Sondheim employed five erudite but seldom-used words: *martyred, cryptic, sullen, passionless,* and *ill-concealed.* His word choices alone show that he's several cuts above, and he made Phyllis just as accomplished.

Shakespeare wrote about the "seven ages" of man, but Sondheim was able to encapsulate the life of an actress in only three steps in "I'm Still Here": "First you're another slow-eye vamp / Then someone's mother / Then you're camp." How true; many a Hollywood starlet once thought she had the world by the tail—and didn't. We can all be humbled by the thought. "Who's That Woman?" is also a reminder of how even the greatest of beauties age (in what was the premier production number of the entire half century).

In "The Right Girl," Buddy says his girlfriend Margie makes him "feel like a million bucks instead of—what?—a rented tux." People do add a "What?" in the middle of a sentence when they don't know what else to say. True, Sondheim obviously added that because he was stuck with an extra musical syllable, but he gets credit for finding a way of making the liability into an asset.

In "Losing My Mind," Sondheim makes an atypical move: he repeats the B section word for word. ("All afternoon, doing every little chore …") But that's apt, because he's referencing a popular song of the day, and in those days, repeating a B section was *pro forma.* That choice does not stop him from coming up with one of his simplest but most effective lyrics that's as bittersweet as dark chocolate: "You said you loved me—or were you just being kind?"

While writing the show, and then through the rehearsal process and the Boston tryout, Sondheim wound up cutting songs and lyrics that lesser songwriters would have insisted were set in stone. In an early version of "Don't Look at Me," Sally sang, "You want to go and hear the throng / Sing every ancient song / With all the lyrics wrong?" In "Can That Boy Fox Trot?" a good song replaced by great one ("I'm Still Here"), Sondheim had Carlotta rationalize her dim-witted lover's deficiencies—"an imitation Hitler but with littler charm"—by arguing, "But who needs Albert Schweitzer / When the lights're / low?"

But arguably the most remarkable lyrics in the entire Sondheim canon occur in the B section of "Uptown, Downtown." Phyllis, referring to her alter ego Harriet, the "nouveau from New Rochelle," sings:

She sits
At the Ritz
With her splits of Mumm's
And starts to pine
For a stein
With her Village chums
But with a Schlitz
In her mitts
Down in Fitz-
Roy's bar
She thinks of the Ritz, oh
It's so schizo.

In a mere forty-one words, Sondheim places seven "its" rhymes (eight, if you count "Ritz" twice) and two pairs of other rhymes. If the average songwriter came up with that, he'd fight tooth and nail not to throw out the song. (Not that the average songwriter *could* come up with that.) But Sondheim, spurred by Michael Bennett, who felt that he could do even better, wrote "The Story of Lucy and Jessie." That's an MVP.

There's been quite a bit of talk over the years that Sondheim hasn't been commensurately appreciated, and that's certainly true. But at least producers and audiences can point with pride to the fact that there have been only nine years in his half-century-plus career where none of his work was heard on Broadway. Since 1987, there's only been one: 1982. It seems that children will listen—and adults have listened, too.

Comeback Player of the Year: Helen Gallagher
No, No, Nanette

In 1970, Broadway was saddened to see Helen Gallagher playing a minor role in the turgid nine-performance flop *Cry for Us All.* She portrayed back-room girl Bessie Legg in 1890s Brooklyn. Gallagher had all of one song, called "Swing Your Bag." It was Bessie's way of saying that when a man betrays a woman, she should shrug it off.

By January 1971, Helen Gallagher had made it back to the top as the leading lady of Broadway's biggest—and unexpected—hit: *No, No, Nanette.* She played Lucille Early, the friend of the nominal lead, Sue Smith, portrayed by Ruby Keeler. Lucille set the plot in motion by telling Sue that her husband was philandering—only to find out later that circumstantial evidence suggested that her husband, Billy, might be doing the exact same thing.

Gallagher was the focal point of the number "Too Many Rings around Rosie," contributed fancy footwork to the number "You Can Dance with Any Girl at All" that she did with Bobby Van, and finished with an extraordinary torch song, positioned center stage and standing still, selling "The 'Where-Has-My-Hubby-Gone?' Blues."

It was a remarkable comeback, topped by Gallagher winning the Tony Award as Best Actress in a Musical. About time; Gallagher was supposed to be a star nearly two decades earlier.

Her Broadway debut came as a chorus member in the Cole Porter flop *The Seven Lively Arts* in 1944. That, however, Gallagher says was substantially better than her next show: *Mr. Strauss Goes to Boston*—"which," says Gallagher, "is where we went to try out and where we should have closed." However, she's ultimately glad she did it, because she began a lifelong friendship with castmate Harold Lang. "He taught me every rotten thing I've ever learned in life. Harold got me drunk for the first time when we were in Boston, took me to my first strip joint when we were in Las Vegas, and took me to my first gay bar over on the East Side. I was the only woman in the room, but I knew every guy in there."

Gallagher was the in the original choruses of *Billion Dollar Baby* in 1945 and *Brigadoon* in 1947. For the former, she was hired by George Abbott, who would use her in his next two shows: *High Button Shoes* in 1947 and *Touch and Go* in 1949. In both, she had small parts, but at least the characters had names, as opposed to the "Dancer" or "Corps de Ballet" labels she had been wearing.

"I loved George Abbott," Gallagher says, "even though he could singe your soul. He had no compunction in telling you what he thought. He'd say to me, 'That was very summer stock.' But I loved him for it." Gallagher also debunks the legend that everyone, always and without exception, called him "Mister Abbott." According to Gallagher, "We all called him 'Mr. A.'"

After *Touch and Go* closed on Broadway it was set for London, and Gallagher was invited to go along. "In that show," she says, "I was what's called a 'HAP'—which is a nice way of saying 'Half-Assed Principal'—because I didn't have all that much to do. So I said, 'I don't want to go to London but I will if you give me that great eleven o'clock number.' So the English—never do business with the English!—sent these contracts around, and every time I got mine, it said I'd get 'a song.' I told my agent, 'Howard, I don't want 'a' song, I want the eleven o'clock song.' They finally had to put it in my contract. But when I got to London, they couldn't send this strange child onstage at eleven o'clock unless they gave her a lot more to do the rest of the night. So I ended up one of the stars of the show."

Upon her return, director John C. Wilson chose her for his 1951 musical *Make a Wish.* The show didn't last long, but Gallagher participated in five songs. Jule Styne, the co-producer, felt she'd be great as Gladys Bumps in the revival of *Pal Joey* he was planning. There she sang "That Terrific Rainbow" and "Plant You Now, Dig You Later" and received a Tony. No question that Gallagher was an integral ingredient in the show's record-breaking run; no Broadway revival had ever lived to see 540 performances.

Styne was so enthusiastic about Gallagher that he wrote a show for her. *Hazel Flagg* was the first (but certainly not the last) movie to be turned into a musical. In this song-and-dance version of *Nothing Sacred,* Gallagher played the title character, who is incorrectly diagnosed as terminally ill. She becomes a media darling in New York, thanks to a newspaper that wants to give her a big farewell.

But the stars weren't in place to make her a star. "Because David Alexander did such a good job directing *Pal Joey,*" Gallagher says, "I insisted that he do *Hazel Flagg.* Well, that was my mistake. It wasn't his fault. The wrong producer, the wrong theater, the wrong leading man. I was a very young 26 and John Howard was a very old 45; but he looked a little like Frederic March, who did *Nothing Sacred,* and that's why he was chosen."

Gallagher was forced to return to supporting roles, taking over for Carol Haney as Gladys in *The Pajama Game* before doing three City Center musicals. Then came the career low when she was the star of the notorious three-performance fiasco of 1958, *Portofino*—about which Walter Kerr wrote that he couldn't say for sure that it was the worst musical of all time because he'd only been going to the theater since 1919.

"Those were the three longest performances of my life," Gallagher says. "We opened on Friday, closed on Saturday. I begged them on my hands and knees to close out of town. They said, 'Oh, no, it'll be okay.' I played an aviatrix, and playing an aristocrat was George Guetary, who'd been born in Egypt and raised in France. He had it better than all of us because, with his thick accent, you couldn't understand a word he was saying—which, for that show, was a blessing. I've never before or since done a show as bad as that. Walter Kerr was right."

Eight long years would pass before Gallagher returned to Broadway. In *Sweet Charity* she played Charity's best friend, Nicky. But Gallagher estimates that she did at least a hundred performances as Charity, because star Gwen Verdon wanted to attend to her two-year-old child, Nicole Fosse. "She'd already had one boy who was living on the West Coast and she felt bad that she was an absentee mother for him," she says. "So when she had Nicole, she decided that she would become a mother and I'd often have to go on for her. That was the most exhausting show. Well, all of her shows were, because Gwen never trusted anyone else onstage—meaning if it was a show that had to be upheld, she'd hold it on her shoulders and wasn't convinced anyone else could. I was so glad every time she returned to Charity. I'd say to myself, 'I did it again, climbing those mountains, and now I can go back to my own part.' It was exhausting. And it's rotten when you're standing behind the curtain and the audience hears 'At this performance . . .' and starts groaning. Well, I knew I'd have them by the end of the performance, and I did. But I still wasn't happy to hear them moan at the beginning."

The producers of *Charity* were also the producers of *Mame,* so when *Charity* closed, Gallagher moved from the Palace to the Winter Garden to assume the role of Mame's dear friend Agnes Gooch. "When I saw Janie Connell as Gooch," she says of the role's creator, "I fell in love with what Janie was doing and the part, too. Gooch takes that show and puts it in her back pocket. What a sneak!"

That she occasionally played Vera Charles in *Mame* says a great deal about Gallagher's versatility. Pretentious Vera and mousy Gooch are hardly the same type. As Billy Bigelow sings (admittedly of a completely different situation), "It takes talent to do that well."

Still, these were all supporting roles. For that matter, even Lucille Early in *No, No, Nanette* is. The only difference is that it didn't seem to be a featured role when Gallagher took the stage.

Gallagher doesn't solely blame *Hazel Flagg* for derailing her road to stardom. "I played Maeve for the entire fourteen-year run of *Ryan's Hope,*" she says, noting the role for which she won three Daytime Emmys. "It probably killed my career in theater," she says, "but I don't care. It made me independently wealthy."

Manager of the Year: Harry Rigby and Cyma Rubin
No, No, Nanette

While these two producers were linked when they began producing *No, No, Nanette,* they certainly weren't when the show opened in New York. By then, they'd become bitter and litigious enemies.

Their names haven't ever since been conjoined, but perhaps enough time has passed for a theatrical statute of limitations to be invoked.

At first, the professional relationship between Rigby and Rubin was, to cite a famous Cahn–Van Heusen song from the 1955 TV version of *Our Town,* "Love and Marriage." But it soon turned to hatred and divorce.

And yet, another line from the song—"you can't have one without the other"—applies. We would have had no *No, No, Nanette* without either Rigby or Rubin.

He had the idea. She had the money. Eventually she decided that money should trump his idea, so she wrested the show away from him. The production that had proclaimed, "Cyma Rubin and Harry Rigby present . . ." suddenly said, "Pyxidium, Ltd, presents." Pyxidium had one officer: Cyma Rubin.

And what's a Pyxidium? Why, says, the dictionary, "the dry fruit of such plants as the plantain: a capsule whose upper part falls off when mature so that the seeds are released." Just another head-shaking moment to add to the many that this production caused.

When Rigby co-produced *Sugar Babies* in 1979, his bio simply read, "He's been around for a while." In other words, the less said about *No, No, Nanette,* the better.

1971–1972

MVPS and Rookies: Andrew Lloyd Webber and Tim Rice
Jesus Christ Superstar

Just around the time when Broadway thought that *Hair* was the future of the Broadway musical, two young men in London were actually creating it.

Andrew Lloyd Webber and Tim Rice started writing in 1965. Their show *The Likes of Us* concerned Thomas Barnardo, the Irishman who had planned to be a missionary but, after moving to London and seeing what poverty was doing to children, created more than a hundred homes for destitute and homeless waifs.

Although Lloyd Webber was a mere seventeen and Rice only twenty, they inherently knew that the best musicals have big characters and big events. The story of Barnardo had both.

Of course, the two were also derivative, as any young writers are. One can tell from listening to the recording made in 2005, long after each of them had become legends, that these neophytes very much appreciated such British musical-theater writers as Lionel (*Oliver!*) Bart and David Heneker of *Half a Sixpence* fame. There isn't a hint of rock anywhere in the piece.

One song in *The Likes of Us*—"Strange and Lovely Song"—sounds amazingly like "Long Ago" from *Half a Sixpence.* (Even at the time, someone may well have noticed and brought it up as the first—but not the last—instance where Lloyd Webber was cited for borrowing someone else's melody.)

The Likes of Us wasn't produced, freeing its song "Love Is Here" to be recycled a decade later as "Travel Hopefully" in *Jeeves.* But Lloyd Webber and Rice's next one certainly got on: *Joseph and the Amazing Technicolor Dreamcoat.* Granted, it was only a twenty-minute show mounted at Colet Court Boys Preparatory School, about six miles from the West End. But their writing about a minor character in the Bible made them aware of a major one.

This time, they'd write a musical about a man who did indeed become a missionary: Jesus Christ. Talk about big characters and big events! But the team wisely didn't make it a sophomoric spoof; not until Herod sang about being "King of the Jews" late in the show did it get silly in the way that people had been expecting and/or fearing all along.

Right from the opening number, Judas's "Heaven on Their Mind," Rice showed that he was going for depth. When Judas sang what he'd like to say to Jesus, he happened to mention, "I've been your right-hand man all along." Nowhere in the Bible is such a relationship suggested, but Rice gave Judas the vital emotion of jealousy. If indeed the apostle had felt that he'd been the most important person in Jesus' life—and later started to fear that Peter was—he might well be motivated to betray Jesus.

Similarly, Mary Magdalene didn't sing a song in which she lustily proclaimed the joys of prostitution. Rice took her seriously, too, and had her sing "I Don't Know How to Love Him," making an audience feel for her.

Mary did, however, know how to calm Jesus, as she did in "Everything's Alright," possibly the first song in 5/4 time to make the Billboard Top 100 Singles (sung by Yvonne Elliman, who would make a career out of playing the Magdalene). Of course, Lloyd Webber's rock-infused but still Broadway-theatrical music was an equally important ingredient.

Because Lloyd Webber and Rice now knew that getting a musical produced was extraordinarily difficult, they looked for a different approach. What if an album of the score could be released as a type of audition tool? Perhaps strong music, lyrics, and presentation would impress producers enough to do the actual musical.

Thus *Jesus Christ Superstar* was first released on two long-playing records in almost plain brown paper sleeves and seemingly gave birth to "the Broadway concept album." But this idea originated more than a dozen years before, in 1955. Would-be producers Sam Vitt and D. A. Brown put on disc *The Body in the Seine,* described as "A Musical Tour de Force through Paris." While the disc boasted "Words and Music by David M. Lippincott," it did not list a bookwriter. In fact, the liner notes started with a mock "Help Wanted" ad: "Musical score requires immediate services of bright, clever 'book,'" it said, actually putting "book" in quotation marks. "Must be mature, sophisticated, and willing to travel," it concluded.

No one will ever know how many (if any) people answered the ad, but *The Body in the Seine* stayed a concept album, thus depriving theatergoers from ever hearing such Lippincott songs as "Love on the Left Bank's a Wild, Wild Thing" and "What the Hell Is So Wide about the World?"

The next concept album, *Clara,* released in 1959, did a little better. At least it got to Broadway under the title *Beg, Borrow or Steal,* albeit for just five performances.

What a profound difference for *Jesus Christ Superstar,* which became a number-one album on the *Billboard* charts and has never been out of print. It led to a few unauthorized concerts before producer Robert Stigwood optioned it as a Broadway musical.

Unlike many of the other Lloyd Webber shows, *Jesus Christ Superstar* was first produced on Broadway and later in London. While it ran a healthy 711 performances in New York, London and hometown pride helped a 1972 production to a record-shattering 3,357 performances—a mark that would be broken only by another Andrew Lloyd Webber musical many years down the line.

Lloyd Webber also deserves extra credit for providing his own orchestrations. In the years and musicals that followed, he either performed this task himself or supervised it with a most watchful eye. Given that it's such a skill in itself, even those millions of people who came to hate Andrew Lloyd Webber because he became immeasurably rich and famous have to be impressed.

Comeback Player of the Year: Phil Silvers

A Funny Thing Happened on the Way to the Forum

Here the word "comeback" is used in a very different way. Phil Silvers literally came back to *A Funny Thing Happened on the Way to the Forum* nine years after he'd turned down the chance to star in the original 1962 production.

Silvers was producer Harold S. Prince's first choice for Pseudolus, the desperate fast-talking Roman slave—essentially an earlier version of Silvers's famous and beloved TV character Sergeant Bilko. But Silvers said no, allowing second choice Milton Berle to accept it. However, not long after the show's first half-page ad in the Sunday *Times* even proclaimed Berle's name above the title, "Mr. Television" dropped out. Only then did third choice Zero Mostel get the role, as well as the acclaim and the Tony as Best Actor in a Musical.

One has to wonder how Silvers felt during the filming of the 1966 film version of *Funny Thing.* There, he was relegated to the secondary role of Marcus Lycus, the pimp who lived next door to Pseudolus's masters. Perhaps the situation did bother Silvers enough to take the lead in the revival.

Perhaps he even needed the work; the year before, he'd appeared in *How the Other Half Loves,* a short-lived Alan Ayckbourn play (is there any other kind in New York?) in which he played someone uncharacteristically nice and sincere.

Before that, in 1960's *Do Re Mi,* he was Hubie Cram, who was, as he proclaimed in a song, "a dreamer, a schemer." Ironically, the show may have wound up a money loser because he atoned for his sins in a big soliloquy at the end of the show. For whatever reason, audiences, despite themselves, liked to see Silvers get away with whatever schemes he planned.

That included Pseudolus's conniving to win his freedom and a buxom young woman at the end of *A Funny Thing Happened on the Way to the Forum.* And for this revival, Silvers won a Tony as Best Actor in a Musical. Better late than never.

Manager of the Year: Kenneth Waissman and Maxine Fox
Grease

Waissman and Fox got their Broadway feet wet by producing *And Miss Reardon Drinks a Little,* the next play by Paul Zindel after he'd won the Pulitzer Prize for *The Effect of Gamma Rays on Man-in the-Moon Marigolds.* As is the case with so many award winners, the follow-up to the smash was a quick fold: 108 performances.

With *Miss Reardon,* Waissman and Fox were fourth- and fifth-billed after three other producers. For their next show—*Grease*—they were the only ones above the title.

The team was introduced to *Grease* at the Kingston Mines Theatre in Chicago. Then the show was actually a straight comedy and not a musical. Waissman and Fox were the ones who saw musical possibilities and urged Jim Jacobs and Warren Casey to add a score to their show.

And so Danny Zuko, the stud who couldn't bring himself to admit that he really loved Sandy Dumbrowski found his singing voice. She did, too, en route to abandoning her high-toned ways for a leather-jacketed persona.

Once the score was in place, Waissman and Fox mounted a production at the Eden Theatre and opened on February 14, 1972. But they soon realized they'd made a mistake. The theater was technically a Broadway house, because it had more than the requisite 499 seats. But it was far from the Broadway district, located on Second Avenue and Twelfth Street.

The reviews weren't strong, and Waissman and Fox were urged to close the show. Both felt that if it moved midtown, *Grease* would find an audience. They were right, for *Grease* wound up breaking *Fiddler on the Roof*'s record-breaking run of 3,242 performances, finishing at 3,388.

With *Grease,* Waissman and Fox gave many future stars their early breaks. Barry Bostwick, Jeff Conaway, Treat Williams, Adrian Zmed, Patrick Swayze, and Peter Gallagher were among the Broadway Danny Zukos. Adrienne Barbeau, Judy Kaye, Jerry Zaks, and John Travolta at various times played various other roles.

After *Grease,* Waissman and Fox regressed a decade and produced a musical about the 1940s. *Over Here!* ran approximately one-tenth as long as *Grease,* and the partnership split.

Waissman continued to produce and would have five more Broadway productions, ranging from disastrous (*Street Corner Symphony*) to solid (*Agnes of God*) to prestigious: *Torch Song Trilogy* won the Best Play Tony in 1983 and ran 1,222 performances. Only two producers can boast of having mounted a play that ran over 1,000 performances and a musical that ran over 3,000; one is David Merrick, via *Cactus Flower* (1,234 performances) and *42nd Street* (3,486 performances); the other is Kenneth Waissman.

Fox toyed with producing *The Tap Dance Kid* in the 1980s but opted to retire from Broadway. But her presence was felt on Broadway in a completely different way during the 1970s. *Grease* set designer Douglas W. Schmidt, taking his cue from the conceit that the show was a reunion of Rydell High School's Class of 1959, wanted to flank the proscenium arch with the yearbook photos of everyone connected with the show.

Fox complied and offered hers, although she didn't want to. During her senior year in a Baltimore high school, she was still going through an adolescent awkward stage when the time came for her to take her yearbook picture. When the proofs arrived, she didn't like any of the pictures. Her mother told her, "Oh, just pick one; you'll never have to look at it again."

Actually, Fox did—from January 27, 1972, through April 13, 1980.

1972–1973

MVP: Bob Fosse
Pippin

Actually, Bob Fosse was the MVP of the world of entertainment in 1973. For in addition to winning two Tonys for directing and choreographing *Pippin,* he captured a Best Director Emmy for *Liza ... with a "Z"* and a Best Director Oscar for *Cabaret.*

No one had ever achieved this triple crown before Fosse did, and no one has since. Frankly, no one is ever expected to do it again—if only because very few directors care to work in all three media, let alone have the power and opportunity to get jobs there.

Fosse took Roger O. Hirson's script and Stephen Schwartz's score and shaped them the way he wanted. Hirson was forty-six to Schwartz's twenty-four, but both saw eye to eye on the story they wanted to tell: a coming-of-age tale about Pippin, son of Charlemagne, the first Holy Roman Emperor. Like so many sons of great men, Pippin has a hard time living up to, let alone surpassing, his father's achievements. They saw him as a flower child.

Hirson and Schwartz felt for the kid, while Fosse saw the tale as "Everybody has to go through stages like that." He wanted us to mock the lad's youthful adventures and indiscretions. He even wanted him to threaten and perhaps commit suicide.

The young Schwartz was outraged. Besides, he felt he knew a thing or two, given his smash off-Broadway debut with *Godspell;* it and *Jesus Christ Superstar* were the only musicals to have a cast album reach the charts in all of 1972. Schwartz and Hirson complained that Fosse's cynicism was not necessarily a good replacement for the empathy.

Fosse did have some humanity, and that was proved by the way he handled actor John Rubinstein, then best known as classical pianist Artur Rubinstein's son. The twenty-five-year-old had appeared on a dozen TV episodes and in a half-dozen films, but only for a few minutes at a time. He had a pleasant voice but no dancing experience at all. Says Rubinstein, "I'd auditioned for him for the *Cabaret* movie for, believe it or not, the Michael York role when there was a chance that Michael might not be able to do it."

Rubinstein says of his *Pippin* audition, "After I sang, he left me onstage while he and the creative team talked. Then he came down the aisle and said 'The part's yours.' He could have gone to an office and had his agent call mine, but he knew that this would be a thrilling moment for a kid, and he didn't want to miss seeing it happen."

But Rubinstein also says he recalls that as early as the Washington tryout, the *Pippin* that Fosse created for him was a cold character to bring to an audience each night.

The fights between the team of writers and the director continued. Producer Stuart Ostrow had to support one or the other. He chose the man who'd already won five Tony Awards starting with *The Pajama Game* and *Damn Yankees.* In the end, the musical, book, and score all got Tony nominated and lost, while Fosse won in his Director and Choreographer categories.

"I'm still not entirely happy with what Bob turned *Pippin* into, but I had a lot to learn then, too," Schwartz admitted in 1998, a quarter of a century later when his musical *Children of Eden* was being readied for a production at the Paper Mill Playhouse in Millburn, New Jersey. But he won't say anything beyond "*De mortuis nil nisi bonum*"—the classic Latin expression for "Of the dead, say nothing but good."

Financially, at least, Fosse's vision helped all of them. When *Pippin* closed in 1977, only six musicals had run longer than its 1,944 performances.

Comeback Player of the Year: Irene Ryan
Pippin

When *The Beverly Hillbillies* finished its 274th episode in 1971, few expected to see much more of Irene Ryan, the feisty Granny Clampett. She'd made a small fortune doing the often top-ranked series for nine straight years, and now, at the age of sixty-nine, could retire to her home in Santa Monica.

But on October 17, 1972, Ryan marked her seventieth birthday by appearing in the final dress rehearsal of *Pippin* at the Imperial Theatre in New York City.

At this point, she was the closest thing that Pippin had to a star. Ben Vereen, the "Leading Player," would become one as a result of this show. John Rubinstein, playing the young title character who was trying to find his "corner of the sky," would have to wait seven years before he won a Tony for

Children of a Lesser God. Jill Clayburgh, who portrayed the single mother with whom Pippin would decide to spend his life, would in 1999 be named by *Entertainment Weekly* as one of Hollywood's 25 Greatest Actresses. But no one saw that coming when *Pippin* opened.

Ryan had had fans long before *The Beverly Hillbillies.* The former Jessie Irene Nobelett was one of Bob Hope's more intrepid USO show entertainers during World War II. But afterward, she merely did a picture or two a year.

Seldom did she have much of a role in any of them. That she did an uncredited bit in 1949's *Mighty Joe Young,* about a giant gorilla, and then in 1952 appeared in *Bonzo Goes to College,* which starred a little chimpanzee, was a metaphor for her declining career—until *The Beverly Hillbillies* called on her to play Granny.

In *Pippin,* she was enlisted to play another grandmother. Berthe gave advice to grandson Pippin. She had one scene and only one number, but it was a showstopper: "No Time at All" had a sixty-six-year-old woman yearning for "67 more" years but appreciating the life she'd had. "I never thought about how much I weighed when there was still one piece of cake," she sang in one of Stephen Schwartz's more piquant lyrics. (Schwartz swears that he wrote, "But it's hard to believe I'm being led astray by a man who calls me Granny" before Ryan was cast.)

Ryan stayed with the show until Saturday, March 10, 1973. In between the two performances, she said she did not feel well enough to continue. She flew back home, where she was later diagnosed with an inoperable brain rumor. Only forty-seven days later, on April 26, 1973, Irene Ryan died. She never knew that she received a Tony nomination.

Her legacy lives on. Because Ryan had no heirs or relatives—and because she'd saved much of her *Beverly Hillbillies* salary—she founded the Irene Ryan Award for college and university students in 1972. Sheryl Lee Ralph and Dan Butler were a couple of the earliest recipients. For many years to come, at least one young man and one young woman will receive a cash prize because of Irene Ryan.

Reliever of the Year: Michael Bennett
Seesaw

Edwin Sherin became famous in the 1990s as the executive producer of TV's *Law & Order.* But more than two decades before, when he was foundering in Detroit as the director of *Seesaw,* Michael Bennett had to step in and lay down the law and provide the order.

When we'd last left Bennett in 1967, he'd lost the Tony for choreographing *A Joyful Noise.* He'd be nominated but lose in each of the next three years for *Henry, Sweet Henry; Promises, Promises;* and *Coco.* But on April 23, 1972, he'd win Best Choreographer for *Follies* and would begin his acceptance speech with, "Well, I don't have to go and play with Ron Fields's Tonys anymore."

Fields had won one in 1967 for his *Cabaret* choreography and two for directing and choreographing *Applause* in 1970. Those would be the last he'd ever win. Bennett had six more on his horizon, including one for co-directing *Follies* that he picked up later that evening.

Now he was part of the Broadway elite and was often asked to help ailing shows. He took a long look at Michael Stewart's adaptation of William Gibson's *Two for the Seesaw,* which had been a 1958 two-character hit about an on-again, off-again relationship. (Hence the title.)

In it, Omaha lawyer Jerry Ryan, who's initiated a separation from his wife, Tess, moves to New York. There he meets Gittel Mosca. She's a would-be dancer who falls in love with him between phone calls to her best friend Sophie and working with her choreographer friend Larry. Jerry's on the phone quite a bit, too, with Tess. She tries to convince him to come home, while he's determined to start a new life, law practice, and relationship with Gittel.

Stewart had decided to add Sophie, Larry, and Tess to the mix, but he didn't give them very much characterization. They seemed to be there simply because musicals are big, and one way to make a show bigger is to add people to the cast.

Cy Coleman and Dorothy Fields, who'd had a success with *Sweet Charity* seven years earlier, and an unproduced musical about Eleanor Roosevelt, followed Stewart's lead. They wrote for Sophie "Ride out the Storm," which she'd sing to Gittel, who feared that Jerry might return to his wife. They also took one of their Eleanor Roosevelt songs, "It's Not Where You Start (It's Where You Finish)" and gave it to Larry. Tess, not inherently musical, and painted as a drudge by Stewart, got no song.

Those who know *Seesaw* will notice that Gittel's choreographer friend had a different name from the one they now know: David. That's indicative of how much Michael Bennett changed the show when he was brought in to replace Sherin and choreographer Grover Dale. Nothing was set in stone, and Bennett would make certain that *Seesaw* would be his very own. He demanded total control and got it.

Bennett also gets credit for bringing in a show doctor that producers Joseph Kipness, Lawrence Kasha, and even George Steinbrenner III (yes, that George Steinbrenner III) might have been hard pressed to get: Neil Simon. Bennett had been the choreographer on Simon's *Promises, Promises,* and was already scheduled to direct the next Simon play, *God's Favorite,* in 1974.

According to Ken Howard, who was portraying Jerry, Simon suggested to Coleman and Fields that they write a song about Gittel's tendency to ruin any relationship. In came "Nobody Does It Like Me," which replaced the less effective "Big Fat Heart." Other than that, however, we may never know exactly what Simon did.

But Stewart's script doesn't include two lines that seem to have a Simon feel. Originally, Larry cooked an Italian meal for Jerry and Gittel. When it burned to a crisp, he said, "Tragedy: the last day of Pompeii, only with noodles." By the New York opening, the dish was changed to a burned souvlaki, which allowed David to say the much wittier, "Tragedy. Greek tragedy."

In "We've Got It," Jerry not only proclaims his good feelings to Gittel, but also begins dancing. The original script didn't include a nice observation Jerry makes while Gittel is astonished that he can dance so well. "Don't look so surprised," Jerry told her. "Fred Astaire came from Omaha, ya know."

That was hardly the extent of the work. Bennett brought in his friend Tommy Tune, not yet well known to Broadway, to choreograph the two big numbers for Larry, who was played by Bill Starr. When Tune had finished them, Bennett had Tune replace Starr in the role.

Bennett did retain Grover Dale's choreography for "My City," in which Jerry is introduced to the sleazier side of New York. But he took "Ride Out the Storm" from Sophie, feeling that a minor character singing it to Gittel deep in the story was not the way to go; he made it into a late act 1 production number that Gittel hears at a night spot. Sophie sang some of it, but a one-song-glory character named Sparkle did most of it. It didn't advance the plot or action in any way, but at least it was entertaining.

The most controversial move that Bennett made was getting a new Gittel. He replaced top-billed star Lainie Kazan with Michele Lee. The word was that Kazan was "miscast," a charge she rebutted in a letter to the *New York Times.* "What could be more perfect than for a Jewish girl from Brooklyn to play a Jewish girl from Brooklyn? So much for my being 'miscast.'"

There was apparently more to it than that—literally and figuratively. Ken Howard, who wrote a self-help book that had nothing to do with show business but with public speaking, nevertheless took time in it to comment on Kazan's unsuitability. He reported that she sang "a terrific song called 'Big Fat Heart'" but "the zaftig beauty of the talented actress encased in a dancer's leotard gave the song an unintentional double meaning."

Even with Bennett's many improvements, *Seesaw* got mixed reviews after its March 18, 1973, opening and was hardly in the clear. It did whatever it could to survive, including having Ken Howard look-alike New York Mayor John V. Lindsay stand in for him during "My City." That got the show some needed attention—but not enough. By December, *Seesaw* was gone after 296 performances—which is 296 more than it would have had had Bennett not come in to save it.

Nevertheless, even four months after the closing, Bennett was remembered at Tony time. He even won over the choreographers of two currently running shows, *Raisin* and *Over Here!*

Speaking of Mayor Lindsay, some might say that he and the Theatre Development Fund should be the MVPs for starting the TKTS booth. The red-and-white-festooned trailer was initiated to sell the Broadway and off-Broadway tickets that hadn't yet been sold at half price.

On the face of it, it was a nice idea. Actually, the booth provided good value for only the first year or so of its existence. When tickets were $15, a $7.50 ticket was a terrific deal. But only seven years had to pass before the top ticket price was $30—and then the deluge.

Now tickets are astronomically priced with an eye to TKTS. Producers now price tickets in the $150 range, feeling that if the show's a big enough hit, they'll get it; if not, well, $75 isn't so bad.

The whole purpose of TKTS has been defeated. These days, one must wait in a sinuously long line to get a bargain that's really no bargain. Had there never been a TKTS booth, there's a good chance that a ticket to a musical these days would be $75, and theatergoers wouldn't have to wait that long at any theater's box office to buy one.

Rookie of the Year: Tommy Tune
Seesaw

He'd already appeared in three Broadway musicals: *Baker Street, A Joyful Noise,* and *How Now, Dow Jones.* But his roles in them were respectively "One of the Killers," "Saw Mill Boy," and "Waiter." Now, thanks to his pal

Michael Bennett's taking over *Seesaw,* Tommy Tune would get the chance to play a character who had a genuine name: David.

All right, David didn't have a last name, but it was still a step up for Tune. As he sang in his second-act showstopper, "It's not where you start, it's where you finish." For Tommy Tune (and yes, that's his real name), it was a marvelous start. As Gittel Mosca's fellow dancer and best friend (read: gay male friend), he had two showstopping numbers in the second act. One was a soft-shoe set to (literally) New York State statutes, while the other was a balloon-filled fantasy.

In 1974, Tune and *Seesaw* had taken to the road (in what many felt was a better production, helmed by Lucie Arnaz and John Gavin). Tune did come to New York on the night of the Tony Awards, and after he was named Best Featured Actor in a Musical, he told the theater and television audience, "Canada, America," *Seesaw* is "not a movie, it's not a television show, it's not a rock concert. It's a Broadway musical and that is something special."

Little did anyone know then how many "something-special" Broadway musicals Tune would provide in the next eighteen years. From playing a would-be choreographer in *Seesaw,* he would become a genuine choreographer and extraordinary director, too. We'll see more of him.

Manager of the Year: Kurt Peterson
Sondheim: A Musical Tribute

At first glance, this honor should go to Stuart Ostrow for *Pippin,* for he revived the Broadway-show television commercial. He revolutionized the way shows were marketed—and added to the budget. Soon the public was assuming that if a show didn't have a commercial, it simply wasn't worthy of its attention.

But the producer of one-night stand better deserves the honor, because he started a vogue for special-event benefits on March 11, 1973, at the Shubert Theatre, where *Sondheim—A Musical Tribute* took place.

Most producers take years—or need them—to produce their shows. Kurt Peterson had six months to put together an astonishing evening that's still being discussed almost forty years later.

In 1972, Peterson was best known as the actor who'd been the young lover in *Dear World* and Young Ben in *Follies.* Out of the blue, he received a call from Joyce Worsley, an administrator at Peterson's alma mater American Musical and Dramatic Academy. She asked Peterson if he could get *Follies'* co-director and producer Hal Prince to be honored at a benefit that would help both the American Musical and Dramatic Academy and the National Hemophilia Foundation.

Actually, Peterson couldn't, for Prince declined. Peterson then suggested Stephen Sondheim, who agreed to attend a small luncheon where a few students would sing and he would say a few words.

Peterson then enlisted Craig Zadan, who was writing a book that would be called *Sondheim & Co.,* to provide material and direct and co-produce with him. He approached every major star and principal who had been in an original Stephen Sondheim show. An astonishing number agreed. Donna McKechnie signed on to choreograph, too. No less than Tharon Musser would design the lights, and Florence Klotz would coordinate the costumes. Warner Brothers agreed to record the event, and Neil Appelbaum, who joined as a producer, designed the poster with a Scrabble motif, to suggest Sondheim's well-known love of games. The Shubert Theatre, where Sondheim's *A Little Night Music* would soon open, was booked.

"When we told Stephen of all that was happening," says Peterson, "his jaw literally dropped. At that point he got fully involved, jettisoned the book idea and brought in Burt Shevelove to direct, telling us, 'If Burt doesn't do it, it's not going to happen.' Although Craig was very disappointed, we both said, 'Yes, Mr. Sondheim.' Craig stayed on as co-producer, though, and did feel some excitement when Sondheim began showing us his trunk songs and agreed that they could be part of the evening."

Everyone was introduced to "Side by Side by Side," where cast members named their peers. ("Chita Rivera!" "Larry Kert!") Sheldon Harnick reminisced about the time he went to a backers audition for *Saturday Night,* Sondheim's first show, soon after he moved to town from Chicago, and that the quality of the work made him fear for his own career. Though Richard Rodgers wasn't there, he sent a telegram saying how much he admired Sondheim's lyrics. (Was he making a statement about Sondheim's music by mentioning only the worth of Sondheim's words?)

The season before, there had been a similar event for Richard Rodgers at the Imperial, but it turned out to be a more quiet affair with not nearly as much hullaballoo. The king wasn't dead, but Broadway was saying, "Long live the king!" to Stephen Sondheim. And Kurt Peterson set the tone for the many elegant and star-studded one-night benefits that were to follow.

1973–1974

MVP: Harold Prince
Candide

For more than a decade, Broadway had been flummoxed by *Candide.* Its seventy-three-performance failure in the 1956–1957 season was a vexing one.

There was much to admire in this musical adaptation of Voltaire's picaresque tale about an optimist who finds that sunniness doesn't pay. It did receive a Tony nomination as Best Musical over the far more popular *Li'l Abner,* which would run almost ten times as long. But that seemed to be a consolation prize to acknowledge Leonard Bernstein's magnificent score.

Candide's original cast album made many wonder if the rest of the show could be salvaged. In 1958, Michael Stewart edited Lillian Hellman's libretto into a concert adaptation—at a time when such revisions were quite rare. It played seven weeks at the Bucks County Playhouse in Pennsylvania, an especially long run for a concert.

Hellman, Bernstein, and lyricist Richard Wilbur did some work for a West End production in 1959, but Londoners took to *Candide* even less. It lasted sixty performances.

Productions popped up here and there in the 1960s, but in 1971, *Candide* was expected to make its triumphant return to Broadway after a three-city tour. Newcomer Sheldon Patinkin (Mandy's cousin), a Second City alumnus, was entrusted to spruce up Hellman's book; he changed so much of it that she demanded her name be removed from it. (It hasn't returned to any major production since.)

The revisal played San Francisco and Los Angeles before dying in Washington that November. But in 1973, Chelsea Theater Center artistic director Robert Kalfin approached Prince about *Candide.* After reviewing the script and score, Prince had a radical idea for it: an environmental circus.

What put that in his head was a 1970 visit to a Bryant Park extravaganza called *Orlando Furioso;* the show had theatergoers move from one ramp and runway to another to follow the story. Prince was excited enough by *Orlando* that when it received an unenthusiastic *New York Times* review, he felt compelled to write to the newspaper complaining about the review and endorsing the production.

Perhaps, Prince thought, *Candide* could be as exciting as *Orlando.* Prince asked his two recent *A Little Night Music* collaborators Stephen Sondheim and bookwriter Hugh Wheeler to think about *Candide.*

To get Sondheim to join the enterprise wasn't easy. Sondheim had promised himself that his days of putting lyrics to other people's music were over. On the other hand, Bernstein was the one who allowed Sondheim to work with him on *West Side Story* when the twenty-six-year-old was a neophyte and even gave Sondheim credit for lyrics that he himself had written. So now Sondheim might be able to do a favor for Bernstein.

Prince, in conjunction with set designers Eugene and Franne Lee, put theatergoers in the "orchestra" on stools, around which the actors would walk. Those in the "balcony" were on bleachers flanking them. To add to the fun, everyone had a chance to get some beer and peanuts before the show.

Even the overture gave a hint that this would be a more fanciful *Candide;* the first violinist who played the "ha-ha-ha-ha" section of "Glitter and Be Gay" made himself sound as if he were a gypsy coming up to a table in a restaurant and zipping through *his* favorite selection.

The result was a show that ran virtually literally ten times as long: 740 performances. It might have run longer had it not been for Local 802, the musicians' union. Prince asked that because the reduced-sized theater could accommodate only eighteen musicians—instead of the usual twenty-five—the unions not ask that the extra seven musicians be paid. The union refused, and seven musicians were paid each week for doing nothing. When *Candide* closed at an approximate $350,000 loss, that figure represented close to the amount of money paid to those idle musicians.

If someone could have broken that stranglehold, he or she would have been the MVP for 1973–1974.

Comeback Players of the Year: The Andrews Sisters
Over Here!

Blond soprano Patty, brunette soprano Maxene, and redhead contralto LaVerne Andrews were once the rage of show business. From the late 1930s until the mid-1950s, they appeared in seventeen movies, recorded over 1,800 songs, and sold more than 80 million records. These included their smash hits "Bei Mir Bist Du Schoen," "Don't Sit Under the Apple Tree," "Rum and Coca Cola," and "Boogie Woogie Bugle Boy."

That last-named hit got them back into the public's consciousness in 1973, when Bette Midler made a new recording. (Thanks to overdubs, she sang all three of the sisters' parts.) But by then, many years had passed since the Andrews Sisters' names had crossed very many people's lips. They were deemed hopelessly passé in a now-rock era. And once LaVerne died in 1967 at a mere fifty-five years old, the act was broken beyond repair.

Like so many in that career-stalled situation, Patty and Maxene were saved by Broadway. Lucky for them that producers Kenneth Waissman and Maxene Fox, who'd had such success with the nostalgia-ridden 1950s-show *Grease,* decided to go back a decade earlier to see if they could mine more riches from theatergoers' memories. And while LaVerne was gone, there was still truth in advertising that "The Andrews Sisters" would be in this new musical *Over Here!*

Will Holt's book told of the DePaul Sisters—Pauline (Maxene) and Paulette (Patty)—who are entertaining GIs during World War II. They're doing adequately, but they know that if they could only find the right third voice, they'd have that oh-so-special sound that would put them over the top. Happily enough, they meet a woman named Mitzi who affords them the perfect blend. What they don't know, however, is that Mitzi is a German spy.

The score for the Andrews Sisters was provided by the Sherman Brothers—the elder Robert B. and the younger Richard M.—who by this point had written such film songs as "Fortuosity" for *The Happiest Millionaire,* "Gratifaction" for *Tom Sawyer,* and, of course, "Supercalifragilisticexpialadocious" for *Mary Poppins.*

The team used genuine, in-the-dictionary words for *Over Here!* and provided a true and exciting big-band sound that couldn't have been predicted from their tween-to-teen-centric films. They wrote exceptionally well for the Andrews Sisters, replicating the jitterbuggy bebop sound that made them famous. (In the published script, however, when citing the three songs that involved both sisters, the brothers took pains "to acknowledge the creative contribution of Walter Weschler.")

The irony is that the non-sister Mitzi—played by unknown Janie Sell—received a Tony Award, while neither Patty nor Maxene even nabbed a nomination. Still, the reason that audiences came for 341 performances to a show that didn't have enough of a story and precious little second act was to see the Andrews Sisters. The stars knew it, and after each show was over, they made sure people had a good time by doing a long medley of their biggest hits.

After the closing performance, Patty spoke for both of them: "Ladies and gentlemen, this has been just about the happiest year of our lives." Maxene later told Dick Cavett on his TV show that after they left the stage that night, Patty said that she never wanted to work with her again.

Rookie of the Year—Janie Sell

Over Here!

Janie Sell must be the only Tony winner whose role asked her to sing the first four lines of the second verse of "The Star-Spangled Banner." That's the one that starts, "On the shore, dimly seen thro' the mist of the deep, Where the foe's haughty host in dread silence reposes."

Don't know it? Sell's character Mitzi did—and that's how she was unmasked as a German spy. "Because," said her accurate accuser, "no real American knows the second verse of 'The Star-Spangled Banner!'"

Not many Americans know Janie Sell, either. And thereby hangs a tale.

In the 1950s, after Gwen Verdon won the Tony for Best Featured Actress in a Musical for *Can-Can,* she went on to star in *Damn Yankees, New Girl in Town, Redhead, Sweet Charity,* and *Chicago,* winning three Best Actress in a Musical Tonys.

In the 1960s, after Tammy Grimes won the Tony for Best Featured Actress in a Musical for *The Unsinkable Molly Brown,* she went on to star in ten more Broadway shows, winning one Best Actress in a Play Tony for *Private Lives.*

In the 1970s, after Janie Sell won the Tony for Best Featured Actress in a Musical for *Over Here!* she went a year and a half without a Broadway role. Oh, there was an undistinguished TV movie called *Wives* and a seventeen-performance stint off-Broadway in *By Bernstein.* But the next Broadway role was the small part of Gladys Bumps in a limited two-month engagement of *Pal Joey.*

Then came ten months of unemployment until Meryl Streep tired of playing the lead in *Happy End*—she'd been doing it for ten whole weeks, after all—allowing for Sell to succeed her. Thirteen days after Sell opened, the show closed.

Sell didn't have a Broadway gig for the next fourteen months, until September 1978, when she replaced one of the two female leads in *I Love My Wife.* That provided her with eight months' work. It was followed by a

TV pilot that didn't sell Sell, and the forty-nine-performance off-Broadway musical *God Bless You, Mr. Rosewater.*

And after that, Janie Sell enrolled in Hunter College to get a degree in psychology.

None of this dour information is meant to suggest that Sell's Tony was a fluke or that she didn't have the talent to continue succeeding. "When I hit my forties, the parts were thinning out," she says with a shrug. "Musicals were different. My shows involved dancing and comedy and most of the newer shows—like *Jesus Christ Superstar* and *Evita*—weren't asking for those skills. I saw the handwriting on the wall. I wasn't going to be offered more parts as I got even older, so I had to do something else."

So count Sell as one of the victims of the dark musical and the British invasion. A marriage to TV writer Patrick Trese gave her a new outlook and a new name: Jane Trese. (It's pronounced "Tracy.")

But then, after she was graduated from Hunter and found employment in an addiction-treatment center, she found didn't like the work. She wound up at Young & Rubicam, the esteemed marketing and communications company—as a receptionist.

The actress who'd starred in *Happy End* may not have felt a happy end was in store for her. But drag out the cliché that uses the words "cream," "always," "rises," and "top." Peter Georgescu, then the company's president, hand-picked Trese to be his assistant. To paraphrase a lyric from *Funny Girl,* "No, it ain't Broadway—it's Madison Avenue." But at least Jane Trese was in a more exalted position.

There would also be one more Broadway semi-burst of glory. When Tom Moore, who'd directed Sell in *Over Here!* was staging *Moon over Buffalo* with Carol Burnett in 1995, he asked his Sell to understudy Jane Connell. Then, when Burnett begged to have each Tuesday off, Moore asked Sell to play the lead role for those performances. Trese gladly did. But she didn't quit her day job.

Managers of the Year: The Shubert Organization
Liza!

One would think that producers would have to mount a show that lasted more than a mere twenty days to be named Managers of the Year. But the difference in this case is not merely that *Liza!* was planned as a limited engagement for the then-very-white-hot Liza Minnelli.

What made the producers significant in this case was that they were Gerald Schoenfeld and Bernard Jacobs, the respective chairman and president of the Shubert Organization. After these two lawyers seized and wrested power from the Shubert family in 1972, they knew they were facing an increasingly barren Broadway.

In the early days of Broadway, the Shuberts—originally, Sam (who died young in a train accident), Lee, and J. J.—had as a matter of course produced several shows a season. But the last show that had the billing "Produced by the Messrs. Shubert (Lee and J. J.)" was *Roland Petit's Ballets de Paris* in January 1954. Now almost twenty years to the day, "the Shuberts"—really Schoenfeld and Jacobs—would get back into the producing business.

They really had to, because independent producers were suddenly few and very far between. If the Shuberts didn't do their own producing, they'd be sitting with more than a dozen empty theaters at any given time. The area was terribly blighted with stores selling pornography and dealers vending drugs.

In the years to come, they'd be instrumental in cleaning up the Broadway district. More to the point, they'd produce big hits (*Godspell; Dancin'; Ain't Misbehavin'; Dreamgirls; Cats; City of Angels*), prestige hits (*Sunday in the Park with George; Jerome Robbins' Broadway; Passion*), modest hits (*Your Arm's Too Short to Box with God; The Act; Song and Dance; Sarafina!; Once on This Island*), revivals (*Fiddler on the Roof; Brigadoon; The Wiz; The Most Happy Fella*), and, of course, flops (*The Human Comedy; Harrigan 'n Hart; Big Deal; Roza; Chess*).

Schoenfeld and Jacobs were known to be ruthless in their dealings, but at least there was still a Broadway on which they and others could deal.

Relievers of the Year: Hugh Wheeler and Stephen Sondheim
Candide

The Tony for Best Book was awarded in 1949 to Bella and Sam Spewack for *Kiss Me, Kate* and in 1950 to Oscar Hammerstein II and Joshua Logan for *South Pacific.* The award then took an eleven-year hiatus before resuming, and it's been given almost ever since. Alas, in 1988–1989, the committee couldn't even dredge up one worthy nominee and completely eliminated the category.

But only one time in all those fifty-plus years has the Best Book prize gone to an author who rewrote. Hugh Wheeler won for reworking Lillian Hellman's original 1956 book for the seventy-three-performance *Candide.*

Voltaire's original novel was light in tone. But Hellman was still smarting from her 1952 appearance at the House Un-American Activities Committee during the Red Scare witch hunts: "I cannot and will not cut my conscience to fit this year's fashions," she famously said.

Now she could get back at these right-wingers by having them excoriated in *Candide.* She heavy-handedly pointed out that Americans were not living in "the best of all possible worlds" any more than Candide was — not when another Senator Joseph P. McCarthy could come on the scene. (Hellman had to be relieved that three months after *Candide* died, so did McCarthy.)

Wheeler provided the lighter touch. He made audiences identify with Candide's plight by suggesting "If it isn't one thing, it's another. That's the 18th century for you!" At the end of the show, after Candide has been drafted, whipped, abandoned, and left for dead, he does manage to retire to a farm where he and his beloved Cunegonde can "Make Our Garden Grow" Then their cow dies of hoof and mouth disease. The audience roared. It's always something, isn't it?

Meanwhile, Stephen Sondheim worked on five songs. He took "Candide's Lament," dropped from the original Broadway production, and transformed it into another lament for Candide called "This World." Some Bernstein music that had never made it into the 1956 production allowed him to write "The Sheep's Song," set in Eldorado, such a nice place that a lion does lie down in peaceful harmony with sheep. And leave it to Sondheim to make a song out of such as subject as an "Auto-Da-Fe."

Sondheim also made "The Best of All Possible Worlds" truly his own. Not only did nothing beyond the title remain, but Sondheim also let some notes that had previously carried Richard Wilbur's words simply stand on their own as little lyric-less orchestral embellishments.

That song had been the opening number, but Sondheim gave the score a more fetching one. He changed what had been "The Venice Gavotte" (with Dorothy Parker's too-singsongy "Lady Frilly" lyrics) into the far more impressive "Life Is Happiness Indeed." Here Candide, Cunegonde, and the high-born Maximilian gave their various philosophies of life; the last-named wasn't as happy because he saw a pimple on his oh-so-beautiful face. But worse fates were to come.

Not quite for this *Candide,* however. Whenever the show is revived, it's the Wheeler–Sondheim–Prince version that everyone does. The Lillian Hellman estate wouldn't have it any other way; its executors prohibit any production of her libretto. They've been influenced by a letter she wrote to Bernstein some time after the revival: "I could not have wanted a hack like Hugh Wheeler to fool around with my work, and I have never been very fond of the work of Hal Prince."

1974–1975

MVP and Reliever of the Year: Geoffrey Holder
The Wiz

Is there anything that Geoffrey Holder cannot do?

The Trinidadian was a member of a dance company when he was seven years old, in 1937. True, it was his brother's troupe, but he did well enough to take it over when he was seventeen, a couple of years after he sold his first two paintings.

He spent virtually the same amount of time on each discipline. Then, when noted choreographer Agnes de Mille saw his troupe perform in the Virgin Islands, she urged Holder to visit New York to audition for Sol Hurok. He sold twenty paintings to pay for the entire company to get to New York in 1954—only to find that Hurok wasn't interested.

Many dancers went back home, but Holder remained and began teaching at the Katherine Dunham School of Dance to support himself. Soon, however, he caught the eye of producer Saint Subber, who made certain he'd appear in his new Harold Arlen–Truman Capote musical *House of Flowers.* By the time the show opened, he'd been recruited to choreograph a dance that incorporated steel drums, instruments that had not been often, if ever, used on Broadway.

The show didn't last, but the marriage that Holder made with one the dancers, Carmen De Lavallade, certainly did; as of this writing, they've been married more than fifty-five years. Together they performed in the Metropolitan Opera Ballet until 1956, when he formed the Geoffrey Holder and Company dance troupe. He did, however take time out in the 1950s to play Lucky in a black revival of *Waiting for Godot,* make his film debut in *Carib Gold,* win a Guggenheim Fellowship for his painting, and sing on an album called *Geoffrey Holder and His Trinidad Hummingbirds.*

That's quite a bit for a man who'd just turned twenty-seven.

So what would the future hold for Holder, who'd already been a professional dancer, dance company founder, stage actor, stage dancer, film actor, singer, and painter? In the next fifteen years, he'd add quite a bit to that résumé. How many others can make the claim that they've been on TV playing a lion in a Richard Rodgers musical (*Androcles and the Lion*) and a genie in a Cole Porter musical (*Aladdin*)? And how about that voodoo priest in a James Bond movie (*Live and Let Die*)? Even if he weren't six foot six, many people would still notice him, saying, "Oh, wait—I know that guy! He did those 'Uncola' TV commercials for 7-Up!"

But the best was yet to come, in 1975. Producer Ken Harper hired him to design the costumes for a black re-imagining of *The Wizard of Oz.* Holder not only agreed to do it, but also made a suggestion that was immediately taken: "You must," he said, "call it *The Wiz.*"

Holder wanted to direct, too, but Gilbert Moses was producer Ken Harper's choice. So Holder went to work dreaming up fanciful costumes; for example, the Tin Man would mostly be made of discarded beer cans.

When Moses was found wanting during the first leg of the Baltimore tryout, Holder was asked and gratefully and graciously took on the directorial assignment. What had been a confused and messy show became a sure-handed one. *The Wiz* didn't receive rave reviews, but it certainly became a popular success. Although songwriter Charles Small didn't adhere to the theatrical standard then in place with perfect rhymes and correct accents on lyrics—a standard staunchly espoused by Stephen Sondheim—Sondheim himself adored *The Wiz.* "It's the one show where you come out feeling better than when you went in," he said.

In a not-so-strong season, *The Wiz* wound up garnering eight Tony nominations—and two for Holder. Never before had a black man been nominated for a Tony for Best Costumes of a Musical, let alone Best Director of a Musical. Needless to say, then, never had a black man won either or both. Holder did, making him our MVP for 1974–1975.

1975–1976

MVP: Michael Bennett
A Chorus Line

He's been a Rookie of the Year and a Reliever of the Year, but now it's time for Michael Bennett, thirty-two years old, to advance to Most Valuable Player.

Bennett was the one who had the goal of doing a show that would display his dancer friends to good advantage. He's the one that Tony Stevens and Michon Peacock called when they were devastated by the quick failure of *Rachael Lily Rosenbloom . . . and Don't You Forget It!* That spurred Bennett to invite eighteen dancers to talk about their lives as dancers into a tape recorder. He spoke first to set the tone.

His Broadway successes had caught the eye of producer Joseph Papp of the New York Shakespeare Festival Public Theatre. Papp wanted Bennett for one project, but Bennett soon talked him into financing this new Broadway animal called "the workshop."

To be sure, Bennett didn't invent it, for it had been an off-Broadway staple for years; even Jerome Robbins had once tried it with musicals. Still, the idea of going into a rehearsal hall without a finished script or score, just to explore, was not an easy idea to sell. But the notion was decidedly downtown enough for Papp to take a chance.

Bennett hired many people who would become part of this show called *A Chorus Line.* He wanted Marvin Hamlisch, not necessarily because he'd recently won three Oscars for *The Way We Were* and *The Sting,* but because he'd been a Broadway dance-music arranger and therefore had an affinity for dancers. (They'd worked together on *Henry, Sweet Henry.*) He believed in Ed Kleban, who'd had no Broadway experience. But Kleban had auditioned one of his musicals for Bennett, who was impressed enough to remember him. And, of course, Bennett is the one who made them into a team.

Bennett enlisted Robin Wagner on sets (not that there'd be many), although he made clear that he wanted mirrors. He also signed Tharon Musser for lights because she'd lit many dance works.

Structuring the tapes as an audition, where dancers would try to get a job from director-choreographer Zach, was Bennett's idea, too. And speaking of auditions, even performers who had participated in the taping sessions and had told their life stories would have to audition to see if they were the optimum performers to play their own lives.

As nine months of workshops wore on, Bennett had to buoy everyone's spirits—and did. This was remarkable, given that everyone was getting a mere $100 a week for days that sometimes lasted fourteen hours. Some became frustrated when he opted to "choose" the auditionees for the mythical musical, because he kept changing his choices so that no one would become complacent. But he certainly knew he wanted Carole/Kelly Bishop in the show; he even bought her out of her contract with *Irene.*

Although Baayork Lee had been a dancer in four Bennett shows, he didn't invite her to the taping sessions. "I wasn't counting on being in his new show, so I auditioned for Bob Fosse for *Chicago,*" she recalls. "When I got home that day, the phone was ringing. It was Michael, who said, 'I heard you were at the Fosse auditions. You start rehearsals with me tomorrow.'"

To borrow a term from boxing, Bennett even took a dive—when during a rehearsal he fell and purposely pretended to greatly injure himself. His actors, he felt, just hadn't been convincing enough during the scene where the character Paul San Marco dropped to the floor in pain. Bennett felt it was the only way they'd learn to be believable when it happened during the performance.

When Bennett wasn't 100 percent satisfied with Nicholas Dante as his bookwriter—the scenes between director Zach and his former girlfriend and former star dancer Cassie weren't working to his satisfaction—he went out and got another. He chose James Kirkwood, because he knew he'd been a child performer and therefore had had much auditioning experience.

Putting off Papp—the boss, after all—from seeing what he was doing wasn't easy, but Bennett was able to keep him away. When Papp finally did see the piece and began believing in it, he suggested the show play the Vivian Beaumont Theatre, which his theater company was running. Bennett wisely turned down the offer, knowing that the Beaumont's thrust stage would not be right for *A Chorus Line.*

Once previews began and *A Chorus Line* seemed a smash hit, Bennett listened to Marsha Mason, who disagreed with a decision he'd made. Bennett felt that Zach would determine that Cassie did not belong in the chorus and would pull focus, and thus had Zach reject her. Mason vociferously pleaded on Cassie's behalf, saying that everyone needed to believe that one could start over again if one needed to. Bennett listened, and this softer ending helped *A Chorus Line* to become a popular success.

Isn't that an understatement? But the bigger astonishment is that Michael Bennett, the quintessential Broadway baby, got the quintessentially un-Broadway Joseph Papp to back the quintessential Broadway musical.

Reliever of the Year: Liza Minnelli
Chicago

When *Chicago* was first announced, a Kander and Ebb musical with Bob Fosse directing Gwen Verdon, Chita Rivera, and Jerry Orbach was expected to be the biggest hit of the season. But by the time it was ready to open in New York after a somewhat shaky Philadelphia tryout, theatergoers were nonstop talking about the musical that had opened off-Broadway and was now moving uptown: *A Chorus Line.*

This was, however, the era when the *New York Times* review was still the be-all and end-all. If the *Times* daily critic Clive Barnes liked it, it was almost assured to be a hit. If Walter Kerr, its Sunday critic, liked it, too, it was virtually home free.

But on June 4, 1975, Barnes said that this new musical had "neither content nor substance" and used these words and phrases: "very little," "few final results," "unfortunately," and "But where does it all lead?"

Then, only four days later, Kerr made matters worse with the words "problem" and "wrong," as well as the phrase "too heavy to let the foolish story breathe."

That "foolish story" told of Roxie Hart, who murdered the lover who was about to abandon her. She then convinced her husband Amos to raise thousands of dollars so shyster (but effective) lawyer Billy Flynn could keep her out of prison.

Both Barnes and Kerr had many good words and phrases for Fosse, Verdon, Rivera, and Orbach and the Kander-and-Ebb score. But *Chicago* had the audacity to demand $17.50 for its best seats when every other musical was charging $15.

Fifty-one days after it opened, *A Chorus Line* played its first Broadway preview on July 25, 1975. *Chicago,* named for the Second City, was suddenly every musical theatergoer's second choice.

Matters got much worse for *Chicago* a mere nine days later. Gwen Verdon, who'd missed some 1966 *Sweet Charity* performances because she swallowed a feather from a boa, had now swallowed a piece of confetti that was stuck in her throat and kept her from singing. That she would require an operation and miss weeks of performances was a severe setback for a musical that wasn't the biggest hit in town. With the unknown Lenora Nemetz subbing for her, *Chicago* would fast run out of steam.

Fosse then made one of the great masterstrokes of his career. He called Liza Minnelli, whom he made an Emmy winner in *Liza with a "Z"* and an Oscar winner in his revolutionary *Cabaret.* Besides, both properties had songs from *Chicago*'s Kander and Ebb—Minnelli's first champion through their *Flora, the Red Menace*. They were the reasons that whenever *South Pacific* was produced, it had to drop the character name of "Ensign Lisa Minelli" [*sic*] that Oscar Hammerstein II glibly put in as his tribute to Judy Garland and Vincent Minnelli's daughter.

No one has a *Playbill* that says, "Liza Minnelli in *Chicago.*" No one has a picture of a marquee that says that, either. Out of deference to Verdon, Minnelli insisted that her name not be used in any advertising. There would simply be an announcement made over the loudspeaker that she'd be subbing for Verdon. (She would, however, record pop versions of the score's "All That Jazz" and "My Own Best Friend.")

Minnelli started rehearsing on Tuesday, August 5, and played her first performance on Friday, August 8. Already she was brilliant. At twenty-nine years old, she was more right for the young and reckless Roxie Hart than the fifty-year-old Verdon. The stare she gave fickle lover Fred Casely after his three seconds of lovemaking conveyed both the contempt and disappointment of "Is that all there is?"

What's more, her voice was perfect for the score; think of "Funny Honey" and imagine her hitting that important note in "He *loves* me so." But, oh, did the audience get awfully quiet in the song "Roxie" when Minnelli talked about "not getting enough love in our childhood—and that's show biz." It was too real a moment for Judy Garland's daughter.

What is regrettable, however, is that when the announcement was made before the show that "Gwen Verdon would not perform," the audience made mock groans and audibly phony "Awwwwwwws." Seconds later, when Minnelli's name was mentioned—and the announcer said it triumphantly—the audience cheered wildly. Theatergoers can be fickle, can't they?

Rookie of the Year: Patti LuPone
The Robber Bridegroom

Of all the credit-card companies, American Express is considered to be the most stringent in accepting applicants. One had better be financially secure if he expects to be given even the lowliest green card.

In 1999, when American Express was running an "Are You a Cardmember?" campaign, it included Patti LuPone on one of its TV commercials. A smiling LuPone was positioned next to a card with her name on it, with the notation that she'd been a "Member since 76."

LuPone turned twenty-seven that year—when the median age for an American Express cardholder was well over forty. What's more, because she was an actress by trade, she was, needless to say, a risk.

And yet, why did Amex dare to give her a card?

Perhaps someone at the company noticed that LuPone had received a Tony nomination as Best Featured Actress in a Musical. That wasn't an easy achievement, given that *The Robber Bridegroom* ran all of fourteen performances. It wasn't a flop; it was always scheduled to play two weeks as a limited engagement from the Acting Company, a troupe of Juilliard graduates who toured the country and made a pit stop in New York.

The Robber Bridegroom, a musical based on a Eudora Welty novella, ran in repertory with three works from distinctly different eras: Anton Chekhov's *The Three Sisters,* William Saroyan's *The Time of Your Life,* and Christopher Marlowe's *Edward II.* In the three, LuPone respectively played Irina, Kitty, and Prince Edward (yes, Prince Edward); the Tony committee was most impressed by her performance in *Bridegroom.*

LuPone portrayed Rosamund, a 1790s Rodney, Mississippi, resident who was utterly bored by rural life. "Ain't nothin' up," she complained in one of Alfred Uhry's lyrics that was set to Robert Waldman's lazy-country music in a git-fiddle-filled score. To make matters worse, Rosamund had a stepmother to rival Cinderella's and a father intent on marrying her off to the first eligible bachelor who came along. Such a home life can drive a young miss into an itinerant traveler's arms, and Rosamund was soon making love to passerby Jamie Lockhart. He was in this neck of the woods to steal every necklace and nickel he could find.

As one of Alfred Uhry's lyrics said about Rosamund, "One night, she's sleeping in the raw. The moon looked down and dropped his jaw." LuPone also made the audience do the same. Recalls Uhry, "There was a scene in which Patti had to appear in the nude. Not only was she game to do it, but once she arrived onstage in the buff, she was absolutely in no hurry to get off. She strategically used her hands to cover the more controversial parts of her body, but while exiting, she seemed to enjoy taking an accidentally-on-purpose fall, so she could have her arms flail out and let everyone offstage get a good look." As LuPone would sing in one of her later hits, "Anything Goes."

But there are other song titles that LuPone would sing in the next three decades that would inadvertently comment on the career she'd have: "High-Flying Adored" (*Evita*), "I'd Do Anything" (*Oliver!*), "God, That's Good!" (*Sweeney Todd*), and "Everything's Coming up Roses" (*Gypsy*). No wonder she made the least impression in *Women on the Verge of a Nervous Breakdown* in 2010; there she had a song called "Invisible," which Patti LuPone cannot be.

Comeback Player of the Year: Bob Fosse
Chicago

In *Chicago's* second act, in "Razzle Dazzle," Billy Flynn sings "give 'em an act that's unassailable; they'll wait a year till you're available."

One has to wonder if Fred Ebb had had this lyric in his first draft. Or did he only think to write it while he and everyone else waited months until the artistically and critically unassailable Fosse was available?

That's almost what Ebb partner John Kander, and producers Robert Fryer and James Cresson, did for Fosse. Although *Chicago* opened on Broadway in 1975, it was scheduled to debut in 1974—and would have, had Fosse not suffered a heart attack that moved the project from the 1974–1975 season to the 1975–1976 season.

The delay cost Fosse and the show plenty of Tony Awards. Is there any doubt that *Chicago,* which lost big to *A Chorus Line,* would a year earlier have wiped the floor with *The Wiz*? *Chicago* certainly would have won Best Musical, Best Book, Best Score, Best Direction, and Best Choreography. But as Roxie Hart says in her number that celebrates herself, "And that's show business."

And while *Chicago* was overwhelmed by *A Chorus Line,* time has proved it just as good a musical as its oppressor. Unfortunately, Fosse's original direction and choreography on *Chicago* were watered down for the 1996 revival. So audiences at the revival have been getting some, but not all, of the Fosse style and imagination. But that's show business, too.

Manager of the Year: Joseph Papp

A Chorus Line

Papp listened to Michael Bennett's radical notion of doing a workshop of a musical. Although Bennett had no writers and only a concept, Papp trusted him. He gave the young director-choreographer free rein at his New York Shakespeare Festival Public Theatre.

For more than a month, Papp agreed to Bennett's demand that he not visit and see what had resulted. Not until the fifth week had ended was Papp invited to see the results—and then he learned that Bennett had only completed two scenes. While other producers might have been infuriated that there's had been so little ostensible progress, Papp kept the faith.

His patience did have boundaries. He did second-guess the project from time to time, but he'd always third-guess himself and allow Bennett to continue. However, after he'd been signing the checks that amounted to more than $5,000 a week for more than nine months, he felt that Bennett had had enough time and now had to show him a show.

Bennett did—a four-and-a-half-hour one. Papp deserves credit for being able to see through the mass of material and know that there was a worthy show there.

Papp had let the Broadway bonanza of *Hair* slip through his fingers, and he wouldn't let it happen again. Even before *A Chorus Line,* he had a surprise Best Musical Tony success with *Two Gentlemen of Verona* in 1972. The Public Theatre had profited from it, but not nearly as much as it would with *A Chorus Line.*

The final cost of the two workshops was $549,526. To move the show to Broadway actually cost more: $588,889. Thus, on a total budget of $1,138,415, a musical came into being that grossed $149,035,253 on Broadway alone, and a profit that reached the pricey neighborhood of $50 million. Bennett's company, Plum Productions, got 25 percent of that, while Papp's New York Shakespeare Festival Public Theatre got the other 75 percent—money that was recycled into numerous productions that made the American theater stronger.

1976–1977

MVP and Co-Comeback Player: Martin Charnin
Annie

First came *Hot Spot,* the 1963 Judy Holliday musical about the Peace Corps. Martin Charnin wrote the lyrics to Mary Rodgers music, and the show, which suffered through an inordinate number of directors, closed after forty-three performances.

It was Charnin's most successful production of the year. In August, the musical version of *The Prisoner of Zenda* would open. How promising *Zenda* looked, with the esteemed Vernon Duke writing the music and Alfred Drake and Chita Rivera starring. It didn't even make it to Broadway, but closed in Pasadena in November.

Charnin's next one, in 1967, would close out of town, too: *Mata Hari* had Vincente Minnelli misdirecting a leading lady who, on opening night, just wouldn't stay still when she'd been shot by a firing squad. Besides, it was an antiwar musical, and producer David Merrick took it to Washington. After years of debates about Vietnam, this was not the show that the nation's capital wanted. That Merrick took it there instead of an antiwar city such as Boston remains one of his rare miscalculations.

Too bad, for *Mata Hari* sported excellent lyrics by Charnin and equally impressive music by newcomer Edward Thomas. However, one couldn't blame Charnin when the chance arose to work with no less than Richard Rodgers on a musical version of Clifford Odets's *The Flowering Peach,* in which Noah (of ark fame) and his family were treated as an ordinary, middle-class Jewish couple. That the librettist would be Peter Stone, fresh from writing the extraordinary book to *1776,* was further inducement.

Two by Two ran longer than all three others combined, of course, especially with Danny Kaye's return to Broadway after nearly thirty years helping to sell many advance theater parties. But Kaye's improvising and staying far from the text, first when he lost faith in the show and later when he was injured, made *Two by Two* one of Broadway's most disgraceful stories.

So Charnin had to be terribly discouraged when *Two by Two* closed on September 11, 1971, after a just-broke-even run of ten months. He had to be singing the show's opening song, in which Noah mourned, "Why me? Why me? Why me?" But little did he know that his life was going to start turning around before the end of the year.

"I went to Doubleday's [book store] to buy a book for a friend, and wound up purchasing a book about *Little Orphan Annie* for him," he said. "But instead, I read it that night and was convinced that it would make a terrific musical." He bought the rights to the material as soon as he could.

When he approached his friends—author and humorist Thomas Meehan and composer Charles (*Bye Bye Birdie*) Strouse—they weren't enthusiastic at all. Not until Charnin carefully explain that this would not be a spoof would they even begin to listen.

Charnin pointed out that Annie in the comic strips had no backstory. What was her background? How did she become an orphan? From that question, the tender story of a spunky kid who's intent on finding her parents—and instead finding a very different kind of parent and love—was born.

"No camp" was the tone that Charnin had set, and Meehan and Strouse found themselves writing sincerely and taking their characters seriously. But they soon found out that very few on Broadway would take them seriously. Yes, Charles Strouse had recently had a Tony-winning musical, *Applause,* but it was winding down after a shorter-than-expected two years. Thomas Meehan had never written a libretto before. His big claim to fame was a collection of humor pieces called *Yma, Ava; Yma, Abba; Yma, Oona; Yma, Ida; Yma, Ava… and Others.* And Charnin's track record didn't instill much confidence.

Charnin has often said that he wrote the show as a response to the Nixon administration—that the nation needed the sun to come out tomorrow after the Watergate scandal. Annie, however, wasn't the only one to believe that credo; Charnin needed to believe it, too, especially when management after management didn't see what he saw in the project. And when he insisted on directing, that made potential producers close the iron door on *Annie.* Through this entire process, Charnin was the one who kept renewing the rights, often borrowing from his friends Jack Lemmon, Jerry Stiller, Anne Meara, and Joe Allen to make payments.

But Charnin wouldn't give up. When Michael Price at the Goodspeed Opera House in East Haddam, Connecticut, said he'd mount the show in his Connecticut theater—but that he wanted one of his staff directors to stage it—Charnin did relent. When no suitable director could be found, Price did the relenting and allowed Charnin to direct.

The scene that opens *Gypsy*—where kiddie talent-show host Uncle Jocko is going mad from many children and one ferocious mother—is only a few minutes long. For Charnin, it was a reality that stretched through weeks as he auditioned hundreds of little girls. Much later on, when he wrote about the horrors of "Little Girls" for Miss Hannigan, the keeper at the orphanage where Annie lives, he probably had much to draw on from those auditions.

Charnin also only had sixteen days to rehearse his cast. Add to this that a thunderstorm knocked out the lights during the dress rehearsal—which lasted five and a half hours and didn't reach the end of the show—and one must be impressed with the lyricist-director's stamina.

There was soon another roadblock. Kristen Vigard, engaged to play Annie, had the sweetness but not the strength of an orphan who'd already spent many semesters in the school of hard knocks. Charnin was the one who had to fire her and had to see something in Andrea McArdle, then playing the small role of Pepper. He promoted her to the lead.

After money was found to continue past Goodspeed, Peter Gennaro became the new choreographer. Here, too, Charnin was responsible for the hire; Gennaro had been one of Jerome Robbins's assistant choreographers on *West Side Story,* in which Charnin, then an actor, played a Jet.

This time, the experience that Charnin had in Washington was quite different from *Mata Hari*'s. And after *Annie* opened on April 21, 1977, at the Alvin, no one was calling it "Charnin's folly" anymore. The reviews were virtually unanimous. *Annie*'s anthem "Tomorrow" was soon adopted as the theme song of Tom Snyder's weeknight TV show *Tomorrow,* but it was heard far beyond that. The vertical sign at the Alvin had its letters changed from A-L-V-I-N to A-N-N-I-E.

Annie received ten Tony nominations, with Charnin nabbing for both director and for his part of the score. He lost the former and won the latter. But there's never been another show that wound up getting two Best Actress in a Musical nominations for performers who hadn't played the roles in the first production. For in addition to McArdle taking over for Vigard at Goodspeed, Dorothy Loudon—the eventual Tony winner—succeeded Maggie Task as Miss Hannigan before the Washington tryout.

When *Annie* closed after 2,377 performances on January 2, 1983, it was the sixth-longest-running musical in Broadway history. But it's been far more pervasive than that. Jerry Herman's *Playbill* bios often mention that every day of the year a woman in a red dress walks down a staircase in a musical. Since the advent of *Annie,* a little girl has done it, too.

It's a rare musical-theater actress who hasn't been in some production somewhere of *Annie.* Certainly, we all now know Catherine Zeta-Jones, Sarah Jessica Parker, Alyssa Milano, Deborah Gibson, and Jamie-Lynn Sigler, but Charnin knew them when they were little girls. "Actually," he says, "*Annie* gave rise to a whole new industry: 'girl-kid agents.' There had been 'boy-kid agents' a decade earlier because of *Oliver!* but once *Annie* hit, there was a need for girl-kid agents."

And how many millions of young girls became fervent musical-theater fans as a result of this show? With thousands of productions in regional, stock, high school, and middle school theaters, *Annie* is one of the reasons that the traditional Broadway musical has survived. And all because Martin Charnin went to buy a nice Christmas present for a friend.

Co-Comeback Player of the Year: Dorothy Loudon
Annie

By the end of November 1977, Dorothy Loudon, in the role of the evil Miss Hannigan in *Annie,* played her 221st performance. That set a personal record for her—for in five previous appearances on the Great White Way, Dorothy Loudon had only been able to amass a grand total of 220 performances.

Although Loudon had had some TV appearances in the early 1950s while she was still a student at Syracuse University, the stage was her goal. By the early 1960s, she was appearing in a stock production of *The World of Jules Feiffer,* directed by a comedian just testing his directorial wings: Mike Nichols.

First came *Nowhere to Go but Up* in 1962. Loudon played the headliner of a speakeasy, the obviously pseudonymous Wilma Risqué. She got to sing the title song—for the Philadelphia tryout, and on Broadway for three New York previews and nine performances. After it abruptly closed, Loudon, among many other cast members, had to be repeating the name of the show.

Luckily, Loudon got a good TV gig. She was handpicked by Garry Moore, who had a popular variety show each Tuesday night on CBS, to succeed Carol Burnett, who was leaving to strike out on her own. But while Burnett was virtually a weekly presence on the show, Loudon would make only eleven appearances over the next fifteen months and would not appear during the show's final three seasons.

There wouldn't be much high-profile work for some time. Loudon did summer-stock tours of *Anything Goes, The Unsinkable Molly Brown,* and *Wildcat.* In 1965, she landed one female role in the first national tour of *Luv,* the hit comedy that the now white-hot Mike Nichols had directed on Broadway. While Nichols wasn't staging the road company, he urged director Jack Sydow to choose Loudon, and that provided her with a year's work.

Nineteen-sixty-seven brought an out-of-town closer—*The Unemployed Saint,* a comedy by Bill (*The Owl and the Pussycat*) Manhoff, in which Loudon played Emily Wabash, a long-suffering wife whose husband, Simon (Shelly Berman), didn't care to work.

Then came the oddly named *Noel Coward's Sweet Potato,* a 1968 revue that lasted forty-four performances. Luckily, Loudon was immediately cast as the over-the-title lead in *The Fig Leaves Are Falling*—but unluckily, the show with the fruit in its title did no better than the previous show that had cited a vegetable. In fact, it ran forty fewer performances and closed on January 6, 1969, not making for a happy new year.

Later in 1969, Loudon portrayed Mabel, an inveterate pony player's girlfriend, in a revival of *Three Men on a Horse* for exactly 100 performances. But that would be her only Broadway credit for the next three years, until a revival of *The Women* arrived in 1973; there she played Mrs. Phelps Potter for an unpredictably short 63 performances. In between, she was the desperately lonely mother Charlotte Haze in *Lolita, My Love,* the Alan Jay Lerner–John Barry musical that closed in Philadelphia, then tried again before closing for good in Boston in 1971.

At least Loudon's personal life was working out. In 1971, she married Norman Paris, the musical director she'd met when both worked on the TV game show *I've Got a Secret.* He was steadily getting musical assignments that may not have been glamorous or high-paying (he was often the musical director for Ben Bagley's *Revisited* records), but, with his work and her club dates here and there, they were getting by. Still, musical theater seemed to be a world Dorothy Loudon wouldn't conquer.

Then when *Annie*'s management wasn't happy with Maggie Task's performance as Miss Hannigan, Loudon was courted. "I almost didn't take it," she said. "I'd been through so much pain that I didn't think I could take another flop. I'd read Walter Kerr's bad review of the Connecticut production and was highly influenced by it. Then I saw how much Marty and Mike [Nichols] and Lewis [Allen, a producer] wanted me and I thought I really should."

When Loudon won her Tony, the audience at the Shubert Theatre was so thrilled that it applauded for fifty-three straight seconds. There's no question that the Broadway community wanted her to have it, for Loudon was up against not only Andrea McArdle, who played the central role in the show, but also Clamma Dale, who had received raves for her Bess in *Porgy and Bess.* One could argue that of the three, Miss Hannigan was the least demanding role.

Not to the voters that year, and Loudon was extraordinarily grateful at the response. As she fervently grasped her trophy, she said, "I had a feeling if I could ever get up here, I could work this room."

Still, Loudon hadn't completely shorn her bad luck. Only thirty-five days after the Tony win, Norman Paris suffered a stroke and died. And while Loudon had given many impressive performances in *Annie,* perhaps none could compare to the one she gave on July 14, 1977, when she returned to the cast. She gave the same extraordinary performance, and only those who had seen Loudon's performance before might have noticed that her smile at the curtain calls was only a millimeter or so less wide. It was her job to entertain, and entertain she would.

Loudon would be offered chances to entertain for the rest of her life. She was now able to pick and choose when she wanted to work. Some say her apotheosis came in 1979 with *Ballroom,* in which she played the widow who found a new life through dancing. She was a well-received Mrs. Lovett in *Sweeney Todd* before starring opposite Katharine Hepburn in *The West Side Waltz,* portraying the addled Dotty Otley in *Noises Off,* and appearing as one of *Jerry's Girls* in the Jerry Herman revue. Her success in *Annie* even made her the star of her own 1979 TV series (albeit a short-lived one) called *Dorothy.*

There are comparatively few Broadway performers who have originated a role in a Broadway musical as well as a Broadway play each of which wound up running more than 500 performances. Loudon is one of them, for *Annie* and for *Noises Off* in 1983. When Hollywood got around to filming both, who replaced Loudon? The woman she replaced on *The Garry Moore Show:* Carol Burnett. Each film suffered from the decision.

Loudon's last appearance on Broadway was sadly curtailed. She was cast as Carlotta Vance, the role Marie Dressler made famous, in a 2002 production of *Dinner at Eight.* She did only the first two previews, for her health would not allow her to continue. Less than a year later, Dorothy Loudon died of cancer.

Rookie and Reliever of the Year: Andrea McArdle
Annie

How many young girls have played the title character in *Annie*? Can we guess, to use a number of which kids are fond, a gazillion?

That number may be mythical, but in a way, it's not far off.

And yet none of them would have had the chance to play the little orphan who gets lucky if the show had not been a hit. *Annie* could have very well been gone for good after its Goodspeed run.

What *Annie* needed was an extraordinary young performer to get it right. Once the creative staff felt that Kristen Vigard couldn't deliver, it had to hope that other orphan, the one playing Pepper, could find the spunk.

Andrea McArdle hadn't had much onstage experience; what kid of twelve did? She'd been in dinner-theater productions of *The King and I* and *The Sound of Music.* She'd done the pilot for *Horschak,* a planned spinoff for Ron Palillo's character in the *Welcome Back, Kotter* series that never spun off.

McArdle's trump card was her appearing in *Search for Tomorrow,* where she had won *Afternoon TV*'s Juvenile Actress Award. That, however, wasn't a pedigree that would guarantee that she could carry a Broadway musical. Buying that billionaire Oliver Warbucks would fall in love with her would only be convincing if we fell in love with her, too.

And we did. The girl from *Search for Tomorrow* began singing "Tomorrow" eight times a week. Because she had the backbone, the sensitivity, the adorable qualities, too, she was the vital component to making *Annie* a smash.

McArdle suffered the fate of so many young performers. Although she soon was portraying the young Judy Garland in a TV movie called *Rainbow,* in the next third-of-a-century her appearances on stage and screen were precious few. To date, she has opened only two new musicals on Broadway—*Starlight Express* in 1987 and *State Fair* in 1996. While she was cast as one of the three leads in the Jerry Herman revue *Jerry's Girls* in 1984, she did not come to Broadway with it the following year; she was replaced by the performer who beat her as Best Actress in a Musical in *Annie:* Dorothy Loudon.

McArdle's only other Broadway appearances have been as replacements in *Beauty and the Beast,* as Belle, and *Les Misérables,* as Fantine, the ill-fated mother of Cosette. Coincidentally, her own daughter Alexis Kalehoff would later play Cosette, too.

Nevertheless, McArdle's place in theatrical history is secure. She was not only at the right place at the right time, she was also the right performer to make Little Orphan Annie the character she needed to be.

Managers of the Year: Mike Nichols and Lewis Allen
Annie

In 1962, Mike Nichols and Elaine May decided to break up their comedy act, but they'd still work together. May had written a play called *A Matter of Position,* in which Nichols would star as Howard Miller, a man so overwhelmed by bills and faulty plumbing that he takes to his bed with his Crayolas and starts filling in coloring books. It closed in Philadelphia without braving New York. Broadway wouldn't know how awful it was for thirty-eight more years, when it was retitled *Taller Than a Dwarf* and lasted fifty-six under-attended performances in 2000.

But in the fourteen years that followed, Nichols turned to directing and showed himself to be far taller than a giant. He received four Tony Awards for directing, as well as three other nominations. Of the five shows that had had open-ended commercial runs, two (*The Apple Tree; The Prisoner of Second Avenue*) lasted a year, two (*The Odd Couple; Luv*) stayed around for two, and one (*Barefoot in the Park*) nearly ran four. In Hollywood, he received a 1967 Oscar for *The Graduate,* a year after he'd been Oscar-nominated for *Who's Afraid of Virginia Woolf?*

And yet his biggest triumph to date came for a production he didn't direct. Spurred by Lewis Allen, a business partner, he saw a performance of *Annie* at the Goodspeed Opera House and wanted to be involved. With lyricist Martin Charnin doing the staging, Nichols offered to become the show's lead producer, and Allen joined the team, as well.

The two existing producers needed them. Irwin Meyer and Stephen R. Friedman had only had the previous season's forty-nine-performance flop *Going Up* to their credit. And while Nichols and Allen would raise only the same $250,000 that Meyer and Friedman had, Nichols's name helped get the Kennedy Center interested in putting up the remainder to get the $800,000–$1 million project first to Washington, and then Broadway.

For Nichols, *Annie* would be half of a unique 1976–1977 Tony parlay. Never before or since has the same person in one year been nominated as Best Director of a Play (*Comedians*) and Best Producer of a Musical—for *Annie*, which he won.

1977–1978

MVP: Yul Brynner
The King and I

April 11, 1978. It's opening night on Broadway for one of Broadway's most beloved stars.

For her last three Broadway appearances, Angela Lansbury has won three Tony Awards as Best Actress in a Musical. First came her title role in *Mame*, her biggest hit, in 1966. Three years later, Lansbury played the eccentric Countess Aurelia, whose values were nevertheless in the right place, in *Dear World.* Despite its 132-performance failure, she won again.

Then, in 1975, she emerged victorious in *Gypsy*, where she portrayed the galvanic Rose Hovick. It's the role that Ethel Merman originated—and yet one that couldn't win her a Tony. Lansbury could.

No question that in a mere dozen years, Angela Lansbury has made quite a Broadway name for herself. Her style and elegance will be perfect for her newest role, Miss Anna Leonowens in *The King and I.* The advertising executives who create the window-card campaign know that using only her first name is enough for today's theatergoer to know which actress they mean; thus the posters simply state, "Angela Is Anna in *The King and I*," before warning patrons, "For 24 performances only!"

And yet when Lansbury opens on a Tuesday night, she sees a sea of empty seats in the less-than-half-full Uris Theatre. Granted, this is Broadway's biggest house, capable of accommodating more than 1,900 theatergoers. But last week it was filled.

Where *IS* everybody? The explanation can be inferred from what's inside a long rectangular box answer at the bottom of the "Angela Is Anna!" window card: "Yul Brynner and Constance Towers star in *The King and I* until April 9 and return on May 2."

The lack of ticket sales does not stem from the fact that Broadway audiences love Angela Lansbury less but that they love Yul Brynner more. The fact that the advertising executives even took pains to mention the dates Brynner was leaving and returning inherently shows that they knew he was the main event of this production. Yes, Towers was mentioned, too, but that was a mere courtesy; good as she is in the role, she of course isn't the drawing card. While Towers gets over-the-title billing, the typeface in which her name is printed is smaller than Brynner's. That rarely happens with performers who are both billed above the show's name.

So despite the inclusion of Towers's name, the management is essentially using the box to say, "We're warning you: No Yul Brynner during those weeks, and we want to head off any angry ticket buyers right now."

Technically, Brynner's success was actually part of the 1976–1977 season, for the production opened at the Uris (now the Gershwin) on May 2, 1977. And while everyone knew for nearly a year that he was the person bringing in the sellout audiences, that fact was incontrovertible once the esteemed Lansbury took over in the 1977–1978 season to tiny audiences.

Would Brynner have ever predicted this when he launched his Broadway career in 1941? He played the small role of Fabian—whom Shakespeare described as "Inhabitant of Illyria"—in a 15-performance run of *Twelfth Night.* His next show, *The Moon Vine,* in 1943, managed to run five more performances. Compared to these, the 142-performance run in the 1946 musical *Lute Song* must have seemed a bonanza for Brynner.

It would be in more ways than one. *Lute Song*'s leading lady was Mary Martin, whose next Broadway musical would be *South Pacific.* (By accepting the role of Nellie Forbush, Martin was also making amends to Rodgers and Hammerstein for turning down their first musical, *Oklahoma!*, in order to do *Dancing in the Streets,* a Vernon Duke–Howard Dietz musical. Served her right; that one opened in Boston eight days before *Oklahoma*! opened on Broadway and closed there eighteen days later.)

Two years after *South Pacific* was a smash, R&H were writing *The King and I* but found that casting the monarch of Siam was turning out to be a royal pain. Martin was the one to suggest Brynner. It would be, of course, the role that would make the shaved-headed actor a Tony and Oscar winner.

Aside from Doug Henning, a magician who was given nothing to sing in *The Magic Show,* no leading man in a Broadway book musical has ever been asked to sing as little as Brynner did in *The King and I.* "A Puzzlement" lasts just a little longer than three minutes. After that, the King sings precious little.

On the other hand, Anna has five songs. More remarkably, four of them became genuine standards: "I Whistle a Happy Tune," "Hello, Young Lovers," "Getting to Know You," and "Shall We Dance?" To be sure, in the last-named the King comes in with a couple of lines, and no, it wouldn't be a showstopper without the King's participation in the dance that follows. But it's primarily Anna's song; she's the power behind the number.

At the end of the first act, after the King has insisted that Anna's head always be positioned lower than his, the two get into a stooping contest. Hammerstein writes one of musical theater's great stage directions: "Who is taming whom?"At the end of the show, we learn who, when the Kralahome, the King's right-hand man, tells Anna, "You have destroyed King."

If Angela Lansbury couldn't get the crowds, then no one could conquer the King. He played almost seven hundred performances in this run—and, happily enough, Broadway hadn't seen the last of him.

Reliever of the Year: Judy Kaye
On the Twentieth Century

In 1973, Judy Kaye, live and direct from Phoenix, landed her first Broadway job as a replacement Betty Rizzo in *Grease.* "That allowed me got up enough money to attend that Sondheim benefit they had at the Shubert that March," she recalls. "At one point, I was standing on the stairs and saw Stephen Sondheim, Hal Prince, Betty Comden and Adolph Green. I said to myself, 'I wonder if I'll ever get to meet any of them.'"

Kaye did—when she worked with all of them.

The first instance came in 1978, through a musical with book and lyrics by Comden and Green (and music by Cy Coleman) that was to be directed by Prince. It was to be called *The Twentieth Century, Ltd.,* for it was based on the 1932 Ben Hecht–Charles MacArthur play *Twentieth Century.* Producer Oscar Jaffee takes in hand mousy Mildred Plotka, changes her name to Lily Garland, and makes her a star. Then her career skyrockets while his sinks. If the plot reminds you of the film *A Star Is Born,* be apprised that that film didn't debut until in 1937. What's more, *Twentieth Century* is a more lighthearted look at the subject.

Producers Robert Fryer, Mary Lea Johnson, James Cresson, and Martin Richards got a blue-chip movie star to portray Lily: Madeline Kahn, a two-time Oscar nominee. And speaking of Oscar, Tony winner John (*Shenandoah*) Cullum was signed for that role.

Kaye was offered the role of Agnes, Lily's maid, but also the chance to become Kahn's understudy. "I turned down the understudy job three times," Kaye says. "Standing by is a very hard job, which I knew because I'd done it at U.C.L.A. I didn't want to do that to myself—to sit around and wait for someone else's misfortune. Yes, the regular performer could get a better job and you could take over, but nine times out of ten, that's not what happens. But Hal Prince wanted me to do it, so I said okay. I signed a six-month contract, so if I were really miserable, I could leave."

Producer Johnson (an heir to the vast Johnson & Johnson fortune) was intent that no one would be miserable. She went to a fortune teller to ask about the fate of *The Twentieth Century, Ltd.* and was told that the musical would be a hit if it had twenty-one letters in its title. That's when it became *On the Twentieth Century.* But after the opening on February 19, 1978, when the critics didn't quite give it a twenty-one-gun salute, Madeline Kahn seemed to lose interest in the role.

And although Kaye was convinced she'd never go on, she did prepare herself just in case. "So," he says, "I'd practice the songs in my dressing room or backstage, and some cast members would say to me, 'Will you go into the wings and let Madeline see what you're doing so she can do it, too?' And I said, 'No, I don't think she'd appreciate that.'"

Eventually Kahn decided to skip a performance. "And," Kaye said, "wouldn't you know it was a night I got there late because my watch wasn't working?" She also admits that she spent too much time at the gym and that she followed it by being engrossed in a film on TV that starred Carole Lombard. (She ironically had played Mildred and Lily in the 1934 film of *Twentieth Century.*)

"When I got there," she recalls, "I found the whole company waiting for me. 'You're going on!' they yelled as they threw the costumes on me. Hal wasn't there, because it was the night the movie of *A Little Night Music* premiered at Lincoln Center, but he sent all the producers, Betty and Adolph to see me do it."

Kaye was uproarious in her opening scene as Mildred Plotka, an accompanist for the self-important Imelda Thornton, who was auditioning for Jaffee. Once Imelda showed that she wasn't up to the rigors of "The Indian Maiden's Lament," Kaye's Mildred had no problem telling her. Imelda (Willi Burke) was livid that a mere accompanist should turn critic and refused to pay her, and Kaye showed that hell hath no fury like a pianist who doesn't get her money.

The fire that Mildred showed Imelda convinced Oscar that the lass had the passion within her to become a great actress—and the fire that Kaye showed proved she could handle the role. Says Kaye, "The reaction the audience gave me—and Comden and Green and the producers gave me afterward—wiped away any fear I'd had."

Kaye went on eight more times in the next weeks, which made her slightly optimistic. "I started to think that maybe, just maybe, Madeline would want to do six performances a week, and I could the matinees—which sounded great to me," she says.

Then came the fateful day on April 24, 1978, when Kaye went into her agent's office to see how she was faring on other auditions she'd had. "The phone rang," she recalls, "and when he took the call, he asked me to step out of the room. I didn't think it had anything to do with me, but some minutes later, he came out ashen-faced, and I realized the call did have to do with me. I said, 'The show's closing! I'm fired!' But he said, 'No, they offered you Lily,' and I literally started jumping around on the furniture. Boing-boing! I knew Madeline was unhappy, but there was no way in God's creation I thought I'd get it. I later found out that Marty Richards was my main champion in endorsing me."

After Larry Kert took over for Dean Jones in *Company,* the replacement got the Tony nomination, but when Kaye took over for Kahn, the original got the nomination. Kaye admits, "I was disappointed. I thought there was at least an outside chance they'd give it to me. But who knows what goes on in those nominating rooms? However, considering what happened, how could I ever complain?" Kaye went out there as an understudy—but sure hasn't been one since.

The 1977–1978 Best Actress in a Musical Tony winner was Liza Minnelli for her barely-leaves-the-stage stint in *The Act.* Many Broadway observers weren't happy with the voting; Minnelli had missed several performances, too. Had Kaye been nominated instead of Kahn, she just might have won. But she certainly wins as Reliever of the Year.

Kaye's next two musicals, both in 1981, ran a total of four performances. *The Moony Shapiro Songbook* closed on opening night, while *Oh, Brother!* ran three times as long. At the 1992 memorial held for her *Brother* castmate David Carroll, Kaye said that she and Carroll enjoyed calling it "the stupidest show on Broadway."

In 1986, she was back as Lily in a road company of *On the Twentieth Century.* Here she didn't get a Tony, but a David. "I was impressed with one man in the company," she says. "He was the one who most seemed to know what he was doing." He was David Green, who proposed marriage within five weeks. They recently celebrated their twenty-fifth anniversary.

A Tony was in Kaye's future, anyway. As she admits, "I'll be the first to say that when I won in 1988 for *The Phantom of the Opera,* it was for my body of work and not solely for my role as Carlotta."

Kaye played Emma Goldman when *Ragtime* opened the Ford Center in 1998. In 2001, she was Rosie, one of the three Dynamos, the 1970s singing group that plays an important role in the plot of *Mamma Mia!* She received another Tony nomination—this time as Best Actress in a Play—for playing the tone-deaf Florence Foster Jenkins in *Souvenir.* Then, when Patti LuPone took a vacation in 2006 from playing Mrs. Lovett in *Sweeney Todd,* Kaye spelled her—and thus checked off that "getting to meet Sondheim" wish.

Because neither *The Phantom of the Opera* nor *Mamma Mia!* recorded original Broadway cast albums—both simply issued their previous London cast albums to American audiences—Kaye has the odd distinction of being in two of Broadway's ten-longest-running shows without having recorded them. What's sadder, however, is that she didn't get to record *On the Twentieth Century.* The vocal pyrotechnics she did at the end of "Babette," Lily's eleven-o'clock number, were far more impressive than what one hears Kahn doing on the album.

Rookie: Richard Maltby Jr.
Ain't Misbehavin'

How could Richard Maltby Jr. be Rookie of the Year, given that he'd been around Broadway for nearly two decades?

Because almost two decades passed before he ever got there.

After he was graduated from Yale in 1959, Maltby had to feel that a prosperous Broadway career was right around the corner. His book and lyrics to *Cyrano,* set to classmate David Shire's music, was such a campus hit that it even got a cast album. Better still, in 1964, Barbra Streisand would record a song from it: "Autumn."

By then, frankly, some of the bloom was off the rose. Maltby and Shire had done an off-Broadway musical called *The Sap of Life* that was sapped of life after forty-nine performances. Aside from contributing a few songs to a revue called *Graham Crackers,* they started and stopped a few other projects.

Perhaps the late 1960s would be better. Streisand recorded their "Starting Here, Starting Now" in 1966, and their musical *How Do You Do, I Love You,* about the vagaries of computer dating, interested a producer. They also landed the job of writing the score for a Queen Victoria–Prince Albert musical called *Love Match.*

The former show died in summer stock in 1967, while the latter one died on the road in 1969. So things looked even bleaker for Maltby and Shire.

Eight years would pass. Then, in 1977, Maltby had a chance to assemble a revue of their material at Barbarann, a Forty-sixth Street nightspot. "It did seem strange," he admits. "Imagine someone saying, 'Let's put together a compendium of your failures.' All I could see initially is that it would be an even bigger evening of failure. And yet, as I started working on it, I decided it could be something different from all the other revues that had emcees and spoken-word filler. Maybe I could structure the songs themselves in a way that seemed to tell a story—the essence of a story-line, an abstraction created without a specific."

That's what he did, using the song for which he and Shire were best known—"Starting Here, Starting Now"—as their title. Maltby directed a cast of three and had the biggest theatrical success of his career. Less than a year later, he'd have a much bigger one.

"Murray Horwitz and I were working on a Fats Waller bio-musical using his songs—at least until we couldn't figure out the second act. We'd decided to put it aside, and then Lynne Meadow," he says, referring to the artistic director the Manhattan Theatre Club, "said, 'Well, you've still got all his songs . . .'"

And that's how *Ain't Misbehavin'* began and set the tone for all the songwriter anthologies that followed.

1978–1979

MVP: Stephen Sondheim
Sweeney Todd

In the first edition of Craig Zadan's book *Sondheim & Co.,* published in 1974, Leonard Bernstein predicted that one day Stephen Sondheim "is suddenly going to write an opera that will knock your eyes out."

Perhaps it was scenic designer Eugene Lee and director Harold Prince who knocked our eyes out when Sondheim's veritable opera *Sweeney Todd* debuted on March 1, 1979. But Sondheim was certainly responsible for knocking our ears out with his score, which is considered his masterpiece.

But as experimental as Sondheim has always been, he and bookwriter Hugh Wheeler actually made *Sweeney Todd* a very straightforward adaptation of Christopher Bond's play. It's one of the most faithful musical adaptations that any play has ever had.

Bond, too, had ex-sailor Anthony and ex-convict Sweeney Todd arrive in London. Both met a Beggar Woman and dismissed her. But Sondheim conceived of having her try to ply her sexual wares to Anthony.

In the play, Bond also had Sweeney return to his old barbershop where Mrs. Lovett was making her terrible-tasting pies. When she heard that he was a barber, she brought out the old razors, to which Bond had him say, "My right hand is complete again!" And while she knew he was the barber who once worked there, all that Wheeler and Sondheim added was that Benjamin Barker was his original name; Bond's play offers none.

But Bond's Sweeney had at least one semi-romantic moment. When Mrs. Lovett showed her interest in him, he lustily kissed her, but only to entice her to get him the Judge and the Beadle who sent him away on a trumped-up charge.

Bond also took us to the fair where Sweeney challenged Pirelli to tooth-pulling and shaving contests, each of which Sweeney won. But in Bond's tooth-pull challenge, Todd actually extracted Anthony's tooth, not one from a passerby with a wicked toothache. Bond also stated that Pirelli's miracle elixir tasted "like chicken shit," instead of the somewhat less graphic "piss" that Sondheim had Sweeney brand it in the musical. Meanwhile, Bond's contest scene took place before, not after, Johanna and Anthony met. The Beadle did not kill Johanna's bird, for she had none.

Most surprising is that Bond's play made Johanna a more savvy character, one who knew the ways of the world. In fact, she was the sexual aggressor with Anthony, who was willing to be a gentleman.

In Bond, Sweeney mock-confessed to the Beadle that he was a thief and he'd show him the jewels he'd stolen if he sat in his chair while he retrieved them. Of course, the Beadle got something else entirely.

One of Sondheim's most controversial songs in the musical was the "Johanna" that Judge Turpin sang as he was flagellating himself. After the first preview, after Prince advised Sondheim to drop it, he reluctantly agreed. But he wanted the world to hear it and asked that it be included in the original cast album. This allowed listeners to accept or reject it at their own pace and on their own terms.

Sondheim's plan worked; the song was included in both the 1989 and 2005 Broadway revivals and has appeared on every subsequent *Sweeney* recording, save the soundtrack, which dropped much of the score.

Given that Sondheim had included "Hear the whips on the galley slaves" (in "Pretty Little Picture" in *Forum*) for a musical comedy, one might infer that it was his idea to have the Judge take a whip to his own back. But the scene comes right out of Bond. His Judge Turpin, however, was less sure of himself than the confident would-be lover in the musical.

The scene in which Pirelli came to Todd's shop to blackmail him, leaving his assistant Tobias downstairs to eat one of Mrs. Lovett's pies, was in Bond, too. So was Todd's murder of Pirelli. In Bond, however, when the Judge first visited Sweeney for his spruce-up, he said that he had a headache, so Sweeney told him a damp cloth on his eyes would ease it—to block the Judge's eyes from seeing what was coming. And while Sondheim and Wheeler dropped this, they retained Anthony's barging in with his romantic woes—causing the Judge to say he'd put Johanna in an asylum rather than see Anthony have her.

In Bond, when Mrs. Lovett came in and saw the dead Pirelli, she, too, came up with idea of popping people into pies. When skirting around this issue with Sweeney, she even said, "Get it?" "Good, you got it," however, came from Sondheim.

So did one of the most dazzling act 1 finales in musical theater. For just when some theatergoers might have started to worry that *Sweeney Todd* was turning into more of an opera and less of a musical, Sondheim delivered a demented waltz in "A Little Priest," the fun-filled, pun-filled paean to murder with more than four dozen clever rhymes.

Bond's act 2 also began with Tobias's promoting the now-successful business and Mrs. Lovett's hoping that she and Sweeney can take some time off by the sea. But Sondheim and Wheeler start here dropped the scene in which the Beggar Woman told Tobias that she suspected foul play in conjunction with the pies.

Sweeney told Anthony to get Johanna out of the asylum on the ruse of purchasing hair. Tobias, sitting downstairs, found a hair and then a fingernail in his pie—and became suspicious. But there was no "Nothing's Gonna Harm You" moment between Mrs. Lovett and Tobias. Nor did he put two and two together by spotting Lovett with Pirelli's purse.

In Bond, the Beadle dropped by because of the stink coming from Lovett's cellar. She put a drug in his drink, and that kept him there—not the harmonium in the parlor.

The rest of the musical doesn't stray far from Bond. Anthony put Johanna in disguise to help her escape from the asylum. A jailer stopped them, and when he couldn't bear to shoot him, Johanna did. She then came to Sweeney's, where he almost slit her throat. The Beggar Woman entered, and Sweeney killed her. When he later discovered that she was his wife—whom Lovett had led him to believe was dead—he danced his pie partner into the oven. A white-haired Tobias then entered and slit Sweeney's throat. End of play.

So in terms of structure—and structure only—*Sweeney Todd* was Sondheim's least adventurous adaptation. But musically and lyrically, it was his most ambitious. When Mrs. Lovett enters and sees "A customer!" she does not tell Sweeney how magnificent her pies are; instead she admits they're "The Worst Pies in London" in a pre-emptive strike; she knows he'd come to that conclusion, anyway. The music has a nervous quality, too, indicating that she's not sure if she's using the right approach.

Mrs. Lovett gets a waltz in "Poor Thing" in which to break the bad news to Sweeney of what happened to his wife. Then there's such moodiness in the music of "My Friends," in which Sweeney is reunited with his barber's tools. Sondheim also provided an art song in "Green Finch and Linnet Bird," and, more amusingly, "Parlor Songs" which parodies those English folk ditties that go on for verse after verse after verse.

No other Broadway songwriter has ever written three songs with the same title, as Sondheim did with "Johanna"—with each melody markedly different. Richard Rodgers was famous for writing the "wrong note" to make music more arresting, but did he ever come up with one as satisfying as the flattened note that Anthony sings in his "Johanna"? It's bittersweet chocolate set to music, and not even the best of Mrs. Lovett's pies could have possibly been as delicious.

Comeback of the Year: Peter Masterston
The Best Little Whorehouse in Texas

In William Goldman's landmark work *The Season*—about the 1967–1968 semester—he devoted an entire chapter to struggling actor Peter Masterson.

In October 1967, the actor born as Carlos Bee Masterson got his second Broadway role, playing the title character in *The Trial of Lee Harvey Oswald.* He hadn't worked on Broadway for nearly four years, ever since he'd had five weeks of work in the 1963–1964 season playing a small role in (Baby/Dainty) June Havoc's *Marathon '33.*

But that would be four weeks longer than Lee Harvey Oswald would run in this fantasy on what might have happened if the alleged killer had been brought to trial for the assassination of President John F. Kennedy.

Goldman took us through rehearsals, previews, the nine performances, and the postmortems. He conveyed the helplessness of a performer who had a wife and two children, one of whom was only sixteen months old.

Nearly a year would pass before Masterson had another Broadway job. And while he may only had the small role of "Smitty," it was in the Pulitzer Prize–winning *The Great White Hope.* With those kids at home, Masterson took no chances and stayed for the entire 546-performance run. But after it closed in January 1970, almost six years would pass before Masterson had his next Broadway role in the weeklong run of *The Poison Tree.*

Masterson's film career was a tad better. He'd appeared in the Oscar-winning *In the Heat of the Night* and later in the Oscar-nominated *The Exorcist* but had an insignificant role in each. He would seemingly get his big break in the film version of *The Stepford Wives,* in which he played one of those Connecticut husbands who reconfigured his wife into a machine. But the expected momentum from that one never happened.

No wonder that Masterson, now in his forties, turned to writing. While reading *Playboy* in April 1974, he came across Larry L. King's article that detailed a crime that occurred in Texas that was, needless to say, not as dark or monumental as Lee Harvey Oswald's. The victim was, according to King's piece, *The Best Little Whorehouse in Texas.* "What a musical this would make," Masterson thought.

King makes very clear in his book *The Whorehouse Papers* that Masterson was the one who found him, encouraged him to do write what would have never occurred to him—the book of a musical—and kept him on an even keel when the entire project looked hopeless. Masterson helped him write it, as well.

Masterson was also responsible for getting his Texas pal Carol Hall to write songs for this country-flavored tale. He also ensured that his wife, Carlin Glynn, would portray the lead, brothel madam Miss Mona Stangley, when the time came for production.

When the show began workshop performances at the Actors Studio, Masterson was the director. And while he knew he needed some help, when Tommy Tune agreed to come on, Masterson at least held on to a co-director credit.

Tune's contributions did help to change *Whorehouse* from an almost-good show to a good one. Carol Hall can still boast that to this day that no female songwriter has ever had a Broadway musical run longer than the 1,584 performances that *Whorehouse* ran.

But as much of a boon as it was to Hall, it was a career changer for Peter Masterson. He'd later direct ten feature films, including *The Trip to Bountiful,* which won Geraldine Page an Oscar.

And that sixteen-month old daughter that Goldman mentioned in *The Season*? She grew up to be Mary Stuart Masterson.

Rookie of the Year: Lucie Arnaz
They're Playing Our Song

In the late 1970s, Marvin Hamlisch kept telling Neil Simon about the problems he was having with his then-girlfriend Carol Bayer Sager. "People claimed she was a free spirit," Hamlisch says. "But there was nothing 'free' about her. She was very expensive."

Simon turned her into the quirky and impossible Sonia Walsk, a would-be songwriter who both entices and frustrates well-established songwriter Vernon Gersh (Robert Klein). Lucie Arnaz managed to capture all her lovable and maddening qualities, while adding a husky voice that sounded just right in dialogue and song.

That's not what's most remarkable about Arnaz. She is, of course, the daughter of arguably the world's most famous female comic—Lucille

Ball—and co-starred with her in sixty episodes of *Here's Lucy.* And yet, Arnaz hasn't a single mannerism to remind an audience of her mother. For that matter, she has none of her father, Desi Arnaz, in her when she performs.

Take a look at Jason Gould, Barbra Streisand's son, in the 1989 film *The Big Picture.* Whether he knows it or not, he's imitating his mother and can't seem to find his own persona. Lucie Arnaz did, to her eternal credit.

1979–1980

MVP: Sandy Duncan
Peter Pan

Some will insist that the MVP this season should be Patti LuPone for her role as Eva Duarte Peron in Lloyd Webber and Rice's *Evita.* And certainly a solid case can be made for La LuPone. She won the Tony and Drama Desk Awards as Best Actress in a Musical.

But after LuPone left the production after sixteen months, it was able to continue for nearly three more years with not-at-all famous actresses playing the role.

What's more, as demanding a role as Evita is—hitting more than a dozen E's in a row can't be easy—LuPone played only six of the eight performances each week.

As *Peter Pan,* Sandy Duncan did eight. What's more, while LuPone missed an occasional performance, Duncan never did. She played every one of the twenty-four previews and 554 performances.

This mark would exceed the total of five other runs of *Peter Pan:* the original production with Mary Martin in 1954–1955 (152 performances) and Cathy Rigby's subsequent four revivals in the 1990s.

But Duncan prides herself on perfect attendance. "I literally have never missed a show in my life, not in fifty-two years," she says, in a voice that challenges anyone to prove her wrong. That includes her Broadway debut in *Canterbury Tales,* her Tony-nominated performance in *The Boy Friend,* and her takeover stints during the runs of *My One and Only* and Chicago.

And while Patti LuPone had to climb stairs to get to the balcony of the Casa Rosada, Duncan had to fly around the stage. That can't be an easy task, but Duncan had to do it under especially difficult circumstances. In 1971, she lost the sight in her left eye. This also short-circuited her TV series, *Funny Face,* which was starting to do well in the ratings. (In the usual good taste that so many rock groups exhibit with naming themselves, some punk musicians in the 1990s called their group Sandy Duncan's Eye.)

Duncan is another of those performers who was born too late. She was capable of carrying a vehicle in an era where few were being written, when the British musical rarely if ever singled out a star.

"Actually," she says, "I'm not that great singing or dancing. I'm really an actress, and I do everything from an actress' point of view. When you're playing Peter Pan, yeah, you're flying around and jumping, but you have to center on who this character really is. Just as comic actors take on *serious* roles—and turn out to be quite good at them—musical comedy performers can act when they're given the chance."

As Exhibit A, Duncan recalled what happened when she was starting out in the 1960s. She auditioned for Louise in a production of *Carousel;* it was to be choreographed by the legendary Agnes DeMille, who had provided the dances for the original 1945 production.

A wistful smile comes over Duncan's face when she recalls what happened. "On opening night," she says, "Agnes came backstage with Philip Burton. She said, 'You were lovely, dear—though you didn't jump as high as Bambi Lynn,'" citing the performer who originated the role.

"And then Philip Burton gave me my favorite compliment of all time when he said, 'But, Agnes, Sandy knows *why* she's jumping.'"

Duncan also knows how important to make the live experience live for first-time theatergoers. At the curtain calls of *Peter Pan,* she would look directly into the eyes of so many kids in the first few rows and tell them, "Thank you for coming!" over and over again.

Duncan aided the Broadway theater in an even more tangible way. She was also one of the performers who helped New York City get back on its feet through one of the "I ♥ New York" campaign TV commercials. While the casts of *Evita, Sweeney Todd,* and *A Chorus Line* were also seen promoting tourism in the Big Apple, Duncan's flying around the city was the capper on the spot.

And while we're passing out MVP Awards, let's give three more for people who never had anything specific to do with Broadway theater but nevertheless helped it immeasurably.

One goes to advertising agency Wells, Rich, and Greene for spurring the "I ♥ New York" campaign. Another gets bestowed on Milton Glaser, the artist who conceived of the now famous logo that involved three letters —"I," "N," and "Y" in a black American Typewriter font with a big fat heart for good measure. The third recipient is Steve Karmen for writing the "I ♥ New York" theme. While it consisted of only twelve notes, that was enough to reiterate the message of "I ♥ New York" three times.

The city needed this campaign. In the late 1970s, New York was enduring terribly tough times, on the brink of bankruptcy. What seemed to be an unending downward spiral started when President Gerald R. Ford refused federal money for a needed bailout, spurring the now infamous *New York Daily News* headline on October 30, 1975: "Ford to City: Drop Dead." Add to this an ever-crumbling Times Square, a 1977 blackout in which looting, vandalism, and arson were at feverish heights, and a rash of serial killings from a deranged David Berkowitz (aka "Son of Sam").

The "I ♥ New York" campaign, however, worked wonders. Tourism skyrocketed, and with the additional moneys and public interest, Times Square was able to get that needed face-lift.

Comeback of the Year: Ann Miller
Sugar Babies

She'd appeared in *Stage Door, You Can't Take It with You, Room Service, On the Town, Hit the Deck,* and *Kiss Me, Kate*—albeit all in Hollywood, and not on Broadway.

And yet Ann Miller did have a couple of Broadway appearances on her résumé. In *George White Scandals of 1939,* she participated in one duet in act 1 and tap-danced in act 2. When Miller left the show after a few months, no effort was made to replace her; both the duet and dance were dropped, implying that no one could follow her.

Miller had far more to do on May 29, 1969, when she assumed the title role in *Mame.* She was the last of four to play it, following Angela Lansbury, Janis Paige, and Jane Morgan, and did it for seven months until it closed on January 3, 1970. Although Miller had seven songs to sing, she took on a little extra work in "That's How Young I Feel," bringing out her tap shoes once again. What had previously been a nice enough number became a genuine showstopper (although it had little to do with the character of Mame).

Ann Miller's first name was actually Johnnie, because her father, John Collier, desperately wanted a son and a junior. The best he could get was Johnnie Lucille Ann Collier.

Young Johnnie suffered from rickets. That may have been a blessing in disguise. Had she not, her mother might not have enrolled her in a dance class, which she hoped would make her daughter's legs stronger. It certainly did, for Miller reportedly at her peak could perform 500 taps a minute.

Perhaps Miller wasn't able to do quite as many during her three-year run in *Sugar Babies,* but her audience was amazed at how many hundred she could still manage. She could still hold a note, too, as was proved as soon as she opened her mouth and sang the *"Iiiiiiiiiiiiiiiiiiiii"* in "I Feel a Song Comin' On."

Of course, a genuine burlesque show meant that Miller had to take part in some less-than-elegant sketches. In a schoolroom sketch, she, as the teacher, asked the pupil (Mickey Rooney) to define the difference between prose and poetry. When he answered "The pros stand on the corner," Miller genuinely looked as if she didn't understand the joke. Ditto when, in a courtroom scene, she admitted to killing her husband and asked the judge, "Are you going to give me a stiff sentence?" and he replied, "If I get a good night's sleep, you can depend on it." Miller's performance-long innocence kept *Sugar Babies* from devolving into a "dirty" show.

Miller made her final significant stage appearance in 1998 at the Paper Mill Playhouse in Millburn, New Jersey. She appeared as Carlotta Campion in Stephen Sondheim's *Follies,* which allowed her to sing "I'm Still Here."

"Actually," says Angelo Del Rossi, then executive director of Paper Mill, "Annie didn't want to do it. I said to her, 'Oh, Annie, for God's sake, you're only sitting around the house doing nothing. Imagine being in front of an audience once again who adores you. Get out here!'"

She did. What was fascinating was seeing her react to the Paper Mill crowd as it went wild with enthusiasm after her number. There was so much gratitude in her face, to be sure, but what was also there was the awareness that this would be the last time she would get this kind of ovation from any audience.

Actually, there would be one more in 1999, for a benefit in London. Says British star Bonnie Langford, "When Ann arrived at the theater, she was this very frail and fragile old woman. I was pained to see her when she struggled to walk up the steps and go backstage for the rehearsal. And then, a few minutes later, a bunch of chorus boys came on the stage. The music struck up, and out came Ann Miller tap-dancing away as if someone else decades younger had inhabited her body. She'd pulled the switch and went into show-biz mode like no one I'd ever seen before or since."

Rookie of the Year: Mickey Rooney
Sugar Babies

Boston Braves pitcher Sam Jethroe was thirty-three and three-quarters years old when he became the oldest Rookie of the Year in baseball history. But he was a youngster compared to our rookie of 1979–1980. Mickey Rooney had just passed his fifty-ninth birthday when he opened in *Sugar Babies* at the Mark Hellinger Theatre on October 8, 1979.

Certainly Rooney had done stage work over the years. In 1970, his starring as the title character in *George M.* (Cohan) garnered him a Straw Hat Award, the prizes summer stock bestowed on performers from 1969 until 1974. He didn't, however, win the same award the next year when he spent the summer portraying W. C. Fields in the unimaginatively (and unfortunately) named *W. C.* (Bernadette Peters played his longtime love Carlotta Monti.)

Now, finally, seven years later, he'd make his Broadway debut in the most opulent and expensive burlesque show ever mounted. After the house lights faded to black and the curtain rose, a well-focused spotlight suddenly pierced the darkness and illuminated Rooney's face. He had a startled expression of "Oh! Are you here already?" before the grin took over, one that said, "Well, yes, why not let's start now? The sooner we do, the more fun we'll have."

And Rooney gave audiences just that. That five-foot-two bundle of dynamite was right at home singing the opening number, "A Good Old Burlesque Show," as the stage burst open with glamorous and scantily clad young women, leering male comics in checkered suits, cops, con men, and bubble dancers. Rooney wasn't above participating in "Meet Me 'round the Corner in a Half an Hour," the venerable sketch in which a lass shows off her wares while bumping and grinding. Later, with co-star Ann Miller, he sang a vivid "I Can't Give You Anything but Love" as part of a Jimmy McHugh medley.

Rooney's *Playbill* bio showed that he was modest about his many accomplishments. The three-time Oscar nominee Rooney simply wrote: "Mickey Rooney . . . formerly Andy Hardy . . . formerly Mickey McGuire . . . formerly Joe Yule, Jr." Nothing more.

Andy Hardy, of course, referred to Rooney's most famous character, spanning seventeen films from 1937's *A Family Affair* to *Andy Hardy Comes*

Home in 1958. Mickey McGuire was both the name he used and the character he portrayed character in more than four dozen two-reelers from 1927 to 1933, when he was seven to thirteen years old. Joe Yule Jr. was in fact his birth name.

After the curtain came down on the final performance on August 28, 1982, Rooney pretty much told the crowd the truth when he said, "No one thought that we would last six months—and we did. No one thought we would last a year—and we did. No one thought that we would last two years—and we did. No one thought that we would last three years—and we did. No one thought that we would last four years—and we didn't."

More to the point, no one thought that Rooney, when he was approaching ninety, would still be performing in front of audiences, this time with his (eighth) wife Jan in an entertainment called, fittingly enough, *Let's Put on a Show!* He certainly did during the entire 1,208-performance run of *Sugar Babies.*

Marilyn Cooper Sometimes getting the lead doesn't lead you in the right direction. Marilyn Cooper had been cast in the second-banana role in *I Can Get It for You Wholesale,* but then director Arthur Laurents decided to promote her to leading lady when he found someone else for the smaller role: Barbra Streisand. Suddenly everyone was noticing Streisand and no one was paying attention to Cooper, whose career languished. She had to wait nineteen years before she won a Tony—for playing a second banana—in *Woman of the Year.* (Streisand has yet to win one—and undoubtedly won't, for that would mean she'd have to appear on Broadway.)

Hal Prince rehearsing *Phantom* The 1980s weren't turning out to be too good for Harold Prince. *Merrily We Roll Along* (1981) lasted two weeks. *A Doll's Life* (1982) and *Play Memory* (1983) each ran three days. In 1985, *Grind* was turning out to be his most successful show of the decade—at seventy-one performances. Had he lost his touch? But then Andrew Lloyd Webber called and said, "Hal, want to stage my *Phantom of the Opera*?"

1980–1990

yne Daly in *Gypsy* The first actress to play Rose in *Gypsy*—Ethel Merman—had been a musical theater star for almost three decades. he second, Angela Lansbury, had already won two Tonys for *Mame* and *Dear World.* Now Rose would be portrayed by an actress whose roadway experience had solely been a supporting role in a twelve-performance play almost a quarter century earlier. But by act 1, scene 2, when Tyne Daly was singing "Some People," she was showing all people that her Rose would bloom with the best of them.

im Walton Sometimes lawyers manage to take over entire companies. In *Merrily We Roll Along,* an actor playing a lawyer—Jerome, who epresented Franklin Shepard, Inc.—took over the role of Franklin Shepard himself. It launched Walton to a three-plus-decade career; the ctor he replaced never performed professionally again.

1980–1981

MVP and Co-Comeback Players of the Year: David Merrick and Gower Champion
42nd Street

During the 1960s, Merrick's *Playbill* bio often ended with, "Since *Fanny* opened on Broadway on November 4, 1954, there has never been a week without a David Merrick production on Broadway."

But by the early 1970s, Merrick had to do some fancy fudging and footwork to maintain that self-imposed record. After all, his *Promises, Promises* was set to end its three-year run on January 2, 1972, while his co-production of *Vivat! Vivat Regina!* wouldn't begin previews until January 13, 1972. Those eleven days would break the week-streak.

So Merrick brought to Broadway the Stratford National Theatre of Canada's production of Georges Feydeau's *There's One in Every Marriage.* He had it play from December 26, 1971 to January 15, 1972—just enough to keep the streak alive.

Vivat! lasted until April 29, 1972, by which point *Sugar* had opened. Although the Stone–Styne–Merrill adaptation of *Some Like It Hot* was hardly a blockbuster, it did manage to run until June 23, 1973. But by then, Merrick had nothing in the pipeline. Until the Gower Champion–helmed *Mack & Mabel* took residence at the Majestic on October 1, 1974, there had indeed been sixty-five consecutive weeks when there was no David Merrick production on Broadway.

After that musical closed surprisingly fast on November 30, 1974, Merrick produced a mere three shows in the next thirty-three months, a true comedown for a producer who as recently as the 1967–1968 season had had six. That "never-a-week-without" record? From *Mack & Mabel*'s closing through August 17, 1980, Merrick *didn't* have a show on Broadway for 240 of those 297 weeks.

Suddenly he was sixty-eight years old, and his next show seemed frightfully old-fashioned: Michael Stewart and Mark Bramble's adaptation of *42nd Street,* using the Harry Warren–Al Dubin songs from the original movie and other properties, too. How could this succeed in the 1980s? Who'd care about star

Dorothy Brock getting injured, with young and untested Peggy Sawyer taking her place to save Julian Marsh's show? The musical's future seemed to be rooted in the style of the two previous years' Tony winners: *Sweeney Todd* and *Evita.*

Broadway moaned even louder when Merrick asked Gower Champion to direct and choreograph. Yes, Champion had helmed seven Merrick shows and never came home without at least a Tony nomination. But his last four shows were utter flops.

However, a second look at these four shows reveals that Champion hadn't fared so poorly. True, in 1976, he had directed and choreographed *Rockabye Hamlet,* a rock version of Shakespeare's play. Cliff Jones's book, music, and lyrics weren't good; he created a character named Honeybelle Huckster to tell us what happened to Hamlet's father: "He Got It in the Ear," she sang to a country twang. When time came for Ophelia to commit suicide, she didn't drown herself but strangled her neck with a microphone cord.

And yet Champion staged *Rockabye Hamlet* in dazzling fashion. In his *Playbill* bio he wrote, "Mr. Champion effects a marriage between the Broadway musical and a rock concert." He did exactly what he set out to do. The look of the show anticipated the future Broadway productions of *The Who's Tommy, Spring Awakening,* and *American Idiot.* Champion's mistake was choosing to stage inferior work, but the failure had nothing to do with his presentation.

Next, in 1977, he reimagined *Annie Get Your Gun* with *The Unsinkable Molly Brown*'s film stars Debbie Reynolds and Harve Presnell. His concept was that a group of performers would greet us, let us know they were about to don different characters along with their costumes, and put on a production of *Annie Get Your Gun.* It wasn't so different from the idea that Peter Stone would have for the show's 1999 revival. The only difference is that that Stone's played Broadway, but Champion's—after engagements in San Francisco, Los Angeles, Dallas, and Miami (cities in which it collected many a rave)—didn't.

Because the New York critics never had the chance weigh in, Broadway believed that the production couldn't have been *that* good. The reason it didn't come in, however, was because Reynolds didn't want to spend months if not years living in New York. Had this production come to Broadway, Champion might well have had a hit.

Champion next played show doctor on the 1977 Kander and Ebb musical *The Act* after Martin Scorsese couldn't solve his then-girlfriend Liza Minnelli's show. Champion made it better and tighter.

The following year he had a "production supervised" credit on Strouse and Adams's *A Broadway Musical,* improving it substantially from its workshop production. The show closed on opening night, but once again, Champion made it flow better.

Still, many assumed that Champion had lost his touch. And weren't there rumors that he wasn't well? So when Merrick phoned, Champion answered the call and agreed to do *42nd Street.*

Merrick went all out. While in the old days he was the general partner who raised money from limited partners, this time he was the sole general and limited partner; for he financed the entire $2.5 million enterprise. He literally had no one to answer to. He allowed Champion to hire forty-eight performers. (The previous new musical to open that year—*Fearless Frank*—had had eight. The next new musical set to open that season—*Charlie and Algernon*—would have ten.)

The cast included two Tony winners: Jerry Orbach and Tammy Grimes. However, one would never know their presence from any of the window cards or three-sheets; the only person's name in evidence was David Merrick's.

During the Washington tryout, Merrick thought Stewart and Bramble's book inept and changed their credit from "book," which promised something cohesive, to "lead-ins and crossovers." That was meant to lower everyone's expectations.

Says assistant-to-the-producer Jon Maas, "There was originally twice as much book. James Congdon played a non-singing gangster whom Julian Marsh would call. He'd show up looking dapper and slightly menacing. Meanwhile, Curt Dawson played Dorothy Brock's boyfriend Pat Denning. But when everyone realized that no one cared what happened to anyone when he wasn't singing or dancing, the gangster became an offstage menace. Dawson was fired and Congdon became Pat Denning.

"'You're Getting to Be a Habit with Me' was originally done as a wicker-wheelchair ballet, the way Champion had staged Cyril Ritchard's number in *Sugar.* Merrick was so desperate that he frantically called me to find Sandy Wilson [the author of *The Boy Friend*] so he could write some new patter lyrics for Tammy Grimes. But then Champion came up with a new staging, so Wilson wasn't needed."

Even Theoni V. Aldredge's costumes went through changes. "The title ballet originally had black and white costumes and the abbreviated version that ends the first act was in grey and white," says Maas. He also notes that "Getting Out of Town" originally had a different tune with Michael Stewart lyrics and was called "It's Time to Leave Town."

Perhaps it was, but would New York welcome such a troubled show? Maas says, "I continually urged Merrick to bring in Comden and Green and he finally told me why he wouldn't: 'Because they'd want to rewrite the whole thing—and they'd be right. Only we don't have the time and I want Gower to focus on the numbers.' Instead, he brought in Marshall Brickman to write jokes." (Whether Comden and Green would have come is another matter. Were they still smarting from that phony ad that Merrick created for their *Subways Are for Sleeping*?)

Meanwhile, the cast and crew were wondering why Champion wasn't attending more rehearsals. Why were Ron Field and Joe Layton surreptitiously around? Didn't Champion's choreography assistant Randy Skinner seem to be the one suggesting new steps and supervising numbers?

Whoever was responsible for *42nd Street,* the fact remains that the show had the same inviting look that Champion had given his other musicals. Of all the director-choreographers of the era, Champion was the one whose shows seemed to say, "Come in! Welcome!" And a hearty welcome was what Broadway would give *42nd Street* for more than eight years.

To be frank, Champion also immeasurably helped *42nd Street* in an unexpected way. On opening night at the Winter Garden, after a tumultuous reception and many curtain calls, Merrick took to the stage to announce, "This is tragic." The audience, still dizzy with delight, laughed and wondered why he looked so serious. They'd soon find out: "No, you don't understand," said Merrick. "Gower Champion died this morning."

Considering all the stunts that Merrick had pulled over the years, some suspected that he might have been making the grandest grandstand play of them all: shipping off Champion to a faraway island and allowing the man to get out of this world alive while claiming he was dead just to boost box-office receipts. For months, many Broadway wags half expected Champion to show up and admit it was all a publicity stunt.

No. Champion was gone, and his specific look for a Broadway musical went with him.

42nd Street won the Tony Award as Best Musical of 1980–1981. It may have been old-fashioned, but it wound up running six times as long as *Sweeney* and twice as long as *Evita.* And while *42nd Street* never became the longest-running musical in Broadway history—*A Chorus Line* saw to that—it would become Merrick's longest-running production, lasting 3,486 performances—642 more than *Hello, Dolly!*'s then record-breaking run.

Alas, Merrick wasn't fully able to enjoy it. In 1983, he suffered a stroke that left him close to speechless. He still had his wits, however, and came up with a clever gambit during *42nd Street*'s eighth year. By then, he'd been forced to move the musical to the St. James Theatre in order for the Majestic to make way for the highly anticipated *The Phantom of the Opera.* Once that white-hot hit opened, Merrick instituted an 8:15 p.m. curtain time for *42nd Street.* His hope was that those waiting in line but denied for last-minute *Phantom* cancellations would find they'd be too late to get into another show—but enough time to see *42nd Street* in toto.

After *42nd Street* closed on January 8, 1989—giving Merrick 436 consecutive weeks on Broadway—92 Merrick-less weeks would pass before he produced his penultimate show: *Oh, Kay!* The rewritten George Gershwin hit with an all-black cast (shades of his Pearl Bailey *Dolly!*—literally) originated at the Goodspeed Opera House but was reworked for Broadway under Merrick's watchful eye. It didn't do well, especially with *New York Times* critic Frank Rich.

But Merrick had carefully watched Rich and his girlfriend, *Times* writer Alex Witchel, during the preview Rich was reviewing. Given that Witchel was making so many comments during the show, Merrick felt that she'd unduly influenced Rich. He took an ad that, unlike the famous *Subways* one, made note of their relationship. Merrick seemed to have the last laugh.

In many ways, it was the last laugh. Once *Oh, Kay!* had closed after less than two months, resumed three months later, and then closed after twelve days of previews, Merrick would not be represented for the next 257 weeks. His final production was simply a rescue mission, providing the necessary funds to bring Rodgers and Hammerstein's *State Fair* to Broadway when the original producers didn't have the money to do it. There was an irony here: when Merrick first struck out as a sole lead producer, he wanted Rodgers and Hammerstein to write *Fanny* for him. They didn't want any involvement with him; now, many years after their deaths, they unwittingly would join forces.

When the Tony nominees were announced a few weeks after *State Fair*'s mildly received opening, the Best Musical nods went to the expected *Rent* and *Bring in 'Da Noise, Bring in 'Da Funk* as well as to the closed *Chronicle of a Death Foretold* and *Swingin' on a Star.* That lineup surprised many, who thought that *Big, Victor/Victoria,* and even *State Fair* had solid chances.

Soon there was another hellishly clever ad from the eighty-five-year-old Merrick: "When the Big Victor is announced, it won't be Fair." But Susan L. Schulman, who was *State Fair's* press representative, cannot give Merrick the credit. "It came from the advertising office," she says. "By then, I'm sorry to say, there was no David Merrick left." He died fewer than four years later, on April 25, 2000.

Co-Comeback Player of the Year: Marilyn Cooper
Woman of the Year

The same day that nineteen-year-old Harriet Marilyn Cooper was graduated as a psychology and communications major from NYU, she immediately went to audition for *Mr. Wonderful* and was cast. Later came minor comic roles in *West Side Story* and *Gypsy;* during the latter, she came to know dance arranger John Kander, who often accompanied her when she auditioned.

She also got to know those shows' bookwriter, Arthur Laurents. So when he was set to direct *I Can Get It for You Wholesale* in 1962, he had her in mind for Miss Marmelstein, the harried assistant to a Fashion Avenue boss.

"Then [composer-lyricist] Harold Rome saw Barbra Streisand on *The Mike Wallace Show,* and was totally bowled over by her," said Cooper. "After she came in and got the part, I didn't know what was going to happen." Cooper even worried for a while that she'd be the understudy, but Laurents chose a newcomer called Louise Lasser instead.

"But," she said, "Arthur had already decided that the show's ingénue should be off-beat, so he had me audition for that. Barbara Harris auditioned, too, but Arthur chose me. I didn't feel bad because I got a lead and," she adds with a laugh, "Barbra did fine."

After *Wholesale* closed, Cooper did a number of industrials and community theater. "My whole life has been a repertory theater," she said. "From big role to small role to big to small—like the one I did in *Hallelujah, Baby!* And then I was Eydie Gormé's understudy in *Golden Rainbow,*" she says, citing the 1968 musical in which Gormé starred with husband Steve Lawrence. "I went on about 50 times, so sometimes it was the Steve-and-Marilyn show."

Two by Two came in 1970, but by the end of the decade, Cooper was an understudy in *Working* and then in *Ballroom.* The latter was especially frustrating, for the show had dozens roles for of late-middle-aged performers.

But shortly after, old friend John Kander asked her to his home to hear his new show, *Woman of the Year.* Cooper was especially impressed when he and lyricist Fred Ebb sang "The Grass Is Always Greener," a duet between two women—one glamorous, one not—who'd married the same man. I thought, 'Oh-my-God, oh-my God, what a song!'"

And what a Comeback Player of the Year performance Marilyn Cooper gave as Jan Donovan, the hausfrau who finds herself meeting her husband's first wife, the glamorous Tess Harding (Lauren Bacall).

"I didn't think the part was big enough to win a Tony," she said of her one-scene role. The voters felt differently, allowing Cooper to give one of the awards' most memorable finishes to an acceptance speech: "I'm a poker player, and I say if you stay at the table long enough, you're bound to come up with a winner"—the perfect line for a Comeback Player of the Year.

1981–1982

MVP: Tommy Tune
Nine

Once Tommy Tune listened to the tape of Maury Yeston's music and lyrics for *Nine* that had been left at his apartment building, he became quite excited. Although the musical version of *8½* had had a number of growing pains, Tune saw possibilities in the story of megalomaniacal movie director Guido Contini. He delivered a production that earned him a Tony for Best Direction in the same season that mentor Michael Bennett competed with *Dreamgirls.*

Nine won the Best Musical prize, too, over the favored *Dreamgirls.* To be fair, *Nine*'s opening only minutes before the Tony deadline helped its cause, but the distinctive look that Tune had given the show helped more. Aside from Raul Julia as Guido—and four young lads who had small roles—the cast entirely consisted of women: twenty-one in all.

Yeston says, "It happened truly because all the women who auditioned were fascinating and Felliniesque, and all the men were basically boring chorus boys who did not seem European. Tune asked us to think about all women, except for Raul. I loved that idea because it meant I could treat the cast as a choral orchestra, have them sing the overture, have them express Guido's mental state, and provide Raul with terrific dramatic authority onstage since he'd be the only man at the center of attention of all the women."

Mario Fratti had already written a libretto for the work, but Tune had another idea for a bookwriter: Arthur Kopit, best known as the playwright who had written the absurdist farce *Oh, Dad, Poor Dad, Mama's Hung You in the Closet and I'm Feelin' So Sad.*

That's not the most logical audition piece for this assignment, but Kopit explains why he got the job: "Tommy suggested me because he'd recently seen my play *Wings,* which investigated the shattered mind of a stroke victim. And because he wanted us to look into Guido Contini's mind, he thought I'd be good for it."

Kopit was. Tune also gets credit for forging a collaboration between Kopit and Yeston that resulted in another show—*Phantom.* While it has never been nearly as successful as Andrew Lloyd Webber's *The Phantom of the Opera,* of course, it still had plenty of productions in the early 1990s and continues to get some.

Relievers of the Year: Raquel Welch (Woman of the Year); Jim Walton *Merrily We Roll Along*

That Raquel Welch had already worked with Stephen Sondheim did not necessarily qualify her to be in a musical; she had played the shoplifter-turned-semi-star in *The Last of Sheila,* the murder-mystery film that Sondheim had written with Anthony Perkins.

Broadway was wary that this actress best known for her measurements could spell Lauren Bacall for even a two-week vacation.

And yet Welch turned out to be the Reliever of the Year for *Woman of the Year.* Her voice, however modest, was substantially better than Bacall's. What she also showed was charisma.

When Bacall opened the show, she was closing in on fifty-seven. And while even front-row patrons might not have noticed with an orchestra pit's worth of distance between them and pink lights caressing the stage, Welch was a full sixteen years younger. It helped the Peter Stone book and Kander and Ebb score, because Tess Harding is a TV anchorwoman—an occupation where age can be a factor.

Welch fared far less well in 1997 when she assumed the lead in *Victor/Victoria*. The role required that she successfully impersonate a man, but Peter Marks of the *New York Times* merely had to take one look at Welch's 37C–22.5–35.5 measurements to lead his review with. "Oh, come on!" The show closed six weeks later.

Our other reliever played two weeks' official performances, too—but not because he was spelling a star's vacation. Jim Walton took over as Franklin Shepard in *Merrily We Roll Along* because original lead James Weissenbach wasn't working out. But two weeks was all the troubled show could run after poor reviews and worse word of mouth for a five-week preview period.

The fate of the show was doubly disappointing because it was the follow-up project for Stephen Sondheim and Harold Prince after their breathtaking *Sweeney Todd* in 1979. But had Weissenbach stayed in the lead, the reviews would have been worse. Walton brought a boyish charm that the egomaniacal character needed.

In the 1989–1990 season, Walton was playing Anthony Hope, the sailor in the revival of *Sweeney Todd* at Circle in the Square Theatre. At the same time, Victor Garber, the original Anthony, was at Arena Stage in Washington, D.C., playing Franklin Shepard, in a revival of *Merrily We Roll Along*. It's one of Broadway's best ironies.

Rookie of the Year: Maury Yeston
Nine

A musical version of a Fellini film—and one of his acknowledged masterpieces?

Composer-lyricist Maury Yeston admits that his musicalization on Federico Fellini's *8½* was one that he never thought would be produced. It was merely what he decided to write when his mentor, Lehman Engel, commanded his BMI Musical Theatre Workshop to select and work on a project as an exercise.

Yeston says that when he was in high school in the 1960s he fell in love with the story of Guido Anselmi, a film director having a midlife crisis. "It wasn't until the early 70's that I came up with the idea of adapting it," he says.

Yeston admits that his title was not the most logical. "I called it *Nine* as a working title—which seemed like the first laugh: *Nine* based on *8½*. Only later did I focus on the character's stunted emotional maturity and figure out nine was a magical age from which he never really wanted to depart."

Actually, thirty-seven turned out to be a magical age for Yeston. On Tony night, he did what even he once thought would be impossible: He beat Stephen Sondheim for the Best Score Tony.

To be sure, Sondheim's *Merrily We Roll Along* had been a two-week flop; his work on the show would be its sole Tony nomination. But by the time voters had received their ballots, the *Merrily* cast album had been long released and had made a terrific impression on its listeners.

Yeston was also pitted against Andrew Lloyd Webber and Tim Rice. They, however, were nominated for a musical they'd written more than a dozen years earlier: *Joseph and the Amazing Technicolor Dreamcoat.* Tony voters prefer to award brand-new scores rather than secondhand ones (*Gigi* in 1974 is a marked exception), so Yeston's victory was not as mammoth here.

However, Yeston's victory over the *Dreamgirls* score—Henry Krieger's music and Tom Eyen's lyrics—was impressive. Not only was *Dreamgirls'* score massive, offering virtual wall-to-wall music, but it also had a powerhouse hit single: Jennifer Holliday's first-act ending aria "And I Am Telling You, I Am Not Going." Much of the nation knew it.

But Yeston's *Nine* had a great deal of music, too. After an overture that was sung rather than "just" played, his all-female cast insisted that Guido (newly surnamed Contini) had achieved as a director feats achieved "Not Since Chaplin." But in "Guido's Song," some nervous patter music showed that Mr. Contini was not nearly as convinced as they—and that he was overwhelmed by personal and romantic problems.

Ambitious musical scenes included "The Germans at the Spa" who distract Guido and the sensuously wicked "A Call from the Vatican," which gave Anita Morris the material to seduce a man. "Unusual Way" and "Simple" became cabaret standards.

Yeston's score was also the only one of the four nominees that had not yet been released as a cast album; it would not be available for months after the Tonys. Thus voters got to hear it only once, in the theater. But that was enough for the majority of them to choose it. This unknown associate professor of music theory at Yale proved that those who teach, can.

1982–1983

MVP: Andrew Lloyd Webber

There once was a book club for Broadway enthusiasts. The Fireside Theatre—later called Stage & Screen Book Club—ran from 1950 until 2003.

In the beginning, the club would send out a little four-page leaflet trumpeting the next month's selection—such as in April 1953, when hardcover copies of Arthur Laurents's recent play *The Time of the Cuckoo* were offered. On the back page was some biographical material on Laurents ("worked for Bloomingdale's department store in the linen section") along with a nice picture of him sporting jet-black hair.

Each month, the back page also offered some filler under the heading of "Fireside Chat." April 1953's filler asked the question, "Have you met Gus the Theatre Cat?" followed by the lines "Gus is the Cat at the Theatre Door. His name, as I ought to have told you before . . ."

There's a sonnet's worth of information there, along with the credit "From *Old Possum's Book of Practical Cats* (copyright 1939, by T. S. Eliot)." One must presume that at least some members of the Fireside Theatre had aspirations of writing a musical, but apparently no one saw the possibilities or found himself able to write a musical version of Eliot's work. Four decades had to pass after Eliot's collection was published before someone saw the possibilities.

Andrew Lloyd Webber had had a marvelous 1970s, what with *Joseph and the Amazing Technicolor Dreamcoat, Jesus Christ Superstar,* and *Evita.* Although *Jeeves* in 1975 couldn't approach their success, it had its moments, too (which is why Lloyd Webber many years later took the B section from *Jeeves'* "Half a Moment" and recycled it for *Sunset Boulevard's* "As If We Never Said Goodbye").

But Lloyd Webber was to have a better 1980s, starting with his idea that Eliot's fifteen poems would make a good musical. Very few people agreed with him. But he didn't have to worry about finding a producer. Just as Rodgers and Hammerstein had done with their fourth Broadway musical (*South Pacific*), Lloyd Webber would now, starting with his fourth musical, produce his own works, too, via his Really Useful Theatre Company, Ltd. Why settle just for royalties? (Lloyd Webber did take on a producing collaborator, a young man who'd struggled with producing new musicals: Cameron Mackintosh.)

The theater Lloyd Webber had earmarked—the New—had never had a true hit; even *Grease* had only run 236 performances in this house that was out of the well-trafficked theater district. When Lloyd Webber was considering it, the New Theatre had been a TV studio since 1977. He, however, saw its thrust-stage seating as ideal for *Cats.*

Lloyd Webber also thought to include a cat that Eliot had written about but discarded: Grizabella, once a ravishing beauty and now a broken-down alley dweller. Wouldn't Judi Dench be terrific in the part?

Perhaps, but five days before the first preview, she injured a tendon and had to leave the show. Elaine Paige, who became a star because of Lloyd Webber's *Evita,* came in. But this was a blessing in disguise for the show's big number, another Eliot poem that wasn't in *Old Possum's Book of Practical Cats.* It had been unpublished and unknown, but after Lloyd Webber and his director Trevor Nunn fit lyrics to it, it became "Memory." Paige's dynamic delivery ensured that "Memory" would become the musical's best-known piece and one of musical theater's most famous songs. It, like all the other songs in the score, was orchestrated by Lloyd Webber, too.

But no one knew what to expect at that first London preview on May 1, 1981. Bonnie Langford, who played the mischievous Rumpleteazer, recalled that the actor playing Mungojerrie, her partner in crime, was fired four days before opening. "We didn't know if we had the biggest hit or the most monumental catastrophe," she remembers. "At our very first performance, after we finished 'Jellicle Cats' and the applause ended, we then very clearly heard an audience member say out loud, 'Rubbish.' I wondered if my career was going to end right there."

No. The London *Cats* wouldn't close until its 8,949th performance on the precise day of its twenty-first anniversary on May 11, 2002. That more than doubled the previous record holder: Lloyd Webber's own *Jesus Christ Superstar,* which performed 3,357 times. The Broadway production of *Cats* ran a month shy of eighteen years, with a then-record 7,485 performances. It wasn't quite the "Now and Forever" that the ads promised, but it was still a grand achievement.

Although one of the plot points in John Guare's play *Six Degrees of Separation* involves a movie of *Cats,* no film was made. Instead, it was videotaped for PBS and home video by Polygram. The company's president, who green-lit the project, was surnamed Sondheim.

Comeback Player of the Year: George Abbott
On Your Toes

George Abbott certainly knew when to write his autobiography.

Mister Abbott was published by Random House in 1963, when Abbott had two of his 1962 directorial efforts still running on Broadway. *Never Too Late,* a comedy about a couple in their late fifties who find they're unexpectedly expecting a child, would run 1,000 performances. The musical *A Funny Thing Happened on the Way to the Forum* would come up only a month's run shy of that mark.

As we saw, Abbott needed help on *Forum,* but the public assumed he'd stage it all: "Dir by Geo Abbott" was on *Forum's* marquee in block plastic letters along with the title. What better evidence to show how important management believed George Abbott's name was to the theatergoing public?

And why not? Abbott had appeared in his first Broadway play in 1913 (when he was twenty-six). Twelve years later, in 1925, he appeared in *A Holy Terror,* a play that he also wrote. A year later, *Love 'Em and Leave 'Em*—another play he wrote—would be his first directing assignment, too.

In 1928, Abbott wrote and directed a play that was called, fittingly enough, *Broadway.* It ran 603 performances, and when it closed in 1928, only thirteen productions had ever run longer. But when Abbott sat down to write his autobiography in late 1962, he'd been involved in eleven productions that had surpassed *Broadway*—including such household-name hits as *High Button Shoes, Call Me Madam, The Pajama Game,* and *Damn Yankees.*

But as soon as Abbott's memoir came out, doom came with it. He then directed an unlucky thirteen flops in an equally unlucky thirteen years. Two of them ran three weeks; two lasted two; three couldn't even play a full week. Granted, during this time span—in 1965—the 54th Street Theater was renamed the George Abbott Theater in his honor. But that playhouse was razed in 1970, making an inadvertent but unpleasant comment about Abbott's current Broadway status.

So after *Music Is,* a musical version of *Twelfth Night,* closed on December 26, 1976, after eight performances, Abbott was deemed all done. Face it: The man had been born during Grover Cleveland's first round as president. Few producers wanted to hire an eighty-nine-year-old man for any job, let alone to helm a musical that would now cost in the millions.

But then in late 1982, producer Roger L. Stevens—himself no kid at seventy-two—had an idea. Why not revive one of George Abbott's hits that the man knew inside out? Abbott was consulted, and he thought *The Boys from Syracuse,* which he had done with Rodgers and Hart in 1938, would be his best shot.

"And Roger was all for it," says John Mauceri, the noted musical director. "That is, until he found out that *The Boys from Syracuse* was an adaptation of Shakespeare's *The Comedy of Errors.* Roger was then the producer for the Kennedy Center, and the year before, they were one of the producers of *Oh, Brother!*—which was *also* a musical version of *The Comedy of Errors.* It had flopped in two days."

On to Plan B. How about *Pal Joey* or *On Your Toes*? "We sent Mister Abbott both scripts," says Mauceri, "and he called back to say that he thought neither one of them was any good. 'But,' he said, 'everyone thinks *Pal Joey* is wonderful, and that *On Your Toes* isn't, so we'd have a better chance with *On Your Toes.*"

Mauceri agreed and became one of the producers for this revival, which would closely replicate the 1936 production.

To be sure, a 1954 revival that Abbott had staged and produced shuttered after a disappointing reception and a mere sixty-four performances. But that was a time when musical comedy was exploding with new shows. Now, during the so-called British Invasion, musical comedy was in short supply.

So at the age of ninety-five, Abbott returned to Broadway at the Virginia Theatre, where he had worked only once before—as an actor in 1955, when he portrayed Mr. Antrobus in a revival of *The Skin of Our Teeth.*

On Your Toes ran 505 performances, enough to then make it the tenth-longest-running musical revival of all time. Of course, one can suspect that the aged Abbott really and truly didn't direct this production, but nowhere in *On Your Toes'* credits can one find the name of an assistant director. There are credits for "Assistant to Mr. DeLiagre" (another producer), "Assistant to Mr. Saddler" (the choreographer), "Assistant to Mr. Balanchine" (the original choreographer), "Assistant to Mr. Martins" (who did the ballets), "Assistant to Mr. Mauceri" (the musical director), "Assistant to Mr. Brown" (the set designer), and plenty of other assistants, too. But there's no credit for "Assistant to Mr. Abbott." Maybe the nonagenarian really did it all himself.

"He certainly did," says Mauceri. "Mister Abbott did have an assistant, but the only thing he had him do was go out to get him a banana and chicken soup for lunch."

Rookie of the Year: Trevor Nunn
Cats

Choosing Nunn as a rookie may seem odd, for the season before, he'd won a Tony for directing *The Life and Adventures of Nicholas Nickleby.* And while that mammoth two-part effort had the scope and feel of an enormous musical, *Cats* was his Broadway musical debut.

Nunn had, however, already directed a London musical. In 1976, he staged a musical version of *The Comedy of Errors* for which he wrote lyrics (and Guy Woolfenden provided music). David Merrick came close to bringing it to Broadway.

More to the point, the famed producer was so impressed with Nunn's abilities that he seriously considered having the thirty-five-year-old—who'd already been artistic director for the Royal Shakespeare Company for seven years—stage his upcoming production of *42nd Street.*

Cats' credits also list Nunn as a co-lyricist on two songs: one "Jellicle Songs for Jellicle Cats," and the far more important "Memory." With the royalties acknowledging his contribution to the latter ditty alone, Nunn may well have been able to retire.

He didn't. Instead, he became the go-to guy for the new British musical: *Les Misérables, Starlight Express, Chess, Aspects of Love, Sunset Boulevard,* and *The Woman in White.* One sees a law of diminishing returns there as the years went on, but Nunn's contribution to the musical theater in the 1980s—starting with *Cats*—remains impressive.

1983–1984

Most Valuable Player: Michael Bennett
A Chorus Line

Michael Bennett was understandably proud of *A Chorus Line.* "They said it's a very New York show; it'll never work on the road," he recalled. "Then it played 102 cities in America and they said they won't understand it in England; it's too American. So then it played England. It played Australia and they said it'll never translate—and then it worked in Japan and in Spain and in Germany."

Nearly eight years after it had opened on Broadway, the nine-time Tony winner was still grossing well enough for Bennett, producer Joseph Papp, and the Shubert Organization to start checking the calendar and counting. Yes, on Thursday, September 29, 1983, *A Chorus Line* would play performance 3,389 at the Shubert Theatre and establish a new record as the longest-running show in Broadway history.

Bennett decided to make that performance an extravaganza. Certainly it would be a black-tie affair—but one that would knock off everyone's black socks, tuxedo shoes, and formal pumps. He planned to invite everyone who'd ever performed the show professionally in New York, on the road, or in another country to perform again. The show's original *Playbill* carried the line "*A Chorus Line* is dedicated to anyone who has ever danced in a chorus or marched in step . . . anywhere"; this performance of *A Chorus Line* would be dedicated to and performed by its alumni and alumnae.

Phone calls were made to 457 performers in those pre-email days, and 332 said they'd be there. Some who were working in other Broadway shows had to negotiate to get the time off. Wanda Richert, about to take over in *Nine,* said when signing her contract that she would have to be excused from the hit on the days Bennett needed her for rehearsals and the performance.

Bennett knew that some *Chorus Liners* had hard feelings for one reason or another, so he smartly defused some potential problems by having a welcoming party on Sunday night. On Monday, four days of rehearsals started, and four dozen tree-trunk-thick wooden pillars were positioned under the stage so that the floor would be able to accommodate everyone and not collapse.

Next door, the dark Booth Theatre would serve as a de facto dressing room, the largest in Broadway history. The original cast would take the actual dressing rooms, while the others would make do here and there throughout the building. To keep everyone occupied when not onstage, a large closed-circuit TV system would broadcast what was happening inside the Shubert at that very moment.

If the original cast felt that developing the show for a mere $100 a week was robbery, they found that *A Chorus Line* pay would now worsen: $50 was all they'd get for rehearsals, dress rehearsal, and performance. Those who came from out of town got to stay "in the center of it all . . . the Milford Plaza" down the street, but those who lived in New York weren't even given subway tokens. Nevertheless, few who participated complained then or later.

Even with these stingy terms, the event that Bennett had in mind would wind up in the pricey neighborhood of $500,000. That was not much less than the cost of the first two workshops that led to a production and Broadway, or the production on Broadway itself.

All for one night?

Yes.

Bennett decided that the current cast of twenty-six would start the show, but when the time came for the chosen seventeen to come forward and stand at the line, the original cast would take over—for a while. Bennett would split up the script and songs among the multitude. He envisioned three Vals, seven Cassies, eleven Pauls, and even more performers onstage to sing "What I Did for Love." An Asian Morales would sing "Nothing" in Japanese, and while few audience members would understand the words she was singing, by now virtually everyone in the house knew the words by heart.

Seven Zachs would run the show, although Robert LuPone, the original, chose not to participate; he's never been sentimental about *A Chorus Line.* Nancy Lane, the original Bebe, would have liked to have attended, but she was taping a West Coast TV series (*The Duck Factory* with an up-and-coming comedian named Jim Carrey). Pam Blair, the original Val, did show for rehearsals but got into a disagreement with Bennett and walked.

So when the seventeen appeared and the electronic sign above the stage said, "The original cast," it wasn't quite accurate. It was, however, close enough to get everyone in attendance to applaud, cheer, and stand, even at the dress rehearsal.

But that was a drop in the applause bucket compared to the reaction at rehearsal's end. As the stage was filled with performers doing Bennett's now-iconic choreography for "One," other performers poured into every aisle in the orchestra, mezzanine, and balcony to do the number there, too. After the show was finished, Bennett came onstage and asked the crowd, "Would you like to see the last number again?" Everyone roared that they would.

The reason for the reprise was that "One" was being taped that afternoon so that it could be broadcast that night on NBC's variety show *Live and In Person.* Apt, isn't it, that Bennett, known for telling many a fib in his lifetime, should show a taped sequence on what was supposed to be a live show?

While $500,000 is a good deal of money for a party, the national attention upped *A Chorus Line*'s grosses; the sum was made back in a few weeks' time. Indeed, many say it wouldn't have run for seven more years if it hadn't had this coast-to-coast exposure. Also helping was *New York Times* critic Frank Rich's statement the next day that "*A Chorus Line* was the best thing that had ever happened to any of us."

After the record-breaking performance, an enormous party in Shubert Alley was marred by a terrible thunderstorm. But it couldn't rain on Bennett's parade. He compared the event to the prom and reunions he never knew from high school; he'd dropped out at sixteen, not long after he was legally able. His lack of education hadn't seem to hurt him any.

AIDS would. Alas, four years to the day of this record-breaking performance—on September 29, 1987—many who'd been in attendance were back at the Shubert for the Michael Bennett memorial service. In many ways, Broadway has never recovered from the loss of this genius, who lived to a mere forty-four years old.

A Chorus Line held on to its record for seven years, until *Cats* broke it. Six years later, *The Phantom of the Opera* surpassed that show. Each had a big cake to celebrate its record-breaking performance.

Rookie of the Year: James Lapine
Sunday in the Park with George

James Lapine had had some nice off-Broadway successes from writing and directing *Table Settings* in 1979 and *Twelve Dreams* in 1981. In between, he'd also staged *March of the Falsettos* to a good deal of acclaim.

But now he'd really be breaking into the big leagues, not simply because he'd work on a musical aimed for Broadway, but also because his collaborator was the most acclaimed musical-theater artist of the age: Stephen Sondheim.

Lapine met the challenge. He's the one who suggested that a musical might be made from Georges Seurat's famous and once-notorious painting *A Sunday Afternoon on the Island of La Grande Jatte.* Even more importantly, he's the one who spurred Sondheim's imagination by pointing out that "the main character is missing—Seurat himself."

So Lapine created a life for each of the painting's subjects, as well as one for George and his girlfriend Dot. (*George,* not *Georges.* Lapine lopped off the S, fearing that *Sunday in the Park with Georges* would suggest more than one man.)

He and Sondheim made George a workaholic in an era long before the term was coined. George felt bad that he couldn't stop working to take Dot to the Folies Bergère—not because he loved Dot less but because he loved his art more.

Dot was made to be superficial. She complained about the bustle she wore but defended her choice by saying that "Everyone is wearing them!" Lapine had George mutter, "Everyone!" to express his disappointment that Dot hadn't learned by now not to follow the crowd, especially when that crowd literally put her in an uncomfortable position.

On to the people in the painting. Giving the Boatman one eye was particularly inspired; the man could thus be belligerent about it, insisting that "an artist lets us see what he wants" and that he sees more with his one eye than many others see with two. In rationalization, there is characterization.

Lapine had two young women—"The Celestes"—come to the park looking for men. One was literally and figuratively fishing, hoping to hook and reel in a man much more than a trout. No one today remembers these ladies or the men whom they made the center of their lives. They had good times then while George was working. But George made much more of his time in the park by concentrating on his art. So when The Nurse looked at Jules, then a preeminent artist, and said dully, "I can never remember their names," the point was made that no one else would as time went on. But many others would come to know Seurat's.

The Old Lady rued that her view has been spoiled, because of "Trees cut down for a foolish tower!" Ah, but the Eiffel Tower is art, too. A famous poem concludes, "Only God can make a tree," and while that's true, only man can make a tower. Interesting, too, that the Eiffel Tower at first got bad reviews from critics; now, for more than a century, it has been an important and beloved work of art. How smart of Lapine to subtly remind us that some people need time to catch up with great art.

Jules urged George to take some time off—not because he primarily cared about him, but more because he was scared that George might eclipse him. Lapine sharply had him tell George, "Go to some parties. That is where you'll meet prospective buyers"—suggesting that even in the nineteenth century, networking was important.

Yvonne, Jules's wife, didn't recognize art when she saw it—as so many hadn't when encountering the works of Lapine and Sondheim. After Dot challenged Yvonne that Jules was simply jealous of Georges, a lesser writer would have Yvonne staunchly deny it. Much better was Lapine's having Yvonne virtually admit that by conceding, "Jealousy is a form of flattery."

Equally smart of Lapine was having Yvonne say to Jules, "We must be going. You know we have an engagement," while he was studying George's painting. Had she not interrupted, Jules might have had the time to see the wonder of George's painting. Here it wasn't Dot but a different woman and her concerns that got in the way of appreciating George's achievement.

After Jules was dismissive and started to leave, Lapine had George say, "Thank you for coming." One wonders how many times Lapine, in the early part of his own career, had to say that to would-be producers who saw a reading of a play and declined to option it. Yes, artists are supposed to show that they're good sports even while they're deeply disappointed.

When George showed his work to a dog, he said, "Look, I made a hat," minimizing his accomplishment, mocking himself, and, for the moment, seeing Dot's point of view. But only momentarily—for George ultimately sees life his way: that is why he completes the line with the wondrous, "where there never was a hat."

That's the whole show in a couplet. No wonder that when Sondheim was settling on titles for his two-volume collection of lyrics that he chose *Finishing the Hat* for the first and *Look, I Made a Hat* for the second.

And that was just the first act. After some fits and false starts, Lapine thought the best option was to move the action up a hundred years and see what had happened to both the island and art. Here we met Marie, Dot and Seurat's daughter, and George, their great-grandson. What skillful writing from Lapine to have Marie remember that Dot bragged how many times Seurat put her in the portrait. Yes, once it became celebrated and valued, Dot certainly wanted to stress her part in it. Where was all her support and understanding while George was painting?

Marie only fleetingly mentioned Louis, her stepfather. The person on whom she dwells is Seurat, and not because he's her "real" father. There are those, in fact, who would argue that Louis's devotion to Marie, in fact, would have made him Marie's "real" father—but Louis is not the one of whom Marie is ultimately proud. Louis's art may not have been "hard to swallow," as Dot had noted of his baked goods, but it was, by its very nature, ephemeral. Seurat's art was longer-lasting, and, if the Art Institute of Chicago has anything to say about it, *A Sunday Afternoon on the Island of La Grande Jatte* will last forever.

Lapine made us realize that if George had succumbed to Dot and had gone to the Follies, he might have wanted to go again—and again. Paris has always been a place that offered good times; if Seurat had got off track and availed himself of all its pleasures, his daughter wouldn't have had a painting that's a source of pride. We've all profited from that.

Comeback Player of the Year: Jerry Herman
La Cage aux Folles

In 1975, Jerry Herman had been snubbed by the Tony nomination committee, who didn't believe his score for *Mack & Mabel* deserved a nod.

It did.

In 1979, Herman had a bigger setback when he wrote the score for *The Grand Tour.* It was a musical version of *Jacobowsky and the Colonel,* in which a meek and mild Jew and an imposing and anti-Semitic Polish colonel are thrust together during World War II. Of course, they come to like and respect each other by curtain's end.

Herman admits that he liked but didn't love the story and only did it because his *Dolly!* bookwriter Michael Stewart asked him. That may be why *The Grand Tour* is one of Herman's lesser scores. Is writing music and lyrics for just any project better than not writing at all? This, Herman's shortest-running musical at only sixty-one performances, would suggest not. But at least it got Herman a Tony nomination.

"But the show was so confused," said cast member Kenneth Kantor. "When we were trying out in San Francisco, we had a scene set in a brothel. There was a great painting of *The Rape of the Sabine Women* on a set that was painted in purple and turquoise around a pink piano. All over the set were little etchings of women in revealing postures.

"Then one day we arrived at the theater and set designer Ming Cho Lee was up on a ladder covering up those etchings. A painting of a Madonna and Child had replaced the Sabine Women, and the set was now brown. The women members of the ensemble who'd been wearing negligees were now being fitted into costumes borrowed from a local production of *The Sound of Music,* because the brothel was now becoming a convent." (The song in the scene, "I Want to Live Every Night," was dropped and earmarked for Herman's Vegas show *Miss Spectacular,* which, as of this writing, has never happened.)

So, after providing Broadway with six musicals in fewer than eighteen years, Herman would be absent for the next half decade. Only after he saw the surprise hit French film *La Cage aux Folles* did he feel inspired to write a new musical. He heard music in the St. Tropez nightclub run by Georges for his longtime lover Albin, whose onstage persona was female impersonator Zaza.

But producer Allan Carr had already secured the rights and signed Mike Nichols and Tommy Tune to co-direct, Tune to choreograph, Maury Yeston to write the score, and Jay Presson Allen to pen the book. The team would Americanize the property, moving it from St. Tropez to New Orleans and calling it *The Queen of Basin Street.*

Happily for Herman—and perhaps for Broadway—that project fell apart. Carr entrusted the property to Herman. And nearly a quarter century after Herman had written a revue called *Parade* in which a vaudevillian sang, "My home is still upon the Palace stage," Herman was at the Palace where *The Grand Tour* had flopped and where he now had one of his biggest successes.

Herman's previous hits had occurred before the 1970s' Stephen Sondheim renaissance. Since Sondheim had reconceived the Broadway musical sound, Herman had seemed retro. Now he'd be pitted against him and his *Sunday in the Park with George* for the 1984 Tony Award for Best Score.

Was Larry Kert's presenting the award an omen? He'd done three Sondheim shows but none by Herman. (Ironically, his last stage appearance would be in a touring company of *La Cage,* but no one knew that then.)

But Kert announced, "Jerry Herman!" and the composer-lyricist bounded onto the stage and said "Thank you" four times before starting his speech: "This award forever shatters a myth about the musical theater. There's been a rumor around for a couple of years that the simple, hummable show tune was no longer welcome on Broadway. Well, it's alive and well at the Palace."

And it was for more than four years. If the building that housed the Palace had not been slated for renovation, the show could have continued. There were plans to move the show to the Mark Hellinger Theatre with Lee Roy Reams assuming the role of Albin/Zaza. But now moving a show was far more costly than it had been only a few years earlier. Carr and his co-producers instead decided to close.

Perhaps if *La Cage* had moved to the Hellinger, its owners, the Nederlander Organization, might not have had to endure its being empty for ten of the next twelve months. Shortly after *Legs Diamond* opened to highly critical reviews, the Nederlanders leased the theater to the Times Square Church and then sold it.

And just as the Hellinger was saying goodbye to Broadway, Herman did, too, as a composer-lyricist. The last song in *La Cage,* "The Best of Times (Is Now)," stressed, "As for tomorrow, well, who knows? Who knows? Who knows?" It would be the last-ever new Herman song in the last-ever new Herman musical on Broadway. He was only fifty-two years old and had many productive Broadway years ahead of him. But going out with a winner was more important to him.

1984–1985

MVP: Yul Brynner
The King and I

As we've seen, Yul Brynner and the King of Siam were inextricably linked. For portraying King Monghut, he'd already won a Tony in 1952 and an Oscar in 1957. But this season he'd also receive a Special Tony Award "honoring his 4,525 performances in *The King and I.*"

Brynner could now boast that he was the only person in history so specifically honored—although Rex Harrison came close; he, too, won a Tony and Oscar for his performance in *My Fair Lady,* and while he also received a Special Tony (in 1969), it was not solely for his Henry Higgins.

"The King" returned to Broadway on December 26, 1984, to play nearly two hundred of those performances. This was extraordinary, and not merely because Brynner was nearing seventy. A month into the run, Brynner, a five-pack-a-day smoker, was diagnosed with lung cancer.

Mitch Leigh, his 50 percent–50 percent producing partner in the revival, wondered if Brynner would cut short the engagement and return home to Normandy. Betty Furness asked him that question in February 1985. Brynner responded, "I preferred two and a half thousand people standing up in the standing ovation at the end of a show and being busy doing eight performances a week than lying down and thinking about the possibility of a death."

Brynner also participated in the TV special *Night of 100 Stars II,* which was taped on February 17 and aired March 10 on ABC. That would be the last time the nation would see Brynner. He was clearly in pain but wore a top hat, which he doffed, and said goodbye.

On June 30, 1985, he played the King for the 4,625th and final performance, grossing a then-all-time high of $605,546. Fourteen weeks later, he was dead.

But he still continued to be a presence in people's living rooms. Before he died, he'd insisted on taping a public service announcement that would be aired posthumously: "Now that I'm gone, I tell you 'Don't smoke.' Whatever you do, just don't smoke."

So Brynner might well have been an MVP in many Americans' lives. We'll never know how many lives the King influenced—and saved.

Manager and Rookie of the Year: Rocco Landesman
Big River

Here's the first leg of one of the most meteoric rises in Broadway history.

No one necessarily expects that a titan of Broadway would have been graduated from Colby College in Maine and the University of Wisconsin. Yale, yes—which was the third school that Rocco Landesman attended. There he became the protégé of Robert Brustein, dean of the Yale School of Drama.

They would work together in 1984 on *Big River,* the musical version of Mark Twain's *The Adventures of Huckleberry Finn.* By then, Landesman had become part of the Dodger Theatricals, which had produced *Pump Boys and Dinettes* in 1982. That country-flavored musical ran for sixteen months and showed that Landesman was interested in a different sound for Broadway.

Thus he's the one who suggested that Huck Finn would not be well served by the usual Broadway composers and lyricists, but by pop songwriter Roger Miller. This proposal was met with a number of raised eyebrows; Miller had an eccentric bent, as was witnessed by his novelty hits "Dang Me" and "You Can't Roller-Skate in a Buffalo Herd." On the other hand, his most popular song was more straightforward: "King of the Road."

By 1984, Brustein had moved from Yale to Harvard, where he helped found the American Repertory Theatre. Landesman's *Big River,* directed by his Dodger partner Des McAnuff, was one of A.R.T.'s early productions. After a stint at the La Jolla Playhouse, *Big River* came to Broadway and played for 1,000 performances at the Eugene O'Neill Theatre, one of the five Jujamcyn Theaters owned by James H. Binger. (He had bought them from William McKnight, who used the names of his three grandchildren—Judith, James, and Cynthia—to furnish the name of the company.)

Chairman Binger was impressed with Landesman and made him Jujamcyn president in 1987. Landesman rewarded him with a string of hits. In 1990 alone, although Jujamcyn owned only five of Broadway's thirty-five active theaters—14.29 percent—it won 100 percent of the thirteen musical categories at the Tonys, thanks to *City of Angels* and *Grand Hotel.*

Binger continued his good relationship with Landesman and pledged that upon his death, the president could buy the organization. That happened in 2004. Landesman stayed with the organization for five more years, until he was offered the position of chairman of the National Endowment for the Arts in 2009. Thus far, he's found it a more difficult job than he ever had on Broadway.

1985–1986

MVP and Rookie of the Year: Rupert Holmes

The Mystery of Edwin Drood

No one had ever won Tonys for Best Book, Best Score, and Best Musical until Rupert Holmes did it with his *The Mystery of Edwin Drood.*

Most musical adaptations say in their credits that they're "based on" or "adapted from" a book, play, movie, or something else entirely. *Drood's* title page said that it was "suggested by the unfinished novel by Charles Dickens." Indeed, Dickens died before he could tell us which of his many suspects might have killed poor Edwin: John Jasper, the choirmaster at Cloisterham Cathedral; Helena and Neville Landless, the brother and sister from Ceylon; Reverend Mr. Septimus Crisparkle; his assistant Bazzard; Princess Puffer, the opium pusher; or even Rosa Bud, who was engaged to marry Edwin but wasn't terribly excited by the prospect.

Holmes could have just inferred—and, mystery writer extraordinaire that he is, created good reason—why one of Dickens's characters did the deed. But he had a better idea, spurred by the many times he'd seen theater audiences react to unanticipated and unplanned stage accidents. What if an entire musical could be built on the premise that the attendees would choose the end of the story by picking out the murderer? That they really couldn't know what would happen would add to their excitement and enjoyment.

Holmes thought the idea so nice that he used it twice. First, audience members would vote to determine which character had pretended to be "Datchery," a detective in disguise. Once they determined his identity, it was on to deciding whodunnit.

At every performance of *Drood,* an audience would hear eighteen songs. Holmes, however, wrote eleven more that could be used—five more for potential Datcherys, six more for possible murderers.

Had a Tony Award been created for Best Orchestrations (which wouldn't happen for eleven more years), Holmes would have probably taken home another Tony, too. For, as if Holmes didn't have enough to do, he provided his own charts, as well. He'd have to console himself with another kind of prize, for *Drood* was the first-ever musical to win the Edgar Award, given by the Mystery Writers of America.

Comeback: Michael Rupert
Sweet Charity

Here's our youngest comeback.

Michael Rupert was a mere sixteen years of age when he portrayed Robert Goulet's nephew in *The Happy Time.* Director-choreographer Gower Champion had originally chosen him for the chorus. But during rehearsals, when the young man whom Champion had chosen wasn't working out, he pressed Rupert, then only fifteen, into service.

Champion's confidence was not misplaced: Rupert came through with a performance that got him a Tony nomination as Best Featured Actor in a Musical.

But the problem with starting out strong is that everyone expects that you'll maintain that pace and keep rising up the theatrical ladder. In the 1970s, Rupert did merely one Broadway show, when he took over for John Rubinstein as Pippin. It was steady employment for two years, but it didn't garner him much attention.

For a while, the 1980s looked worse: a six-week run in *Shakespeare's Cabaret* was all Rupert could claim on his Broadway résumé. Luckily, an off-Broadway gig (alas, with only an off-Broadway salary) came along for a while—Marvin in *March of the Falsettos*—and he got some months of work out of it.

Finally, four years later, Rupert was back on Broadway as Oscar Lindquist. He's the nervous wreck who meets (Sweet) Charity Hope Valentine (Debbie Allen) on a broken elevator, takes her to church (in a manner of speaking), falls in love with her, finds out about her past, still offers to marry her, but then rescinds the offer.

It's a role that demands that we like and understand this complicated, neurotic man who breaks our heroine's heart. Rupert played it with the right balance of vulnerability and common sense.

On Tony night, the thirty-four-year-old Rupert was named Best Supporting Actor in a Musical. Those obsessed with awards couldn't help noticing what might slip by the rest of us: Rupert had won a Tony for playing Oscar, while Goldie Hawn had won an Oscar for playing Toni (in *Cactus Flower*).

1986–1987

MVP: Betty L. Corwin

Theater on Film and Tape Archive

Les Misérables was the season's big hit, to say the least. It may last forever. But Betty Corwin's work will certainly last forever.

Friday afternoon, August 22, 1986. The phone rings in Corwin's office. Madeline Gilford is calling on behalf of *Rags,* the musical on which she's associate producer. "We're closing tomorrow," she says.

Corwin is, of course, sad to hear it. *Rags* was one of the most anticipated Broadway musicals of the season. It had a book by Joseph (*Fiddler on the Roof*) Stein, music by Charles (*Annie*) Strouse and lyrics by Stephen (*Godspell*) Schwartz. Who'd have predicted only four performances?

Gilford wanted more than condolences from Corwin; she wanted her to green-light the taping of *Rags* for Theater on Film and Tape Archive in the Billy Rose Theater Collection at the New York Public Library for the Performing Arts.

"I said to Madeline, 'Are you crazy?'" Corwin recalls. "It's a Friday in summer. I can never get all the permissions that quickly."

Before any taping can proceed, Corwin must get approvals from Actors' Equity, the American Federation of Musicians, the Dramatists Guild, the International Alliance of Theatrical Stage Employees, the Society of Stage Directors and Choreographers, and United Scenic Artists—not to mention from everyone associated with the production.

On the small chance that she could reach the necessary people (on a day when many were already leaving for the Hamptons or the Jersey Shore), how many would give permission? And even if they did: was there enough time to hire a video truck, a video director, camera and sound personnel, and others who'd coordinate with the stage producers and their crews?

Nevertheless, Corwin got it done. *Rags* now sits in the TOFT Collection (as The Theater on Film and Tape Archive is known). "That taping allowed many people to see it," Corwin says. "It may well have led to its getting five Tony nominations."

Corwin could have been any season's MVP since 1970–1971, when she started arrangements to have Broadway and off-Broadway shows taped. But her yeoman work in rescuing *Rags* from complete extinction is the reason we'll choose her for this season.

Her first taping was the now-forgotten 1970 off-Broadway musical *Golden Bat,* a Japanese import. But its producers were Broadway heavyweights: Kermit (*The Diary of Anne Frank*) Bloomgarden and Arthur (*The Golden Apple*) Cantor. They were amenable to Corwin's noble experiment.

They'd known her for years. As a young woman, Corwin worked in many producers' offices, which resulted in her getting free tickets to Broadway. "Laurette Taylor in *The Glass Menagerie,* all those wonderful Katherine Cornell performances," she recalls. "I was distraught that they couldn't be seen again."

Although Corwin admits that agent Helen Harvey gave her the idea to tape shows, Corwin did the work and drew up a formal proposal in 1969. "I started calling up the unions," she says. "Getting everyone to agree took almost two years. We did *Golden Bat* on a $200 budget and used the cheapest cameraman in town."

Corwin found she'd have to abide by a number of caveats. "I had to promise that we'd protect the tapes from piracy; we'd only let them be viewed at the library; and they would be viewed under supervision."

Not every Broadway show is routinely taped. "We look for outstanding quality of some kind—writing, acting, directing or design; qualities of uniqueness which may have historical importance; a balance among types and styles of theater; revivals; unusual stagings; important cast changes; and shows that demonstrate theatrical traditions of other countries. We even tape mime and choreography that don't naturally lend themselves to other forms of documentation."

Ethnic and minority concerns are important, too. "When Diahann Carroll took over in *Agnes of God,* we taped it with her, even though we had already done it with Elizabeth Ashley. We usually don't tape the same production twice—we barely have the money to tape it once—but we thought this was significant."

There's a five-figure cost to taping every show, and that's with simply a two-camera taping. For *The Phantom of the Opera* and *Miss Saigon,* three would be used, and for *Jerome Robbins' Broadway,* four.

"We make the cameras see as your eyes would," she says. "We always start with a wide shot so that you can view the entire panorama as the audience saw it. Later, we zoom in for important close-ups. We try to tape a Wednesday matinee, so in case we run into technical problems, our crew can stay and try again that night."

Corwin retired in September 2000, but not before taping nearly three thousand Broadway, off-Broadway, and regional productions. "We have the record-breaking performance of *A Chorus Line.* And if you wanted to go to the other end of the spectrum, we have 20 minutes of *Moose Murders,*" she says, referring to the infamous 1983 one-performance flop.

But how did *Moose Murders* meet the criteria of "outstanding quality? And does only twenty minutes exist because Corwin stopped the taping when she saw how terrible the show was? "No," she says. "Joel Siegel, the critic for ABC News, would give us all the press reels that he got, and that was one of them. Believe me, otherwise we wouldn't have taped it."

Comeback Player and Reliever of the Year: Donna McKechnie

A Chorus Line

For a solid decade, Broadway saw no sign of Donna McKechnie. After she originated the iconic role of Cassie in *A Chorus Line* and won a Tony as Best Actress in a Musical, she, along with much of the original cast, took the show to California in April 1976.

What had she been up to since then? She'd barely been up at all. McKechnie unfortunately spent much of the late 1970s and early 1980s in bed dealing with rheumatoid arthritis.

It seemed to be a woefully sad ending to a career that included her appearing in the original casts of *How to Succeed; Promises, Promises; Company;* and *A Chorus Line.*

For the last three, her choreographer was Michael Bennett, whom she married on December 4, 1976. That surprised most of the Broadway community, which had ample anecdotal evidence that he was gay. But considering all that Bennett and McKechnie did for each other, they had, as *A Chorus Line*'s lyricist Edward Kleban wrote for another show, "The Next Best Thing to Love"—which, in true friendships, is love that's just as valuable.

Not the kind good enough for marriage, however. The two initiated a divorce a little more than a year later.

McKechnie has said that her biggest challenges have been "arthritis and getting divorced twice—once at 20, and once at 106." She felt that old during 1977 and 1978 when she often crawled out of bed and along the floor. A radical diet, alternative medicine, and a health regimen of sixty pills a day slowly got her back on track.

On June 18, 1979, McKechnie opened an off-off-Broadway play called *Wine Untouched* and managed to do all fourteen of its performances. She spent 1980 developing and touring a nightclub act and did a Chicago production of, appropriately enough, *I'm Getting My Act Together and Taking It on the Road.* Nineteen-eighty-one had her in Ohio doing Sally Bowles to the then-unknown Billy Crystal's Emcee in *Cabaret.*

A move to Los Angeles meant a few films, TV episodes, and plays. Then in 1983, Bennett called her to be part of the record-breaking *A Chorus Line* extravaganza. McKechnie agreed, setting the table for her return to the Broadway production as Cassie for an eight-week run in 1987.

She wound up staying eight months, giving new theatergoers who had missed her the first time the chance to savor what she originally brought to the show.

Says McKechnie, "I enjoyed it so much more this time around. When it originally opened, we'd all been through this hard time creating it. Then we had all that attention and were asked to do a million things. The company was not happy, for there was strife and bitter jealousy. After I left, I said to myself, 'What a shame; here's the most important show in my whole career, and I can't look back at it with fondness.' But when I came back, there was a very friendly cast there, almost sibling-like, who was thrilled they were getting to do it with me. How many get a second chance like that?"

Rookies of the Year: Alain Boublil, Claude-Michel Schonberg, and Herbert Kretzmer
Les Misérables

Robert Lindsay
Me and My Girl

"Les Miz," as it became chummily known, neatly condensed Victor Hugo's mammoth 1862 novel about Jean Valjean's desperation, second chance, and redemption. His turning his life around failed to impress Inspector Javert, who believed "once a criminal, always a criminal." Their lives became complicated by the student revolution of 1832 that terrorized Paris. The romance between Valjean's ward Cosette and young Marius—not to mention Éponine, the young woman who loves him—made for great musical drama.

Bookwriter-lyricist Alain Boublil and composer Claude-Michel Schonberg had a score to match it. When the show was first produced in France at a sports arena, the collaborators must have been thrilled that so many people were seeing their show.

Little did they know how many millions more would thrill to their score and show. "It's not just that the music is wonderful," says longtime Broadway observer John Harrison. "It's that the music has somehow been infused with a spirituality."

While such a score doesn't lend itself to Top 40 hits, an unexpectedly inordinate amount of music found its way into the public's consciousness. That includes "On My Own," sung by desperate prostitute Fantine in the original French production but switched to Éponine in the London and subsequent editions. And if it weren't for "I Dreamed a Dream," Susan Boyle might have never had her late-in-life career.

"Do You Hear the People Sing?" could have been adopted as a national anthem of some worthy country. It also sounded majestic enough to be the first-act closer, but Boublil and Schonberg had an even greater anthem in mind: "One Day More," which stirringly reminded us of what was at stake for every one of our major characters. On a lighter note, "Master of the House," sung by the corrupt Thenardiers, started out sounding like Kurt Weill and ended up more reminiscent of Scott Joplin.

Although *Les Misérables* was of course a French creation, many thought of it as another "British musical," because its lack of book and continually sung music was reminiscent of Andrew Lloyd Webber's shows. Others were reminded of Lloyd Webber in a different context. For weren't the opening notes of Valjean's "Bring Him Home" stolen from a theme in the humming chorus in act 2 of Puccini's *Madama Butterfly*?

There had to be a British influence of another kind: translation. Most of the lyrics were supplied by Herbert Kretzmer, a former theater critic for London's *Daily Express,* who had written lyrics for the West End musicals *Our Man Crichton* and *The Four Musketeers.* Luckily, he wrote songs for Charles Aznavour, which brought him to the attention of *Les Miz* producer Cameron Mackintosh.

The 1987 Tony race pitted the heavily favored *Les Misérables* against the somewhat less heralded *Me and My Girl* in nine categories: Musical, Book, Score, Director, Actor in a Musical, Featured Actor in a Musical, Featured Actress in a Musical, Scenic Design, and Costume Design.

Aside from Costume Design—in which *Starlight Express* emerged victorious—*Les Miz* bested *Me and My Girl* in every category.

Except one.

Although Colm Wilkinson's Jean Valjean and Terrence Mann's Javert received rave reviews along with their nominations, Robert Lindsay won the prize—and deserved to.

Me and My Girl was a London import, too, but quite different from the serious West End musicals that Broadway had been importing. It was a carefree revisal of a 1937 London musical that took us inside the handsome castle that belonged to the Harefords.

Here family solicitor Parchester had news for Maria, the Duchess of Dene. Although the recently deceased titular head of the Harefords was thought not to have had a genuine heir, he in fact had sired an illegitimate son: Bill Snibson, who was raised by his mother in lower-class London. In other words, "Not Our Kind, Dear."

The moment Lindsay entered, he had the audience's sympathy. The actor was wise enough to know that if he entered as a low-class blowhard, the audience not only wouldn't like him, but would also want him taken down a peg.

But the shy and nervous way in which Lindsay came down the marble steps allowed audience members to relate to his plight. Every one of us has had the experience of walking in a room where we don't know anyone and we're afraid of what these people are thinking of us. Lindsay had us feel for him as he stood there hat in hand, nodding "hello" almost imperceptibly to the Duchess and others whom he considered his betters. He made an ever-so-tiny social gaffe by occasionally lifting up a thumb, in his world a symbol for "Everything's all right," but one that was considered vulgar by the so-called high-borns here.

The Duchess wants Bill to become educated and acculturated. Lindsay showed he wasn't thrilled about it, but he didn't resist—again gaining our sympathy for showing an open mind. But when the Duchess insisted that he give up his fiancée—fish-cleaner Sally Smith—that's where he drew the line.

Bill swore that nothing would part them, and while Lindsay had Bill stand up for his rights, he was never obnoxious to the Duchess. Lindsay made clear that Bill would give up his title and fortune for The Woman He Loved. (One can see why this was a British hit only a year after Windsor and Wally's affair.)

Lindsay turned out to be a wonderful song-and-dance man, too—astonishing for a man whose previous credits included *The Cherry Orchard, The Lower Depths,* and *Hamlet.* What a shame that, as of this writing, Robert Lindsay has never made another Broadway appearance.

1987–1988

MVP: Andrew Lloyd Webber
The Phantom of the Opera

Say what you will about Andrew Lloyd Webber: he had respect for the Old Guard. So when he decided to write a musical of Gaston Leroux's *The Phantom of the Opera,* he went to a librettist-lyricist whose three previous musicals ran a total of twenty-six performances: Alan Jay Lerner.

This was—and wasn't—the same Alan Jay Lerner who wrote *My Fair Lady.* But Lerner wasn't appreciative enough, if a certain story is true. It may well be apocryphal, but it deals with the oft-maintained claim that Lloyd Webber borrows melodies from other composers. Lerner was supposedly asked early on in the writing of *Phantom* if he'd yet heard any of Lloyd Webber's music for it; Lerner was said to reply "Probably."

Lloyd Webber eclipsed Jerry Herman as musical theater's most cited tune thief. The number of times that "tune detectives" have mentioned that he's lifted from Puccini has possibly surpassed even the worldwide performances of *Phantom.* Soon after it opened in London on October 9, 1986, people alluded to songs from *Brigadoon, The Fantasticks,* and *How to Succeed.* Even Billy Crystal's character in *Forget Paris* pointed out that "The Music of the Night" sounded like "School Days" to him.

Phantom mostly succeeded on its music, production and, yes, falling chandelier. But how skillful Lloyd Webber was to come up with a title song that had enough of a rock sensibility to appeal to younger theatergoers while also maintaining the majesty of classical work. In "Prima Donna," he showed he was capable of a soaring and beautiful melody worthy of opera singers.

Lloyd Webber was so proud of his score that he made a radical move with the original cast album. Each disc's songs were programmed as one and only one track, so that no selection of them was at all possible, because Lloyd Webber wanted listeners to hear the show as one continuous piece of music. Anyone who liked a song well enough to play it again—or who wanted to scoot ahead—would have to stand by his CD player, press a certain button, and learn the timing so he could hear what he wanted.

Apparently a good number of people complained, and/or returned their discs to stores while griping that they must have received a defective copy, what with number "1" always staying on the track display. Later copies tracked the songs individually.

By then, plenty of people had heard the score the way that Lloyd Webber wanted them to, albeit in the theater. After its opening at Her Majesty's Theatre to virtually unanimous raves, theatergoers have kept it there ever since. It may even still be there when the time comes for the theater to be renamed *His* Majesty's Theatre.

Phantom made plans for a January 26, 1988, opening at the Majestic Theatre on Broadway. The budget was a record-setting $8 million, but the advance sale was a then-astonishing $18 million. After winning seven Tony Awards, it was en route to taking in over $795 million at the Majestic box office, easily making it the highest-grossing show in Broadway history. More than fourteen million people have attended the show, and many New Yorkers who are now in graduate school have never seen anything else on the Majestic marquee for their entire lives.

Worldwide, *Phantom* has grossed an estimated $5 billion. It may well be the world's all-time most successful entertainment venture; even *Avatar,* Hollywood's highest-grossing film, has collected "only" $2.7 billion.

Over 65,000 performances of *Phantom* have been seen by 100 million people in 27 countries and 144 cities. And since it became the longest-running show in Broadway history in 2006 (when it surpassed Lloyd Webber's own *Cats*), each and every performance has set a new longevity record.

It also set another record: not until fourteen years had passed did it start using the TKTS booth to sell discounted tickets.

Comeback: Harold Prince
The Phantom of the Opera

For many moons, it was one of the most astonishing careers in Broadway history. Since he began producing in 1954, how many days had Hal Prince not been represented on Broadway? To quote a line from his 1981 production of *Merrily We Roll Along:* "Damn few."

Harold S. Prince was a mere twenty-six years old when he started producing on Broadway. For the longest time, he looked as if he'd never stop. Take a look at how many consecutive days his name appeared in a Broadway *Playbill.* (The first date cited represents the first preview.

Decade One:

May 13, 1954–November 24, 1956: *The Pajama Game* (co-produced)

May 5, 1955–October 12, 1957: *Damn Yankees* (co-produced)

May 14, 1957–May 24, 1958: *New Girl in Town* (co-produced

September 27, 1957–June 27, 1959: *West Side Story* (co-produced)

June 28, 1959–November 22, 1959: Prince's name not in a Broadway program — 147 days

November 23, 1959–October 28, 1961: *Fiorello!* (co-produced)

October 29, 1961–December 19, 1961: Prince's name not in a Broadway program — 51 days

December 20, 1961–December 8, 1962: *Take Her, She's Mine* (co-produced)

May 1, 1962–August 29, 1964: *A Funny Thing Happened on the Way to the Forum* (produced)

Thus the thirty-six-year-old Prince's first decade on Broadway—May 13, 1954–May 12, 1964—saw him represented on Broadway for 3,453 days and missing 198. His percentage of days represented was 94.58 percent.

Prince's Broadway résumé included a few other shows that weren't needed to help the consecutive days' streak: *Tenderloin* and *A Call of Kuprin,* which he produced, and *A Family Affair,* which he directed.

Decade Two:

May 8, 1962–August 29, 1964: *A Funny Thing Happened on the Way to the Forum* (produced)

August 30–September 16, 1964: Prince's name not in a Broadway program—17 days

September 17, 1964–July 2, 1972: *Fiddler on the Roof* (produced)

March 28, 1972–August 12, 1972: *A Funny Thing Happened on the Way to the Forum* (non-Prince revival that said on title page. "Originally produced on Broadway by Harold Prince")

August 13, 1972–December 4, 1972: Prince's name not in a Broadway program—113 days

December 5, 1972–January 13, 1973: *The Great God Brown* (directed)

January 14, 1973–February 14, 1973: Prince's name not in a Broadway program—30 days

February 15, 1973–August 3, 1974: *A Little Night Music* (produced and directed)

The forty-six-year-old Prince's second decade on Broadway—May 13, 1964–May 12, 1974—saw him represented on Broadway for 3,492 days and missing 160. His percentage of days represented was up to 95.62 percent.

There were many other shows that Prince co/produced and/or directed that weren't needed to help the consecutive-days streak. He produced and directed *She Loves Me, "It's a Bird, It's a Plane, It's Superman," Cabaret, Zorba, Company,* and *Follies,* which would make a startling résumé for anyone. He also produced *Poor Bitos* and *Flora, the Red Menace* and directed *Baker Street.*

Decade Three:

February 15, 1973–August 3, 1974: *A Little Night Music* (produced and directed)

March 4, 1974–January 4, 1976: *Candide* (co-produced and directed)

December 31, 1975–June 27, 1976: *Pacific Overtures* (produced and directed)

June 28, 1976–December 26, 1976: Prince's name not in a Broadway program—181 days

December 27, 1976–May 21, 1977: *Fiddler on the Roof* (non-Prince revival that said on title page, "Originally produced on Broadway by Harold Prince")

April 13, 1977–March 19, 1978: *Side by Side by Sondheim* (produced and directed)

February 9, 1978–March 18, 1979: *On the Twentieth Century* (directed)

February 6, 1979–June 29, 1980: *Sweeney Todd* (directed)

September 10, 1979–June 26, 1983: *Evita* (directed)

June 27, 1983–October 4, 1983: Prince's name not in a Broadway program—66 days

October 5, 1983–September 2, 1984: *Zorba* (non-Prince revival that said on title page, "Originally produced on Broadway by Harold Prince")

The fifty-six-year-old Prince's third decade on Broadway—May 13, 1974–May 12, 1984—saw him represented on Broadway for 3,492 days and missing 247. His percentage of days represented was 93.24 percent—a slight dip.

However, the percentage would have been far worse without the non-Prince revivals. Take away that 1976 *Fiddler,* and he would have been absent for 287 straight days; remove that 1983 *Zorba,* and he would have suffered 288 additional ones. The percentage would have dropped to 84.26 percent—still a solid "B," but not an "A."

What's more, the number of other shows with which he was involved dropped to six: He directed *Love for Love, Some of My Best Friends, End of the*

World, and *Play Memory.* He produced and directed *Merrily We Roll Along* and co-produced and directed *A Doll's Life.* Let's throw in a seventh with Prince's strangest credit: he provided a voiceover for *The Moony Shapiro Songbook,* the show that closed the Morosco Theatre, from April 21 through May 3, 1981.

But notice that the majority of these Prince-associated shows would not be ones that would enter the repertory. Perhaps that was an omen for the decade to come:

Decade Four:

October 5, 1983–September 2, 1984: *Zorba* (non-Prince revival that said on title page, "Originally produced on Broadway by Harold Prince")

September 3, 1984–March 24, 1985: Prince's name not in a Broadway program—202 days

March 25, 1985–June 22, 1985: *Grind* (produced and directed)

June 23, 1985–September 13, 1987: Prince's name not in a Broadway program a whopping 812 days, much more than two years

September 14, 1987–October 11, 1987: *Roza* (directed)

Let's stop here to take a quick audit of how the fifty-nine-year-old Prince was doing after *Roza* opened on October 1, 1987—and closed a mere ten days later. Out of 1,379 days, Prince's name had NOT been on a *Playbill* for 1,014 of them—making for a woeful in-*Playbill* percentage of 26.47 percent. Take away the *Zorba* revival, with which he had nothing to do, and the number of missing days balloons to 1,157 while the percentage drops to a pitiful 16.10 percent.

But even then, Prince couldn't have been too concerned—and not because he had just directed a revival of *Cabaret* that was just about to debut on Broadway. By then, the London production of *The Phantom of the Opera* that he'd directed had already celebrated its first anniversary as the biggest smash hit in the West End—and it was Broadway bound. So add those Broadway figures into play:

October 7, 1987–June 4, 1988: *Cabaret* (directed)

January 9, 1988–current: *The Phantom of the Opera* (directed)

Thus Prince ended Decade Four on May 12, 1994, with 72.24 percent—a low "C," which wasn't so terrific, but impressive when one considers the rebound. His directing of such hits as *Kiss of the Spider Woman* and *Show Boat* and the well-regarded *Parade* and *Candide* revival added to his comeback.

And Decade Five, from May 13,1994, to May 12, 2004? Thanks to *Phantom* alone, the seventy-six-year-old Prince scored a perfect 100 percent. Decade Six could turn out to be exactly the same. Octogenarian Harold Prince is back getting "A's"—and is back on the A-list.

Reliever: Bernadette Peters
Into the Woods

She'd been the above-the-title leading lady in her previous three Broadway shows. True, her billing had her respectively follow Robert Preston in *Mack & Mabel* in 1974 and Mandy Patinkin in *Sunday in the Park with George* in 1984. For *Song and Dance* in 1985, however, she was the only one billed above the title. And after that show provided her with her first Tony and she left after thirteen months, Betty Buckley took over—and the show closed in a month.

So why would Broadway star Bernadette Peters now take a supporting role in a musical? Because *Sunday*'s authors Stephen Sondheim and James Lapine, who'd written this new musical called *Into the Woods,* needed her.

During the tryout at the Old Globe in San Diego, Ellen Foley played the witch who prevented a baker and his wife from having a child. But the couple was the main event. Now Peters was asked to take over to add some star power to a less-than-starring role.

They gave her top billing, however—and she took it. But the part was too small to be considered for a Best Actress Tony (which went to her castmate Joanna Gleason for portraying the Baker's Wife) and too large for the Best Featured Actress category. For the first and only time since 1972, in four previous Broadway appearances and three yet to come, Peters would not be acknowledged with a Tony nomination.

Into the Woods was not Peters's most dynamic rescue of a show, however. Back in 1961, she was playing Rose's favorite daughter, Dainty June, in the national company of *Gypsy.* The role only lasts until act 1, scene 9, which leaves a young actress with nothing to do for the rest of the show.

One night, however, Peters had to return in the second act, because the young actress playing Agnes, a new chorus member that Rose had recruited for her vaudeville act, was incapacitated from a backstage accident. Peters took her place. (Actually, having the actress who plays Dainty June also portray Agnes is a good idea—for Rose might very well choose for the act a girl who would look just like her once-beloved daughter.)

Wakefield Poole, who was director Joe Layton's assistant on *George M!* in 1968, was impressed by the young Peters. In his memoir *Dirty Poole,* he recalled that once during rehearsals, he happened to spy her notebook. "Bernadette had maybe 30 lines of dialogue in the whole show, so she had written things down to help her," he wrote. "She'd made up an entire scene where George comes into her room late one night and sits on her bed. He talks about his ambition and his love for his family. It continued, expanding her every moment in the show to help her overcome the brevity of her scenes. She'd done this on her own."

Perhaps it was something she'd learned to do while she was studying at the Professional Children's School. Gene Castle, one of the original newsboys in *Gypsy,* was a classmate. "Once when we were on *The Sid Caesar Show* together, I could see that she was all business—and I mean that in the best sense of the word," he says.

Peters showed that she was a pro in 1971 when she did a summer-stock tryout of a musical called *W. C.*—which referred to the performer named Fields and not a toilet (although the toilet is where the show eventually landed).

One night in Storrowtown, Massachusetts, the heavens opened during the second act, and astonishingly heavy rains poured onto the metal roof of the theater. Mickey Rooney, portraying Fields, broke character to acknowledge the rain, cocking a hand to his ear to indicate he couldn't hear what Peters said. He tried to turn the show into a burlesque, but Peters stayed true to her character and wouldn't allow Rooney to spoil the show.

By then, Peters knew that theater didn't always mean smooth sailing. Her first Broadway job was understudying a role in a dim-witted comedy called *The Girl in the Freudian Slip.* She was not asked to substitute for anyone during its four-performance run. She did land her own role in *Johnny No-Trump* in 1967, but the play closed after one performance.

Peters's big break came after first choice Sandy Duncan decided not to star in *Dames at Sea* but opted for *Canterbury Tales* instead. As star-in-her-eyes would-be star Ruby, Peters proclaimed, "I'm a dancer and I just got off the bus, and I want to be in a Broadway show!"

She would accomplish that goal many times. *Dames at Sea* led to *George M!,* which resulted in her getting the lead of Gelsomina in the musical version of *La Strada.* That, too, closed on opening night—meaning that two of Peters's first three Broadway shows closed after a single performance.

It hasn't happened to her since. Peters won her second Tony in 1999 for playing the title role in *Annie Get Your Gun,* the role originally written for Ethel Merman. Irving Berlin, aware that Merman was famous for holding a note for an inordinately long time, wrote in "Anything You Can Do," "Any note you can hold, I can hold longer." As noted earlier, Merman's recordings show that she held the note for ten seconds in 1946 and nine seconds in 1966. Peters actually held the note for those two lengths of time combined: a full eighteen seconds.

Peters's last role as reliever came in 2010, when she succeeded Catharine Zeta-Jones in *A Little Night Music.* Her performance, especially her haunting rendition of "Send in the Clowns," got raves. Send in Peters when you want a star to originate or relieve.

1988–1989

MVP and Comeback Player of the Year: Jerome Robbins
Jerome Robbins' Broadway

What would it take to get Jerome Robbins to return to Broadway after almost a quarter-century absence?

Quite a bit, as it turned out. Robbins was not interested in starting a new musical from scratch but did agree to do a retrospective of his biggest successes.

Fine, said the heads of two producing companies (the Shubert Organization and Suntory International Corporation) and three producers (Roger Berlind, Byron Goldman, and Manny Azenberg). Anything to get this esteemed director-choreographer away from the New York City Ballet and back to Broadway where he belonged.

Then Robbins demanded that he could hire sixty-two performers and twenty-nine stagehands.

...all right, said the producers, albeit a little more softly.

Then he insisted on not the standard six weeks of rehearsals, but twenty-two.

At this point, at least one of the producers must have been as apoplectic as Hinesy in *The Pajama Game:* "Twenty-two weeks! Do you expect me to, awwww, I would trust him, I would trust him . . ."

And trust Jerome Robbins they did, to the tune of an $8 million budget and a weekly running cost of $350,000 at a time when most musicals cost half that. No wonder that ticket prices had to zoom to an all-time high of $55.

Robbins was well known as a difficult taskmaster. Said Jason Alexander, who'd emcee the evening, "It's safe to say that anything you've ever heard about Jerome Robbins is true. At first I wondered why he doesn't have an ulcer or a heart condition, but he gets out his volatile energy by exorcising his demons religiously, so there's nothing eating away at him at the end of the day."

After good if not spectacular reviews and a Best Musical Tony, the price went up to $60 that November. All to no avail. *Jerome Robbins' Broadway,* despite a 633-performance run, closed at a $4 million loss.

But it was one of the worst seasons in Broadway history. The show's only real competition was *Black and Blue,* a revue that was never a hot ticket, but with far less expensive running costs that kept it alive for 829 performances. *Jerome Robbins' Broadway* won twice as many Tony Awards—six to three, including Best Musical—but *Black and Blue* was able to outrun it by five months (and still lost money).

A number of people could have created and performed *Black and Blue.* Jerome Robbins had to be there for *Jerome Robbins' Broadway.*

1989–1990

MVP: Cy Coleman
City of Angels

The idea came to composer Cy Coleman. One night in 1981 when he was watching *The Maltese Falcon* on late-night TV, he realized that there'd never been a 1940s private-eye musical.

Coleman also knew that he was the one to compose it, for he was the only Broadway composer with the requisite jazz background. He'd be able to emulate the murky and pulsating sounds of David Raksin's score to Laura or Miklos Rosza's *The Strange Love of Martha Ivers*. He could also write the hard-hitting sound that would characterize a cynical detective.

The composer then went to Larry Gelbart, who had co-written *A Funny Thing Happened on the Way to the Forum* in 1962. "Larry's musically inclined," Coleman said. "He can play the clarinet and sax, and I knew I wouldn't have any problems describing the music to him. If I told some other writers that I was going to do a jazz score with a completely different sound from even the Broadway jazz I'd written, they would have either misunderstood or assumed I simply meant pastiche. Larry got what I meant when I told him I wanted to score the show like a film and avoid conventional thirty-two-bar songs."

Gelbart's excellent book for *City of Angels* had a detective simply known as Stone asked by the wealthy Mrs. Alaura Kingsley to find her missing stepdaughter Mallory. After that's established, we learned that this was actually a plot that was in the mind of a writer named Stine. But that was literally another story—and one with which Gelbart and Coleman had a great deal of fun, constantly juxtaposing one set of characters with the others.

To be sure, Billy Byers would help with the orchestrations that created the dark mood (although there was a touch of Nelson Riddle every now and then in the scenes with Stine and his wife, Gabby). But Coleman not only came up with the right sound for his melodies; he also did his own vocal arrangements. That was especially valuable in the mood-setting scatting that started the show.

Coleman also made time for some mellifluous sounds for a late-1940s easy-listening radio group called the Angel City 4 that often punctuated the action.

It wouldn't have been a true film-noir score without a chanteuse singing in a smoke-filled nightclub. Think Ann Sheridan crooning "Who Cares What People Say" in *Nora Prentiss* in 1947, or Rita Hayworth (actually, Anita Ellis) in "Put the Blame on Mame" in *Gilda* in 1945. Coleman saved his best melody for Bobbi, with whom our Detective Stone was once in love. "With Every Breath I Take" had an angular but accessible melody that showed remarkable range. In a kinder, gentler musical era of radio play and TV variety shows, it would have become a certified standard.

Considering that Coleman started out as a pop composer—"Witchcraft," "The Best Is Yet to Come," and "When in Rome" were his—Broadway had to be thankful that he didn't make the same decision that Burt Bacharach, another pop giant, made about Broadway. Because he found writing for a musical too difficult—even though his *Promises, Promises* was a big hit—he said adieu.

But Coleman, who saw his terrific score for *Wildcat* wither because of a bad book and unreliable star, and *Little Me* die because of an even more unreliable star, continued. *Sweet Charity* was his first hit, in 1965–1966, but it was overshadowed that season by *Mame* and *Man of La Mancha*. In fact, the runs of those three Coleman musicals combined didn't last as long as Bacharach's *Promises, Promises*. And yet Coleman persevered.

Never mind that *Seesaw* was trumped by *Raisin* in 1973–1974, *I Love My Wife* by *Annie* in 1976–1977, and *On the Twentieth Century* by *Ain't Misbehavin'* in 1977–1978. Coleman never turned his back on Broadway but kept on with new ideas and projects.

A great part of his legacy is that he was, as *Ragtime* lyricist Lynn Ahrens once said, "an equal-opportunity collaborator." No late twentieth-century composer gave as many chances to women and fledgling writers.

Coleman's first four Broadway musicals had female lyricists: *Wildcat* and *Little Me* with Carolyn Leigh; *Sweet Charity* and *Seesaw* with Dorothy Fields. One could argue that Coleman was the lucky one to get the chance to work with Fields, who had written such standards as "I Can't Give You Anything but Love," "On the Sunny Side of the Street," and "I Won't Dance"—not to mention her conceiving and co-writing the book for *Annie Get Your Gun*.

But when Fields teamed up with Coleman to write *The Small World of Charity*, as it was then called, she hadn't had a Broadway show in almost seven years. Yes, that one—*Redhead*—did win a Tony, but few would offer it as Exhibit A of Fields's best work. When she began work on *Charity*, she was nearing sixty—and was not that far from seventy when she did *Seesaw*. Coleman was nearly a quarter-century younger than she, so he might well have worried, rightly or wrongly, that Fields was past her prime. But Coleman didn't and wound up writing two fine scores with her, as well as that Eleanor Roosevelt musical that didn't get on.

Granted, Coleman wrote his next show, *I Love My Wife*, in 1977 with a well-known theatrical name: Michael Stewart. But while Stewart was an acclaimed bookwriter (for *Bye Bye Birdie*, *Carnival*, *Hello, Dolly!* and *George M!*), he was an unknown quantity as a lyricist. But Coleman trusted that Stewart could write lyrics as well as book, and *I Love My Wife* was one of Coleman's biggest hits.

Then Coleman worked with another female lyricist—as well as a male one—when he joined Betty Comden and Adolph Green for *On the Twentieth*

Century in 1978. Lord knows they were tried-and-true, but Coleman was soon back working with another female and untried lyricist: Barbara Fried on *Home Again, Home Again* in 1979. Alas, the show didn't work out and shuttered in Connecticut, and while plenty of award-winning composers would have stopped taking phone calls from the novice who didn't deliver a hit, Coleman didn't give up on Fried. They continued to work on the show and almost successfully jump-started it again four years later under the new title *Thirteen Days to Broadway*.

For *Barnum* in 1980, Coleman again worked with the now-experienced lyricist Michael Stewart and the not-very-experienced Mark Bramble as bookwriter. True, Stewart and Bramble were said to have been romantically linked, but even so, Coleman again showed his willingness to work with someone new.

After he helped as "creative consultant" to another female songwriter (who was better known as a singer)—Miss Peggy Lee, on her bio-musical Peg in 1983—Coleman worked with an acclaimed man of letters, A. E. Hotchner, who'd had a big success with his *Papa Hemingway* biography in 1966. But Hotchner wasn't an established Broadway lyricist, and no matter how accomplished one is in one field, he won't automatically be capable of writing a good Broadway musical.

This was proved when *Welcome to the Club*, about men who have been sent to alimony jail by their wives, was a quick flop in 1989. But once again, Coleman didn't give up on his collaborator. He and Hotchner reworked the show several times, first retitling it *Exactly Like You*, and subsequently *Lawyers, Lovers and Lunatics*.

For *City of Angels*, Coleman once again took a chance with a comparative rookie. David Zippel's résumé pretty much consisted of a few off-Broadway revues and a couple of songs for Barbara Cook, but he had had no Broadway experience. Coleman said, "David had published some songs with my publishing company, so I'd been watching his work for some time." Coleman's trust in him turned out to be well placed.

After Coleman returned to work with Comden and Green on the Tony-winning *The Will Rogers Follies* in 1991, he once again gave a break to a relative unknown lyricist, Ira Gasman. His sole theatrical credit was the 1973 cabaret show *What's a Nice Country Like You Doing in a State Like This?* which had had an off-Broadway run in 1985. The Life dealt with a seedy subject, those who lived outside the law on the old Forty-second Street, but that allowed Coleman to bring his funky pop, jazz, and Broadway sound to the neighborhood.

Through it all, he proved his range. Does the man who created the jaunty polka "Our Favorite Son" for *The Will Rogers Follies* seem to be the same composer of the tender waltz "Real Live Girl" in *Little Me?* The operetta-infused "Our Private World" in *On the Twentieth Century* would never be confused with the aggressively brassy "Big Spender" in *Sweet Charity*. The countrified "Someone Wonderful I Missed" in *I Love My Wife* bears no resemblance to the thoroughly infectious "Come Follow the Band" in *Barnum*—which asked the perfectly justifiable question "Ain't it drivin' you crazy?" The melody sure did to years' worth of theatergoers.

How apt that Cy Coleman, who spent nearly half his life in the theater, should go out with a show called *The Life*. He died expectedly on November 18, 2004, only three days after he'd been honored at a benefit at the Rainbow Room. He lived to the age of seventy-five, a number that's associated with both diamond and platinum—good words to describe his music and his career.

Reliever of the Year: Maury Yeston
Grand Hotel

In Baxter's Beauties of 1933, the second half of the film spoof *Movie, Movie*, George C. Scott plays a Ziegfeldian producer, Spats Baxter, who listens to his composer Dick Cummings's latest song. "Dick," he says earnestly, "that's the best song you've written today."

The line amuses because in all those Hollywood backstagers of yore, the seemingly impossible was always achieved in no time flat by anyone who worked on a Broadway musical.

But Maury Yeston almost matched Dick Cummings's rate of speed after he came home one night, played his answering machine messages, and heard, "Yeston, this is Tune. I have a suite in the Ritz-Carlton in Boston in your name. Come."

The reason was that director-choreographer Tommy Tune's *Grand Hotel* had just opened to not-so-good reviews. Songwriters Robert Wright and George Forrest weren't coming up with new material fast enough.

Yeston could. "What the piece needed," he says, "was an opening that would explain what the evening would be." Hence his minor-key masterpiece,

"The Grand Parade," to underline each character who came through the revolving door of the most luxurious hotel in 1928 Berlin.

"Then," Yeston adds, "there had to be a character-song for each of the main characters that could define each and provide enough musically and lyrically to create winning performance."

He wrote a riveting song for each of the show's main characters. For Kringelein, the bookkeeper who wanted one last fling before death, he wrote the touching "At the Grand Hotel." When desperate businessman Preysing decided to commit an illegality, Yeston had him sing "Everybody's Doing It."

The young Flaemmchen needed an optimistic song that suddenly turned realistic before returning optimistic, and Yeston responded with the flapperish "I Want to Go to Hollywood," which had a dour midsection where the miss acknowledged that she wanted "to wear nice shoes" but that that was often impossible in her current economic conditions: "when things get broken, they stay broken."

Says Yeston, "It also provided a glimpse of the hideous economic state of Weimar Germany outside the hotel's doors."

For fading ballerina Grushinskaya, who believed that the penniless Baron loved her, Yeston wrote the exultant "Bonjour, Amour." To show how this impacted her devoted assistant Raffaela, Yeston created the haunting "22 Years." And if that wasn't enough, for the Baron he wrote not only the lush ballad "Love Can't Happen," but also the frenetic "Roses at the Station," which he sang as he lay dying.

Yeston made it happen both musically and lyrically in only a few weeks' time. Even Spats Baxter would have been impressed.

Comeback of the Year: Michael Jeter
Grand Hotel

"If you've got a problem with alcohol or drugs, you can't stop, you think life can't change, and that dreams can't come true, then I stand here as living proof that you can stop. It changes a day at a time, and dreams come true."

So said Michael Jeter on June 3, 1990, seconds after he won his Best Featured Musical Actor Tony. Minutes before that, he'd performed his showstopping "We'll Take a Glass Together" with Brent Barrett. There he was, swinging around, on and above a brass rail, as his character literally celebrated his good fortune, punctuating it with a number of high kicks before jumping up into Barrett's arms. It was a great tribute to striking it rich and making a nice friendship (in that order).

But even before this stunning number, Jeter had won the audience's sympathy for Otto Kringelein, the wage slave who could hardly believe that he, a Jew, had gained admittance into the Grand Hotel—even if he was only destined to spend his last dying days there. He was charming when he fox-trotted with the young and beautiful Flaemmchen (Jane Krakowski). Later, when she had to admit that she was pregnant and the father was nowhere to be found, how tender he seemed when he offered to carry the typewriter for the expectant mother.

But take a look at the 1979 movie *Hair*, where Jeter plays a young man who's been summoned by his draft board for possible induction. In order to avoid a stint in Vietnam, he pretends to be homosexual, down to painting his toenails red.

Then look at pictures or videos of Jeter as Kringelein, who was approaching retirement age.

That he was twenty-seven when he filmed *Hair* is not surprising. That he was only thirty-eight when he portrayed Kringelein is what's astonishing.

Has anyone aged so terribly in less than eleven years? Well, that's what comes from too much pills and liquor—and other stuff, too.

In the decade between *Hair* and *Grand Hotel*, Jeter appeared in only five feature films and four TV movies, made seven guest appearances on TV series, and was a regular on a TV series that lasted seven episodes. He made no Broadway appearances during that entire span.

In the decade after *Grand Hotel*, Jeter was courted to appear in five TV movies (including playing Mr. Goldstone in the Bette Midler *Gypsy*), for thirteen guest appearances on TV series, and for fourteen feature films, and he was a regular on the TV series *Evening Shade*, appearing in all ninety-eight episodes.

A Broadway success can turn a career around very quickly. So can getting off drugs.

Rookie of the Year: Tyne Daly
Gypsy

She'd appeared on Broadway once before—in 1967 for all of twelve performances in a play called *That Summer—That Fall*.

But during that summer of 1989 when Tyne Daly was announced as Rose for the upcoming revival of *Gypsy*, many expected that she'd fall and fail in one of Broadway's most demanding roles.

Many of those who didn't see Daly in the role—and only got to hear her on the cast album—might assume that she had failed. Daly's voice was never her strong suit; no one would ever buy or download *Tyne Daly Wishes You a Merry Christmas* or *Tyne Daly Goes Latin*.

To make matters worse, Daly was ill at the time the album was to be recorded. In the pop world, the powers-that-be would have postponed; in the cast album universe, you're lucky to get studio time and you go in and finish in one day.

Many of those who saw Daly, however, were very much impressed with the single-minded force-of-nature bravado she brought to the role. It's her acting that got her all the awards that year, and there were few around Broadway who begrudged her getting any of them.

Alan Cumming in *Cabaret* *Cabaret* was almost a third of a century old in 1998, but Alan Cumming made it seem brand-new with his pansexual take on the Emcee. More to the point, Cumming made it seem a more important role. When Joel Grey originated it, he won a Tony–as Best Featured Musical Actor. After Cumming re-envisioned it, his Tony was as Best Actor in a Musical.

Julie Taymor For centuries, people portraying animals onstage simply zipped themselves into animal suits. Then Julie Taymor came along and had a quite different way of "costuming" animals–which is one reason why *The Lion King* ruled the Tonys and Broadway for years to come.

1990–2000

Tim Rice One of life's most bitter pills to swallow is when you and your partner split, and you don't do nearly as well. That was the fate facing Tim Rice after he and Andrew Lloyd Webber stopped working together. Without Rice, Lloyd Webber had four new long-run Broadway musicals in the 1980s, while Rice had none. Ah, but in the 1990s, the tables turned, as Rice turned out songs for Disney's *Beauty and the Beast, The Lion King*, and *Aida*.

Chita Rivera in *Spider Woman* She's considered one of the nicest people in show business, but that didn't preclude Chita Rivera from playing the venomous title character in *Kiss of the Spider Woman*. An actual black widow spider's life expectancy is a year; Rivera's Broadway career has been more than sixty years longer.

1990–1991

MVP: Heidi Landesman
The Secret Garden

In 1988, Heidi Landesman got hold of the 1986 British concept album of *The Secret Garden* and eagerly put it in her CD player. The Frances Hodgson Burnett novel on which it was based was one of her childhood favorites.

Many times young Heidi Ettinger had read about little orphan Mary Lennox, who's sent to rural England to live with her uncle Archibald. She's disappointed to learn that he's become a virtual recluse since his wife died. As for Uncle Neville, he isn't at all avuncular.

Mary rebels by treating the staff badly. Once Mary learns that Uncle Archibald's wife died in a garden—and that it has since been locked and camouflaged so that no one can find it—she endeavors to reclaim it. What she also discovers in her search is that she has an infirm cousin Colin, who's been abandoned by his father. But Mary is able to transform everyone's lives as well as the garden that had been left to die.

As Landesman examined the CD booklet, she didn't recognize the names of the writers, aside from the fifth (!) lyricist, Will Holt. He'd worked on seven Broadway musicals, only one of which—*The Me Nobody Knows*—was a hit.

The CD left her unimpressed. So, as the good producers of yore did, Landesman decided to start from scratch and put together a team to write a new musical version of *The Secret Garden*.

At this point, Landesman did have two blue-chip producing credits: she was second-billed on *Big River* and first-billed on *Into the Woods*. Among the former's seven Tony Awards was one for Landesman herself, for Best Scenic Design. She often designed; her providing both the set and the costumes for Marsha Norman's Pulitzer Prize–winning 'night, Mother would be important to *The Secret Garden*.

For Landesman called Norman and asked her to write the book and lyrics. As her composer, Norman chose Lucy Simon, sister of Carly, but also sister of talk-show host Joanna, who recommended her for this project. R. J. Cutler—a man, incidentally—was chosen to stage it. But after the production in 1990 at Virginia Stage in Norfolk, Landesman decided that

Susan H. Schulman, who'd staged the successful 1990 revival of *Sweeney Todd* on Broadway, should succeed Cutler.

The show was budgeted at $6.2 million, and money raising went reasonably smoothly. Here even Landesman would admit that having her then-husband, Rocco Landesman, president of Jujamcyn Theatres, as co-producer was helpful.

And so, fifty-five years after Burnett's friends had erected a "*Secret Garden* Fountain" featuring Mary and Dick in Central Park, sixty streets south at Jujamcyn's St. James Theatre, Heidi Landesman's creation opened. It wasn't a smash hit, although it did manage to run 709 performances and win three Tonys. One was for Heidi Landesman—not the one she most wanted as producer of the season's Best Musical. But winning her second for Set Design helped ease the pain.

Since *The Secret Garden*, Landesman has concentrated more on set design (eight Broadway productions) than on producing (just *Moon over Buffalo*). She divorced Landesman in 1997 and reclaimed her maiden name of Heidi Ettinger. She's been so billed for *Triumph of Love*, *The Sound of Music*, *The Adventures of Tom Sawyer*, *Dracula: The Musical*, and *Good Vibrations*.

Manager of the Year: Cameron Mackintosh
Miss Saigon

When Cameron Mackintosh announced that he'd bring *Miss Saigon*, his latest London smash—written by the *Les Misérables* team—to Broadway, there was enough public interest to secure a $25 million advance.

This update of *Madama Butterfly*, set in 1970s Vietnam, would be an exact replication of the London production. Coming to Broadway was Lea Salonga (who once played Annie in Manila). She'd again play Kim, the Asian woman who has a child by an American soldier. When she discovers that he'd married after he returned home, she gives the child to him and his wife and kills herself.

Also coming to Broadway would be Jonathan Pryce, reprising his Eurasian "Engineer" who latches on to Kim and her half-American son in hopes he can reach the United States.

But would Pryce reach the United States? Alan Eisenberg, the executive director of Actors' Equity Association, wasn't happy that Pryce wore prostheses that slanted his eyes and that he applied heavy makeup to make him appear Eurasian.

"The casting of a Caucasian actor made up to appear Asian is an affront to the Asian community," Eisenberg said. "The casting choice is especially disturbing when the casting of an Asian actor in the role would be an important and significant opportunity to break the usual pattern of casting Asians in minor roles."

Mackintosh reminded Eisenberg that the Engineer was Eurasian. True, Pryce couldn't provide the "Asian" part of the equation, but he did have the "Eur"—which any Asian-American actor wouldn't have. Given that the Engineer was of mixed race, would only a mixed-race actor be allowed to play him in New York?

Eisenberg held fast and moved on to another issue. Salonga was playing an Asian. Actors' Equity had plenty of Asian-American actresses who could play her. Mackintosh said he'd try to find a replacement, but after holding auditions not only in the States but also in Canada, he said that he couldn't find one.

Yes, you can, said Eisenberg. Mackintosh not only said no, but said no *Miss Saigon*, too. He would cancel the production and return the $25 million.

That caused everyone at Actors' Equity to rethink their stance. In this era of mega-musicals, *Miss Saigon* could conceivably run ten years. Pryce and Salonga wouldn't stay with it forever. Think of all the Asian American performers who would have jobs after they left.

Twelve Asian American Engineers did in a run that was only two months shy of ten years. And while there had allegedly been no suitable Kims during the original auditions, suddenly nineteen were found worthy during the run to play the part. But give Mackintosh credit for sticking to his guns. Of course, one does pick up a lot of power when he's already brought *Cats*, *Les Misérables*, and *The Phantom of the Opera* to Broadway.

Rookie of the Year: Daisy Eagan
The Secret Garden

That the eleven-year-old gave a terrific performance as Mary Lennox in *The Secret Garden* and won the Best Supporting Actress in a Musical Tony are only two of three reasons that Daisy Eagan gets this award.

The musical had been struggling before the Tonys, but once this little winner got to the podium, she cried tears as big as lemon drops. Buddha make a miracle! The audience in TV Land was moved enough to go to their telephones and order tickets. Suddenly business skyrocketed.

Come to think of it, perhaps Daisy Eagan should have been named this season's MVP.

1991–1992

MVP: William Finn
Falsettos

William Finn started his career by writing the music and lyrics for an amazing collection of songs for *In Trousers*.

At first glance, it seemed to be the story of an epileptic; after all, the opening song was called "Marvin's Giddy Seizures."

But what had seized Marvin was the need for sex from a man, and no longer sex from His Wife, as the script identified her; Finn didn't even feel the need to dignify her with a name.

Marvin's boyfriend had one: Whizzer Brown. And to a melody as intoxicating as "Milord," Marvin described his joy at having sex with him in "Whizzer Going Down."

Of course, his new liaison brings much anguish to His Wife. Finn wrote a heartbreaking song called "A Breakfast over Sugar" where no affection was expressed between the two. Lyrically and even musically, Finn was able to convey that these two had been fighting all night and had little fight left in them. They hoped to get through the morning without additional harm. Later His Wife sang that "The only thing that's breaking up is my marriage, but me, I'm breaking down."

Finn had a unique take on childhood, too, imagining the stream-of-consciousness thoughts that might go through a baby's head when he's hungry: "I need my breakfast now!" Marvin as a Child roared, before he criticized his mother: "She's a lousy chef. I don't want miracles from heaven—just some eggies over spinach over toast." What she ultimately gives him doesn't please him: "This is shit, this isn't breakfast. I could crack your feet."

Ira Weitzman and André Bishop, respectively the musical-theater program director and artistic director at Playwrights Horizons, believed in Finn. His music sounded fresh, new, contemporary, and yet wasn't rock. They gave *In Trousers* two productions in 1979; a third came under different management in 1981. None could last a month, despite its having one of the most original and exciting scores in decades.

The reason? Many deemed the impressionistic lyrics inscrutable ("Stay clear of love and jail") and full of non-sequiturs ("I am wearing a hat. After winter I'll marry.")

Still, Weitzman and Bishop encouraged Finn to continue. He started a sequel called *The Pettiness of Misogyny*, which was renamed *Four Jews in a Room Bitching* by the time it was given a workshop in February 1980. It was clearer, but not clear enough.

Maybe a bookwriter would help.

Enter James Lapine. He would later provide the book and direction for two of Sondheim's longest-running shows—*Sunday in the Park with George* and *Into the Woods*—but first he'd prove just as important to Finn for this new show, which would be renamed *March of the Falsettos*.

Lapine did more than just name "His Wife" "Trina." He urged Finn to make clear what was going on from Marvin's first lyrics. So Finn blatantly wrote, "I divorced my wife, I left my child and I ran off with a friend."

And yet Marvin didn't run off never to be seen again. "I want a tight-knit family," he insisted. "I swear, we're gonna come through it."

"We're" included Jason, Marvin, and Trina's son, who now worried that he'd grow up gay just like dear old Dad. What Marvin didn't see was that "we're" would also include Mendel, the psychiatrist whom Trina would see professionally, then socially, then romantically.

It was all set to quirky music and lyrics. In the so-called Golden Age of Musicals, one wouldn't run across such song titles as "My Father's a Homo" and "Everyone Tells Jason to See a Psychiatrist." And yet Finn found room to write "The Games I Play," a song that had "That's-the-single" written all over it.

Even in the much clearer version, Finn's work could be hard to interpret. Michael Rupert, who played the bisexual Marvin, says, "We all asked Bill what 'March of the Falsettos' meant and he'd never get any more specific than 'It's about sexuality.' The rest of us decided that the falsetto voice is an 'outsider's' voice, and that's what we went with—that we were outsiders."

If that was deliciously complicated, *Falsettoland*, the third jewel of the triple crown, had a plot that exacerbated matters. Finn and Lapine originally called it Jason's Bar-Mitzvah, for it would deal with the complications of planning an event to be attended by an ex-husband, an ex-wife, his lover, her psychiatrist husband, and, of course, Jason. That the lad is facing an event where he's supposed to be a man prompts some hard questions about masculinity, too.

But there would be another plot complication that the 1980s brought to the writing: This strange new "gay cancer" that was afflicting gay men. Whizzer, Finn decided, would contract AIDS. While *Falsettoland* wasn't produced off-Broadway until 1990, it took place in 1981, when so many men were meeting much-too-early deaths. Finn and Lapine wisely dovetailed the two stories, culminating in Jason asking to have his bar-mitzvah party in Whizzer's hospital room. He becomes a man partly by judging a man by his worth and not his sexuality.

Off-Broadway, *March of the Falsettos* ran eight months in 1981–1982, but *Falsettoland* had less long a run in 1989–1990. The following year, Graciele Danielle did both shows in an evening that she called *Falsettos*—and got a rave review from Frank Rich in the *New York Times*.

André Bishop, who'd since moved to Lincoln Center Theater, offered Finn the Mitzi Newhouse Theatre, an off-Broadway-sized house. But Finn wanted *Falsettos* on Broadway—and wanted Lapine to direct it, too.

Many were wary that this long evening could succeed on Broadway. If each of these musicals couldn't independently have a sustained run off-Broadway, how could they together have any type of run in a theater more than three times the size?

But Finn held out and got what he wanted. *Falsettos* spent more than a year on Broadway, an impressive run given the subject matter. And while Lapine's shaping the material, creating a book out of songs, and directing it to perfection makes him a strong contender for the MVP award, Finn gets the oh-so-slight edge and the award for creating the characters in the first place, writing the entire score, and holding out for Broadway.

When Finn accepted his second Tony of the night for Best Score—minutes after co-winning for Best Book—he praised many connected with the production before stating, "I'm a miserable person." Whether he is or not, he certainly had the admiration of millions around the world for taking a frank look at a subject that had not dared been musicalized. There have been many serious gay musicals since, and Finn is a prime reason why.

Manager: Roger Horchow
Crazy for You

We all know today that one doesn't need a store to sell high-end merchandise; that's what the Internet is for (among other things). But in 1971, selling pricey items to people who couldn't actually see or touch them—and had to rely on a catalog—was a somewhat radical notion.

Roger Horchow's not having bricks and mortar at his disposal didn't deter him from sending out a handsome, four-color mail-order catalog that purveyed plenty of upscale wares.

The Horchow Collection, he called it, and if anyone in, say, Duarte, California, inferred from the Dallas postmark that there was a big Horchow store in Big D that rivaled Neiman-Marcus, so be it. Just as long as a consumer had an American Express card or a checking account, he and Horchow could do business.

After seventeen years of wildly exceptional growth, Horchow had his fortune and sold his business to Neiman-Marcus. Now what?

Well, he always was a big Gershwin fan and wished he could have seen such musicals as Gershwin's *Girl Crazy* in 1930. He was only two years old when it opened and three years old when it closed, so how about a revival? He'd pay for it.

The Broadway savants he consulted admitted that the Gershwin score—with such marvels as "Bidin' My Time," "Embraceable You," "But Not for Me," and, of course, "I Got Rhythm"—was still doable. But, oh, that trite book by Guy Bolton and John McGowan! Who in the 1990s would be interested in Manhattan playboy Danny Churchill's going to Custerville, Arizona, where he'd transform a farm into a dude ranch? That he fell in love with Molly Gray, the town's postmistress, seemed just as trite. Who would care when Danny's old girlfriend Tess showed up on the scene to get back her man?

Many whom Horchow consulted did say that if someone came in to revamp the book, maybe, just maybe, *Girl Crazy* could work.

Whatever Horchow wants, Horchow gets. Ken Ludwig, who'd had a recent Broadway hit with *Lend Me a Tenor*, came in. Danny became Bobby; Molly, Polly; Tess, Irene. Ludwig added the complication that Bobby holds title to the farm owned by Polly's father, Everett Baker, and plans to foreclose to start his theater. That makes Polly hate him, of course, so Bobby adopts a disguise and pretends to be Broadway impresario Bela Zangler. Polly does fall in love with Bela, but then the real Zangler comes to town ...

Horchow liked what he read—as well as Ludwig's inserting some other Gershwin hits ("They Can't Take That away from Me," "Someone to Watch Over Me") and obscurities ("The Real American Folk Song," "What Causes That?"). Of the eventual $8.3 million budget, Horchow was confident enough to put up nearly $6 million. The gamble paid off, for *Crazy for You*, as the new show was called, opened strong and ran for 1,622 performances.

Such a hit usually makes everyone involved very happy. Perhaps director Mike Ockrent and Susan Stroman were just kidding around two years later when they said they could see Horchow taking over as Everett when Carleton ("Aba-Daba Honeymoon") Carpenter went on vacation. Horchow, who'd worked closely with American Express during his merchant years, knew that "Membership has its privileges." So does producing. He took the challenge.

So on September 19, 1994, at this performance (number 1,079) the role of Everett Baker usually played by Carleton Carpenter was played by Roger Horchow. Ditto for the next seven shows. Horchow gave a deliciously amateurish performance that was just a little on the stiff side. All in all, however, he was as endearing as *Crazy for You*.

1992–1993

MVP, Reliever, and Comeback Player of the Year: Chita Rivera

Kiss of the Spider Woman

About time we got to Chita Rivera, isn't it?

Dolores Conchita Figueroa del Rivero was born on January 23, 1933, attended Balanchine's School of American Ballet, and toyed with changing her name to Chita O'Hara. "That," recalls her first agent, Richard Seff, "was because she loved Maureen O'Hara so much."

But it was Conchita Rivero who joined the ensemble of Can-Can in 1953. Not until 1955 did the newly christened Chita Rivera get to originate her first role in the utterly forgotten musical version of Seventh Heaven. The following year, she joined Sammy Davis Jr. (professionally onstage and romantically off stage) in *Mr. Wonderful*, the slam-bang musical comedy that looked terribly antiquated when it opened exactly a week after *My Fair*

Lady on March 22. (*Mr. Wonderful*, not *Fair Lady*, should have opened on the Ides of March.)

Yet a listen to *Mr. Wonderful's* original cast album shows that Rivera sings her one song—"I'm Available"—in her distinctive style with that sly-wink voice that's full of confidence. She'd already found her persona before she appeared in three landmark musicals in each of the next three decades: as Anita in *West Side Story* in 1957; Rose in *Bye Bye Birdie* in 1960; and Velma Kelly in *Chicago* in 1975.

The Rink (in 1984) wasn't a musical for the ages but at least afforded Rivera with a long-overdue Tony. At the time, she was a still-youthful fifty-one and had many good years ahead of her.

But a big setback occurred during the run of *Jerry's Girls*. On April 7, 1986, Rivera was involved in an automobile accident in which she broke her tibia and fibula. Twelve pins had to be inserted into her leg. Thirteen days later, *Jerry's Girls'* producers decided to close the show—as many a Broadway observer closed the book on Rivera's career. Even Gwen Verdon admitted, "I remember saying at the time, 'Well, that's that. I suppose we'll never see Chita dance again."

Never underestimate Rivera. She worked hard, and while nearly a year had to pass, she did start dancing again. By 1988, she was heading a tour of *Can-Can*.

However, when Harold Prince, Terrence McNally, John Kander, and Fred Ebb were readying their *Kiss of the Spider Woman* for its tryout in Purchase, New York, in May 1990, they didn't call Rivera—although each of them had already worked with her. Lauren Mitchell played Aurora, the favorite actress of Molina, a gay window dresser who'd been imprisoned for having sex with a young man who didn't tell him he was a minor. Aurora would come to life in Molina's fantasies and replicate scenes from her films for him.

Neither Mitchell nor the show made much impact. What was expected to be a quick tune-up for Broadway instead was the first musical to ever close in Purchase.

Not forever, but for a two-plus-year delay. Next time Rivera was chosen to open *Kiss of the Spider Woman* first in Toronto in June 1992 and then at the Shaftesbury Theatre in London on October 20, 1992. Having Rivera in the cast motivated Kander and Ebb to write "Where You Are," one of the show's best songs.

Suddenly the flop of 1990 was the hit of 1992. Rivera brought the show to New York for a May 3, 1993, opening, jump-starting it to a two-plus-year Best Musical Tony run. Here was the performer who'd been written off after the accident now winning a Tony as Best Actress in a Musical, too.

What's also been said about Rivera through her six-decade career is that she was often hired because she had a reputation for being cooperative. Producers and directors on the fence about casting her or another choice would be heard to say, "Oh, let's go with Chita. We'll have smooth sailing."

Of course Rivera's good nature was hardly the main reason she was signed. She got roles because she had star quality, could do the work superbly, and always would—no matter what the worth of the show. But being nice didn't hurt.

Many in her position could have become bitter. Hollywood neglected her. No one else has seen two roles she originated go to other performers, both of whom won Oscars for them: Rita Moreno, *West Side Story*; Catharine Zeta-Jones, Chicago. When the original cast album of *Chicago* was recorded, her second-act opener, "I Know a Girl," was dropped. Both she and Gwen Verdon had a duet, "I Am My Own Best Friend"—but when Liza Minnelli subbed for Verdon, Minnelli wanted to sing the song alone. "Liza really wanted to do it that way," Rivera said diplomatically, sounding as if it really was a good suggestion.

Says Arthur Laurents, *West Side Story's* bookwriter, "One day, when we were rehearsing the 'A Boy Like That / I Have a Love' sequence where Anita agrees to help Maria, I noticed that her dead lover's jacket was hanging on a hook, so I suggested to her that she touch it on her way out. Now, a hundred years later, she's still mentioning it when anyone ever brings up West Side Story. Chita doesn't want anyone to think that she thought it up or that she wouldn't give credit to the person who did."

Wakefield Poole, who worked on the video sequences of *Bring Back Birdie*, wrote in his memoir that the 1981 four-performance flop was "disastrous. I can't remember one pleasant thing about it other than getting to know Chita, who'll do anything for you."

Says Lada Edmund Jr., who played a *Bye Bye Birdie* teenager, "I once did something onstage that Chita didn't like, and she came up to me, took me aside and said, 'People behave differently when they're nervous. Some are jackasses. Some are professional. You be professional.' And I've tried to be that ever since."

Adds Sara Gettelfinger, who appeared with Rivera in *Nine*, "What's wonderful about Chita is not that she's just one of our greatest actresses, singers, and dancers, but that she's such a great human being. I'm so impressed at how she's so disciplined but has a sense of humor that says you can't take yourself too seriously, that you have to keep it light while keeping it real. I understand why everyone always wants to hire her."

Nine, produced in 2003, was Rivera's first Broadway revival. Here she portrayed Liliane La Fleur, the producer of director Guido Contini's newest film. At one point, she was asked to stand on a table that was at a raked angle—and, twelve pins be damned, she did it with ease. At the end of the show, when each of the sixteen women in the cast went to kiss Young Guido on the cheek, Rivera kissed each of his cheeks. Leave it to her to always give a little more.

No one was surprised that Rivera had accepted "only" the featured role; she was, after all, seventy years old, although her trim figure belied the fact. What no one knew, however, was that in 2005 Rivera would embark on the most arduous challenge or her career when she was nearing seventy-three: *Chita Rivera: The Dancer's Life*.

In it, Rivera talked about starting out as a gypsy—the term for a Broadway dancer who goes from show to show to show. (In the 1950s, there was enough work for dancers to dare to do that.) "It's a good word, gypsy," Rivera said.

In fact, Rivera had even played a genuine Romany Gypsy in the 1964 musical *Bajour*. Add that credit to her playing a French woman (*Seventh Heaven* and *Nine*), a Puerto Rican (*West Side Story*), a Hispanic (*Bye Bye Birdie* and *Bring Back Birdie*), a British monarch (*Merlin*), an Italian American (*The Rink*), and a South American (*Kiss of the Spider Woman*). Far from Broadway, she even played a Chinese-American in a summer-stock Flower Drum Song. That represents a great number of nationalities, but has any critic ever complained that this chameleon was miscast?

In the revue that was the apotheosis of her career, she sang, danced, and dominated. Never in any of her fifteen Broadway shows had she ever had as much to do—and she was never older when she'd attempted it. But Rivera performed as if very few years had passed since she'd first visited Broadway. Despite her age, she didn't seem to break a sweat or lose a breath.

She also gave late choreographer Peter Gennaro some additional and unexpected credit. While Jerome Robbins had been heralded thousands upon thousands of times for his choreography in *West Side Story*, Rivera was the one to say, "Peter Gennaro choreographed every step of 'The Dance at the Gym' and 'America,' and has never gotten the credit he deserves."

Rivera offered more musical-theater history than one could get in any classroom. She also showed what a person can accomplish when she won't bow to adversity, takes meticulous care of herself, and refuses to stop working. Even those audience members who are loath to give Automatic Standing Ovations stood at the end of this show. They were happy to stand tall not just for a star who's a survivor, but to recognize her half-century-plus of Broadway history.

And during her curtain call, Rivera could be seen doing what she'd been doing for decades: she'd find a young person in the audience and give the kid a wink that said, "You and I just shared something special, didn't we?" Chita Rivera doesn't just give her all while performing; she also needs to make someone feel special after the performance, too.

1993–1994

MVP: Robert Jess Roth

Disney's Beauty and the Beast

"So, Michael—when are we going to do a Broadway show?"

That's the question that freelance director Robert Jess Roth kept asking Michael Eisner, the chief operating officer of the Walt Disney Company.

Eventually Eisner listened, and that yielded four Broadway musicals that each played more than four years—including the inaugural attraction, *Disney's Beauty and the Beast.*

Roth was a kid from River Edge, New Jersey, who quickly fell in love with Broadway. "In the 1970s," he says, "I saw Bette Midler's *Clams on the Half Shell Revue*, *Pippin* a dozen times, *Equus* and *A Chorus Line* not many fewer. I loved *La Cage*, too."

The goal was to become a director, and he went to Rutgers University's Mason Gross School of the Arts. There he met Matt West, a choreographer, and Stan Meyer, a designer. All worked on a production of William Finn's *In Trousers*.

Once Meyer was graduated, he landed a job as an art director in Disneyland. "Stan suggested I come out there," says Roth, "and though I was interning at Playwright Horizons, I did."

His first directing assignment was a parade. "It was called *Hooray for Disney Stars* and was promoting four Disney afternoon TV shows," he admits. Next he was asked to stage a musical based on the upcoming *Dick Tracy* film for a Disneyland presentation. "But Warren Beatty wouldn't let me see the movie in advance. So [studio head] Jeffrey Katzenberg, said, 'Oh, just make up your own Dick Tracy story and plug in the Stephen Sondheim songs.'

"That resulted in *Dick Tracy Diamond Double Cross*, which was really a thirty-minute Broadway musical. Jeffrey and Michael Eisner saw it before they even saw the movie and really liked it. So we all thought we should get them to do a Broadway show."

The trio even had a name for the new arm of the company: Touchstone Theatricals, citing the firm's division geared to adult comedies. "I wrote a letter to Michael saying Disney should be on Broadway," Roth says. "I quoted figures to let him see that Broadway makes money and that so many musicals could be adapted from Disney's rich library."

Roth thought he had a chance, because he knew that Eisner had been a theater major in college and had been with Paramount Theatre Productions. "He's the one who had to fire Michael Bennett after he offered to help out on *My One and Only*," he says. "So I made my pitch to him, only to hear him say that it was a big investment in money and time for so little return, and that he didn't think the company should put its resources there. And while he changed the subject to encouraging the three of us to pitch more shows for the parks, he did say, 'You can ask me this question again.'"

Roth did after he, West, and Meyer had created a rock-and-roll version of *The Nutcracker*. "And when he liked that," says Roth, "I said, 'Now can we do a Broadway show?'"

When Eisner challenged back, "What would it be?" the triumvirate thought and chose *Mary Poppins*. Eisner gave some seed money, but soon after they'd started, the movie of *Beauty and the Beast* opened. Good reviews greeted the story of Belle, an inveterate reader whose father is captured by the Beast; after she trades places with him and becomes the Beast's hostage, she changes the Beast for the better.

"Michael asked me if I'd seen it," says Roth. "I said I had and had loved it—so he suggested we try adapting it. But I wondered how you could show onstage the way the spell was shown in the movie, where the members of the Beast's staff were immediately changed into objects. So when I asked how all these people could change in an instant, Michael said, 'Yeah, you're right. Keep going on *Mary Poppins*.'"

But the following day, Eisner once again suggested *Beauty and the Beast*. "We asked for a video," Roth recalls, "but that part of the company said no, so we all went to a movie theater and spent the whole day there seeing the picture over and over and taking notes by a little flashlight."

That the *New York Times'* Frank Rich said it was "the best musical of the season" helped. "Jeffrey told Michael that Andrew Lloyd Webber was making a billion from *Phantom*, so maybe we should do this."

They asked Roth, West, and Meyer to make a proposal independent of composer Alan Menken and scriptwriter Linda Woolverton. (Lyricist Howard Ashman had died.)

Roth had admired Broadway costume designer Ann Hould-Ward's work on *Sunday in the Park with George* and *Into the Woods*, so he asked her to meet with him, West, and Meyer. The foursome eventually realized that the Beast's staff didn't need to quickly change; they could change a little bit at a time into objects. Lumiere would not be a candelabrum, but a person with an affliction who was slowly losing the battle.

Meyer did 140 black-and-white drawings that Roth put on slides. But, thinking that he should have more in his arsenal, he hired Jim Steinmeyer, who'd helped magician David Copperfield with his illusions, to create one for him. Because Chip, the son of housekeeper Mrs. Potts, was turning into a teacup, Steinmeyer arranged to have him sit in an open box where the bottom half of his body seemed to be missing.

"When Michael, Jeffrey and [Disney president] Frank Wells, came," says Roth, "I started talking, but I could see that Michael wasn't paying that much attention. He kept looking at Chip. He wanted to know how we did that illusion."

Roth plowed on, and when he concluded, he recalls that Eisner whispered to Katzenberg, and then to Wells. "And then," he says, eyes widening, "he turned to me and said, 'Okay.' I didn't get what he meant for the longest time."

He meant yes. Roth met with Menken and Woolverton, who approved of the places where he suggested additional songs. "I was really sweating through my clothes, though," says Roth.

He perspired more at one of the first tryout performances in Houston when the enchantress in the opening scene got stuck in the air and when Belle's father crashed into the scenery and lights went out. As the mishaps mounted, Eisner asked him to address the crowd. "I was sweating so much that as I walked onstage, I could hear the squish of water in my shoes."

But the worst was over for the $13 million musical. *Disney's Beauty and the Beast* opened on April 18, 1994, at the same Palace Theatre where Roth had sat mesmerized by Bette Midler and *La Cage aux Folles*.

It didn't close until July 29, 2007. At 5,461 performances, it was the fifth-longest-running Broadway musical. Since then, Roth has staged eighteen subsequent productions. "The first year alone, we did five: Los Angeles, Vienna, Australia, and two in Japan," he says. "I did a re-imagining in 2010, but I'm not the slightest bit bored by the show. I'm still impressed to find over and over again that emotion and love are the same in any language. Audiences all over the world have responded the same way. And," he says, "among the thousands of actors I've worked with, I'm now casting actors who, when they were kids, tell me that Beauty and the Beast was their first Broadway show."

When asked about the gestation, Roth mentions his many other collaborators many times. But he's the one who kept saying to Eisner, "So, Michael—when are we going to do a Broadway show?" And that led to *The Lion King*, *Aida*, and *Mary Poppins*—not to mention the rehabilitation of the New Amsterdam Theatre, which was an important building block in the rejuvenation of West Forty-second Street. That makes Robert Jess Roth an MVP.

Rookie of the Year: Audra Ann McDonald
Carousel

In her dressing room at Carousel, Audra Ann McDonald had a picture of Barbra Streisand on her closet and a picture of Judy Garland on her mirror. "I've got both of them motivating me at all times," she'd said.

Lord knows how many performers today have pictures of McDonald on their closets and mirrors to motivate them.

Less than a year after she was graduated from Juilliard, McDonald got the role of Carrie Pipperidge in the revival of *Carousel*. It was a true change of pace for McDonald, who'd played Evita and Aldonza in regional theater. "I'm used to being beaten and raped and dying in shows," she said. "So Julie Jordan was the part I wanted. Only they wanted me for her best friend."

McDonald was doing a tour of *The Secret Garden* when she was called in to audition, so she flew in. Then came more flights for callbacks. "I was so exhausted at my last audition that after I sang 'Ms. Snow,' I fainted dead away." She got the part after that. "They were probably afraid I'd drop dead on the stage if they auditioned me again."

Although McDonald won the Best Featured Actress in a Musical Tony for *Carousel*, she was just getting started. She received a Best Featured Actress in a Play Tony for *Master Class*. McDonald then got a second Best Featured Actress in a Musical Tony for *Ragtime*.

In 2000, McDonald received her fourth nomination for playing an updated Medea in *Marie Christine*. Throughout awards season, she stated unequivocally that she wouldn't win. "I don't think anyone thinks that I need another Tony," she's say. And indeed, she didn't win.

Not that year. But in 2004, the Tony voters decided she did need another Tony and gave her a fourth award for playing Ruth Younger in *A Raisin in the Sun*. Perhaps some of those pictures on young performers' closets and mirrors have her holding one, two, three, or four of those trophies.

Comeback and Reliever: Tim Rice
Disney's Beauty and the Beast

There are many murderously painful aspects to show business, but one of the worst is being half of a team, breaking up, and then seeing your partner to go on to great success while you muddle through.

It happened to bookwriter-lyricist Tim Rice. After he and composer Andrew Lloyd Webber wrote three of the most popular musicals of the 1970s—*Jesus Christ Superstar*, *Joseph and the Amazing Technicolor Dreamcoat*, and *Evita*—they split.

Since *Evita's* first preview on September 10, 1979, at least one Lloyd Webber musical has been on Broadway each and every day—the longest streak by far that any artist of any kind can claim. But as the 1993–1994 season started, Tim Rice had been represented by only one new Broadway musical in that same time span: *Chess*, which had a disappointing run of sixty-eight performances in 1988.

Rice wasn't, of course, living hand-to-mouth. His still-robust royalties from those three 1970s hits saw to that. And whatever had happened to *Chess* on Broadway, it had been a solid London hit from its 1986 opening, running almost three years. What's more, his musical *Blondel*, based on the life of a twelfth-century French troubadour, ran almost two years in two West End venues.

Still, compare Rice's 1980s successes to Lloyd Webber's *Cats* and *The Phantom of the Opera*—easily the two most successful musicals of all time.

No one knew then that Rice, not Lloyd Webber, would have two of the most successful musicals of the 1990s: *Disney's Beauty and the Beast* and *The Lion King*.

Rice was summoned to buttress the lyrics to the stage version of *Beauty and the Beast* because original lyricist Howard Ashman had died in March 1991, eight months before the film's debut. The plans were that, in addition to the eight songs from the film, Rice would add eight more lyrics to Alan Menken's music.

First was "No Matter What," in which Belle's father, Maurice, gave her unconventional nature a vote of confidence. "Me" was the vainglorious Gaston's love song to himself. (It was a worthy successor to Lancelot's "C'est Moi.") "Home" had Belle reflect on her imprisonment by the Beast. "How Long Must This Go On?" saw the Beast rage that his punishment did not fit his crime. It was soon followed by "If I Can't Love Her," his soliloquy of frustration that ended the first act.

"Maison des Lunes" hatched Gaston's devious plan to make Belle his own. "A Change in Me" saw both Belle and the Beast slightly moving from their previously intractable positions. Finally, Rice provided the lyrics for the transformation scene.

Truth to tell, none of Menken and Rice's new songs reached the popularity of Menken and Ashman's "Belle" and "Be Our Guest," which had received Oscar nominations, or the title song, which had won the Oscar as Best Song from a Motion Picture. But Tim Rice's work enhanced *Beauty and the Beast* and was appreciated enough by Disney that, five years later, when it needed new songs for *The Lion King*, it called on him again.

1994–1995

MVP: Andrew Lloyd Webber
Sunset Boulevard

Go to the Tony website, call up Best Score, and look at the first five seasons. Aside from 1947–1948, when no award was given, each season simply had a winner with no nominees announced.

Then go to 1994–1995, and once again you'll see the same layout: a Best Score winner and no other nominees.

However, there is a profound difference between the two situations. In those first five seasons, the Tonys weren't bestowing any nominations in any category.

Kurt Weill's *Street Scene* in 1946–1947 didn't have to officially battle *Finian's Rainbow* and *Brigadoon*; it was announced as the outright winner. Similarly, Cole Porter's *Kiss Me, Kate* in 1948–1949 didn't duke it out with *Magdalena*, *Love Life*, and *Where's Charley?* Those three didn't get as much as a nod.

Frank Loesser, the Where's Charley? composer-lyricist, probably didn't feel disappointed at losing to Porter, but he must have felt cheated two seasons later when Irving Berlin's *Call Me Madam* beat out his *Guys and Dolls* for Best Score. (Bet the Tonys wish they could have that one back.)

For 1949–1950, few would begrudge *South Pacific* the prize, but a kinder, gentler system would have had nominations in place. That way, such worthies as *Lost in the Stars*, *Regina*, and even *Gentlemen Prefer Blondes* could have been recognized.

But in 1994–1995, when the Best Score was *Sunset Boulevard*—music by Andrew Lloyd Webber, lyrics by Christopher Hampton and Don Black—it didn't win because the Tony committee didn't draw up a list of nominees. It won uncontested and outright, because giving a nomination to the one and only other original score that season—*Lamb Chop on Broadway*, with music by Stormy Sacks, lyrics by Rob Battan—would have been too humiliating.

Lloyd Webber had been eligible for Best Score eight other times. He must have come to the ceremony reasonably cocky only during the *Evita* and *Cats* years, in which he indeed won. He had to be a little less certain about *Jesus Christ Superstar* and *The Phantom of the Opera*, for each time he was battling Tony darling Stephen Sondheim, respectively for *Follies* and *Into the Woods*. (Sondheim won both times.)

For that matter, Lloyd Webber probably didn't expect to hear his name called after the envelope (or folder) was opened during the years of *Joseph and the Amazing Technicolor Dreamcoat*, *Song and Dance*, *Starlight Express*, or *Aspects of Love*. But on Tony night, 1995, Lloyd Webber had known for three solid weeks, ever since the nominations had been announced, that he was the de facto winner.

The composer also deserves credit for starting, continuing, and completing the project. Betty Comden and Adolph Green tried musicalizing the 1950 hit film but eventually abandoned it. Stephen Sondheim has often said that he was once interested—but then he had a conversation with Sunset's director and co-writer Billy Wilder. Faded silent-movie star Norma Desmond, Wilder said, should be the subject of an opera, not a musical, because she was "a fallen queen." Sondheim thought Wilder had a point and scratched *Sunset Boulevard* off his list of possible musical adaptations.

In the mid-1950s, two neophyte composer-lyricists had tried an adaptation. Dickson Hughes and Richard Stapley worked hand-in-glove with the film's original star, Gloria Swanson. Nothing came of it, mostly because Paramount Pictures, which held the rights, wouldn't release them to the novices.

But in the 1990s, Lloyd Webber was by now the most successful musical-theater composer of his era (and every other). He had no problem securing the rights. And although Amy Powers, the first lyricist he engaged, didn't work out, he persevered.

Frankly, even if there had been an abundance of Best Score nominees in 1994–1995, Lloyd Webber, Hampton, and Black would have most likely won the award. From the first brooding notes of the Prologue, Lloyd Webber captured the murky sound of old-world Hollywood melodrama. When struggling writer Joe Gillis and his friends suggested "Let's Have Lunch," Lloyd Webber's melody was breezy, pre-rock 1950s that suggested people who believed they were swingers. The pulsating sounds of Joe's driving his car at full speed to elude his creditors were apt, as well.

Once Joe pulled into Norma Desmond's garage and met the fallen queen, Lloyd Webber and his lyricists gave their all. "With One Look" showed Norma's delusion in still believing that she was at the height of her beauty. Compare this with her second-act vulnerability, when she arrived at the studio where she once reigned supreme. She started "As If We Never Said Goodbye" in timid fashion. But she became the Norma of old before song's end. (Note, too, that she used "the royal we." But that also is appropriate to a queen, even if she's fallen.)

Sunset Boulevard was not a financial success, but it's the closest thing Andrew Lloyd Webber has had to one since *The Phantom of the Opera* opened lo those many years ago. *Whistle down the Wind* closed in Washington in 1997 during its pre-Broadway tryout. In 2000, The Beautiful Game ran less than a year in London, the shortest Lloyd Webber run in a quarter century, since the thirty-eight-performance run of Jeeves in 1975. Lloyd Webber rallied with *The Woman in White*, which reached 500 performances in London but a mere 109 performances on Broadway.

In 2004, a British satirical musical revue called *Zipp!* did an "Andrew Lloyd Webber Tribute," in which, said narrator and creator Gyles Brandreth, "we go through the entire Andrew Lloyd Webber canon—though in reverse chronological order, working back to the ones you actually know—and like."

Reliever and Comeback Player of the Year: Jerry Lewis
Damn Yankees

When you saunter down the passageway between Forty-fourth and Forty-fifth streets to enter the Minskoff Theatre, are you aware that you're walking in "The Jerry Lewis Arcade"?

That's what producer Alexander H. Cohen was planning to christen the walkway when his production of Jerry Lewis in *Hellzapoppin'* would open at the Minskoff on February 13, 1977. The only problem was that Jerry Lewis in *Hellzapoppin'* closed in Boston twenty-two days earlier. Until he died in 2000, Cohen called Lewis "the worst mistake I ever made."

Lewis fought quite a bit with Cohen, in keeping with his reputation for being belligerent. "One time I asked him about his previous partnership with Dean Martin," says longtime radio and TV host Joe Franklin. "He actually punched me in the mouth."

That sounds as if he'd be perfect casting for the Devil. But Mr. Applegate in *Damn Yankees* isn't evil incarnate. Audiences have to like him, too, in spite of themselves.

Audiences did like Lewis, who made his official debut in a Broadway musical on March 12, 1995, only four days before he would mark his sixty-ninth birthday. The closest Lewis had ever been to appearing in a Broadway musical was his one-man show at the Palace in January 1953. (He also starred in *Living It Up*, the film version of *Hazel Flagg*, semi-assuming the role originated by Helen Gallagher after it was reconfigured as Homer Flagg.)

Mr. Applegate has only one song: "Those Were the Good Old Days," in which he mourns the loss of guillotines, scalping (heads, not tickets), and stock market crashes. Lewis did the song-and-dance routine with panache and then extended the hat-and-cane part for more stage time.

He did add his screeching trademark "Layyy-dee" when he greeted Meg Boyd. But vintage Lewis was exactly what attendees of a musical in its second year wanted to see: legendary celebrity first, show second.

Lewis kept *Damn Yankees* running for an additional five months before taking it on tour and then to London. And not once was there a report that he'd punched anyone.

1995–1996

MVP and Rookie of the Year: Jonathan Larson
Rent

December 16, 1985. The ASCAP Workshop, New York City, where new musical-theater writers perform their songs for a panel of pros. Tonight it's Jonathan Larson's turn.

The twenty-five-year-old songwriter performs songs from his work-in-progress *Superbia*, inspired by George Orwell's *1984*. A panel of musical-theater experts will assess: bookwriter Peter Stone, director Tony Tanner, and composers Charles Strouse and Nancy Ford. When Larson finishes, he learns that Tanner and Strouse aren't impressed while Stone and Ford certainly are. This leads to a heated discussion—one that gets flaming hot when the other young songwriting students in the class get to air their perceptions. Musical-theater hell breaks loose, as sides are taken. The commotion lasts close to a half hour, and Larson looks pretty embarrassed by the whole mess.

No one knows that in a little more than ten years, Larson will have the biggest hit on Broadway—or that the young man won't live to see it.

If Stephen Sondheim had died ten days before his thirty-sixth birthday, we would have been denied a dozen more musicals from him, starting with *Company*. Had Richard Rodgers met the same fate, we would have lost the five final musicals he wrote with Lorenz Hart and all nine with Oscar Hammerstein II.

So one can only imagine what we lost from Jonathan Larson's all-too-premature death on January 25, 1996. This happened when his friends and relatives were giving thought to how to celebrate his upcoming thirty-sixth birthday on February 4.

There was much to celebrate. Never mind that *Superbia* went unproduced, that *J. P. Morgan Saves the Nation* got only one small production, and that *30/90* (later called *Boho Days*), while meeting with a few little productions, had stalled. *Rent* was now being mounted at the prestigious New York Theatre Workshop. Larson's new version of *La Bohème* had for the last three years been developed at the theater and was just about to play its first preview.

Then Larson unexpectedly died of an aortic aneurysm. Show business often carries with it tremendous heartbreak, but this was one of the cruelest blows it ever dealt.

Rent was not Larson's idea; his friend Billy Aronson had the inspiration to do a new *La Bohème* that centered on New York's many struggling and starving artists. Larson, however, thought it should become about the residents of Alphabet City, and not, as Aronson had suggested, the Upper West Side.

Aronson later dropped out, but Larson continued to write the book, music, and lyrics that dealt with AIDS, drug addition, transvestism, homosexuality, civil disobedience, and vandalism. However, after the show opened to raves, dramaturge Lynn Thomson came forward to say she was a big factor in *Rent's* success. We'll never know what happened after Larson said—if or when he did—"Hey, Lynn, would you read this and make some suggestions?"

Whatever the case may be, Jonathan Larson gets credit for motivating an entirely new generation of theatergoers to enter a Broadway theater—and/or sleep outside it while waiting to get tickets. "Rentheads," these individuals were called. Had any musical before this had so many groupies that they required a name?

Larson did not die in vain. His family established the Jonathan Larson Award. It gives hope to bookwriters, composers, and lyricists that they won't always be living existences much like the characters in *Rent*.

Comeback Player of the Year: Julie Andrews
Victor/Victoria

She opened three Broadway musicals in six years: *The Boy Friend*, *My Fair Lady*, and *Camelot*. She might have squeezed one more in there, if *Fair Lady* hadn't been such a mammoth hit. The New York and London engagements took more than three years of her life.

But after Julie Andrews left *Camelot* in April 1962 after 500-plus performances, she did one Broadway musical in the next third of a century. Hollywood kept her that busy with nineteen films, two TV movies, and two TV series.

By 1995, Andrews was sixty, long past prime time for Hollywood actresses. More to the point, Blake Edwards, her husband of twenty-seven years, was seventy-three and was no longer a top-of-the-line Hollywood director.

So here would be a return to Broadway for her and a debut for him. What other options did they have besides retiring?

Besides, Andrews could finally win that Tony that had been denied her: Mary Martin had won for *Peter Pan* in *The Boy Friend* season; Judy Holliday had beaten Andrews's Eliza with her Ella in *Bells Are Ringing*; Elizabeth Seal's

Irma La Douce had bested her Guinevere. So by bringing her 1982 semi-hit film *Victor/Victoria* to the stage, Andrew could finally get that Tony. It'd look good next to her Oscar and Grammy (for *Mary Poppins*) and Emmy (for *The Julie Andrews Hour*).

Actually, Andrews deserved the Tony. The way she moved around the stage showed an elegance and grace that proved that she was a natural musical-theater performer. When Tony Randall appeared in *Oh, Captain!* one critic said that the star's dancing "tortured the air." Andrews's every move enhanced it.

But the show wasn't much good. So when the Tony nominations were announced on May 6, 1996, *Victor/Victoria* received only one nomination—for Andrews. Two days later, the nominee made an announcement after the matinee: "I have searched my heart, and find that I cannot accept the nomination, when the rest of the company has been so egregiously overlooked."

Since that statement, the word *egregious* has become a mainstay of Broadway observers' vocabularies each year at awards season.

Andrews asked that her nomination be withdrawn. Did she think she'd be taken seriously? Did she think she'd win anyway? Did she care?

Only Andrews can say for sure. But many Broadway observers were surprised when she didn't win and Donna Murphy's name was announced as the Best Actress in a Musical. Murphy was wonderful as Mrs. Anna in *The King and I*, but had Andrews stayed in the race, she would have won.

At least Andrews got a Drama Desk Award out of it. Not that the Drama Desks were so generous to *Victor/Victoria*; it bestowed only two other nominations on the show: Outstanding Featured Actress in a Musical to Rachel York, who won, and Outstanding Set Design to Robin Wagner, who didn't.

But Andrews didn't attend the Drama Desk Awards. If they had thrown a few more her show's way, who knows?

If Andrews demanded to be taken off this ballot as Comeback Player of the Year, Carol Channing would have received the honor by virtue of her third Broadway run in *Hello, Dolly!* Many mocked Channing for doing the role when she was almost seventy-five years old. But wanting to love and remarry can happen at any age, can't it?

Those who scorned Channing need to be reminded that earlier in the year at Madison Square Garden, an entertainer known as Gary Glitter appeared in *The Who's Quadrophenia*. The fifty-one-year-old singer portrayed a teenager.

Managers of the Year: Jeffrey Seller, Kevin McCollum, and Allan S. Gordon

Rent

When people see that *Rent* author Jonathan Larson had a sister named Julie Larson McCollum and that Rent was co-produced by Kevin McCollum, they automatically assume that she was related by marriage, which is how this young producer got the rights to one of Broadway's all-time bonanzas.

Not at all. Despite having the same atypical last name, the two are not related in any way.

What Kevin McCollum and his producing partner Jeffrey Seller and Allan S. Gordon did for *Rent*—and Broadway—was one of the most significant audience-friendly moves. They decided to offer $20 tickets to the first twenty people who showed up at the box office.

Such deep discounts weren't uncommon in the past, but they were always for the seats far in the upper reaches of the mezzanine or balcony. Rent's management, though, instead would offer $20 for the first two rows of the orchestra. First come, first served, first class. It's a rare show that now doesn't have a similar lottery, opening the doors to Broadway to those who otherwise wouldn't be able to afford it.

Seller and McCollum have since gone on to produce two other Tony-winning musicals: *Avenue Q* and *In the Heights*. Both, like *Rent*, have an urban rock sensibility. But one can't pigeonhole the duo; they also, surprisingly enough, produced Irving Berlin's *White Christmas*.

1996–1997

MVP and Manager of the Year: Walt Disney Corporation

The New Amsterdam Theatre

May 15, 1997. New Amsterdam Theatre. The people flocking in certainly are interested in seeing this first preview of this modern oratorio *King David*.

After all, its authors, Alan Menken and Tim Rice, have quite a pedigree by now. Their *Beauty and the Beast* recently celebrated its third anniversary and will celebrate many more (ten more, in fact).

But even Menken and Rice's staunchest fans—indeed, even Menken and Rice themselves—might well admit that they're more interested in seeing the theater than the show.

For this is the first legitimate attraction at the New Amsterdam Theatre in more than sixty years, since *Othello* had played a three-week engagement in 1937. To better put into perspective how much time had passed: Othello had been played by a white actor. (Walter Huston, in fact, most famous for playing the grizzled old and wise prospector in *The Treasure of the Sierra Madre.*)

Then it became a place where one saw, as Dimitri Weismann said of his own theater in *Follies*, movies and blue movies. When that's the bill of fare, all too often management doesn't care about keeping the property in tip-top shape. Little by little the place was crumbling and rotting.

The Nederlander Organization bought the property for $5 million in 1982 and planned to restore it in the 1980s, but after seeing that the most important supporting beam was severely damaged, it opted to bow out. Imagine how many millions it would cost to restore the house.

$34 million, in fact, which is what the Walt Disney Corporation was willing to spend to have a permanent home for any of its shows (including its upcoming production of *The Lion King*).

King David is nice enough, and in the years to follow, it will get a few productions here and there. But the raves go to the theater, a reclaimed Art Nouveau masterpiece. The boxes on each side of the stage once again bloom with the flower motifs they originally had: buttercup, goldenrod, lily, and violet. The proscenium arch is surrounded by fully restored paintings, many of peacocks, which is fitting, for this theater and the Walt Disney Corporation have every right to be as proud as peacocks.

Only one problem: Here and there are plastered little signs that give information on seat locations and restrooms. All have Mickey Mouse on them, and they make the place look, well, Mickey Mouse. But it's a small price to play to have one of Broadway's most glorious theaters back in business and, more importantly, back to its former glory.

Comeback: *Chicago*

In 1976, *Chicago* landed an impressive eleven Tony nominations.

It didn't manage to win a single trophy. Never before had a musical scored so many nominations without bringing home at least one. Meanwhile, *A Chorus Line* won nine.

Chicago *did manage to run 936 performances—which represented about 15* percent of the run that *A Chorus Line* would have. It was officially a hit, in that it repaid its entire investment to its backers, but no one got rich from it.

And no one would have ever expected that it would have a stunning and unprecedented renaissance a couple of decades later.

It was only supposed to be a weekend concert at Encores!—the newly established series for musicals that probably didn't warrant a full-fledged revival.

That turned out not to be the case. The audience was taken by surprise at how much they loved the musical and even the stripped-down production. As murderess Roxie, Ann Reinking didn't seem to be any older than she was when she'd closed the show in 1977. Bebe Neuwirth's sardonic personality was perfect for double murderess Velma. James Naughton brought plenty of swagger to their lawyer, Billy Flynn. Joel Grey, as Roxie's cuckolded husband Amos, reminded us how good he could be in supporting roles.

The media attention that now surrounds such controversial characters as O. J. Simpson and Jim Bakker was given as a reason for Chicago's rebound. Many a theatergoer nodded when Billy was about to conduct a trial and said, "It all show biz, kid." Yes, we learned that many a night in our homes as we watched the news.

But *Chicago* mostly scored because it's a superb musical. How smart of director-choreographer and co-bookwriter Bob Fosse to structure it as a vaudeville. He knew that if he put Roxie Hart in a "realistic" musical, audiences wouldn't be able to get behind, as Billy Flynn unapologetically calls her, "a common criminal." Vaudeville and razzle-dazzle, as the song went, carried the day.

The vaudeville approach also helped Kander and Ebb to write of an era they remembered from their youth. The score had echoes of Sophie Tucker ("When You're Good to Mama"), Bert Walker ("Mr. Cellophane"), Eddie Cantor ("Me and My Baby"), and Helen Morgan ("Funny Honey").

To date, *Chicago* is the only musical to win more Tonys for its revival (six) than for its original production (none). Never before had a Broadway musical that had failed to win a single Tony turn into a Best Picture Oscar winner. More impressive still, this revival passed the 6,137 amassed by the musical that humiliated it in 1976: *A Chorus Line*.

Rookie and Reliever of the Year: Elaine Paige
Sunset Boulevard

The First Lady of the British Musical Stage was the third to play Norma Desmond. Glenn Close opened the show on November 17, 1994, and won a Best Actress Tony for it—mostly, it was said, for her acting. When Betty Buckley succeeded her in July of 1995, she was well received—mostly for her singing. When Elaine Paige took over in August of 1996, she had both the acting and vocal chops.

Although Paige had been performing professionally for three decades (and had been a London star for two of them), *Sunset Boulevard* marked her Broadway debut. Paige turned out to be worth the wait. What thought she'd given Norma Desmond. She seemed to have imbued every word and gesture with hours of analysis.

Not that resembling Gloria Swanson, the original Norma in the 1950 film, was a prerequisite, but Paige happened to look a good deal like her. She had the same long, open rectangular face displaying those man-hungry teeth.

Paige did have her detractors. Some accused her of being over-the-top, but Norma Desmond is an over-the-top character. Others complained that she was occasionally too British in delivery and gesture, but Norma is an affected woman and would not have been above sounding affected.

And then there was the height issue. Addison De Witt in *All about Eve* had once told Eve Harrington that she was "too short for that gesture." Some said that Paige, a mere four feet eleven—"and a half," she insisted—was not tall enough to play Norma. After all, when she walked down the famous staircase, Paige could barely be seen over the banister. Once she got on the main floor, however, this wasn't a particular problem.

Paige—née Elaine Bickerstaff—got her first professional assignment as one of the urchins in the pre-London tryout of *The Roar of the*

Greasepaint—the Smell of the Crowd, which then starred Norman Wisdom and Willoughby Goddard. While the show would have a respectable 232-performance run on Broadway in 1965, this first edition closed before it got to London. Says Paige, "I can still remember what I felt on closing night when we were all singing songs called 'A Wonderful Day Like Today' and 'Nothing Can Stop Me Now' when we knew that this was not a wonderful day and that the show was stopping. My reaction was beyond poignant. How I wept!"

But then Paige made an Oscar-winning movie—in a manner of speaking. "I appeared in *Oliver!*—barely," she says. "Look carefully in 'Consider Yourself' and 'Who Will Buy?' and you just might see me. Even though I did nothing to speak of in the film, being in it taught me a great deal. Because those two numbers took months to get right, I saw that nothing less than perfection will do for some directors."

Paige left her urchin phase in dramatic fashion, for she next appeared in *Hair*. "Because I felt very vulnerable in those days, I was one of the last to take my clothes off," she says. "I got teased a lot for not doing it. Then one night Gary Hamilton, one of my castmates, said, 'Come on; I'll stand near you and I'll give you my hand to hold.' That gave me the courage. The problem is that once we were both naked onstage, it was hardly his hand that he gave me to hold."

Next came *Jesus Christ Superstar*. "Half the cast was stoned half the time. I don't know how those people could do that and then get onstage and give any kind of performance," she says evenly. "Often they went on after having many glasses of wine, too. I just wouldn't be able to do it."

Roar of the Greasepaint tangentially returned to her life when she auditioned for Evita. "I sang 'A Wonderful Day Like Today,'" she says. "I've since noticed that I used to audition with songs that had the word 'day' in them—'On a Clear Day' and 'Yesterday,' too. I've also noticed that two of the characters I've played have had my initials—Eva Peron and Edith Piaf." And while Paige hasn't shown us her impression of Elvis Presley, she did at least play Sandy in the original West End production of *Grease*.

Once she was cast in *Evita*, Paige was surprised to find that her face would have to be slathered with wax. "It was to make a model of my face that could be put in the casket at the beginning of the show," she says. "Being waxed like that was very difficult, because I suffer from claustrophobia. But I didn't fight it. Again, I was impressed by the director's seriousness of detail. Only those in the dress circle would have been able to see that face, but that was still enough for them to do it. By the way, that wax mask is still one of my favorite souvenirs."

Perhaps more arduous was climbing to the balcony of the Casa Rosada. "There was just this little ordinary wooden ladder back there, and I was supposed to climb it while wearing this enormous dress," she says. "I couldn't possibly do it alone, so a man backstage had to steady me by actually sticking himself under my dress and helping me up. That was embarrassing, but he got me up there."

Once she was in place, there was another challenge—and not just to sing "Don't Cry for Me, Argentina." Paige says, "Hal Prince told me to glide to the microphone as if I were on roller skates, which took some practice."

Alas, what Prince couldn't do was give Paige the chance to glide on Broadway. "Hal said to me, 'I'll make you a Broadway star with *Evita*,' but there was such trouble with Equity that I didn't come over," she says. "And later when *Cats* was coming to America, as much as I wanted to do Grizabella here, they didn't even try to bring me. Same thing with *Chess*, which was harder, because that was written with me in mind." (She and lyricist Tim Rice were once romantically linked.)

At least there was *Sunset Boulevard*—and Elaine Paige got the most out of it.

1997–1998

MVP: Julie Taymor
The Lion King

November 14, 1997. Opening night of *Children of Eden* at the Paper Mill Playhouse in Millburn, New Jersey. Stephen Schwartz and John Caird have respectively reworked their score and book to their biblical musical that had a mere three-month run in London in 1991.

Hopes are high that the reviews will be good and that *Children of Eden* will make the twenty-five-mile journey across the Hudson River and onto Broadway.

It might have, too, in a different season. But this morning, the reviews for *The Lion King* were published.

And why does a musical based on a Disney cartoon pose an unbeatable challenge to a Bible story? To be sure, *The Lion King* was a most popular animated film in 1994. It was a fresh variation on what is considered the world's greatest play: *Hamlet*. Here, Lion King Mufasa is killed by his brother Scar, to the horror of Prince Simba. Unlike in Shakespeare, however, Simba is made to believe he's responsible for his father's death and runs off in disgrace.

But the Bible is, after all, the world's best-selling book. Shouldn't it have even more appeal? And Schwartz and Caird's work was usually as good and often superior to what *The Lion King* offered in its book, music, and lyrics.

The reason has a great deal to do with the way each musical depicted the animals that were vital to the story.

Children of Eden's animals romped around the garden of paradise in Gregg Barnes's perfectly decent costumes. Actors wore headpieces to suggest birds, mammals, and reptiles. For a giraffe, a large cardboard cutout of a neck and head was eased into view thanks to a wire that was all too visible.

Meanwhile at the new New Amsterdam Theatre on Broadway, Julie Taymor showed substantially more imagination—and genius. Her giraffe was a man who walked on four very thin stilts; he wore a many-feet-tall neck and head unit. While "two heads are better than one" has been a bromide for eons, Taymor took it literally and had an actor wear an animal head atop his own. Then, by having the actor stoop over and walk with two glorified canes, the illusion was created of a giraffe that gingerly walked through the jungle.

Another actor would suggest a zebra by wearing a zebra head on his right shoulder and positioning the rest of the zebra's body behind him. Yet another performer would run across the stage while holding a device that had three gazelles on it, creating the illusion that they were running, too. Other gazelles came courtesy of an earthbound deus ex machina, a large tricycle that another actor pedaled.

There's always been a theatrical stigma to playing the back half of an animal. But Taymor's actors played an animal's hind legs while maneuvering an enormous puppet as the front half of its body. That ameliorated the situation, for the actor could still be seen. That human beings were plainly visible was an asset, not a liability, to Taymor. It was all part of the unique theatrical experience. Another bromide—"Behind every good man is a good woman"—could be paraphrased thus: Behind every puppet was an actor. Both cases involved a good deal of manipulation.

Taymor designed the musical's many masks, too—which she would have actors use in battle scenes as shields. And although Taymor didn't take a book credit, she was responsible for making some helpful suggestions to bookwriters Roger Allers and Irene Mecchi. Make Simba more like a moody teenager. Have his friend Nala's leaving home seem more permanent and less mercurial.

Taymor was the one to choose Hans Zimmer, Mark Mancina, and Lebo M. to augment the score—and to keep Zulu sensibilities in place, even down to not translating the lyrics. She wanted the percussionists, flautists, and kora players to be visible on each side of the stage.

As for Elton John and Tim Rice, who'd written the abbreviated score for the film, Taymor urged them to write more songs, such as a comic one for the hyenas and a musical descent into madness for Scar.

Taymor also wanted to create stronger female characters for the piece. While the film opened with a man singing about "The Circle of Life," she had a woman deliver it while arguably the most arresting opening sequence in Broadway history occurred. "The Circle of Life" had all these aforementioned animals and more come down the aisles and bound onto the stage. It was—and continues to be—a thrilling sequence.

With a six-pack of credits on one of the biggest hits in Broadway history, Julie Taymor is a lock for this season's MVP. She gets sole credit for designing the costumes, puppets, and masks and for directing. Add to that her "additional" credit for music and another for lyrics.

While Geoffrey Holder was the first man and African American to win for the unlikely combination of Best Director of a Musical Tony and Best Costume Design—and deliver the Best Musical—Taymor became to first woman to match that trifecta.

But Taymor also got a nomination for her "additional music" to the *Lion King* score. (She and her collaborators, however, couldn't take the prize from the extraordinary achievement that lyricist Lynn Ahrens and composer Stephen Flaherty gave *Ragtime*.)

As of this writing, *The Lion King* is the sixth-longest-running production in Broadway history, closing in on 6,000 performances. It has grossed $4 billion. And while *Children of Eden* continues to be one of the most popular musicals in the stock and amateur arena, it still hasn't made it to Broadway.

Manager of the Year: Garth H. Drabinsky
Ragtime

Don't forget: Joseph Stalin was once named *Time* magazine's Man of the Year, too.

Like George Abbott, Garth H. Drabinsky wrote his autobiography at the right time. In Abbott's case, as we saw, he wrote it before he had a long string of flops. In Drabinsky's, he wrote *Closer to the Sun* in 1995, four years before the law caught up with his financial irregularities.

"Producer for producer, Garth was the best," says Richard Maltby Jr., who worked on Drabinsky's final Broadway outing, *Fosse*, in 1999. "He was totally committed to creating a work of art. He would do anything to make it happen, spending whatever money was necessary.

"If you worked for him, you were by definition the best available, and he made sure he supported you. He wasn't the questioning type who stood over your shoulder. And he was smart. He gave me a suggestion that made 'Mr. Bojangles' a better number."

Maltby then stops and sighs. "And then, the morning after we opened *Fosse* in Toronto, the Mounties came into the offices and sealed them. Garth was almost arrested," he adds, shaking his head. "It's sad that he was operating a kind of a theatrical Ponzi scheme."

Yes, but Broadway got a new theater out of it. For his production of *Ragtime*, Drabinsky would build on Forty-second Street a theater merged from the barely used Apollo and Lyric theatres.

The theater he was planning for his production of *Ragtime* turned out to be as big as Drabinsky's ego. At 1,839 seats, it would be second only to the Gershwin in seating capacity. "And," Drabinsky said, "the theater will be available for naming opportunities."

Given that *Ragtime* had a song called "Henry Ford," not much time passed before Drabinsky's new theater was called the Ford Center for the Performing Arts. But one gets the impression that Drabinsky would have sold naming rights to Kaopectate.

Soon after the 1998 opening, Drabinsky declared bankruptcy and the theatre has since changed hands many times—not to mention a name change from Ford to Hilton to Foxwoods. Meanwhile, Drabinsky was changing residences to get away from the law. However, for the brief, shining season of 1997–1998, Garth H. Drabinsky made Broadway a bigger place.

Rookie of the Year: Alan Cumming
Cabaret

Joel Grey won the 1966–1967 Tony for Best Featured Actor in a Musical for playing the Emcee of the Kit Kat Club in *Cabaret*. It was certainly considered one of the most memorable performances in the postwar era.

After he won, Cabaret's producer Harold Prince took Grey's name from below the title and put it high above it.

For months, Prince knew that above the title was where Grey belonged, given his riveting, talk-of-the-town performance. Prince, however, didn't want to spoil Grey's chances of getting a Tony, which probably would have happened if he'd been upped to the Best Actor category.

Grey soon had the title role *George M!* (as in Cohan). Both he and the show were at best a modest success. But not long after, Grey was repeating his Emcee for the cameras. That resulted in a 1972 Oscar. No question that Grey owned the role.

In 1975, Grey's *Goodtime Charley*, in which he played the Dauphin to Ann Reinking's Joan of Arc, couldn't last three months. In 1979, *The Grand Tour*, in which he portrayed the meek but wily Jew who tames a tough Gentile during World War II, couldn't last two. So Grey would come back in 1987 by playing the Emcee in a Broadway revival of *Cabaret*.

It lasted a disappointing 261 performances. The next revival would run more than nine times as long—and Alan Cumming's reinterpretation was a prime reason why. Grey had played the Emcee as a white-faced asexual puppet. Cumming, in conjunction with his director Sam Mendes, underlined the fact that the Emcee worked in a decadent club where anything went. Under those circumstances, he'd seen everything and had become a raging pansexual who'd been in on the action. Cumming was creepy, but an audience couldn't take its eyes off him.

He was rewarded with a Tony—but certainly not as Best Featured Actor in a Musical. This time, it was Best Actor in a Musical all the way. Cumming proved a variation on a very famous theatrical cliché that a featured part can seem a starring one if a star plays it.

1998–1999

MVP and Reliever of the Year: Richard Maltby Jr.
Fosse

With all the retrospectives that had been cropping up in recent years, how about one that featured Bob Fosse's work?

Certainly Gwen Verdon, the four-time Tony winner who was also Fosse's widow, thought it was a good idea. She started pitching the notion in 1995.

Fosse himself had, in 1978, done a show in which one new dance simply followed another: *Dancin'*. It lasted more than four years. So imagine how much more successful an evening of his greatest dances would be—from *The Pajama Game*, *Damn Yankees*, *Bells Are Ringing*, *New Girl in Town*, *Redhead*, *How to Succeed*, *Little Me*, *Sweet Charity*, *Pippin*, *Chicago*, *Dancin'*, and even his last show, the unsuccessful *Big Deal*.

Garth Drabinsky, now established as a major Broadway force, sponsored a workshop in Toronto in the summer of 1996. The timing couldn't have been better, for in the spring of that year, Encores! had revived Fosse's *Chicago* to tumultuous reviews. That musical would move to Broadway come fall, and maybe this new Fosse revue could nestle nearby.

But the workshop didn't work out, although no one could understand why. Marty Bell, Drabinsky's vice president of creative affairs, had an idea: call Richard Maltby Jr.

"Because I'd directed and created and, with Murray Horwitz, co-conceived *Ain't Misbehavin'*," says Maltby of the 1978 Tony-winning musical, "people assumed I knew how to do a revue."

Maltby watched a tape of the workshop and understood why artistic advisor Verdon and director Chet Martin began with one of *Dancin's* most beloved production numbers: "I Wanna Be a Dancin' Man."

"It was a logical idea, because Bob was if nothing else a dancing man," he says. "But by the fifth number, I was getting pretty bored, and thought 'Bob Fosse has to have been better than this.'"

Maltby began to see why. "Bob of course never expected these numbers to be strung together back to back. Doing 'Dancin' Man' up front revealed his bag of tricks, and the numbers that followed reiterated those tricks. I felt the show would have to keep the cat in the bag of tricks for as long as it could."

Martin departed and Maltby began restructuring Fosse. "I decided to hold off the signature material and start the show as far afield from it. First we'd have the most unrepresentative Fosse dances so we could get slowly to the Fosse vocabulary. Only when people were getting desperate to see what they had come to see all along would we give it to them."

Malty opted to begin with "Life Is Just a Bowl of Cherries" ("Bob's favorite song," he says), sung by Valarie Pettiford. "Behind her, I had the cast doing little dance elements from some of the numbers, but not full-blown dances," he says. "It wasn't until seven minutes into the show that you got a big Fosse number."

Even that was an unfamiliar one, "Because it was 'Bye Bye Blackbird' from *Liza... with a 'Z,'* which had only been seen on TV once many years before," Maltby says. "It was very subtle for Fosse. Then we did a percussive number from *Dancin'* that was rowdy, and represented who he was when he was growing up as street kid."

Fosse had made that clear many times. When he was interviewed by Pia Lindstrom in 1980, he said, "I started at thirteen in very cheap night clubs in and around Chicago—stripteases—and I haven't recovered since." His parents, he said, "really didn't know what I was doing."

"He got into dancing because a girl he was interested in was taking lessons," says Maltby. "But when the girl dropped out, he was intrigued enough to stay."

Maltby was also applying the lessons he'd learned from *Ain't Misbehavin'*. "Underneath the surface of a show like this, there should be a biographical feel," he says. "So up front we had the numbers that suggested what life was like for Bob when he was a kid growing up in Chicago. To represent those burlesque houses, we did 'Big Spender'—again a number that has some little finger and body moves that are 'Fosse famous' but there's no real dancing per se in it. To show his introduction to Hollywood, we did 'From This Moment On' which he did in *Kiss Me, Kate.* And not until twenty-five minutes in did we do 'Dancin' Man,' after which the curtain came down for the first intermission."

Act 2 was reserved for the joyous parts of Fosse's career: "'Shoeless Joe from Hannibal, Mo' (from *Damn Yankees*), "Steam Heat" (*The Pajama Game*), and "Rich Man's Frug" (*Sweet Charity*) were all exuberant," says Maltby. "And act 3 was reserved for the last part of his life when he often explored how depraved a human being could be. So we had the war sequence from Pippin and the darker moments from *All That Jazz*, his thinly veiled biography. We had numbers in which Fosse showed what he thought attracted people to each other; they had no sentimentality attached."

Maltby did decide to end on an upswing. "'Mr. Bojangles' had a ragged old vaudevillian and a young one who represented the spirit of dance. And even though Bob wasn't big on eleven-o'clock numbers, we had one with 'Sing, Sing, Sing.'"

It worked, says Maltby, "because of this subterranean structure that actually held these numbers together and gave a greater sense of story. An audience really does feel it, whether it knows it or not."

All this didn't come easily. "I actually had to ask Gwen not to attend rehearsals," he says. "She sat there gloomily disapproving and no one could do any work if he did any variation on what Fosse had done. Although when she did a scene, she would change anything. I was actually more protective of Fosse's material than she was."

Rookie: Jason Robert Brown
Parade

Parents say no to their children all the time. So when Daisy Prince, daughter of Hal, insisted that her daddy listen to this new songwriter named Jason Robert Brown, he didn't have to.

But Prince did. Once he listened, he didn't sign Brown to write the score for his new musical *Parade* simply appease and please his daughter.

Brown's collection of songs, under the title *Songs for a New World*, was produced at the WPA Theatre off-Broadway when he was twenty-five. The pièce de resistance was "Just One Step," a song in which a woman threatens to throw herself off the balcony of her high-rise apartment because life is not worth living any longer. The reason? Her husband won't buy her a new fur coat.

Actually, she's aware that her husband has long since stopped loving her, but that seems to bother her less. Brown lets us see the woman has tried this suicide threat before, and now the husband is intent on not giving in to her.

The woman winds up revealing much more about herself than she planned. Once she admits that she's no longer the pretty young thing she once was, she realizes that she'd better not remind him of that. Bringing up that his mother never liked her probably wasn't a good idea, either. Eventually the woman gets so worked up that she inadvertently slips. Be careful what you wish for.

It wasn't an easy song to write, but Brown captured perfectly the heart, soul, and mind of the woman. Now he'd have a much bigger challenge. Prince wanted Brown to provide the score for the sad and difficult story of Leo Frank. He was a Jew living and working in Atlanta in 1913 when he was accused of murdering a young girl. Most people now believe he was not guilty, but anti-Semitism was greatly responsibly for his being convicted and sentenced to death.

His wife, Lucille, begged the governor to commute his sentence, and he did, to life imprisonment. Some of Georgia's citizens wouldn't have that. They kidnapped Leo Frank and hanged him.

How fresh Brown's score was can be gleaned from the show's final song. Said the *Playbill*, "All the Wasted Time"—Leo and Lucille Frank.

Any seasoned theatergoer could see in advance what that song would be: a mournful realization of all the time that was lost from Leo's unfair imprisonment. No: Leo and Lucille had a dull marriage until trouble hit. Only then did they both have something to fight for, and only then did they come to love each other. "All the Wasted Time," then, meant the time when they had each other at home and could have spent those precious days and years loving each other.

Parade couldn't march beyond eighty-five performances, but Brown won the Tony for Best Score. Never in the fifty-three-year history of the awards had a musical run so short a time and won that prize.

1999–2000

MVP and Comeback Player of the Year: Susan Stroman

Contact and *The Music Man*

Many Broadway dancers decide to choreograph only after they are physically unable to perform eight times a week.

Not Susan Stroman. When she was growing up in Wilmington, Delaware, she was figuring out dances as much as she was doing them. And while an occasional extraordinary high schooler is given the chance to choreograph the school musical, Stroman even talked her way in choreographing halftime shows at the school's football games.

In 1975, when Stroman was majoring in theater at the University of Delaware, the touring company of *Seesaw* came to town. As she says, "When I saw Tommy Tune and all those balloons and girls in 'It's Not Where You Start, It's Where You Finish,' I just couldn't wait to get to New York and do numbers like that. I quit school."

So when Stroman made her Broadway debut as a dancer in *Whoopee!* on Valentine's Day, 1979, she viewed it as a means to an end. Fifteen months later, she was dance captain of *Musical Chairs,* in which the audience watched an audience watching a musical. But she was also its assistant choreographer and director—and a member of the team that hired Scott Ellis as a performer.

Many regional jobs followed for both. Ellis was a cast member in Kander and Ebb's *The Rink,* and impressed the team with his acumen. Might he try directing a revisal of their first flop, *Flora, the Red Menace*? Might Susan Stroman choreograph, as well?

Stroman didn't expect the show to be seen by many. After all, the Vineyard Theatre, little more than an L-shaped room, was at the time located on East Twenty-sixth Street at Second Avenue. But by then, Kander and Ebb were Broadway royalty, and a parade of pros attended. They included Hal Prince, who'd produced three of their first four musicals.

Prince was impressed with Stroman's work and offered her the chance to choreograph the production of *Don Giovanni* that he was directing at New York City Opera. Stroman didn't abandon Ellis, however; she was his choreographer and co-conceiver of the 1991 off-Broadway hit *And the World Goes 'Round: The Songs of Kander and Ebb.*

A year later, Stroman made the A-list, after Frank Rich of the *New York Times* anointed her work on *Crazy for You.* "Extraordinary," he called her, with a "winning style" by which she "works her magic ... to bring out specific feelings in the music and lyrics." He concluded, "It is the big numbers in *Crazy for You* that people will be talking about."

Stroman seemed to be leading a charmed life. *Crazy for You* lasted four years, during which time she and Mike Ockrent, its director, fell in love and married. By then she'd won Best Choreography Tonys for *Crazy for You* and a 1994 revival of *Show Boat.* That year, she and Ockrent collaborated on *A Christmas Carol* at Madison Square Garden that returned each holiday season for ten straight years.

Then came two Broadway flops—*Big* in 1996, *Steel Pier* in 1997. You know Broadway wags: Has Susan Stroman lost her touch? Had we overestimated her? Did we make her believe she was invincible when she wasn't? Had it all gone to her head too soon?

These doubts were ameliorated by a choreographic success with *Oklahoma!* in London in 1998. But Stroman had much more on her mind to worry her. Ockrent had leukemia.

She juggled caring for Ockrent with working. André Bishop, Lincoln Center's artistic director, helped by saying, "Come here and develop whatever you want."

Stroman called bookwriter John Weidman, with whom she'd collaborated on *Big.* (One of the marks of a champion is working again with someone you still believe in even if you had a flop together.) Together they decided to do a piece that involved far more dance than book. *Contact,* it would be called.

Many musicals have been based on people: *1776, Gypsy,* and *Fiorello!* So was *Contact,* albeit on someone who wasn't famous. Stroman had seen a woman in a yellow dress in a nightclub stand on or near the dance floor and silently dare men to approach her. Many did and were rejected; others were accepted, but only for a dance or two.

"I'm convinced that she wanted to make contact," says Stroman. In her new show, this woman became their "Girl in the Yellow Dress" (Deborah Yates), who wound up making contact with a lonely man (Boyd Gaines) in a most unexpected way.

Their second piece of inspiration wasn't anonymous. It was *The Swing,* the 1767 painting by Jean-Honoré Fragonard. Stroman and Weidman designed a servant—master–mistress triangle that wasn't what it seemed at first glance or assumption.

They had their opener and closer. For the middle, they concocted "Did You Move?" Karen Ziemba portrayed the wife of a 1950s mafioso who took her to a Queens restaurant but demanded that she not say a word or even get up from her seat. She smiled and submissively obeyed—until his was back turned. Then she broke into some stunning Stroman choreography that fully expressed her inner spirit.

Ziemba admits, "When we did the workshop, I didn't know what to think. So I called people I really trusted and said, 'I want you to see this because I just don't know about it. Do you think it's worth staying in?' I mean, I'd do anything for Susan, but I guess I needed some buoying," she conceded. "And I was relieved when they told me they thought it was very moving and that I was good in it."

Contact was an immediate hit after its October 7, 1999, off-Broadway debut at the Mitzi Newhouse Theatre. But Stroman couldn't completely enjoy the victory, because Ockrent's health was steadily failing. On December 2, he died at the age of fifty-three.

Weeks later, Stroman was coping in the best way she could—as she prepared *Contact*'s move upstairs to Lincoln Center's Broadway-sized house, the Vivian Beaumont. As soon as that show settled in, Stroman was directing and choreographing rehearsals for *Meredith Willson's The Music Man,* as it was officially called.

While she did a magnificent job with the warhorse—"76 Trombones" was especially effective—she saved her ace trump for the end. Noticing that the people of River City took pride merely in seeing their kids in a marching band—and never mind how well or terribly they played—Stroman had the inspired notion of having the entire cast come out at show's end and play trombones. (Almost everyone: anvil salesman Charlie Cowell played the anvil.) No one in the forty-member cast was very good, but that was the fun of it. Certainly some improved over the 699-performance run.

Contact and *The Music Man* allowed Stroman to become the first director-choreographer to receive four Tony nominations in the same season: two for direction and two for choreography. When athletes are said to "beat themselves," that usually means that they made foolish errors that were beneath their abilities. Stroman's beating herself—with *Contact*'s choreography winning over *The Music Man*—was a very different kind. Barring the unlikely event of a tie, she was destined to beat herself. (The voters opted not to give her the directing trophy for either show; they bestowed the prize on Michael Blakemore for *Kiss Me, Kate.*)

At the Lucille Lortel Awards, where Stroman was named Best Director of a Production—play or musical—for *Contact,* she gave her gratitude to André Bishop. Said Stroman, "He told me, 'If you have an idea, I'll develop it,'" which, she said, "provided me with an escape every day." She then broke into tears as she remembered those last months of Mike Ockrent's life.

Hugh Jackman The highest compliment a movie star can pay Broadway occurs when he could make millions doing a movie and "settles" for hundreds of thousands doing a Broadway show. Hugh Jackman, then white-hot from appearing in the X-Men series as a superhero, was a superhero to Broadway, not only for delivering a galvanizing performance as Peter Allen in *The Boy from Oz,* but also for playing a gay man and not worrying about any possible consequences.

Christina Applegate The biggest cliché in show business is the star who breaks her leg, thus allowing the understudy to go on and become a bigger star. It almost happened when Christina Applegate injured herself while doing *Sweet Charity* out of town. The understudy took over, but the show closed in Boston—until Applegate wouldn't say die and, broken foot or no broken foot, returned to the show.

2000–2010

Sutton Foster in *Thoroughly Modern Millie* In the 1997 revival of *Annie,* she had four small roles: a dog catcher, a maid, a radio inger, and a Star-to-Be. That last one turned out to be the most accurate, for in five years, Sutton Foster would play the title role in *Thoroughly Modern Millie* and thoroughly become a star.

Stephen Schwartz In 1976, Schwartz had three long-run musicals on Broadway: *Pippin, The Magic Show*, and *Godspell.* After three lops, he came up with *Wicked*–which will run longer than all six of those put together.

2000–2001

MVP: Lonny Price
A Class Act

He didn't quite do what MVP Anthony Newley did in 1962–1963, but he came close.

For while Lonny Price didn't co-write the songs of *A Class Act,* he matched Newley's 1963 *Stop the World* achievement of starring, directing, and co-writing a show's book.

Both music and lyrics came from Edward Kleban (c. 1939–1987). Although Kleban was certainly best known (solely known, really) as the Tony-winning lyricist of *A Chorus Line,* he spent most of his life writing both music and lyrics. While he worked on an inordinate number of other shows, he never saw another one of his musicals produced.

By the time Kleban died, Price had already had a busy theater career. Not long after he won a 1979–1980 Theatre World Award for his off-Broadway debut in *Class Enemy,* he was one of those young performers chosen by Harold Prince and Stephen Sondheim for their *Merrily We Roll Along.* Following that, Price performed on Broadway in three plays and one musical (*Rags*). He then portrayed the title role in two different versions of *The Apprenticeship of Duddy Kravitz,* but neither came to town. Nor did the musical in which portrayed Jimmy Durante.

"That's one reason why I started directing," Price says. "I saw people in charge making bad decisions and I was at their mercy. There's only so much you can take if the sets are stupid or the lights are wrong or you're opening before you're ready. I just didn't want to be a victim anymore."

Price admits, however, that he fell into direction. "I was performing in *The Immigrant* at the American Jewish Theatre when artistic director Stanley Brechner asked me to recommend directors for *The Education of H*Y*M*A*N K*A*P*L*A*N.* So I gave him a list, and he said, 'What about you?' I swear, I had never thought of it. An actor was all I wanted to be. But I thought, well, if I don't do a good job, I'll just be another actor who tried it, and maybe I'll have learned something."

One person impressed with *H*Y*M*A*N K*A*P*L*A*N* was Ira Weitzman, the musical-theater program director at Playwrights Horizons. So he sent Price a tape of Kleban's unpublished and unperformed songs. Price admits that although he admired the songs, he didn't have any idea what to do with them.

But in 1993, after he was introduced to Linda Kline, Kleban's longtime partner, she had him again listen to the songs and encouraged him to collaborate with her on a show that featured them. "Actually," says Price, "Ed left his songs to Avery Corman and Wendy Wasserstein for a period of five years—enough time, he thought, for them to create a show. But they didn't, so the songs reverted back to Linda."

Price and Kline immediately agreed that the show should have nothing to do with *A Chorus Line.* They both feared that the memory of that show would upstage the new one. Instead, they embarked on a musical about a fictitious songwriter named Harold who's having a nervous breakdown—partly because Kleban had written a song about a insecure man named Harold: "Harold is nice, so shy behind the glasses, you'd hardly know he was there," went the lyric.

But after doing readings at Musical Theatre Works, where Price was now artistic director, both Joe (*Cabaret*) Masteroff and Stephen Schwartz urged the pair to name the names. "They said no one cares about a fictitious songwriter," says Price. "But they might care about the man who wrote the lyrics to *A Chorus Line.*"

Still, Price was reluctant to put such "characters" as Michael Bennett and Marvin Hamlisch on stage. Bennett was dead, but Hamlisch was alive and asked to see the material. Once he approved it, Price and Kline proceeded.

They structured the show as Kleban's memorial service, reiterating that he left his songs in his will to his friends, including former girlfriends Lucy and Sophie. Lucy was the one most based on Kline, while Sophie somewhat resembled Susan Stamberg, a National Public Radio reporter (as well as many other women Kleban knew).

"I was glad I was writing a musical that had a platonic love story, one that's somehow romantic yet not sexual," says Price. "I've had that experience with plenty of women—Daisy Prince, Robyn Goodman, and Erica Slezak among them. Close relationships of that nature have never been explored in theater, musical or otherwise."

That led to Sophie singing the show's most extraordinary song, "The Next Best Thing to Love," in which she pointed out that people who are very close friends have what is actually love, too. (For a while, *The Next Best Thing* was the title of the show. *Fridays at Four* and even the no-frills *The Kleban Project* were also considered.)

But *A Class Act* seemed right, too, because some of the musical concentrated on Kleban's experiences with a class: the BMI Musical Theatre Workshop, the foremost training ground for those who want to write for the theater, then helmed by former musical director Lehman Engel. So audiences saw the scene where Engel asked his students (as he did in real life) to write a song for Blanche DuBois of *A Streetcar Named Desire* fame. He also asked them not to use the title "The Kindness of Strangers," which caused a student to punch his notebook in frustration, for that was the title he'd already chosen and thought so clever.

And perhaps *A Class Act* was chosen for another reason. In the second act, there was a historically accurate scene in which Bennett told his cast that he was calling their new show *A Chorus Line* rather than just *Chorus Line*—because that would put it first in the *New York Times*' alphabetical listings. *A Class Act* would do the same.

The ups and downs of writing for Broadway were carefully detailed. At the end of the first act, Kleban comes to Toronto to work on the revival of *Irene* but is so headstrong that director John Gielgud fires him. As Kleban walks off in defeat, the orchestra plays a musical quotation—the vamp from *A Chorus Line*'s eleven-o'clocker, "One (Singular Sensation)." It came out soft and subtle, but it was there to indicate that better times were coming.

The second act opened with the cheerful "Better," a song that is optimistic but not in the same style of "I Got the Sun in the Morning (and the Moon at Night)." Instead, Kleban admitted, "I've been naughty, I've been nice. I've been naughty once or twice. Twice is better."

In actuality, "Better" was conceived as a pop song, but Price and Kline wisely turned it into a genuine production number, in which Kleban and his friends could celebrate the good fortune that had recently come their way. Kleban, in fact, had particularly good news: "Barbra Streisand is recording one of my songs!"

This actually happened. Streisand did record one of Kleban's songs. And the song, in fact, was "Better." The downside of the story was that after she'd recorded it, she decided not to release it.

Price and Kline succeeded where so many dozens of other writers of so-called jukebox musicals had failed, for they made the preexisting songs seem as if they had been specifically written for the script. Many an audience member might have assumed that Kleban was alive and well and writing songs for his life story.

Price had never intended to star in *A Class Act.* Peter Scolari was the chosen star, but he bolted shortly before rehearsals began. His replacement departed almost immediately after. Lynne Meadow, the artistic director of the Manhattan Theatre Club, where *A Class Act* would debut, suggested Price take over. Recalls Price, "After we'd bandied about a number of names that no one really liked, she said, 'Your direction may be great, but if you don't have the right guy in the show, you're going to have a big, big hole. She knew Ed very well and said I reminded her of him."

Price was superb, too, in playing a nebbishy neurotic. A lesser talent would have made the character speak too loudly and carry big shtick. But Price kept his characterization honest and made Edward Kleban a complicated and real person. Of course, he didn't have to argue with the director on how to interpret the character.

Comeback Player of the Year: Mel Brooks
The Producers

As Melvin Brooks, he wrote some sketches for Leonard Sillman's most successful revue: *New Faces of 1952.* But after that, Mel Brooks's books for *Shinbone Alley* in 1957 and *All-American* in 1962 respectively ran forty-nine and eighty-six performances.

In between the hit and the flops, Brooks had had great television success as one of the writers of *Your Show of Shows* on 139 episodes from 1950 through 1954. That series was New York based, but television was becoming more Hollywood-centric. Brooks had to move west.

That worked out well. Would you believe that Brooks created the TV series *Get Smart*? But his zany humor was just finding itself. His first-ever film, *The Producers,* won him the 1968 Oscar and Golden Globe for Best Original Screenplay.

However, Brooks originally had other plans for *The Producers.* "I originally conceived it as a play without music called *Springtime for Hitler;* then I went to my first choice of producers, Kermit Bloomgarden," Brooks says, referring to the esteemed producer who gave the world both dramatic classics (*Death of a Salesman, The Diary of Anne Frank*) and musical ones (*The Most Happy Fella, The Music Man*) — not to mention everyone's favorite cult flop, *Anyone Can Whistle.*

The plot, as down-and-out producer Max Bialystock told accountant Leo Bloom, was "Step One: We find the worst play ever written, a surefire flop. Step Two: I raise a million bucks. Lots of little old ladies out there. Step Three: You go back to work on the books, two of them—one for the government, one for us. You can do it, Bloom; you're a wizard! Step Four: We open on Broadway. And before you can say 'Step Five,' we close on Broadway! Step Six: We take our million bucks and fly to Rio!"

But neither Bloomgarden nor anyone else had been as enthusiastic about *Springtime for Hitler* as Brooks had hoped. "Every producer I approached said there were too many different scenes and sets," he recalls. "They kept asking, 'Can't you set the whole thing in one office?' No, I couldn't."

That it might be a film didn't occur to Brooks. "Sidney Glazier was the first one to say it was a movie," he recalls. "We got a bite at Universal. Lew Wasserman loved it but wanted me to make it *Springtime for Mussolini,* but I held out for Hitler. Finally, Joe Levine loved it and said he'd do it as-is. Ever since then, I've been on the fast track."

Not in the 1980s and 1990s, however. Brooks's Hollywood career wasn't going well, and so, like hundreds of others, he made the move east that would make him the toast of another world once he began work in earnest on a musical version of his still most famous and beloved property *The Producers.*

Brooks had Thomas Meehan co-write the book. The two came to know each other in 1973, when Meehan was one of five writers who penned a TV script for Brooks's wife Anne Bancroft (*Annie, the Women in the Life of a Man*). "Back then," Meehan says, "Mel said he'd like to work with me sometime, but it wasn't until after I wrote the book to *Annie* that he actually did call." They co-wrote the films *To Be or Not to Be* in 1983 and *Spaceballs* in 1987.

While the show would eventually carry the credit "Music and lyrics by Mel Brooks," he didn't originally plan to write the score. Brooks had asked Jerry Herman to do it. But Herman, who had been content to rest on his laurels for quite some time, not only declined, but also said that he believed Brooks could do it. After all, hadn't he written that marvelous "Springtime for Hitler" song? So Brooks took up the challenge.

Had Brooks and Meehan only inserted songs into the existing screenplay, *The Producers* might well have turned out just as splendidly. But they made a concerted effort to deepen the property. While the film's Leo was clearly an accountant with no particular goals, the musical's Leo harbored ambitions to be a producer before he even set foot in Max's office.

Max, however, wouldn't make it easy for him. Although Leo admired Max's wide-brimmed black hat, Max wouldn't allow him to wear this "producer's hat" until he felt Leo was truly worthy.

New complications arose after *Springtime for Hitler* became an unexpected hit. Leo flew off to Rio with secretary Ulla, leaving Max alone to face the unpleasant legal music. But Leo eventually returned, for Max had become both a father figure and friend to him. All was forgiven—even to the point where Max allowed Leo to wear a "producer's hat."

Smartest of all was the decision to expand "Springtime for Hitler." In the film, it was a single number that lasted less than three and a half minutes; in the musical, it led to others in what was nearly a nine-minute sequence.

"That was Susan's suggestion," says Brooks, referring to Susan Stroman, the choreographer Brooks had hired when he'd chosen her husband, Mike Ockrent, to direct. But after Ockrent died in 1999—and Stroman got four Tony nominations later that season for directing and choreographing *Contact* and *The Music Man*—Brooks allowed Stroman to stage the entire production.

Stroman says that Brooks was a good collaborator. "Don't forget, he's used to collaboration because he came from *Your Show of Shows,* where everyone sat around a table and pitched in. I did worry that because he'd spent his life making fun of women, as well as every other minority, that he might be difficult. But he treated me with the utmost respect because he was coming into the world of the theater, in which he knew I'd had success."

One of the first was dropping Lorenzo St. DuBois—"L.S.D."—as the actor who'd play Der Führer in *Springtime for Hitler.* With it went the song "Love Power"—most probably, however, because John Morris, not Mel Brooks, had originally written it. This would be an all-Brooks score.

In a manner of speaking, anyway. Brooks ran all his melodies by Glen Kelly, who merely got credit as "Music arranged by." We'll never know how many times, when Brooks was humming his melodies, Kelly said, "Well, Mel, how about this note instead?" before playing it and having Brooks say, "Yeah, yeah! Keep it in!" (Brooks has gone on record stating that Kelly wrote the "Unhappy" section of "I Want to Be a Producer," but little else.)

Another change involved the flop that we see Max Bialystock produce at the beginning of the show. While it became *Funny Boy*—a musical version of *Hamlet*—it was originally *Hey, Nebraska!* whose opening number audiences would see. "It was an obvious rip-off of *Oklahoma!*" Brooks now admits. Also dropped was a sequence where Leo went to Rio and, in a restaurant, felt so guilty that everyone he saw—the hat-check girl, the waitress—looked like Max to him.

One thing did not change from the original film. Once again, Brooks would make a vocal cameo during "Springtime for Hitler." As one of the actors mouthed, "Don't be stupid, be a smarty. Come and join the Nazi party," Brooks's voice, which had been dubbed into the film, was now—older and scratchier—played over the sound system.

On Tony night, many wondered if Brooks's show could eclipse the ten wins held by record holder *Hello, Dolly!*—whose score had been provided by the songwriter who had turned down *The Producers:* Jerry Herman.

Goodbye, *Dolly!*; *The Producers* nabbed twelve, including Best Book, Best Score, and Best Musical. More to the point, this would be the only time in Tony history that one and only one new musical won every prize. The only Tonys that *The Producers* didn't take home all went to a revival, *42nd Street.*

Said Brooks, "Movies, no matter how good they are, leave the theaters in a couple of weeks. With a hit musical, I can drop in and see a whole audience of people who love what I've done for a long time." Six years, in fact.

Reliever of the Year: Reba McEntire
Annie Get Your Gun

Geographically, who was born closer to where Annie Oakley was born: Broadway star Bernadette Peters, or country star Reba McEntire?

Has to be McEntire, right? After all, Oakley was this rustic southern girl and McEntire probably was, too, while Peters seems Manhattan all the way.

Not quite. True, Peters was born in Ozone Park, New York, only about a dozen miles away from the Broadway she'd conquer, and McEntire was born in McAlester, Oklahoma. But Oakley, you may be surprised to learn, was not born south of the Mason-Dixon Line, but in Darke County, Ohio, about halfway up the state near the Indiana border.

So Peters was born about 650 miles away from Oakley's birthplace; McEntire's hometown is about 850 miles away.

Of course, the legend of Oakley, and the way she's been portrayed—especially in *Annie Get Your Gun*—is country and rustic all the way. That's why McEntire seemed to be such a good fit as the most famous female sharpshooter. Lending her country twang to Irving Berlin's songs made for a delightful variation on a theme.

Audiences, especially her country fans, flocked to see her. No one much minded that she wasn't skilled in knowing how to develop a character, and one-note in compared to Peters's layered performance. Peters beautifully calibrated Annie's growth. She was a word-slurring hillbilly at the beginning but grew into an extraordinary young woman. Just as Annie was turning from illiterate to a real reader, Peters displayed the confidence of someone who knows she's becoming a better turned-out person. After three months' time had passed in the script, Peters convinced that she was genuinely three months smarter than she'd been in the previous scene. More and more, she became self-actualized.

But McEntire was fun and games, and she kept the revival alive longer than it would have lasted after Peters's departure. Those qualities qualify her as Reliever of the Year.

Rookie of the Year: David Yazbek
The Full Monty

Actually, Adam Guettel was first approached to do the score for the Broadway version of *The Full Monty,* the surprise film hit of 1997. Why anyone would think that the composer of the highly ambitious *Floyd Collins* would be right for this show is quite the mystery.

Guettel knew enough to turn it down but made a suggestion that turned out to be an inspired one: David Yazbek.

Who?

The two had played together in a band, which gave Guettel ample opportunity to hear Yazbek's music. Between songs, Guettel found himself enjoying Yazbek's quirky sense of humor, too.

Credit goes to bookwriter Terrence McNally, who could have felt that a Broadway novice was beneath him, a four-time Tony winner. But he let Yazbek's talent make the decision for him.

The film took place in Sheffield, England, a once-prosperous steel town. Now that the factory has closed, it's home to too many unemployed men. McNally, in order to make the story more relevant to American audiences, wisely reset it in Buffalo, where times have been just as tough. Six men are so unsuccessful in finding work that they're willing to dance naked in front of any townsperson willing to pay admission to see them.

The musical demonstrated from its first moments that it wouldn't be Broadway-by-the-book. Orchestrator Harold Wheeler created a swingin' big-band medley rather than an important-sounding overture. It was Yazbek's music, however, that guided him to that conclusion.

The first song, "Scrap," in which the unemployed husbands mourn their fate, sounded as if it were postmodern Jerry Bock, what with its angular and irregular lines. It contrasted nicely with the following song, "It's a Women's World," a raucous rave where these same men's wives celebrated their good fortune at having good jobs.

In "Man," Jerry, a divorced father who's terribly behind on child support, suggested the naked-performance scenario to his friend Dave, saying that men take action. To punctuate that, Yazbek included some of Elmer (*How Now, Dow Jones*) Bernstein's potent *The Magnificent Seven* theme. (Old-timers recognized it as the one-time Marlboro cigarette TV commercial.)

There was gallows humor in the suicide-drenched "Big Ass Rock"; ribald fun in "Big Black Man," about male endowments; and many laughs more in "Jeanette's Showbiz Number," sung by the men's seen-it-all boozy accompanist.

Yazbek showed, however, that he was also capable of writing a beautiful ballad. "You Walk with Me" took place after one would-be stripper, mama's boy Malcolm, feels devastated that his mother has died. Malcolm is secretly gay, although he's only begun to acknowledge that to himself, and to Ethan, one of the other would-be strippers. At the cemetery, Malcolm sang a song that was a genuine hymn, and a most beautiful one at that.

The song by itself didn't move the action forward as good show songs should, but forward motion arrived midway, when Malcolm faltered and Ethan picked up the song. Once they sang together, the audience knew that they would succeed as a couple. The song was successful independent of gender, for its message was one of love: "Are you alone there in the valley? No, not alone—for you walk with me. Never alone, for you walk with me."

In a score that mostly made the audience laugh, here was a song that made it cry. Not bad for a rank Broadway rookie.

2001–2002

MVP: Dick Scanlan
Thoroughly Modern Millie

He contracted AIDS in the late 1980s, when such a fate usually meant a death sentence. But in an article for *The Advocate* in 2002, Dick Scanlan said, "It is absolutely true that your outlook adds to your longevity. I chose to keep investing in my future—even when I had no future."

In the early 1990s, Scanlan did take solace in a rented summer house in Southampton, where friends would visit. Alas, Scanlan wasn't enough of a host to have more than two videos on hand. It was either *Caligula* or *Thoroughly Modern Millie,* and more often than not, his friends chose *Millie* (which speaks well of them).

Repeated viewings made Scanlan more and more impressed with the property. While *Millie* was not a highly regarded film, Scanlan saw stage-musical possibilities. The native of Bethesda, Maryland, understood the goals of Millie Dillmount and Miss Dorothy Brown in coming to the Big City in hopes that every dream will come true.

For Scanlan, each one would.

It wasn't easy. When Scanlan first summoned the nerve to track down original screenwriter Richard Morris, he found that the man didn't even want to talk with him, let alone collaborate.

Scanlan, however, wouldn't give up and kept calling. Morris had written *The Unsinkable Molly Brown,* so there's good possibility that he was impressed by Scanlan's Molly-like "I-ain't-down-yet" indomitability. Eventually, Morris agreed to see Scanlan, and the meeting went so well that he agreed to collaborate on a new book. Unfortunately, Morris died on April 28, 1996, but Scanlan wouldn't abandon the project.

He interested Michael Mayer, the eventual director, and in 1997, both of them approached Jeanine Tesori to coordinate the music. Later they'd ask her to write a little. Later still they asked her to write substantially more. The dozen songs she composed had lyrics by Scanlan.

Without him, there'd be no *Thoroughly Modern Millie*—and high school drama teachers would now have a much harder time choosing their spring musical. After all, a show that has three fat parts for girls—Millie, Miss Dorothy, and Mrs. Meers, the harpy intent on enslaving them—is going to be a high school favorite now and forever.

Rookies of the Year: Greg Kotis and Mark Hollmann
Urinetown

May 2001. It's the opening-night party of an off-Broadway show. The theater's artistic director gets up to make the usual thank-you speech. Then he goes on to say that his job isn't an easy one, because he's sent so many unsolicited scripts that turn out to be terrible.

"Like this one," he says, squeezing the script between a thumb and forefinger, as if he were holding a skunk by the tail. Then, as he lets loose his fingers so that the script can drop into a trash can he's carefully situated next to him, he gives the name of the show: "*Urinetown.*"

Some of the party attendees jeer; others moan as if to say, "What's happened to musical theater?" And true, getting past that title isn't easy. It's even worse than *Home Sweet Homer,* the musical version of *The Odyssey* (!) that lasted a day in 1976.

Composer Mark Hollmann and bookwriter Greg Kotis—who both collaborated on the lyrics—did want to find another name. The best they could ever come up with, however, was *You're in Town.* Ultimately they felt that that title would be unfair to the public, who wouldn't be able to infer from *You're in Town* what was really on the authors' minds: a musical about "A Gotham-like city sometime after the Stink Years" when people must pay to urinate.

The tyrant Caldwell B. Cladwell (a pun that suggested clothes do make the man) runs the Urine Good Company. His dictate is that citizens will be imprisoned (or worse) if they don't use his pay toilets. These johns are well enforced by Officers Lockstock and Barrel—some nice wordplay there—and Cladwell's vigilant employee Penelope Pennywise, who insists, "It's a privilege to pee," and "If you got to go, you got to go through me," which offers even better wordplay.

The situation rankles Bobby Strong, who will fight Cladwell to the death. Unfortunately, Strong has strong romantic leanings, too, and the object of his affection is Cladwell's daughter Hope. Their first love song, "Follow Your

Heart," has an inspirational title, but its three-quarter waltz tempo is more careful than swirling. In fact, Bobby is killed before the final curtain—to our surprise and Hope's agony.

Does it sound as if there's a little *Romeo and Juliet* in the story? The authors in essence admitted their plot was not new when they had Lockstock sing, "In the end, it's nothing you don't know."

But it was. Kotis admits that he got the idea when he was on a trip to Europe and only ran into pay toilets. What would happen if the entire world were like that—even down to the bathrooms in your own home? Of course, someone would get rich from the pay-toilet franchise, but what about the people who couldn't afford to pay?

We've all been in situations where we've desperately needed to find a bathroom and have run the risk of embarrassing ourselves. However, none of us thought to write a musical about it.

Urinetown won over jaded theatergoers right from the start. A police officer brought a doleful-looking man onstage. Where was he escorting him? To the piano, in fact; the "criminal" was the show's musical director, and already theatergoers were chuckling.

The overture began, and many knew from its first five dissonant notes that Kurt Weill's music, *à la* his *The Threepenny Opera,* was being homaged. But Weill and early collaborator Bertolt Brecht even in their most radical moments wouldn't have dared to write a show in which urination was a central issue.

There would be many minor-key Weill mockups in Hollman's music, as well as a march and a couple of gospel numbers. But who expected a Hungarian czardas to show up in a Broadway musical? The number where Cladwell's victims celebrated him has to be the first time the Stockholm syndrome had ever been put into song. The score sounded as if it had been written by a postmodern Tom Jones and Harvey Schmidt.

The musical started its life in 1999 on Stanton Street, a spot that most New Yorkers wouldn't be able to find. It was then an entry into the 1999 New York International Fringe Festival. Finally, *Urinetown* set an opening date of Tuesday, September 11, 2001, at Henry Miller's Theatre. We all know why that didn't happen. After its rescheduled opening on September 20, it ran 965 performances. That's an astonishingly good number for a show with that title.

Ever since the success of *Urinetown*—Tonys for book, score, and John Rando's direction—the show has become the poster child for the musical that goes from long-shot to long run. Many a theatrical hopeful says, "I'm writing (or doing) a show that's part of a summer festival—you know, like where *Urinetown* started."

There's a sad irony to what happened while *Urinetown* was running. Real-estate moguls (who might have something in common with Cladwell) forced the show out of Henry Miller's Theater in order to build a skyscraper. Moving to another theater would incur too many additional expenses (thanks to unions).

But *Urinetown* was hardly forgotten. Regional and foreign productions abounded. (In Berlin, it was called *Pinkelstadt.*)

Then it turned out to be a surprisingly frequent choice of high school drama directors. Many ambitious shows are said to have piss and vinegar, but *Urinetown* has the most right to the claim. It was a privilege to see.

Reliever of the Year: Sutton Foster
Thoroughly Modern Millie

Clichés become clichés because they're usually true. Take the famous show-biz story of a star who becomes incapacitated, allowing her understudy to save the day. It can happen. It does.

It certainly did during rehearsals of *Thoroughly Modern Millie* at the La Jolla Playhouse in October 2000. Newcomer Erin Dilly had been signed to play Millie Dillmount, the young miss who comes to the big city to follow her heart and dreams.

To be sure, Dilly had big shoes and costumes to fill, for Julie Andrews had played the part in the 1967 movie musical. If Dilly could pull it off, it would be a sparkling Broadway debut.

But during rehearsals, Dilly fell ill. Her understudy, Sutton Foster, stepped into rehearsals just so that the cast could continue working.

Foster had had some Broadway experience. She'd been a replacement in *Les Misérables* and the 1994 revival of *Grease.* Although she'd been picked as "Star-to-Be" in the 1997 revival of *Annie,* by now Foster had to believe that that might not be her destiny. In fact, she was back in the chorus for her next show, *The Scarlet Pimpernel.*

And after that closed, Foster had few options, so when she was offered the chance to understudy Dilly in Millie, she accepted it.

As rehearsals progressed, management and creators became more and more impressed with what their substitute was doing. By the time of the first scheduled official run-through in a University of Southern California–San Diego lecture hall, Dilly still wasn't well enough to perform. And while Foster was still on book for the dialogue scenes, she was fully prepared to do the songs and dances.

"But even in those books scenes," says Joshua Ellis, the La Jolla press agent at the time, "Foster gave Millie a wide-eyed innocence that expressed a surprise that it all could be happening to her."

What Foster brought to the show convinced the creators that Sutton Foster would have to be their new leading lady. Lyricist Dick Scanlan and composer Jeanine Tesori were so inspired that they were moved to write "Gimme, Gimme" an eleven-o'clock number to show case Foster's abilities. The former understudy came through there, too.

The song was one of the most important building blocks in the musical, for it gave Foster another showstopping moment—and just might have given her the ammunition that won her the Best Actress in a Musical Tony Award.

Dilly, by the way, wasn't the first choice of management: Kristen Chenoweth was. She did the workshop but opted not to continue with the show once she was offered her own sitcom. *Kristin* lasted eleven episodes.

Given that Chenoweth, a Best Featured Actress Tony winner for *You're a Good Man, Charlie Brown* has yet to secure a Best Actress Tony in three more tries, one must wonder if she views *Millie* as a missed opportunity. On the other hand, eleven episodes of a sitcom named after you is a nice compliment and it means a good deal of money in the bank.

2002–2003

MVP and Manager of the Year: Margo Lion
Hairspray

She'd experienced many a good morning while growing up in Baltimore. That could be one reason why Margo Lion responded so enthusiastically to the 1988 film *Hairspray,* made by fellow Baltimorean John Waters.

The elegant-looking, beautifully coiffed Lion was born into money and inherited her parents' fortune in the way no child wants to: her mother and father were killed in a plane crash. Waters was a step below—from a solid upper-middle-class background.

One would never know it from his work. He began his film career in 1969 by writing and directing a $2,100 film that he named *Mondo Trasho.* Then came *Pink Flamingos,* in which a three-hundred-pound transvestite named Divine concluded the film by eating freshly made dog feces that had just been deposited on the street. (Talk about cleaning up after your dog!)

Lion, meanwhile, became a producer of prestige projects: *Angels in America, The Secret Garden,* and August Wilson's *Seven Guitars* on Broadway; plays by Terrence McNally and David Mamet off-Broadway, as well as *Garden of Earthly Delights,* an avant-garde dance piece by her cousin, the well-regarded choreographer Martha Clarke.

Waters had, however, become a bit more mainstream over the years. In 1988, his film called *Hairspray* still starred Divine in a female role of Edna Turnblad, a 1962 Baltimore hausfrau. But the story centered on her chubby teenage daughter Tracy. The lass believed that blacks should have the opportunity to dance and be seen on *The Corny Collins Show*—a fictitious version of a local *American Bandstand*—not just on "Negro Day" but on each day of the week.

Lion had recently dealt with the African-American experience, too, and not just through Wilson's play. She had spearheaded the 1992 musical *Jelly's Last Jam,* about Creole jazz pioneer Jelly Roll Morton and his inherent prejudice against his own people. Perhaps Waters and Lion did have more in common than one might assume.

Jelly's Last Jam was an expensive proposition for Lion. She worked on it for eleven tortuous income-impaired years. Producers are supposed to raise money, not invest their own, but Lion took a home-equity loan on her apartment and put a Matisse up as collateral to help get the show on. She took a wild chance on an off-Broadway writer-director named George C. Wolfe, who delivered the artistic goods. *Jelly's Last Jam* opened in 1992, got many good reviews, and ran 569 performances—but not nearly long enough to pay back its $5 million investment.

In 1997, *Triumph of Love,* with which she became emotionally as well as financially involved, failed quickly. That hurt, because it had been so well received at her hometown's regional theater, Center Stage. "I really thought about leaving the business," Lion says.

And yet she also thought about a musical version of the 1995 film *Clueless.* "But Scott Rudin said I'd never get the rights to it," she recalls. "He suggested that I should do *Hairspray* instead. Actually, Scott held the rights to it and wanted to use Marc Shaiman, but it didn't happen."

Not then, anyway. Although Lion had seen the film of *Hairspray* and had been underwhelmed by it, she watched it again. "And this time, it clicked," she said.

So did the musical version. Although Lion had to raise twice as much money as she did for *Jelly's Last Jam,* she did it—and wound up with the seventeenth-longest-running musical in Broadway history. Most surprisingly of all, she delivered a Broadway musical that even counter-culturalist John Waters liked.

Comeback Player of the Year: Harvey Fierstein
Hairspray

It was one of theater's best rags-to-riches stories. Harvey Fierstein—a gay, overweight, croak-voiced transvestite who was not attractive by conventional standards—didn't have to wallow off-off-Broadway paying for his own readings and productions. He made the highly unexpected leap to Broadway with his ambitious *Torch Song Trilogy,* which he wrote and in which he starred.

That the lengthy gay play ran was remarkable enough, but that it was the longest-running non-musical in a decade was even more remarkable. And who would have bet on Tony night that Fierstein the he'd win prizes for Best Actor in a Play, let alone Best Play?

He'd get another Tony his next time out—for the book of *La Cage aux Folles.* After it opened on August 21, 1983, Fierstein would have, for the next twenty-one months, two gay-themed shows on Broadway.

In a way, there's no surprise that Fierstein's subsequent Broadway play didn't do well; statistics show that the average Tony-winning playwright's subsequent offering runs only a fourth as long. Fierstein, however, would have certainly settled for that, for it would have meant that *Safe Sex* ran nine months. Instead, it ran nine performances.

So Fierstein tried another musical. *Legs Diamond.* The show in which Peter Allen didn't just need to star but had to write the music and lyrics, too, was one of the most reviled shows of the postwar era. Whenever a show has more previews (seventy-two) than performances (sixty-four), something's wrong. The Nederlanders, who owned the Mark Hellinger Theatre, where it played, were so discouraged by it that they sold the theater.

Fierstein took off the entire 1990s from Broadway and did some minor film work. But when *Hairspray* needed an actor to play Edna Turnblad—an overweight, croak-voiced transvestite who was not attractive by conventional standards—there was no other person to whom any casting director would go.

So Fierstein became, like Tommy Tune, the only person to win Tonys in four separate categories: two for acting in both a play and a musical and two for writing both a play and a musical.

Rookie of the Year: Marissa Jaret Winokur
Hairspray

In *Follies,* Carlotta Campion sings about the life of an actress:

"Top billing Monday; Tuesday, you're touring in stock."

Yes, but it works the other way around, too. As 2002 began, Marissa Jaret Winokur's big claim to fame was for appearing in the Oscar-winning *American Beauty.* That doesn't seem to be so bad a credit on the face of it, but she was hardly the star. Her character was known as "Mr. Smiley's Counter Girl," a lass who worked the drive-through window at a fast-food establishment. She'd been noticed for having said, "Whoa! You are so busted!" to a wife who'd been discovered cheating on her husband.

Not much to brag about. But *Hairspray* needed a fresh face on a heavy-set girl, and the available Winokur could offer that—as well as a solid voice to handle Marc Shaiman's 1960s pop-rock score. Almost every Broadway season has a "new girl" who's highly championed, but rarely if ever has she been hefty and with a face that traditionally wouldn't have launched a thousand ships.

Never mind that Winokur was pushing thirty when asked to portray the sixteen-year-old Tracy Turnblad. She was superb. You don't beat someone playing Rose in *Gypsy*—Bernadette Peters—if you aren't.

And when Winokur was doing her one *American Beauty* scene in1999, would she have ever believed that four years later, she'd be winning a Tony while her director on that project—the Oscar-winning Sam Mendes—wouldn't even be nominated for one (for *Gypsy*)? As Comden and Green wrote in *Fade Out—Fade In,* "Democracy and fame can come to all girls."

2003–2004

MVP: Hugh Jackman
The Boy from Oz

The Boy from Oz opened to mediocre reviews but did manage to run 364 performances.

Hugh Jackman starred in every one of them. In an era where so many performers call in sick for little more than a paper cut, Jackman didn't disappoint the audiences who were first and foremost coming to see him and only secondarily interested in this bio-musical of songwriter-entertainer Peter Allen (1944–1992).

Jackman also gets credit for not being afraid to portray a gay man. He let another man kiss him directly on the mouth and didn't shy away for any of the many long seconds. Many an actor, even in the twenty-first century, is still fearful that if he plays a gay man and gives a quite public display of affection, he could easily be typecast as gay. This is true even of gay actors. But Jackman, who leads a heterosexual life, wasn't afraid. When you've got the talent and looks, you can do that.

Two standbys—Michael Halling and Kevin Spirtas—had been hired for Jackman. But when the time came for the star's well-earned vacations—February 1–6 and March 28–April 2, 2004—management didn't bother to choose which of those men would replace him. And while the producers could have opted to put in a celebrity for the times Jackman would be away—as the *What Makes Sammy Run?* management did with Paul Anka when Steve Lawrence wanted a break—the producers simply closed the show for those weeks. When the management does that for you, you know you're a Most Valuable Player.

Jackman would cavort with the audience and would especially bond with an arbitrary woman in the front row, calling her by name and returning to her a few scenes later. Each one of those might well remember him and the show for as long as she lives.

It wasn't the only way that Jackman was "loving and giving," as one of his lyrics went. He was equally attentive after each performance. He was one of the best at signing autographs at the stage door, talking to the fans who requested them, and showing that he was in no hurry to get away. That made him Broadway's newest goodwill ambassador, too.

The rest of Broadway agreed. It asked Jackman to host that year's Tony Awards—for the second year in a row. (A year earlier, Jackman had been, at thirty-four, the youngest-ever male solo host for the show.)

When time came for the Best Actor in a Musical Tony, Jackman sauntered off into the wings and waited to hear the results that most Tony observers felt was a foregone conclusion. As a result, when his name was announced, he didn't have much of a walk to the stage. What he did have, however, was a long wait before he could speak. Not only did Jackman get thirty-eight seconds' of applause, he also got a standing ovation, which doesn't often happen to an awardee unless he's getting a lifetime-achievement prize.

In his acceptance speech, Jackman said that he had seen *The Boy from Oz* five years earlier in his native Australia: "I thought it was the best role I've seen for a guy in a long time." He also said he was proud that *The Boy from Oz* was "the first Australian musical to make it to Broadway." It wouldn't have made it here without him.

Every winner gets thirty seconds to speak before the orchestra conductor taps his baton and instructs his band to play; it's Tony's subtle way of telling the winner, "Get the hell off. You've had your thirty seconds of fame." But not even a piccolo dared to peep during Jackman's two-minute-and-forty-seven-second-long speech. That orchestra knew a Most Valuable Player when it saw one, too.

Rookies of the Year: Robert Lopez, Jeff Marx, and Jeff Whitty

Avenue Q

At the beginning of 2003, precious few in the Broadway community had heard of Robert Lopez, Jeff Marx, and Jeff Whitty.

That certainly wasn't the case by the end of 2004.

But long before 2003, those in the Lehman Engel BMI Musical Theatre Workshop had heard of Lopez and Marx—and wanted to hear more of them. That class full of budding composers and lyricists soon learned to look forward to the times when Lopez and Marx would raise their hands and say, "Yeah, we have a new song that we'd like you to hear."

Some of them belonged to *Kermit, Prince of Denmark,* in which the famous frog substituted for *Hamlet.* That allowed for such songs as "There's More Than One Pig in the Sea." When they tried to sell the project to the Jim Henson Company, they were rejected. So dreams of writing for Kermit, Miss Piggy, and all the rest gave way to creating their own personae for puppets.

Unlike most everyone else in the class, they weren't necessarily out to write a Broadway musical, but a series that they could sell to TV. It would take its inspiration from *Sesame Street,* with which they'd grown up, and make it grow up, too. Instead of children's concerns, their series would follow the anxieties of recent college graduates who were trying to find their footing in the world.

And while the approach would be as sunny and optimistic in style of the famed PBS series, the subject matter would be markedly different—say, the ramifications of ignoring a jury-duty summons. If that question wasn't pointed enough, Marx and Lopez wrote a song in which characters wondered about the size of their neighbors' incomes.

They invented Princeton, who, soon after he's graduated, meets Kate when he moves to Avenue Q. (Hey, there's a title!) Romance might very well bloom, although it would be a harder road for Paul and Nicky, who'd be patterned after the famous Bert and Ernie from the series. Whether or not they'd admit to being homosexual would be part of the plot.

And just as Sesame Street had an occasional genuine human being, so, too, would *Avenue Q:* For their engaged couple, they chose the names Christmas Eve (that's a woman) and Brian.

Luckily, Marx had once worked as an intern at *Sesame Street,* and through an employee's recommendation, he met puppeteer Rick Lyon. He asked him to sing one of the project's songs at BMI. After Rick and his puppet had performed, the class kept saying that they really enjoyed watching both puppet and master, so the creators inadvertently found the look of their show.

This was audacious. *Avenue Q* would dare to challenge the time-honored *bunraku* policy of masking the puppeteers in black to create the illusion that only puppets were on stage. This new approach would allow audiences to shift their eyes from the puppets to the actors whenever they wanted. Why mask actors in black? There was nothing to mourn in this show.

Lyon then invited his puppeteer pals John Tartaglia, Stephanie D'Abruzzo, and Jennifer Barnhart to join in. And while the clever book, tuneful music, deft lyrics, and smart staging would all be admired, *Avenue Q* would get a big boost from having puppeteers who'd worked together in harmony for more than a decade.

When a reading of *Avenue Q: Children's Television for Twentysomethings* yielded more theatrical than television interest, *Avenue Q* was on its way to becoming a Broadway musical. But Marc and Lopez wisely knew that they'd be so busy writing songs that they could well use a bookwriter. An agent's recommendation got them Jeff Whitty, who took their characters and forged more of a plot. Now Princeton's main goal would be to find his purpose in life. Whitty also changed Paul's name to Rod and shamelessly took the name of former TV star Gary Coleman, now down on his luck, and made him the super of one of Avenue Q's less inviting tenements.

Marx and Lopez's agent also represented director Jason Moore, and soon he was on board. Momentum steadily picked up, and the adventurous Douglas Aibel at the Vineyard Theatre thought it right for his theater. Within months, *Avenue Q* was a Broadway show, and would be for six years. Even then, it didn't close, but moved to cozier confines off-Broadway.

And why not? Lopez and Marx's score was mostly upbeat and catchy—and audacious. Their "Everyone's a Little Bit Racist" got laughs of recognition from the crowd. They could be tender when that feeling was called for ("Fantasies Come True"), but soon they were writing a deranged waltz for Rod, who wanted everyone to know about "My Girlfriend Who Lives in Canada." (Oh, no, she didn't; in fact, she didn't exist.)

There was rock ("Purpose"), soul ("You Can Be as Loud as the Hell You Want") and a fine, fine melody line in "There's a Fine, Fine Line"—Kate's song of disappointment in Princeton. All of the characters had been out of school only a few years, and yet they were already saying what so many much older people have said so often: "I Wish I Could Go Back to College." Lest it seem as if these characters could wallow in self-pity, they had a perky melody to go along with their credo, "It Sucks to be Me." Meanwhile, Whitty's book made audiences truly care about the puppets.

The lyrics were often monosyllabically simple, but they had to be for a "kid's show" spoof. At the same time, these co-lyricists were wildly funny, as was shown by a reference to a Hoover vacuum cleaner that was hardly a product placement paid for by that company. Their talent could be described by quoting one of their own creations, Lucy the Slut, when she referred to breasts: "Yeah—they're real."

Best of all was "Mix Tape," in which Kate inferred that Princeton liked her from the titles of the songs he'd selected to record on a tape for her. And while the songs did start out romantically—"Kiss the Girl," "Ma Cherie

Amour"—they soon seemed less promising to Kate when she learned that "I Am a Walrus" and "Yellow Submarine" were included, as well.

Finally, *Avenue Q* made Tartaglia and D'Abruzzo members of the theater community. Both have revisited Broadway and off-Broadway a number of times. The show changed their lives, as was shown when D'Abruzzo accepted her Theatre World Award as one of the season's outstanding debuts: "This is the first award I've received since I was named Burger King Employee of the Month."

Comeback Player of the Year: Stephen Schwartz
Wicked

While Stephen Schwartz brought a new pop-rock sound to Broadway, he admits that in one sense, he was highly influenced by both *Bells Are Ringing* and *Funny Girl.*

Not that those shows had anything to do with his creating *Pippin, Pippin* (as it was then called) at Carnegie Mellon in 1967, when he co-wrote the music and lyrics with fellow student Ron Strauss. But when the time came to put his name on it, Schwartz chose the pseudonym Lawrence Stephens instead of using his real name.

"It wasn't that I was trying to hide that I was Jewish," he insists. "It was that Schwartz is the punch line in many Jewish jokes. *Funny Girl* uses Private Schwartz from Rockaway to get a laugh. *Bells Are Ringing* has Judy Holliday mention Ethel Schwartz in 'Drop That Name.' Besides, I thought Schwartz was too common a name, and I still think I should have kept Lawrence Stephens or even Stephen Sanford, another name that I was considering. But then I changed it back to Stephen Schwartz, and after a while, it got too late to change it."

That's because Schwartz had an immediate success after he was graduated in 1969 and came to New York. His agent Shirley Bernstein (Leonard's sister) told him that a new comedy called *Butterflies Are Free* needed a song for its hero to sing, and if he cared to write one, she'd submit it. Schwartz did just that, never dreaming he'd be the winner. But he was. His lovely little song "Butterflies Are Free" not only appeared in all 1,128 Broadway performances, but also in the 1972 film version.

The credit was well noted when Bernstein had Schwartz audition *Pippin, Pippin* for producers Edgar Lansbury and Joseph Beruh. Although they chose not to produce that show, they did think that Schwartz would be right for another project. Their show, *Godspell,* was an off-Broadway smash in 1971 and moved to Broadway in 1976.

Pippin, which debuted on Broadway in 1972, was another smash. Ditto *The Magic Show* in 1974. For almost one solid year—June 17, 1976, to June 12, 1977—Stephen Schwartz had three shows on Broadway. He could have had a fourth, too, had David Merrick brought in *The Baker's Wife* instead of closing it in Washington after an anguished six-month cross-country tryout.

That was the beginning of a bad time. *Working,* a project that Schwartz originated and directed—and for which he provided five of its fifteen songs—didn't work out. It lasted twenty-four performances. And then the man who once had three musicals currently running on Broadway would reappear there only fleetingly for the next quarter century.

Rags, for which he wrote lyrics to Charles Strouse's (best) music, was a four-performance flop in 1986. *Fosse* used two of his songs. But that was it for a twenty-five-year span.

Not that Schwartz went hungry; he went Hollywood. He started working with Alan Menken and wrote lyrics to *Pocahontas* in 1995, later winning two Oscars (one for the song "Colors of the Wind"). The following year, the team did *The Hunchback of Notre Dame,* which got each of them an Oscar nomination. In 1999, Schwartz then wrote the entire score to *The Prince of Egypt,* got two Oscar nominations, and won for the song "When You Believe."

Around this time, Schwartz heard about Gregory Maguire's novel *Wicked,* which retells *The Wizard of Oz* from the so-called Wicked Witch's point of view. It essentially asked, "If you had a green face and everyone made fun of you while you were growing up, wouldn't you turn out anti-social?" And while we're asking questions: Is Glinda really as lovely as she seems? Doesn't everyone have a dark side?

"I love when a writer takes a new look at a story we all know and sees something entirely different in it," says Schwartz.

He would take a chance on Winnie Holzman, whose theatrical experience was limited to writing the lyrics of one song in *A... My Name Is Alice.* But Holzman had done reasonably well in Hollywood, too, albeit on the small screen. She'd created and written for the hit series *My So-Called Life* and wrote many episodes of *Once and Again.* Schwartz's confidence in Holzman was not misplaced; she brilliantly distilled 406 pages into a workable length.

Schwartz also credits Holzman for spurring his writing of one of the musical's most important songs. During one of their work sessions, she happened to use the expression "for good," meaning "once and for all." Schwartz seized on the idea that the expression of course has another meaning: "for the better." So, when previous enemies Glinda and "Wicked" witch Elphaba realize the worth of their friendship, each establishes that she's been changed "For Good."

Glinda (Kristin Chenoweth) had a bouncy first-act number, "Popular." Elphaba (Idina Menzel) got a dynamic first-act closer, "Defying Gravity," which became so entrenched in Broadway's consciousness that even the creators of *Shrek* had their evil Lord Farquaad sing that no one "is ever gonna bring me down."

As of this writing, no original Broadway original cast album of the new millennium has surpassed *Wicked* in sales. And while Schwartz, Holzman, and *Wicked* itself didn't win Tonys—as all succumbed to *Avenue Q*—certainly *Wicked* has become the far more popular show, seen by millions more (and making substantially more millions, too).

Manager of the Year: Robyn Goodman
Avenue Q

Robyn Goodman started out as an actor and was part of the original cast of *When You Comin' Back, Red Ryder, Red Ryder* in 1973. Appearances at Lincoln Center, Playwrights Horizons, and the Public Theatre followed.

But as early as 1976, Goodman showed an interest in producing. While in London that year, she gave a number of American plays their American premieres.

Then in 1980, Goodman co-founded Second Stage with Carole Rothman. The mission was to take plays that had been less than successful the first time around and give them a second chance.

Although the theater had four different homes in the next dozen years, Goodman and Rothman had great success with revivals and added some new plays, too.

Then, after thirteen years, Goodman decided to become supervising producer of the TV soap opera *One Life to Live*. That lasted four years, during which time Goodman's goal was to become an independent commercial theatrical producer.

She was one of the first to see the potential of *Avenue Q* when it played the Vineyard Theatre. Many felt the show had no chance—"Puppets on Broadway?"—and predicted an early demise. They were wrong.

As of early 2011, every one of Goodman's five off-Broadway productions has received at least a Lucille Lortel nomination for Best Play or Musical. *Bat Boy* won in 2001, although *Altar Boyz,* with 2,032 performances, turned out to be the most successful.

On Broadway, four of Goodman's five subsequent productions have been given a Best Musical or a Best Musical Revival Tony Nomination. She's won twice, for *Avenue Q* in 2004 and *In the Heights* in 2008.

When that former show's victory was announced, Goodman, along with dozens of others connected with *Avenue Q,* bounded onto the stage of Radio City Music Hall. Although she was the second-billed producer behind Kevin McCollum, he insisted that she be the one to make the acceptance speech. "I guess it doesn't suck to be us," she said, paraphrasing an important *Avenue Q* song. No one disagreed.

2004–2005

MVP, Comeback Player and Rookie of the Year: Christina Applegate
Sweet Charity

Walter Willison recalls that when he was directing a California production of *The Grass Harp,* a local reporter came to interview the cast. The musical has a number of children in it, and the reporter asked one six-year-old, "Do you want to be an actress when you grow up?" The child calmly replied, "I'm already an actress."

The child was Christina Applegate, who would become a well-known actress nine years later, in 1987, when she started a ten-year run in as the not-so-bright bleached-blonde teen Kelly Bundy in the sitcom *Married... With Children.* Unlike so many young performers, however, Applegate did not just fade away. In 1998, she became the title character in *Jesse,* which ran three seasons. Many feature motion pictures, TV movies, and appearances came along, too.

What audiences probably didn't know was that Applegate had been a big Bob Fosse fan since her youth. So when she heard that Barry and Fran Weissler were planning a Broadway revival of his *Sweet Charity,* she made it known that she'd be interested. An actress who'd made her feature film debut in *Jaws of Satan*—and had appeared in *Mars Attacks!* and *Jane Austen's Mafia!*—could use the prestige of a Broadway musical.

Applegate was aware that the Weisslers, in planning their *Sweet Charity,* had already contacted Jenna Elfman (who didn't do well by a workshop), Jane Krakowski (who thought that Charity was too stupid), and Marisa Tomei (who wasn't very interested). Applegate wasn't proud. She'd assume the role of "The Girl Who Wanted to Be Loved," per Neil Simon's book, Dorothy Fields's lyrics, and Cy Coleman's music. She even turned down the chance—and the money—to star in the film *Charlie and the Chocolate Factory* to do it.

Charity is not an easy role to do night after night, as Helen Gallagher told us earlier. The dance-hall hostess has five songs of her own and participates in three others. She also must dance in six. During the original 1966 run, Gwen Verdon dropped her opening number "You Should See Yourself" from time to time, and "Where Am I Going?" now and again. In the 1986 revival, Debbie Allen chose not to do the four-plus minutes of "Charity's Soliloquy." But the thirty-three-year-old Applegate was determined to do them all.

Actually, thirty-three was a little young for the role. One aspect of Charity's character is that time has already ticked off many opportunities that she might have had in terms of both jobs and men. Gwen Verdon looked the part when she created it at age forty-one; Applegate appeared as if she still had a few more chances at a better career and a good relationship.

On the other hand, Applegate may have looked a little older by the time she reached Broadway, for few things age a person faster than trying out a musical. And Applegate would endure one of the most trying tryouts in Broadway history.

One wouldn't expect that from a frozen show. But Applegate didn't expect to break her foot on March 11 during the second leg of the tryout (after Minneapolis and before Boston) at a Chicago performance. In what would be a harbinger of her resiliency, she continued singing and dancing for twenty minutes before the pain demanded that her understudy Dylis Croman take over.

That seemed to be the end of the $7.5 million production. For the Weisslers, it was a most uncomfortable déjà vu; nearly ten years earlier, their production of *Busker Alley* had closed in Tampa when its star Tommy Tune broke his foot.

The Weisslers were determined not to have this unfortunate history repeat itself and asked Charlotte D'Amboise, currently portraying Roxie Hart in their long-running *Chicago,* to take over. D'Amboise had already been told some months earlier that when Applegate left the production, she'd be their first choice to take over. Now she was getting that chance much earlier than expected.

D'Amboise learned the part in time for the Boston opening on March 22. She wound up getting a better review from the *Boston Globe* than the show itself did. But a not-so-funny thing happened at the Broadway box office. Once Applegate withdrew, the advance sales suddenly lost their momentum and many who'd bought tickets asked for refunds. The Weisslers decided only three days later to add their *Sweet Charity* to the list of the dozens of shows that had closed in Boston. Sunday, March 27, would be the final performance.

Applegate wouldn't have it. In the middle of her physical therapy and Pilates, she started making phone calls to get the money that would keep the show alive. Doctors had told her that returning in a month's time was not impossible, even likely. Perhaps if the tryout continued with D'Amboise—and if her replacement could be enticed to do a few Broadway previews until she was enough healed—the show could go on.

On Tuesday, March 29, the announcement was made that *Charity* would begin previews on April 11 prior to a May 4 opening. That the show would debut only two weeks late was rather miraculous, but not as much as the lineup of Charities: D'Amboise would play her from April 11 to 17, and then Applegate would return for good.

Although Applegate and the Weisslers stayed mum on her financial contributions, her co-star Denis O'Hare (who played Oscar, the man who almost loved her) told a 2010 Drama League luncheon that "Christina put up a million dollars of her own money to save the show."

That was hardly her only contribution. The first scene of the show demands that Charity fall into the orchestra pit. Applegate did it. She survived the scene where Latin lover Vittorio Vidal knocks her on her backside. She then arose and stomped steps worthy of a flamenco dancer in "If My Friends Could See Me Now." At any moment, an audience would have pardoned her if she'd hit the floor and crawled, but she never needed to.

There was an inadvertent irony in "There's Something Better Than This," when she and her dance-hall co-workers Nickie and Helene were considering new occupations. When Nickie asked her, "But, baby, what can you do?" Applegate had already proved that she could do—and was doing—quite a bit. Only those who had seats near the front would see that after doing each demanding number, she'd limp off into the wings.

In an era when so many performers call in sick, Christina Applegate demonstrated that she still believed the show must go on.

Reliever of the Year: Charlotte D'Amboise
Sweet Charity

Anyone who's been promised a job and then has it mysteriously and suddenly taken away understands how Charlotte D'Amboise must have felt. So does everyone from the substitute teacher to the office worker who fills in until the real replacement can be hired.

D'Amboise's star dressing room turned out to have a very short lease. "That's the way the theater is," she told the *New York Times*. "You have to have a big name."

What *Sweet Charity* did have was a big-hearted savior when it needed it.

2005–2006

MVP: Bob Martin
The Drowsy Chaperone

Many 1920s musicals concluded with a couple getting married. *The Drowsy Chaperone*—a valentine to 1920s musicals—could be said to have *started* because a couple was getting married.

For if Canadian writer Bob Martin hadn't popped the question to Janet Van De Graaff in 1998, his friends Don McKellar, Lisa Lambert, and Greg Morrison wouldn't have given him a stag party. They would have had no motivation to write a few risqué songs and sketches that spoofed the engaged couple.

Their little musicale turned out to be one of the best wedding presents any couple has ever received—because it led to a Broadway hit eight years later.

For Martin not only liked the little presentation, but also suggested that he and his pals expand it into a full-length show. He'd co-write the book with McKellar while Lambert and Morrison would do the score. They first called their show *An Accident Waiting to Happen* after one of their more felicitous songs but eventually settled on *The Drowsy Chaperone.*

Martin's idea was that there might be a musical about a man who was a big fan of musicals of the 1920s. He conceived a character simply known as Man in Chair—a role he'd play if the show amounted to anything.

At first, Man was a deejay for a radio show devoted to Broadway musicals. He specialized in shows that preceded the rock revolution. "Ah," he says, "if only today I could hear a score by someone like Rodgers and Hammerstein—or Gable and Stein!"

The latter team turned out to be the fictional authors of that fictional titanic 1920s hit *The Drowsy Chaperone.* Luckily, there was a bootleg made of the whole show, and Man would now play it for his listeners—as the stage was filled with the actors, costumes, and sets that Man remembered.

The plot of the musical-within-a-musical had a diva, still named Janet Van De Graaff, ready to give up her lucrative musical-comedy career in favor of a marriage to Robert Martin. (Yes, their names were retained.) Janet was glad that she was getting married, because she didn't "want to show off no more." But the excellent joke was that she did show off aplenty, for during this song she changed costumes, did cartwheels and high kicks, played water-filled drinking glasses with a spoon, charmed a snake, and twirled not only a rope, but also a baton and hoops, too, and spun plates on tall poles the way such artists did many a Sunday night on *The Ed Sullivan Show.* Then she held a note so long that she made Ethel Merman seem like Susan the Silent in *Finian's Rainbow.* And all that was before she exited and then reentered to do her inevitable encore.

Nevertheless, she claimed she was quitting show business, which made her blustery producer Feldzieg (get it?) quite worried. For one thing, some gangster financiers wanted to see their investment protected, so they pretended to be pastry chefs to get closer to the action. So Feldzieg hired Adolpho, a Latin lover, to break up Janet and Robert's marriage. Added to this was Underling, a butler who gave many a dour frown when his boss Mrs. Tottendale made unreasonable or stupid demands—all to show that he had better taste than she. Underling eventually got the chance to dance a little with an attitude of "unaccustomed as I am to public dancing, now that I've been called upon to do it, yes, I can, just as I can fulfill any request you make of me. Just leave everything to me."

Other colorful characters included Feldzieg's dim-witted blonde Kitty, some bridesmaids, and a maid of honor who turned out to be a rather drunken chaperone whose brain had seemingly been marinated in 100 percent proof gin. (Her actual name was never divulged, no more than Man in Chair's was.)

Man admitted to his listeners that "the characters were two-dimensional and the plot is well-worn" and that was certainly truth in advertising. The musical-within-a-musical was purposely written as silly piece of fluff that mirrored what musical-theater entertainment was like way back when. There were puns from the pastry chefs with plenty of pastry imagery: "One cannoli hope." "Now you're in truffle and there's muffin you can do about it." There were gags that got groans (He: Have you ever spent any time in a coma? She: No, but I have a cousin in Seattle.) But the groans were affectionate, with even a little tinge of "That was clever!" in them.

As the show developed, Martin and McKellar dropped the concept of Man hosting a radio show. The character instead became a simple agoraphobic who talked aloud about his passion for musicals, and the audience he saw in his mind was aptly played by the real audience who'd come to see the show.

Martin gave Man in Chair a gay sensibility, but a closeted one. He became deeply ashamed when he made an inadvertent double entendre, such as when he mentioned that one 1920s chorine caused men in the audience to have accidents. We're the ones with dirty minds, he pointed out, when he testily explained that what he meant was that they spilled their drinks.

Man also experienced embarrassment when he got a little too close to the onstage hunky men whom he so admired. Finally, when he made a passing reference to porno, he was suddenly sorry that he'd revealed so much of himself. The Broadway audience enjoyed seeing him get so flustered, for it didn't care whatever this closeted man had in his closet. And yet Man did mention having a wife at one point—and got a laugh after he asked the crowd, "Are you surprised I was married?"

Actually, Martin hadn't created Man in his own image. He wasn't a (you should pardon the unfortunate expression) show queen. Whenever he was asked by theater writers to cite musicals he enjoyed, he could come up with little more (and nothing more obscure) than *The Music Man.*

But it was Martin's show. As Man, how he cared for this 1928 musical! He was aghast when a performer on roller skates came perilously close to falling over. And when he joined Janet and Robert on "An Accident Waiting to Happen," he eventually pulled back, for he saw that they were getting romantic and he was the fifth wheel. He would often applaud the performers, too, in that slow and deliberate kind of handclapping that said, "Oh, come on, admit it: that was great."

Martin made cleaning a record (yes, record) an act of love. With the fervor of an Egyptologist trying to decipher the Rosetta stone, Martin was hilarious as he tried to figure out a word on the cast album that was obscured because some cast member had accidently dropped a cane during the recording. What delight he showed as he wiggled a forefinger in the air when the gangsters danced their "Toledo Surprise." He steepled his hands over his nose as he intently watched a scene, and his face was full of disappointment when the show was too silly even for him. But Martin's little-boy face also beamed when he heard a beloved joke that he'd heard hundreds of times—but each time, for the first time.

Man in Chair glumly observed that in the real world, nothing ever works out and that he needed *The Drowsy Chaperone* to take him away from its dreary horrors. But the musical that played the Marquis Theatre for nineteen months made Bob Martin and many others very happy people indeed.

Manager of the Year: Roy Miller
The Drowsy Chaperone

So another musical has opened out-of-town to rave reviews, which means that Roy Miller, the associate producer at the Paper Mill Playhouse in Millburn, New Jersey, must now decide whether or not to make the trip to see it.

This time, the show in question is in Toronto and has the funky title of *The Drowsy Chaperone.* Given that it's 1999, musical comedy hasn't yet made its Broadway comeback. So what's a guy to think of a show that brands itself as a sophisticated musical—except that the "ph" in the word "sophisticated has been replaced by "tw" to morph the word into "so-twist-icated"?

The Drowsy Chaperone played a Fringe Festival, where many a musical opens and closes forever—but this one continued at Theatre Passe Muraille, a small off-Broadway-like playhouse. Then mogul David Mirvish picked it up in 2001 and brought it to his Winter Garden (a fascinating space above a legit theater that has artificial flora and fauna flowing from the ceiling).

More good reviews followed, which Mirvish faxed to theaters in the United States—including Paper Mill.

"We'd always get these great reviews," Miller recalls, "to the point where you'd say, 'Yeah, sure'—because you'd been disappointed far too often before. I can't count how many times I traveled to see a show that had received big bouquets from the local critics and found they didn't deserve them."

Miller wasn't impressed with the credits of the creative staff. Co-bookwriter Bob Martin was part of the sketch comedy group Skippy's Rangers. DonMcKellar co-wrote the Canadian TV show *Twitch City.* Greg Morrison had musical-directed *Pochsy's Lips.* Lisa Lambert had provided songs for a musical called *Ouch, My Toe.*

Because Miller's friend Paul Mack lived in Toronto, he sent him to see the show. Wasn't Miller surprised when Mack called and said in a low, I'm-serious voice, "Roy, you'd better get up here."

Miller did, but, as he recalls, "When I got into my seat for the matinee, I was almost saying, 'Okay, go ahead: Make me laugh. I dare you.' Except," he says, still sounding surprised, "I fell on the floor laughing, especially at this Man in Chair who commented on the mythical actors who played the roles in the mythical show *The Drowsy Chaperone* and their private lives. His comments weren't the type you'd find in a 1920s musical; they were more like ones you'd read in *Broadway Babylon.* Bob Martin delivered them all with what I'd call sinister enthusiasm. What I also loved was that an audience didn't have to know anything about musicals to like it; people just needed to know something about people."

Mack asked Miller if he wanted to co-produce the show, but Miller told him he was, after all, representing the Paper Mill Playhouse. He went back and told Angelo Del Rossi, then the theater's executive producer, that this was definitely a property he should see. So Del Rossi went to Toronto and saw a performance with Kaye Ballard, on her off-night from *The Full Monty,* which was playing downstairs. "And they both adored it," Miller reports. Nevertheless, when Miller told Del Rossi that he and Mack were interested in producing it commercially, the boss gave his employee the green light.

In October 2004, Miller and Mack offered forty-five minutes of *The Drowsy Chaperone* at the National Alliance for Musical Theatre. Martin both directed and played Man in Chair. Also in the cast were Danny Burstein (Adolpho), Christine Ebersole (The Drowsy Chaperone), Georgia Engel (Mrs. Tottendale), Richard Kind (Feldzieg), Christopher Sieber (Martin),

Christianne Tisdale (Van De Graaff), and Lea DeLaria as Trix, the aviatrix who literally provided a deus ex machina ending by easing down from above in her aeroplane and solving everyone's problems.

Alas, not enough money was raised, causing Mack to eventually withdraw. Miller would not be denied, although he knew by this point he would not be able to raise the millions necessary to chaperone *Chaperone* to Broadway. Who could?

One of the more successful producers to whom he sent the script and score was Kevin McCollum, who had produced two previous shows by unknowns—*Rent* and *Avenue Q*—and had profited handsomely from them.

"I have to admit that I didn't get around to reading it for a full year," McCollum admits. "Once I did, I signed on."

McCollum was billed first and Miller second among the six above-the-title producers. Martin agreed to a new director, so Casey Nicholaw took over that job and choreographed, too. He retained Martin, Burstein, and Engel, and engaged Tony-winner Sutton Foster as Janet and future Tony-winner (for this role) Beth Leavel as The Drowsy Chaperone.

In late 2005, *The Drowsy Chaperone* opened in Los Angeles, where it enjoyed a successful run and critical reception. Good wishes were forthcoming, but far more importantly, so was money. But there was no available Broadway theater to house the potential hit. McCollum, Miller, and the others resigned themselves to reluctantly postpone until the 2006–2007 season.

But then Andrew Lloyd Webber's *The Woman in White* found that mediocre reviews and audience indifference were fast catching up with it. Its closing after a humiliatingly short run of 109 performances allowed *The Drowsy Chaperone* to open at the Marquis Theater on May Day, 2006.

It received thirteen Tony nominations and won five, including Best Book and Best Score. Don't those two categories automatically mean Best Musical? Actually, as the years have gone on, Tony voters have actually been saying that Best Musical means Best Show and Production. It's not just the writing; it's the whole ball of wax that's considered. *Jersey Boys* won.

The New York Drama Critics Circle, however, chose *The Drowsy Chaperone* over *Jersey Boys.* That may be because even the most rarefied of critics could relate more to that Man who loves musicals than to four guys who wanted to sing early 1960s rock.

And so *The Drowsy Chaperone* stayed on Broadway for 674 performances—only one performance shy of the original production of *Irene* in 1919. That musical, which featured the song "Alice Blue Gown," was one that Man in Chair would have undoubtedly enjoyed.

Rookie of the Year: John Lloyd Young
Jersey Boys

"Talent is lovely," says agent Richard Seff, who helped to make Chita Rivera a Broadway star. "But nothing beats being in right place at the right time."

John Lloyd Young had both the talent and the timing—and another break, as well, that led to his getting the prime role of the 2005–2006 season: Frankie Valli, the linchpin of the Four Seasons in *Jersey Boys.*

There could have been a musical about the Four Seasons ten years earlier or ten years later, but it came to fruition during the time when thirty-year-old Young was auditioning, understudying, ushering here and there, and getting an occasional role. When he heard about the *Jersey Boys* producers' hunt for a Frankie Valli sound-alike, he knew he had the requisite falsetto that would make him conquer "Sherry," "Big Girls Don't Cry," and several other enormous hits that the group had had.

But he didn't get the part. An actor named David Norona did. Young was a close second.

Not close enough.

Jersey Boys was quite successful during its run at the La Jolla (California) Playhouse in October 2004. Ticket demand caused the show to be extended three times. Norona was getting a good deal of attention playing Valli and was soon offered a TV series called *Inconceivable.* Considering the salary and visibility that a performer gets on a TV series compared to what he gets for eight shows a week on Broadway, no one can blame Norona for taking the television job.

Young is glad and grateful that he did. Norona got ten episodes of employment from *Inconceivable.* Young got 800-plus performances of *Jersey Boys* as well as the Outer Critics Circle Award, the Theatre World Award, the Drama Desk Award—and the Tony Award. In fact, at the Theatre World Awards, which honors twelve newcomers a year, Harry Connick Jr. of *The Pajama Game* quipped that he was glad to win something in the face of Young's sweep.

During many a performance, Young's rendition of "Can't Take My Eyes Off You" actually got many in the audience to stand. Not at the end of the performance—right then and there following the song. If that ever happened to Merman or Martin, no history book has reported it.

2006–2007

MVP: Christine Ebersole
Grey Gardens

In a sense, Edith Bouvier Beale (1917–2002) led a double life. She didn't do it simultaneously, but consecutively.

Her first life involved the pleasure and privilege one would expect from a first cousin of Jacqueline Bouvier (Kennedy) and Lee Radziwill. She was born on Madison Avenue, attended Miss Porter's School, and made a stunning debut at the Pierre Hotel in 1936. Admittedly, her father had abandoned the family five years earlier, but she and her mother, affectionately known as "Big Edie," still lived well at Grey Gardens, an East Hampton showplace.

The second part of Beale's life, however, was far different. The estate went to ruin. Lest there be any doubt about that, one only need see the documentary *Grey Gardens* made by the Maysles brothers in 1975. Raccoons came and went at will inside the house. A cat was seen urinating on a bed. And none of this particularly unnerved a fifty-eight-year-old "Little Edie" or seventy-eight-year-old "Big Edie." They simply ate their meals, in which Wonder Bread seemed to be the main course.

Bookwriter Doug Wright, composer Scott Frankel, and lyricist Michael Korie decided that in their musical adaptation, their leading lady would in the first act play middle-aged Big Edie in 1941; in the second, she'd change characters and become the middle-aged Little Edie in 1973, a couple of years before the documentary made their lives public.

But playing a cultured pearl in the first act—and shattered glass in the second—would be a great challenge for even the most gifted actress. And yet, in act 1 Christine Ebersole blithely played the jovial hostess who was preparing her daughter's engagement party to Joseph P. Kennedy Jr. She breezed through as if her character didn't have a true care in the world.

Actually, Big Edie did have one. The authors took the liberty of keeping her husband Phelan Beale on the scene, but just barely. Ebersole smartly showed that Big Edie knew that Phelan wasn't in love with her anymore but brushed that off as something that routinely happens in every marriage.

Then in act 2, Ebersole became Little Edie, full of neuroses, skittish behavior, and the dour desperation of a wasted life. Right from her act 2 opener, "The Revolutionary Costume for Today," she made her mouth into a grim line and then miraculously turned it into a zigzag.

In both acts, Ebersole sang, danced, and acted extraordinarily. But her finest moment might have come at the show's end, when she was simply standing still. She was out the door, preparing to leave her mother and start a new life—but then she heard her mother call her. Would she go and forge her own life, or retreat back into the filthy home?

For many long, long seconds, Ebersole certainly had the audience wondering, and the tension was palpable. One could see her thinking: Shall I stay with the mother who bore me and bores me? And then one saw Ebersole succumb, as if to say, "Where'm I gonna go?"

Walter Newkirk, who was one of Little Edie Beale's few confidants during her darkest years (and has since written two books about her), says, "I went into that theater thinking that no actress could possibly be able to bring the very eccentric Little Edie Beale to life. But Christine Ebersole certainly did it. She was fantastic in every way."

The critics agreed, and so did the awards committees. Some people had carped a few years earlier when Ebersole won the Best Actress in a Musical Tony for her brief role as Dorothy Brock in the revival of *42nd Street.* "I spent much of the second act making phone calls in my dressing room," Ebersole had admitted. But few if any begrudged her the many Best Actress in a Musical prizes she got for her roles here.

Rookies of the Year: Scott Frankel and Michael Korie
Grey Gardens

While lyricist Michael Korie and composer Scott Frankel thought there were musical possibilities in the 1975 documentary *Grey Gardens,* they had to admit it had many grey areas.

First, the songwriters had to ask themselves the question that a *Merrily We Roll Along* chorus had once asked of Franklin Shepard: How did it happen? The once-elegant Beales of East Hampton—Edith and her daughter Edie—were now recluses who neglected their estate and lived in cat-infested poverty.

Korie and Frankel were pleased that the documentary also intrigued Doug Wright. How wonderful that a recent Best Play Tony and a Pulitzer Prize winner (for *I Am My Own Wife*) was at least interested in writing the book of their musical.

"But until we had a solution to the past, Doug Wright would not commit to collaborating," says Korie. "He wouldn't write the book, even though he was intrigued enough to have many meetings—all of which ended where they began: nowhere."

In a subtle sense, the past was actually there in the documentary. The camera's panning across old photographs and news clippings showed Edie as debutante. The oil portraits of Edith and her once-husband Phelan said a great deal about their posh existence. True, Phelan's leaving could have sent both Beales into a tailspin, but such a fall from privilege to squalor and delusions seemed to beg another explanation.

"A definite answer was not necessarily 'our' answer," says Korie. "It's just that in order to have an 'after,' we needed a 'before.' But we didn't have a clue how to do it. There are no camera close-ups in a musical onstage. To mingle past and present simultaneously would have been *Follies.* The thought of a Greek Chorus made us all tired."

Korie and Frankel were in danger of losing Wright. They went to a restaurant to brainstorm. It happened to be a place with white paper tablecloths and glasses full of crayons—"for bored children and childish adults," says Korie.

And creative types. "Scott began to doodle," says Korie. "Idly, he drew two boxes, rectangles, one on top of the other, with a white space in between. Then, getting interested, he wrote a date into each of the rectangles—on the top, 1941. The bottom, 1973. He said to me, 'Look at this' and I said, 'That's it. That's our show.' Two acts, each told in their own time period, with an intermission in between where thirty years would pass. The gray fog of forgetfulness and myth clouding the reasons of Act One would lead to the small tragedy of act 2."

The writers also realized another exciting possibility: the passage of thirty years between the acts meant that the actress who played Big Edie in act 1 could be double-cast to play Little Edie, all grown up in act 2. "In addition to being a unifying concept of the show," says Korie, "it would provide an opportunity for a leading actress of the musical theater to do something spectacular. At that moment, we had no idea how spectacular that performance would turn out to be," he adds, meaning Christine Ebersole.

Korie ripped the paper tablecloth off the table. The songwriters brought it to Wright, who saw what they saw and officially signed on. Says Korie, "In this first act of the past, he immediately grasped an opportunity to forge the myth, originate dialogue and situations based on the truth—but not cinema verité—and a chance to stylize the past in the manner of a Philip Barry drawing room."

The three spent a winter weekend in Cape Cod, where each of them brought every scrap of history about the Beale family they had found. "It's there that we learned about Joseph Kennedy Jr. and his brief romance with the young Edie Beale, and the legend they had been—or almost had been—engaged," says Korie. "It was then a short leap to the concept of a lawn party in Grey Gardens to celebrate the engagement of Little Edie Beale to the eldest Kennedy son and navy hero."

Joseph P. Kennedy Jr. was earmarked by his father, Ambassador Joseph P. Kennedy, for the presidency of the United States. Those who know their Kennedy history might assume that Joe's death in action in World War II sent the Beales on their downward spiral.

But Wright, Frankel, and Korie went for a more psychologically interesting idea. When "Big Edie" discovered that her own husband was leaving her, all her emotional fuses were blown and she sabotaged her daughter's happiness so that the young woman would never leave her. So Big Edie hinted to Joe that her daughter was promiscuous and scandal-prone.

The young achiever couldn't risk being married to someone who could block his road to the White House. Joe's value system was shown in one of Wright's sharpest lines: After Big Edie said, "You love her very much," Kennedy answered, "She's the reason I'm here." That's quite a different statement and sentiment from "I love her and I can't live without her."

While Wright mentioned nothing about Joseph P. Kennedy Sr.'s alleged affair with former movie star Gloria Swanson, one can infer that young Joe had heard all the rumors and knew that scandal was to be avoided at all costs. So, then, must he avoid Little Edie, too. This dramatic turn was much more involving than the almost deus ex machina move that true life provided by killing Joe. If both Beale women were assuming that Little Edie could become the First Lady of the Land—and saw that possibility disappear in a day—the heartbreak could cause them to lose their minds.

That Frankel and Korie solved the inherent problem with the show would not alone make them Rookies of the Year. They also get the award for writing an arresting score. What's more, after a successful stint at Playwrights Horizons before going to Broadway, they dropped a half-dozen songs and added two new ones. Frankel showed he was up to recreating the easy-listening sound of the 1940s in the first act. That Big Edie believed she had a good singing voice and liked to entertain afforded song opportunities, too.

Korie was equally adept in writing lyrics that aped the novelty numbers of the day. "Hominy Grits" was a takeoff on the type of song that erstwhile white songwriters wrote in a southern black style. "Two Peas in a Pod" was a list song that incorporated period references ("Like Crosby and Hope; a rosy complexion and Ivory Soap.") They also made room for an Irving Berlin–like ditty, "Will You?" in which one questioned the depth of her partner's love.

In the second act, Frankel's music changed to sound theatrically quirky whenever either of the Beales sang. Many brooding chords reflected and commented on the Beales' hand-to-mouth existence. Many musicals have title songs that celebrate; this show almost had a title tune—"Entering Grey Gardens" was the actual name of it—that was distinctly and dissonantly eerie. It wasn't meant to be the one a theatergoer would leave humming; it was meant to set the ominous mood, and did just that.

Grey Gardens had to be two shows in one, and Scott Frankel and Michael Korie succeeded in writing two scores in one.

Comeback: Mary Louise Wilson
Grey Gardens

Her first three Broadway musicals, all in the 1960s, were *Hot Spot; Flora, the Red Menace;* and *Noel Coward's Sweet Potato.* None of them became a household name, and certainly not one of them was a hit.

The 1970s were kinder. At least Mary Louise Wilson got to play a Tony-winning role—although she wasn't the one to win a Tony for it. She took over as loveable lush Marge MacDougall in *Promises, Promises.* Later she was dressy Tessie Tura, one of the second-act strippers, in the 1974 Angela Lansbury revival of *Gypsy.* There were stints in three plays, too, including the much-heralded 1975 revival of *The Royal Family.*

But the entire 1980s brought Wilson only four Broadway plays for a total of twelve months' employment. That's enough for an actress to develop a one-woman show, which Wilson did with Mark Hampton. She portrayed Diana

Vreeland, the *Vogue* editor-in-chief, in *Full Gallop.* She played it for eleven months and won a 1995–1996 Drama Desk Award for her efforts.

Wilson did get the chance to play Fraulein Schneider in the 1998 blockbuster revival of *Cabaret* but only stayed with it for five months of its six-year run. A few off-Broadway roles followed, as did a limited-engagement Broadway run of *The Women.* But in 2006, after she'd passed her seventy-third birthday, theatergoers weren't expecting to see much of Mary Louise Wilson.

That, however, is precisely when the best role she'd ever have in a musical suddenly arrived: Big Edie Beale, the seventy-eight-year-old recluse who didn't seem to notice that her entire world had fallen apart. She'd sit in bed most of the day reminiscing about the glory days of Grey Gardens when she believed she could sing reasonably well. In fact, she still believed she could.

The way the role was conceived, Wilson wouldn't show up until the second act, and she had only two songs in which she took the lead. But these were enough for her to make a strong impression.

"The Cake I Had" took its inspiration from the oft-misquoted line about one's wanting "to have his cake and eat it, too." (The actual expression is "eat your cake and have it, too," which makes more sense.) Edie, in one of Broadway's jauntiest songs of denial, said that she was very happy with her life. When daughter Little Edie mused that her life had been less fulfilling and that she should have done more, Wilson barked one of Michael Korie's best lyrics, "You had two hands. You could have modeled gloves."

Wilson got the chance to show Big Edie's sentimental side in "Jerry Likes My Corn," a song that displayed quite a bit of character and subtext. Jerry was a local high schooler who dropped by Grey Gardens from time to time and was the closest thing to a friend that the women had. Wilson had such pride in her voice when she sang, "Jerry likes the way I do my corn." She was able to ever-so-subtly guide the audience into hearing the most important of Korie's words—such as "I boil it on the hot plate," which showed how far this family had fallen from the days when maids traversed their ornate kitchen.

Wilson got our sympathy for Big Edie when admitting that her sons had abandoned her and when she detailed her medical condition. But Wilson bravely took the lady on an upswing when she sang, "Then quick as a wink, I'm in the pink, 'cuz Jerry likes my corn."

And Tony voters liked Mary Louise Wilson enough to name her the Best Featured Actress in a Musical for 2006–2007.

Reliever of the Year: Rupert Holmes
Curtains

More than two decades before their backstager *Curtains* arrived on Broadway, John Kander and Fred Ebb wrote a song about "Collaboration." An early demo recording of the show displayed an important aspect of writing a musical.

As Kander played his melody that was in the same tempo and spirit as "Comedy Tonight," Ebb sang the song. One lyric about the process of rewriting—"We made it better"—suddenly made Kander stop playing the piano. And, for the first time in the song, we heard Kander's voice drolly noting that "We made it shorter."

The absence of music underlined their point that the simple act of cutting a show is often one of the most important improvements that collaborators can make.

One of biggest improvements that Rupert Holmes made when adapting the late Peter Stone's original book to *Curtains* was to make it shorter. Given that the rule of thumb is that each page of script loosely translates to one minute of stage time, Stone was in the process of writing an extremely lengthy show. An April 1, 1986, draft weighed in at 176 pages. That would have meant a nearly three-hour-long show, not counting the intermission.

Curtains owed much of its existence to *Woman of the Year,* the musical that Stone, Kander, and Ebb wrote in 1980. While standing at the back of the Colonial Theatre during its Boston tryout, the collaborators remarked that it was a beautiful showplace. Wouldn't it be fun to actually see a musical that was set in this very theater during its pre-Broadway tryout?

Stone, in addition to winning a Tony (for *1776*) as well as an Oscar (for *Father Goose*) and an Emmy (for *The Defenders*), had also nabbed an Edgar—the highest honor afforded by the Mystery Writers of America. That was for his 1964 screenplay for *Charade.* Perhaps the show set at the Colonial could be a murder musical?

Kander and Ebb remembered a show they'd started with Abe Burrows in 1971: *Tango Mogador* (as in Morocco) concerned the French Foreign Legion. Perhaps they could recycle that musical's material as the musical that's trying out in Boston when the murders were suddenly committed.

For a while, the new musical was called *Who Killed David Merrick?* Perhaps that was wishful thinking, for all three writers had worked for the notorious producer on musicals that had terribly shaky tryouts. (Kander and Ebb toiled on the 1968 failure *The Happy Time;* Stone in 1972 labored on the just-squeaking-by hit *Sugar.*) But *Who Killed David Merrick?* gave way to *Curtains,* although the collaborators weren't too subtle in renaming their murdered producer David Mishkin. (How interesting that a producer named Mishkin—Chase—did eventually show up on Broadway. But she began her Broadway career in 1996, long after Stone conceived the producer's name of his fictional show.)

David Mishkin would never show up on the scene, but his biggest backer—one wealthy but vulgar Carmen Nussbaum—would. She'd deal with the likes of general manager Oscar Katz, bookwriter Stan Cates (and his wife Laura), composer Aaron Fox, lyricist Georgia Guerney, director-choreographer Christopher Belling, and his assistant Bonnie Lee. She'd also tangle with the cast, including stars Jessica Cranshaw and Harry Winslow, featured player Nikki Ellis, and gypsy Charlene LeMay.

The one who bothered her most of all, however, was Daryl Grady, the critic for the *Boston Globe,* who had hated her production of a new French Foreign Legion–themed musical called *Sand.*

After the murder, Detective Salvatore Cioffi of the Boston Police Department arrived at the theater. He adored musicals and bought all the cast albums, so he was thrilled to be meeting some of his all-time heroes. But Cioffi had to put his ardor aside to investigate. "I need everyone out here onstage," he said, followed by the famous tinkling vamp of "One" from *A Chorus Line.* Indeed, all the principals then formed a line, came forward, and shared their inner thoughts with the audience, if not with Cioffi.

Belling admitted that Mishkin had fired him. Carmen divulged that she got him rehired on the condition that he give her daughter Elaine—who'd renamed herself Bambi—Nikki's part. (But, as an Ebb lyric went, "Nikki gave him nookie.") Oscar had been caught stealing. Stan was upset at all the changes that had been enforced on his "beautiful play." Harry wanted out of his ironclad contract because he'd been offered a good soap. Laura had discovered that her husband had been sleeping with Charlene, who was also sleeping with Mishkin, at whom she was furious because he wouldn't leave his wife. Aaron and Bambi had a thing, too, and so did Laura with Grady, at least when he and Stan were at Yale. But Daryl never lost his ardor for Laura.

Cioffi's first observation about this case? "Is a puzzlement!" Ebb also adapted the last lines of Billy Bigelow's "Soliloquy" for him to sing: "I'm sworn to resolve it / and take it and solve it / or die!"

After Mishkin's death, Stone had Belling ask the company to give some tributes to the dead man. "Johnny, you did five shows with him," he said to a stagehand. "What do you have to say about him?" Johnny answered, "The Shuberts are worse." That line would ensure that half the theaters on Broadway wouldn't welcome this musical.

Stone later toyed with putting Joe Papp and then Fran and Barry Weissler in the Shuberts' place. But he also wasn't above naming two of the lowliest of stagehands "Bernie" and "Gerry"—the respective first names of Jacobs and Schoenfeld, who were then running the Shubert empire.

Some of Stone's lines were pure routine musical comedy. (Carmen: "Have you any idea how much this show is going to cost?" Daryl: "How much?" Carmen: "Don't ask.") There was an easy shot about Andrew Lloyd Webber's writing a musical about a Mexican earthquake. Stone also wrote the most inside joke ever to invade a musical: when Stan phoned the president of the Dramatists Guild to complain, he said, "Hello, Peter?"—for at that time the guild's president was one Peter Stone.

What's often been said about collaboration is that a lyricist often takes a bookwriter's lines and turns them into a song. It happened in *Curtains,* for this draft had Cioffi telling the cast, "I just hope you know how lucky you all are" to be in show business. That spurred Kander and Ebb to write "Show People," in which Cioffi started singing that sentiment before the staff of the show reiterated it.

After a while, Stone, Kander, and Ebb decided to change *Sand* to a commedia dell'arte musical called *Harlequinade.* Ironically, a Broadway-bound commedia dell'arte musical called *Comedy* did indeed close at the Colonial in Boston, albeit in 1972. But would someone as crass as Carmen Nussbaum put money into a commedia dell'arte musical?

We'll never know. Stone died in 2003 and Ebb in 2004, so *Curtains* appeared to be permanently closed. But Scott Ellis, who'd directed Kander and Ebb off-Broadway in *And the World Goes 'Round* and on Broadway in *Steel Pier,* itched for the chance to stage it. Who could write both book and new lyrics?

Rupert Holmes, our 1985–1986 MVP on *The Mystery of Edwin Drood.* He read what Stone had and thought the first mistake was setting the show in "Time: Now." He suggested that the show remind us of the good ol' days. Besides, how many shows went out of town anymore? In the previous twenty years, four had come to Boston—the same number that had come there in 1959 alone.

First, Holmes did some tiny cosmetic work. He changed a first name (Salvatore became Frank), two last ones (Nussbaum to Bernstein; Gurney to Hendricks), and even a spelling (Nikki was shortened to Niki). Stan,

Laura, Harry, and Charlene were dropped. More importantly, Holmes had Aaron and Georgia previously married and divorced, but still a songwriting couple. Carmen and Oscar were married co-producers—at least until he was murdered at the end of the first act.

Now their musical would be *Robbin' Hood,* with the famous British legend adapted to the American West. (Holmes wrote the lyrics to the new music that Kander wrote for it.)

But star Jessica Cranshaw stinks—and she's the one who's murdered. The way it happened was pure Rupert Holmes, a clever gambit that only the biggest crime-novel fans would have thought of.

Holmes dropped "Collaboration," so no work needed to be done on the lyric "The wait for critics is a bitch, but we get approval from Frank Rich—even though it isn't Sondheim." (Two measures of "Comedy Tonight" then punctuated the point.) He excised "Out-of-Town," in which chaotic theatrical adventures were catalogued. One of them was "Some big backer's girlfriend says, 'I was depressed' (by the show)." One can imagine that this line came from a similar criticism Ebb once had to endure from some angel's not-so-angelic girlfriend. Holmes also dropped Nussbaum's "It's All Because of Me," her paean to herself—and undoubtedly the only song in musical-theater history that used the phrase "creative scumbags."

Some changes had to be made to accommodate 1959. For "Show People," the lyric about audiences—"honest to God, they jeer Sherlock Holmes and cheer Sweeney Todd"—became a lyrics about detectives: "They fancy this life; they jeer Sherlock Holmes and cheer Mack the Knife." The lyric "The audience paid 50" shows how long this show struggled to get on. Now tickets were twice that. Holmes changed the number to "plenty."

"I put two million in and I expect three million back," said Nussbaum. Holmes's Bernstein dropped each figure by a million, but even a single million was more than twice the money needed for a new musical in 1959. Her stating that "I'd do the Kama Sutra with a Jerry Herman score" had to be changed, for Herman was a nobody in 1959. Holmes had Richard Rodgers replace him. And while Carmen had told of a producer who lost his shirt trying to produce something artistic—"He mounted Robert Wilson—I don't mean it like it sounds"—she now used Samuel (pronounced Sam-you'll) Beckett in his stead.

Curtains played 511 performances, which isn't theatrical chopped liver, but this was no longer the era when 500 performances meant a hit. Still, Holmes did the work that got *Curtains* opened.

2007–2008

Co-MVP and Rookie of the Year: Lin-Manuel Miranda
In the Heights

Some critics and audience members left *In the Heights* with skeptical smiles on their faces. A winning lottery ticket providing a happy ending was too far-fetched for them. After all, the odds of winning $96,000 are estimated from one in 360,000 to one in 890,000, depending on how many people play and how many others choose the same numbers you do.

But winning a lottery was an apt metaphor for this unexpected hit. For what were the odds that Lin-Manuel Miranda, a Latino with no Broadway experience whatsoever, would be able to conceive a viable story for a Latino musical, let alone find the right Latina librettist (Quiara Alegria Hudes) to write it with him?

Miranda and Hudes would tell the story of the oddly named Usnavi, who was raised by his *abuela* (grandmother) in Washington Heights, a conclave for immigrants from the Dominican Republic. Usnavi has found a modicum of success in owning his own bodega, but he wonders if he'd be happier in the Dominican Republic, where his family originated. A young, attractive woman named Vanessa, however, is one reason why Usnavi prefers to stay put.

A subplot involved Nina, who's just finished her freshman year at Stanford University. However, Nina has kept from her very proud parents that she doesn't expect to return for her sophomore year.

That was the crux of *In the Heights.* Said Miranda, "There's a whole group of immigrants you grew up with who had your parents' traditions. Then you went to school and found a completely different set of traditions. We had to find ourselves between the margins." He would write a show "for those who don't know where they belong or how many traditions they should keep."

Miranda planned to write both music and lyrics for the show and to star as Usnavi—a lad who was named because his father saw the words "U.S. Navy" on the ships that docked near where they lived. And yet the closest connection Miranda had with Broadway was that he shared a birthday (January 16) with Ethel Merman.

So how could this young man in his twenties interest producers in even providing seed money for a musical that would apparently have a limited audience? How many Latinos even thought of trekking downtown to see a Broadway musical? How many traditional theatergoers would want to know about the goings-on in Washington Heights? Even after *In the Heights* was chosen to be part of the Eugene O'Neill Festival in 2005, where would the money come from to mount even an off-Broadway production?

And yet all those dreams came true when *In the Heights* opened off-Broadway on February 8, 2007, at 37 Arts. But to many theatergoers, this Thirty-seventh Street house was Siberia. Few wanted to travel to a playhouse between Ninth and Tenth avenues on a remote block on which nothing else of interest sat. As a result, despite encouraging reviews, there were plenty of empty seats during the disappointingly short five-month run.

To be sure, when *In the Heights* closed, its producers were promising a future on Broadway. But didn't every set of off-Broadway producers say that about their closed shows to save face?

Not this time. Miranda and Hudes, along with director Thomas Kail and choreographer Andy Blankenbuehler, made some cuts and changes. On Valentine's Day, 2008, this valentine to uptown life began at the Richard Rodgers Theatre and officially opened on March 9 to strong reviews. Ben Brantley of the *New York Times* called Miranda "a singular new sensation."

That description was a paraphrase from the final song of a Pulitzer Prize–winning musical—*A Chorus Line*—but it was a much later Pulitzer Prize–winning musical that inspired Miranda to write *In the Heights.* At age seventeen he saw *Rent* and reasoned that if a starving East Village resident could write a musical about his friends and neighbors, so, too, could he paint a picture of the place where he was living.

Miranda began writing while at Wesleyan University and, in seven years' time, saw his artistic lottery ticket win. (He also did concede, however, that *The Phantom of the Opera* had some influence, too: "At the end of the day, it's about an ugly songwriter who can't get girls to notice him," said the diminutive Miranda. "I was like 'That's me!'")

Soon after its Broadway opening, *In the Heights* received a lucky thirteen Tony nominations. A few weeks later at Radio City Music Hall, Whoopi Goldberg announced that the show had been chosen Best Musical. Dozens of producers and cast and staff members poured onto the Radio City Music Hall stage. But one man literally towered above them all with his feet literally off the ground—because lead producers Kevin McCollum and Jeffrey Seller had hoisted Lin-Manuel Miranda onto their shoulders.

By then, *In the Heights* had won the Outer Critics Circle and Lucille Lortel awards as Best Musical. Miranda's songwriting yielded a Tony, too, and his performance won Theatre World, Clarence Derwent, and HOLA awards, as well as a Drama Desk award, for the organization voted that *In the Heights* had that season's Outstanding Ensemble.

Miranda's opening number for *In the Heights* was in rap (although it took a decidedly non-belligerent approach), so Miranda decided to write his Tony acceptance speech in the exact same style: "I used to dream about this moment / Now I'm in it/ Tell the conductor to hold the baton a minute," he began, alluding to the fact that each winner gets thirty seconds of thank-you time before the musical director strikes up the band to drown out an overly lengthy speech.

Musical director Elliot Lawrence didn't interrupt Miranda when he began acknowledging one of Broadway's blue-chippers: " Mr. Sondheim, look: I made a hat where there never was a hat," Miranda said, citing what Seurat says in *Sunday in the Park with George;* at first, he minimizes and mocks what he's just painted before having to stand in awe of it. But, Miranda added, "It's a Latin hat at that."

There was more in common between Miranda and Sondheim than one might have noticed at first glance. After all, Sondheim's first musical, *West Side Story,* had Latino characters on Broadway fifty-one years before Miranda's showed up there. And the following season, when Arthur Laurents planned a *West Side Story* revival where the Puerto Rican–born Sharks would sing and speak in Spanish, Miranda was chosen to provide the translations.

When *West Side Story* was first produced in 1957, some of the Sharks were played by actors with the last names of LeRoy, Gavin, Murray, Norman, and Schwartz. The *Playbill* for *In the Heights,* however, sported such surnames as Gonzalez, Gomez, Lopez, De Jesus, Merediz, Dacal, and, of course, Miranda.

Most had backgrounds similar to their characters'; Mandy Gonzalez, who played Nina, was the daughter of a migrant worker. So as valuable as Miranda was as a writer and performer, he was also significant in conceiving a show that would provide years of employment for the Latino acting community. His musical would also be the first Equity production that would play Puerto Rico.

In the Heights would run 1,184 performances, but only partly because the Latino audience was now big enough—and affluent enough—to attend a musical that spoke to their own experiences and concerns. The issues of assimilation were ones that many attendees who ever questioned their place in the world could relate to. At the end of *In the Heights,* Miranda's Usnavi sang, "I'm home," about his neighborhood. But by then, "I'm home" also referred to a street more than ten dozen blocks below Washington Heights—as Broadway became a new home for Lin-Manuel Miranda.

And beyond. Miranda ended his closing-night speech on January 9, 2011, by saying:

> Now I know how obsessed some of y'all are gettin',
> But listen, *In the Heights* ain't closin'. This is spreadin'.
> Yeah. And up here, on this lectern,
> One day, you'll be somewhere Midwestern.
> Somewhere, chillin' in some outer theater lobby—
> Some little high schooler's gonna be playin' Usnavi!
> I don't know how to brag this—
> That little white kid is gonna know / What a Puerto Rican flag is!

And he will.

Co-MVP: Patti LuPone
Gypsy

What? Another production of *Gypsy*? Fewer than five years after the last one with Bernadette Peters? It was playing on Broadway as late as 1990, too, at the end of its run with Tyne Daly. Could the town take yet another production?

Yes, when Patti LuPone early in the season, in a summer offering from Encores! showed that she'd be as accomplished as Rose as most everyone had assumed.

City Center was filled with *Gypsy* savants who knew that before the show they'd better get their purses and backpacks out of the aisle, for there was a fifty-fifty chance that Patti LuPone would soon be storming down it.

And when LuPone did, she got wild applause from her first words—"Sing out, Louise!" of course—as she stormed down the stage-left aisle of the theater. The commotion continued as she reached the stage and as she climbed the stairs onto it. LuPone then kept her back to us for a long time as she fussed over Baby June, and neither the star nor the kid moved a muscle until the last theatergoer gave his last handclap.

All this came from the people who could only fantasize that LuPone would someday play this role—but were certain she wouldn't, at least not during her foe Arthur Laurents's lifetime. She was once scheduled to do a play of his, *Jolson Sings Again*, and when she decided not to do it, financing fell though, and Laurents was miffed. He refused to let her play *Gypsy* in any top-notch venue.

Ah, but because the Ravinia Festival in Highland Park, Illinois, works under a different type of contract, Laurents couldn't prevent LuPone from doing it there under Lonny Price's direction. Once word (and, of course, bootleg videos) got out on how magnificent LuPone was, Laurents had to take pause. He not only decided to forgive her, but to direct her, too.

In that first scene, LuPone had utter revulsion when looking at Balloon Girl and, when threatening Uncle Jocko, brought plenty to her line worthy of Sweeney Todd: "Desperate people do desperate things." So when she popped the Girl's balloons (which looked used, as if the kid and her mother had recycled them from gig to gig), LuPone wasn't malevolent but had a business-as-usual air. She was inured to doing what it takes to make her kids (KID, really) get ahead.

Already she was wonderful, and she hadn't sung a note. So imagine the audience's glee when she did start. In "Some People," LuPone's low notes were as deep and delicious as bourbon. For all that talk about how much she doesn't enunciate, LuPone sure underlined each syllable and rhyme in "some humdrum." What perfect timing, too, on slamming the door on the song's last word ("Rose," of course).

Then, while she and the kids were on the road "recruiting" boys, all LuPone needed was a Dracula cape, considering the way she turned her hands into claws and slowly but deliberately reached to snag each lad. Soon after, when she said to Herbie, "You like me, but you don't want show business," she made it sound as if she were actually saying, "Now, how could you ever explain such a ridiculous idea to people? Who can't love show business?" In "Small World," she sang, "I'm a woman with children" with an air of "What a coincidence!" as if the thought had just hit her, and not that she'd had been carefully tallying in her head the reasons why Herbie should hook up with her. By this point, she had already proved that that this Rose wasn't just a woman with children, she was also Patti LuPone in the role that she was destined her to play.

LuPone's ferocity was in place. In the hotel-room scene (which was strangely abridged, with no confrontation with and pseudo-rape by the landlord), LuPone hit one of her Farmboys on the head with a pie plate;

as one might expect from LuPone, she didn't pull the punch. Then came the Chinese restaurant scene where Herbie begged her to put the kids in school—causing LuPone to snarl, "So they can be like other girls, cook and clean and sit and DIE." Rose was not one of those people who could be content to sit by a swimming pool bought by an Andrew Lloyd Webber payoff for not doing *Sunset Boulevard* in New York.

Later, after June had eloped with Tulsa and a Farmboy had said, "The act's washed up," LuPone showed Rose's indomitable nature just by her raised eyebrow. Oh, no, she wouldn't have that. Once she launched into "Everything's Comin' Up Roses," she added extra brass to an orchestra that was already sporting plenty.

But as act 2 began, LuPone showed she wasn't creating an out-and-out monster. When this Rose watched the execrable Mme. Rose's Toreadorables perform, LuPone's face said, "How can I possibly say anything good to these kids about their efforts, as much as I'd like to? They DO need to be praised or at least encouraged." And that face kept searching in vain for something good to say. One could also feel her thinking that if she did find it, she worried that she might not be able to make it sound convincing.

And so LuPone excelled, right through to and including the character's breakdown in "Rose's Turn," which conquered, despite having a strange little cut in it. And yet, immediately after it, she was back to being the Rose we knew and did *and* didn't love, rallying with a finger point when she told Louise, "Just trying out a few ideas you might want to use"—with a subtext of, "I have some great suggestions here, and you'd be a fool not to take them."

Suddenly Broadway felt it'd be a fool if it didn't offer Patti LuPone the chance to actually play this for an extended run on Broadway. If the reaction at City Center was hot in July, it was hotter still the following March at the St. James.

Once she reached the stage and flummoxed Uncle Jocko enough so that she could order, "Mr. Conductor, if you please!" she looked right out into the orchestra pit—where there was no orchestra pit, for this birthed-at-Encores! production still had the orchestra situated behind her. But one could see in LuPone's eye that she liked looking out and making eye contact with some theatergoer sitting center in the house, giving him a thrill that Right Now, This Very Second, Patti LuPone Is Looking at YOU! Now, that's a star, too.

At the top of the second act, the audience wanted to applaud LuPone for all she'd achieved in the first act (and in the last third of a century). But the star was having none of it and plowed on with her dialogue. She'd received her entrance applause an hour and a half earlier, and now she was simply a performer at work, there to do the show. It was "Applause? Later, when I'm finished."

And when Rose was backstage at Wichita's one and only burlesque theater and was forced to give up the dream, LuPone showed she wasn't ready. After she said, "We lasted till the very end. No one can say we didn't try!" the look LuPone gave Herbie (Boyd Gaines) was one that said, "Herbie! Please! Do something! I don't mean it! It can't be the end! It just can't be!" Some years earlier, LuPone had sung as Norma Desmond, "I can say anything I want with my eyes," and that's what she did here.

Not that LuPone was perfect. When Herbie asked her, "Honey, don't you know there's a Depression?" she quickly adopted a phony low voice and said, "I read *Variety,*" as if she were telling us, "Here's the punch line in case you don't recognize it." When she promised Herbie that she'd keep her promise to marry him, she extended one arm, put her fingers below table level, and crossed them. That's not as interesting as what Roses usually do, fully believing at that moment that they plan to keep their promises—and only later finding out they can't go through with them.

But just as there are good stones and bad stones, there must be bad moments among the good. LuPone was the reason this production got to Encores! and then to Broadway for 332 performances.

Reliever of the Year: Cheyenne Jackson
Xanadu

He had replaced the male leads in *Aida* and *Thoroughly Modern Millie,* but he wasn't getting attention from the critics or the suits who'd long stopped attending those shows.

Then, in 2004, Cheyenne Jackson appeared in the New York Musical Theatre Festival's presentation of *Altar Boyz.* He played Matthew, who, along with Mark, Luke, and Juan (and Abraham), spread God's word through wholesome bubble-gum rock songs. The spoof was a smash and would move to an open off-Broadway run. But Jackson, although invited to make the move, got a better offer.

The powers-that-be of the incoming musical *All Shook Up*—about an Elvis-like entertainer named Chad—noticed that Jackson had an early-Elvis body and a natural Elvis-like sneer. They offered him the role of the drifter who motorcycles his way into a small Midwest town and brings this new art form called rock-and-roll with him.

Presley's songs, both famous and lesser-known, were shoehorned into a convoluted book that, librettist Joe DiPietro admitted, also borrowed a female-passing-for-male subplot from *Twelfth Night. All Shook Up* ran only 213 performances, but Jackson was noted as one of Broadway's most handsome and muscular leading men.

In spring 2007, Jackson didn't have prospects for a Broadway show. But then *Xanadu,* Douglas Carter Beane's spoof of the wretched 1980 film musical, had a setback during its June previews. James Carpinello, best known as Tony Manero in Broadway's *Saturday Night Fever,* had been cast in the lead of Sonny, a record-cover designer who dreamed of opening a roller disco. During one rehearsal while roller-skating, he fell and severely injured his left foot. Someone had to be found in a hurry, and the producers settled on Jackson.

But he didn't know how to roller-skate.

Jackson admits he fell quite a few times during rehearsals and previews but didn't do much damage to his six-foot-three frame—"even though that's a long way to fall," he said. The show's opening had to be postponed from June 26 to July 10, but Jackson quickly learned to roller-skate—and learned the part—to avoid another postponement.

At first, Jackson was to play the role only until Carpinello returned. But his reviews were excellent, and by October, management quietly revealed that the part was his for as long as he wanted it. He stayed for the entire 512-performance run.

Jackson, who's since become an important character on the TV series *Glee,* is an out and proud gay who married his longtime partner, Monte Lapka, in 2010. He does have one regret about his sexuality, however. "When I was a kid, I was always disappointed that I never got the opportunity to play Annie," he says. And he means it.

Manager of the Year: André Bishop and Bernard Gersten

South Pacific

When *South Pacific* closed on January 16, 1954, the curtain did not come down for a final time. It was the production's way of saying that metaphorically, the show would never close.

Maybe that's why, even in a revival-happy era, *South Pacific* had not seen a new Broadway production in more than a half century. It had "never closed."

There had been a limited-engagement revival at the State Theatre in Lincoln Center in the summer of 1967, but no open-ended run. One reason was that, despite its Tony- and Pulitzer Prize–winning pedigree, *South Pacific* was very much of its era.

Once upon a time, when Lieutenant Joseph Cable sang that we're not born with a bias, but that we're all "Carefully Taught" to be prejudiced, people were shocked. This may have been one of Broadway's shortest songs—less than a minute and a half long—but it packed one of the biggest wallops. It opened the eyes of many people who would never again be able to re-shut them. Long before the twentieth century ended, interracial marriage had ceased to be an enormous issue in many American households.

But the wonderful thing about old works of art is that they function as their own peculiar time machines. They can take us back to a different era and show us the way things were—and why they're no longer that way. So *South Pacific* still did have merit—as well as that unforgettable Rodgers and Hammerstein score.

Over the years, the Rodgers and Hammerstein office had had many requests for a *South Pacific* revival. Some were dismissed out of hand, but quite a few producers were given the rights to stage a production outside of Broadway. If the production passed muster, it could be brought to New York. None did.

But then André Bishop and Bernard Gersten, respectively the artistic director and executive producer of Lincoln Center Theater, had an idea. They approached Theodore S. Chapin, R&H's president and executive director, and said the magic words that caught his eye, ear, and soul. Lincoln Center Theater would mount the show with an orchestra that had just as many pieces as the original production had: thirty, with not a synthesizer among them. This would allow Rodgers and Hammerstein's work to be heard in all its glory. Compare this to *A Catered Affair,* the next musical to open after *South Pacific.* It had nine musicians in attendance.

To gild the lily, when the audience entered, it wouldn't see the musicians in the pit, for they'd be covered by flooring. Once the overture started with those strains of "Bali H'ai," however, the flooring would slide back and show every musician at work.

Bishop and Gersten could afford to hire so many musicians partly because Lincoln Center Theater may well be the most successful and financially sound not-for-profit theater in the country. Certainly this was not always the case. An inordinately high number of producers had tried and had failed in dealing with its mainstage Vivian Beaumont Theater and its second-space Mitzi E. Newhouse Theater.

Robert Whitehead and Elia Kazan, responsible for six unsuccessful productions downtown at a makeshift theater from 1963 to 1965, were gone before the new facilities at Lincoln Center could even open. They were followed by Herbert Blau (1965–1967), Jules Irving (Amy's father; 1967–1973), and Joseph Papp (1973–1977). When Papp bailed out, both the Beaumont and the Newhouse sat empty for more than three years.

Richmond Crinkley tried next and stayed until 1984. Then Gersten arrived with artistic director Gregory Mosher. Gersten's still there, and Bishop succeeded Mosher in 1992. Asking for members (who'd pay an annual fee) rather than subscribers made a great difference; allowing members to choose when they'd like to attend instead of being locked into subscriber dates made a profound difference. That Bishop and Gersten produced dozens of excellent productions that have won Tonys, Drama Desks, and other awards of course helped, as well. *South Pacific* was one of them, with seven Tonys and five Drama Desks, including Best Musical Revival.

And yet, at first glance, one might not have thought that Bishop and Gersten were such good managers when one looked at their schedule. *South Pacific*'s previews were to commence on March 1, 2008, prior to an April 3 opening—thirty-three days later. In contrast, the original production of *South Pacific* opened in New Haven on March 10, 1949, traveled to Boston on March 14, and opened on Broadway on April 7, 1949—only twenty-eight days after that first performance. That a set-in-stone revival needed five days more to ready itself than the original production seemed odd, especially when the original had to restage a major number, cut two songs and some dialogue, and have its authors write a new song ("This Nearly Was Mine")

But Theodore S. Chapin explained the extra time by uttering one word: "Computers."

2008–2009

MVPs: Hunter Bell and Jeff Bowen
[title of show]

If television could have a show about nothing, why couldn't musical theater?

[title of show] told of Jeff Bowen and Hunter Bell, "two nobodies in New York." Jeff composed songs that few heard. Hunter wrote plays that producers nixed.

But in 2004, when the two learned that the New York Musical Theatre Festival—an annual showcase for new works—was looking for material, they decided to spend their next three weeks writing a show.

And their musical would be about writing a musical.

"We could put this exact conversation in the show," Bell suggested.

"Wait," Bowen said, trying to understand. "So everything I say from now on could actually be in our show?"

"Yeah," replied Bell.

"Like this?" Bowen tested.

"Like this," Bell agreed.

Just as there's cinema verité, here was musical-theater verité. Where the application asked for *[title of show],* Bowen and Bell filled in the space with those exact three words in brackets. Many a quip, observation, complaint, and profane word that they uttered became part of their musical. They'd become a part of it, too, in playing themselves.

They also wrote in a part for Stacia Fernandez, who, of course, played a character named Stacia. All three performed a pre-festival tryout in the summer of 2004 at the Manhattan Theatre Source. But before they could moved to the New York Musical Theatre Festival that had inadvertently spurred the show. Fernandez decided to accept an understudy assignment in *The Drowsy Chaperone.* That forced Bowen and Bell to find a replacement in Heidi Blickenstaff—and a character that was suddenly named Heidi.

Later, to establish the tension that many productions have when two actresses vie to be a leading lady, a new part was written for Susan, because Susan Blackwell got the role. Heidi was held in greater esteem because she had twice appeared on Broadway while Susan had less luster because she worked in an office.

But the four seemed to get along as well as Jerry, George, Kramer, and Elaine did in that other show that was built on "nothing." *[title of show]* equally demonstrated why living in New York is such fun, for a person has ample opportunity to make friends who have common goals and who enjoy the creative process.

There'd never been a musical with so many inside jokes. Who was this Mary Stout that was mentioned, anyway? Indeed, the program included a two-page glossary to explain the more arcane references. (However, to explain them all might well have taken a glossary as long as the New Testament.)

And yet the inside jokes didn't stop the little four-person musical with no set to speak of. The year 2005 brought stints at the Eugene O'Neill Theater Center and off-off-Broadway's Ars Nova. Then came an invitation from the prestigious Vineyard Theatre, where *Avenue Q* originated. It opened on February 26, 2006, and was to close on April 24 but did so well that an extension was announced.

But all this newfound success did involve some extra drama. Early in the script, Bowen told Blackwell, "We'll replace you when we get to Broadway." It was a joke—then—but it did foreshadow the show's most chilling scene: once the possibility of Broadway was suddenly not an impossibility, Bowen and Bell had to consider the advantages of casting a genuine star who was interested in Blickenstaff's role. Of course, the guys wanted to be loyal to Blickenstaff, but what did that mean in the world of show business? As the character Cameron Drake said when winning his Oscar in the film *In and Out,* "I'd like to thank my agent and my new agent."

During a photo shoot that no one ever dreamed would happen, Blickenstaff pseudo-off-handedly mentioned that she knew there'd been serious talk about replacing her. When this actually happened to Patsy Barton (Judy Garland) in *Babes in Arms*—also for monetary reasons—Patsy had to work hard to hold back her tears. Blickenstaff, though, was steely. She was hurt, to be sure, but she was strong because she'd been around and knew the business. While she was bitterly disappointed in the guys' apparently not standing by her, well, Brice, that's life in the theatuh. She knew that Irving Berlin lied about show business: NOT "everything about it is appealing."

So while *[title of show]* could be said to have been the great-grandson of those Mickey-and-Judy "Let's put on a show!" movies, it had a far more realistic take on show-biz jealousy, rivalry, and treachery. The authors had to grapple with selling out their principles in order to sell seats.

But Bowen, Bell, and smart director Michael Berresse replaced neither Blickenstaff nor Blackwell, and audiences were able to bask in everyone's success. Actually, replacing Blickenstaff with a star might well have thrown the show off balance. Rodgers and Hammerstein originally hoped that Mary Martin would play Laurey in their new show *Oklahoma!* but, as both men later attested, had Martin accepted the job, they would have written for a star, and the show would have turned out to be much different—and probably not nearly as good. Had either Blickenstaff or Bell been replaced, *[title of show]* would have lost its biggest trump card: Theatrical Dreams Can Come True for the Lowly-Profiled but Supremely Talented.

On October 1, 2006, the show closed at the Vineyard, but Bell and Bowen wouldn't close the books on it. There was a whole new world out there on YouTube, and they'd use it to keep the fires burning on *[title of show]* by creating *The [title of show] Show.* They did more than a dozen episodes that said the two had daydreams that the show was Broadway bound. But by doing these videoblogs, Bell and Bowen showed what they really had was good old-fashioned stick-to-it-iveness.

The vblogs created quite an Internet stir and became so popular that producer Kevin McCollum, who had already taken an option on the property, decided to exercise it. He booked the Lyceum Theatre on Broadway.

[title of show] opened on July 17, 2008, and only ran 102 performances. But the authors of shows that had opened at the New York Musical Theatre Festival the same time as Bowen and Bell's (and closed a few days later) had to look on with great envy.

The script had said from an early draft, "Maybe we'd transfer immediately to the intimate Radio City" and "Make Broadway my permanent address." Neither statement turned out to be entirely true, but the show had advanced to a high point on the theatrical food chain. When Jeff wrote the lyric "We could win a Tony Award," he probably thought he was joking. And while he didn't win, Bell was at least nominated for Best Book.

Bell and Bowen also get credit for bringing greater attention to the New York Musical Theatre Festival (NYMF), which continues to blossom and expand. Even audiences in North Dakota learned what NYMF was, for in March 2011, the Fargo-Moorehead Community Theatre produced *[title of show].*

A Chorus Line said that it was "dedicated to anyone who has ever danced in a chorus or marched in step . . . anywhere." *[title of show]* could have dedicated itself to anyone who had ever dreamed of writing a Broadway musical. It showed each budding author that success is possible if he insists on making it happen.

Rookie of the Year: Brian Yorkey
Next to Normal

In a manner of speaking, bookwriter-lyricist Brian Yorkey was not making his Broadway debut when *Next to Normal* opened on April 27, 2009. Although he didn't have a single Broadway credit, he'd been represented at the Golden Theatre for the past six years.

For when Yorkey's BMI-Lehman Engel Musical Theatre Workshop buddies Jeff Marx and Robert Lopez were writing their musical *Avenue Q*, they named one of their characters Brian Yorkey. True, as time went by, they dropped his surname, but the first name of Brian (and the character) stayed in the show.

But Yorkey, of course, had greater ambitions than to be merely mentioned on Broadway. And with composer Tom Kitt, he did—as bookwriter and lyricist of *Next to Normal*.

The musical was mostly played on a slick black floor, though there should have been a rug on it to indicate all that this family has swept under it. For the longest time, an audience couldn't be if Di or her husband Dan is the crazy one.

There was a flashback when we saw him propose to her. She said, "Dan, this is crazy," and he blithely said, "Maybe it is!"—the way we all do when we want to brush aside someone's objection as a small one. Ah, but when we returned to the present, we saw that this family learned that their decision to get together did lead to something crazy—and now it couldn't be blithely rationalized.

They tried to play down any difficulties. "Did you take you meds?" one party asked another, using the euphemism "meds" to make them sound less ominous. But "meds" are drugs, pure and not-so-simple. That added poignancy to the line "Most people who think they're happy haven't thought about it enough."

Also wise was that Dan and Di's daughter Natalie was told by her wannabe boyfriend Henry, "I believe I can be perfect for you." Already the girl, not to mention her parents, knew that no one can.

The musical decisions were equally wise. A powerful and omniscient doctor was described as "a rock star," and rock was the appropriate music that composer Tom Kitt gave him. A song about electroshock therapy was done in a hard-rock manner, too. The choice of music was right for parents who came of age in the early 1980s.

Normal is too much to hope for in any family these days, and the best we can begin to hope for is next to normal. Even with an up-tempo ending, the show didn't have a happy ending and didn't purport to.

It's often been said that a musical can become a hit if it has three showstoppers. *Next to Normal* had those, but it also had two guaranteed gasps from the audience—one in each act. Each gasp showed that the audience at the Booth Theatre connected to and came to care about the characters that director Michael (*Rent*) Grief staged to maximum advantage.

Yorkey and Kitt beat the favored Elton John's *Billy Elliot* for the Best Score Tony. But no one was expected to surpass Alice Ripley's wondrously accomplished performance as Di. No one did, for Ripley showed the anguish of a fate worse than death. The audience gave her an enormous amount of applause and plenty of "Whoos!" too. But no reaction made as strong an impression as those gasps.

Manager of the Year: David Stone
Next to Normal

His first Broadway production was called *What's Wrong with This Picture?* Critics said "Plenty," and the play, albeit by upcoming playwright Donald Margulies, lasted twelve performances.

So David Stone did what many fledgling producers do: he turned to revivals. He delivered decent productions of *The Diary of Anne Frank* in 1997 and *Man of La Mancha* in 2002. But both failed to become hot tickets.

For those, he was the top-billed producer. For *Wicked,* he was the fourth. Even being in that slot, however, meant plenty of money and prestige for Stone.

But as longtime Broadway observer Howard Gradet says, "I've noticed that one can't go more than 48 hours without running into some reference to *The Wizard of Oz.*" So a musical that would draw on it would seem to have been a good commercial bet.

Stone was back to being lead producer in 2005 for *The 25th Annual Putnam County Spelling Bee,* a feel-good tuner with a score by Tony-winner William (*Falsettos*) Finn. Following that, he was second-in-line with *Three Days of Rain,* a serious and moody play that had already had an off-Broadway run. What made it a safe bet was that Julia Roberts would be in the cast.

But *Next to Normal* was hardly a safe bet, and here's where Stone showed his producing mettle.

For one thing, he attended a presentation of the show when it was known as *Feelin' Electric* at the New York Musical Theatre Festival in 2005 and was moved enough by the show's potential to become its guardian angel. He saw it through a title change, an added character, and an hour's shortening. Then he helped bring this new *Next to Normal* to off-Broadway.

The revamped show opened on February 18, 2008, at Second Stage, where it lasted a month. The voters of the Outer Critics Circle—the organization of non-mainstream critics—awarded the show its Best Score prize. But the majority of reviews were decent if unexciting. Said Ben Brantley of the *New York Times,* "*Next to Normal* has the shape (and many of the details) of a disease-of-the-week television movie. And though it gives off hot sparks of original wit, the show also sinks into what feels like warmed-over social satire, with detours to the giddy brink of camp."

Usually, that's the end for a show in New York. The feeling is: you had your chance. But Stone believed that *Next to Normal*—undoubtedly the only musical in Broadway history to include the words "intestinal obstruction"—still had a future. He simply treated the Second Stage production as a pre-Broadway tryout.

Next stop for *Next to Normal* would be Arena Stage. The Washington-based theater was producing shows that season in Arlington, Virginia, while its home was being refurbished, but it made room for *Next to Normal.*

The authors worked on the show, dropping, among other songs, one that took place in Costco. Now the reviews were substantially better: "The future of American musicals," insisted Peter Marks in the *Washington Post.* But bringing *Next to Normal* to Broadway—even with a relatively inexpensive $4 million budget—was still quite an iffy proposition.

Stone and his three partners, along with Second Stage, gambled and won. *Next to Normal* ran 733 performances. Despite his optimism and faith in the show, even Stone would have probably never predicted that it would be the eighth musical to win the Pulitzer Prize.

2009–2010

MVP: Joe DiPietro
Memphis

On the morning that the 2009–2010 Tony nominations were announced, *Memphis* garnered eight nominations, of which co-lyricist and bookwriter Joe DiPietro received two.

On the morning that the 2004–2005 Tony nominations were announced, DiPietro's *All Shook Up* got none at all.

And while both musicals demonstrated how 1950s rock-and-roll helped pave the way for racial integration, there was a profound difference between the two shows. *All Shook Up* was set "during the summer of 1955," in "a small you-never-heard-of-it town somewhere in the Midwest" in the nation's "squarest state." And yet act 1, scene 2, showed white Jim Heller (Jonathan Hadary) having a heart-to-heart conversation with black Sylvia (Sharon Wilkins) in her roadside nightclub.

In the squarest state in the union? In 1955? And how did a black woman wind up owning a nightclub in such a time and place, anyway? If she did, wouldn't it cater to blacks only—either because only blacks would want to go there, or because the blacks weren't allowed in the town's white clubs?

When Chad (read: Elvis Presley) arrived in town, four councilwomen denounced him. Two of them were white; the other two were black. How did they get elected in the squarest state in the union in 1955? Non-traditional casting could be the reason, but a show about race can't afford the luxury of that democratic practice. In a show such as this, everything must literally be black and white.

DiPietro learned from his mistake, and four years later in *Memphis,* he portrayed realistic 1950s black–white relations. When white fledgling disc jockey Huey Calhoun (Chad Kimball) entered an all-black club hoping to hear more of the music that inspires him, the blacks in attendance all bristled. Huey had to do some fast talking and piano playing before they accepted him.

Huey's mother (Cass Morgan) was scandalized when she discovered who his new friends were. "Your calling is playing race music for white folks?" she sneered. She was more horrified still when she inferred that his new girlfriend was a black singer named Felicia (Montego Glover). Huey didn't care and told

Felicia, "I'm tired of sneaking around as if you're a bad thing." He proved it in act 2, when he kissed her on nationwide TV.

DiPietro opted for a happy ending for everyone in *All Shook Up.* Not in *Memphis.* The lack of truth made the former show an also-ran, and the addition of truth begat the winner of four Tony Awards, including Best Musical.

Producer George W. George, who had had a good 1964 with *Any Wednesday, Dylan,* and *Ben Franklin in Paris,* many years later had the idea for *Memphis* and gave it to DiPietro. "It's pretty much the story of Dewey Phillips, a real Memphis deejay of the 1950s," says DiPietro. "Although I added some elements of Alan Freed, too."

George encouraged DiPietro to find a composer. "I knew all the good ones who'd been working on Broadway or towards it, but I wanted someone who understood the world of rock 'n' roll, too," DiPietro says. "So I wrote the story and some lyrics and gave the script to my agent Scott Yoselow, who said, 'I know managers of rock acts. I'll try to get you someone.'"

Not long after, DiPietro got a call out of the blue from David Bryan, who identified himself as the keyboardist for Bon Jovi. While DiPietro knew the group, he didn't quite know or remember where Bryan fit in it. A look at an album allowed him to realize, "Oh, yeah, the blond guy."

One might not assume that a rock-group member would have composed the music for a musical of Francine Pascal's wildly successful tween favorite *Sweet Valley High.* But he had. And although that show didn't get beyond a small workshop, Bryan was up for trying another musical. He told DiPietro, "I hear every song you've written in my head."

That was all very nice, but DiPietro needed to hear substantially more than that. He asked Bryan to set a song to music. "I figured it'd be a while before I heard from him again, if I ever heard from him at all," says DiPietro. "Only one day passed before a FedEx package arrived with the melody to my lyric 'The Music of My Soul.' Not only did I call and tell him that I liked it—because it bridged authentic rock with theater music—but I also told him that he picked the perfect song to set to melody, because at this point it was the most important song in the show."

DiPietro also reiterated the facts of theatrical life to Bryan. "I told him it would be really hard, but he didn't get discouraged. I think he's just as optimistic a guy as I am."

However, DiPietro admits that when he told producers that Bryan was composing, they'd say the dreaded semi-complimentary, "That's interesting."

As he recalls, "Not interesting enough for them to put up money. David wasn't Rod Stewart or Elton John."

They did manage to have their world premiere of *Memphis* at the North Shore Music Theatre in Beverly, Massachusetts, in 2003 and then another production at TheatreWorks in Palo Alto, California, in 2004. But five years of stops and starts had to pass to get to Broadway. No fewer than seven production companies and eleven individuals were listed as producers, with four production companies and eleven other individuals getting "produced in association" credit. It's a wonder that when they all tromped onto the stage of Radio City Music Hall to get their Tonys, the floor didn't cave in.

And to think that the show DiPietro jump-started was originally given very little chance by the Broadway establishment. It had no stars, unlike the incoming *The Addams Family* with Nathan Lane and Bebe Neuwirth. It didn't have the cachet of a famous director-choreographer, such as Twyla Tharp, who was coming in with *Come Fly Away.* If rock was what certain theatergoers wanted, there'd be *American Idiot* to fill that slot, thanks to the pedigree of the group Green Day and the name recognition from the millions upon millions of albums sold.

But *Memphis* was the one that won the Best Musical Tony and sold more tickets than any of those others.

Rookie of the Year: Douglas Hodge
La Cage aux Folles

George Hearn, Walter Charles, Keene Curtis, and Gary Beach all had something in common when playing Albin and his onstage alter ego Zaza in *La Cage aux Folles.* They were excellent in portraying a female impersonator.

But Douglas Hodge, who headed the 2010 Broadway revival, did all of them one better. He portrayed someone who seemed genuinely female. While he looked as if he were a combination of Millicent Martin and Peggy Cass, he always displayed the heart and soul of a genuine woman.

Male-to-female transsexuals often observe that they've been "trapped in the wrong body." Hodge showed a man who didn't feel trapped at all. This Albin/Zaza knew that he was a woman down deep and the wrapping on the package didn't matter.

Hodge started quietly during his first song, "A Little More Mascara On," when he changed from civilian to entertainer. But by the time he morphed into a woman, his "Za-ZA is here!" was quite loud. The man had found his voice—and it was a woman's. Later, when he tried to come across as "Uncle Al," he was itchy-scratchy uncomfortable. That's how much of a woman he was.

Of course, more than a quarter century had passed since the original production opened on August 21, 1983, and the extra years (and a glut of gay characters on TV) had helped heterosexual audiences become more accustomed to a man/woman. Originally, composer-lyricist Jerry Herman smartly had Georges and Albin declare their love through a quick reprise of a song that had just been performed by their son Jean-Michele and his fiancée Anne. That the melody had been established and that the reprise lasted only two and a half minutes helped heterosexual theatergoers to remain at ease.

In 2010, however, Albin and Georges (Kelsey Grammer), in conjunction with impressive choreographer Lynne Page, turned that two-and-a-half-minute reprise into a genuine production number. Georges and Albin were unapologetically affectionate, unashamed, and unworried. Once again, Hodge's reaction was blushing-bride effective.

The original production had had George Hearn's Albin and Gene Barry's Georges walk off arm in arm at the end of the show. True, in the revival that had played five years earlier, Gary Beach and Daniel Davis kissed—just as Kelsey Grammer and Douglas Hodge did here. But Hodge threw himself into it with an extra zest. So even those who came solely to see the far more famous Grammer may well have left the theater talking about Hodge.

During that expanded reprise of "With You on My Arm," Hodge sauntered offstage left and suddenly returned by doing a few back flips across the stage. What a surprise, for he didn't seem limber enough to accomplish that. But by the time he did the third flip, even the most myopic audience member would have noticed that a double was doing these pyrotechnics for him. A second after the ringer had bounded offstage right, Hodge reappeared stage left, standing tall with a look on his face that said, "I know we didn't fool you at all, but didn't that bring a smile out of you?"

Yes.

Comeback Player of the Year: Kelsey Grammer
La Cage aux Folles

There is, of course, no play or musical more associated with theatrical bad luck than *Macbeth.* And one could prove it by Kelsey Grammer.

His Broadway debut came in 1981 through a production of "The Scottish Play" that had starred Philip Anglim and Maureen Anderman as the Macbeths. Grammer was Lennox, a nobleman with seventy-nine lines. The revival, however, couldn't even reach seventy-nine performances, but died after sixty-one.

Grammer was a nobody then, but that wasn't the case in 2000, the next time he did *Macbeth.* This time, he'd have almost ten times as many lines—719—for he was playing the title role in a production that happened simply because he wanted to do it. Such a situation arose because of his fame as Dr. Frasier Winslow Crane, MD, PhD, APA, thanks to 263 episodes and an eleven-year run on *Frasier* on NBC.

However, there was a profound difference between portraying a sitcom shrink and the Man Who Would Be King. The reviews for both Grammer and Terry Hands's production were lethal. Shakespeare's shortest play got its shortest commercial run; the drama that will forever be intertwined with bad luck ran, fittingly enough, thirteen performances.

Ten years later, Grammer would brave Broadway again, but not in a play by the Bard. He'd play Georges, the owner of a second-rate St. Tropez nightspot called *La Cage aux Folles* and the longtime lover of Albin, the club's star.

This was a somewhat surprising situation. Georges was the (you should pardon the expression) straight man and by far the less flashy role. Albin had always been the star of the show, and the part helped George Hearn get a Tony in 1984 and Gary Beach a Tony nomination in 1995. Georges, on the other hand, got only a Tony nomination for Gene Barry in 1984 and no nomination at all for Daniel Davis in 1995. (Although, in Davis's case, his being fired from the show a few weeks before the nominations were announced must have had something to do with the snub).

And yet Grammer—by far a bigger name to Americans than Douglas Hodge—was willing to take the part. There was some discussion about the two switching roles after six months or so, but as it turned out, that switch wouldn't happen. Grammer seemed to content to stay with Georges and played the role for a full year.

Because he was easily the biggest star to play Georges in New York, he got entrance applause. He nodded to the audience to acknowledge it, but he wasn't accepting it as TV star Kelsey Grammer, but as Georges, the emcee of *La Cage aux Folles*—the nightclub, and not the musical. More surprising was that he, not Hodge, got the final bow. In a way, that was fitting, for Grammer wisely played his role as if it were just as important as Hodge's.

Stars who are good actors do that.

Epilogue

And then there are the categories for which awards aren't given, but achievements—both positive and negative—get entered into the history books.

Such as "Led League in Errors." Of course there are those who feel that the Tony Nominating Committee leads the league in errors each and every year. But if we're centering on individuals, we know who'd have committed the most errors during the 1970–1971 season: Danny Kaye.

The star eventually lost faith in *Two by Two* and started ad-libbing to "help" the musical. Once he injured his leg and was forced to do the show from a wheelchair, Kaye added even more off-the-cuff remarks. He would make a reference to *No, No, Nanette*—which was quite the anachronism coming from Noah (of the ark fame) in a show set in long-ago biblical times.

At least Kaye's shenanigans ended after a few months of performances. Broadway is still feeling the ramifications from the 1988–1989 league-leader in errors. The Nederlander Organization at first leased, and then sold, the Mark Hellinger Theatre, one of Broadway's most beautiful houses, to the Times Square Church. Broadway was going through doldrums then but has since rebounded; today, the Hellinger would be a prime house, and the Nederlanders must kick themselves for not having as much faith as—well, a member of the Times Square Church.

"Hit into Most Triple Plays" would have to go to Eaton Magoon Jr., who, in the 1960–1961 season, wrote the book, music, and lyrics to *13 Daughters.* It lasted twenty-eight performances—which was twenty-eight times as long a run as his next show, *Heathen!* in 1972. To be fair, Magoon only co-wrote the book to the latter show while providing all the music and lyrics. Magoon was a native Hawaiian, and both musicals were set in his home state—suggesting that you shouldn't necessarily "write what you know."

Best Slugger would have to go to Nicol Williamson, who, in the 1975–1976 season, slugged castmate Jim Litten after the curtain calls of their show *Rex.* Litten had said, "Well, that's a wrap," while Williamson thought he heard, "Well, that was crap"—and took what he considered appropriate action. Two wrongs never make a right, but one must at least give Williamson some credit for standing up for his show.

On a more upbeat note, there's a category called "Led League in Doubles." The 1967–1968 winner would have to be Jule Styne at that year's Tony Awards. In the category of Best Actress in a Musical, there was a tie between Leslie Uggams of *Hallelujah, Baby!* and Patricia Routledge of *Darling of the Day*—each of whom sang Jule Styne music in her show.

Never before or since has a composer provided the music for two Best Actresses in the same year. The likelihood is that no one ever will, for what are the odds of another tie in this category, and that the same composer would have furnished both actresses' material?

Speaking of Uggams, there's the "Sophomore Jinx." It isn't an official category, but a time-honored baseball superstition—that after an exceptional rookie year, a player will slump terribly. One can prove it by Uggams, for after making her Broadway debut in *Hallelujah, Baby!* and winning the aforementioned Tony, she next appeared in a musical version of George Bernard Shaw's *Caesar and Cleopatra.* Richard Kiley, himself a recent Tony winner via *Man of La Mancha,* played Caesar to her Cleopatra.

The score was written by Ervin Drake, who also suffered the sophomore jinx; his rookie outing was the score for *What Makes Sammy Run?* Drake's songs, taken on their own, were melodious and lyrically well crafted. However, few of Cleopatra's songs sounded right. There's a 1940s supper-club feeling to "The Wrong Man('s the Right Man for Me)" both in music and in lyrics. ("His work comes first / At times, I could burst.") "Many Young Men from Now" was too ingénue-ish for a queen of Egypt. "I Cannot Make Him Jealous (I Have Tried)" was a line that comes directly from Shaw, but the melody was stock Broadway.

Her First Roman, as the musical was called, could manage only seventeen performances. Uggams never again originated a role in a high-profile book musical.

Finally, every year there's an All-Star Game, and every year there's a musical with plenty of star power. What's the starriest in the fifty seasons we've chosen? A look at the credits for this 1966–1967 show might provide the answer: David Merrick (twenty-four Tony nominations, five wins, one special award) presents Mary Martin (three Tonys) and Robert Preston (one Tony and one Oscar nomination) in *I Do! I Do!* Book and lyrics by Tom Jones and music by Harvey Schmidt (one Tony nomination each and *The Fantasticks,* then poised to become the longest running musical in off-Broadway history). Directed and choreographed by Gower Champion (five Tony Awards and one other nomination). Based on the 1952 Tony-winning play *The Fourposter.*

Has any musical in these past fifty years had the star power to match this one that, coincidentally, dealt with fifty years of marriage?

But *I Do! I Do!* lost the Best Musical Tony to *Cabaret* and ran less than half as long (560 performances to *Cabaret's* 1,165). As any fan of the 1969 Baltimore Orioles and New York Mets can tell you, the team that's expected to win everything doesn't always emerge victorious.

But come to think of it, everyone in this book is an All-Star.

Acknowledgments

Thanks to my agent Linda Konner, who's also the love of my life.

Thanks to "Al" Skip Koenig, who's overly generous with information and functions as the best informal editor anyone could ever have.

Thanks, too, to Val Addams, Ken Bloom, Michael Buckley, Wayne Bryan, Jay Clark, Bill Cox, Brian Drutman, Joshua Ellis, Larry Fineberg, Alan Gomberg, Marc Grossberg, John Harrison, Kenneth Kantor, Richard A. Lidinsky Jr., Robert LoBiondo, Peter J. Loewy, Jon Maas, Joe Marchese, Kevin McAnarney, Marc Miller, Dick Minogue, Richard C. Norton, Rick Pender, Paul Roberts, Howard Rogut, David Schmittou, Jim Seabrough, Bob Sixsmith, Ron Spivak, Ryan Stotts, Robert Viagas, Dan Vitetta, Walter Willison, and the late, great David Wolf. They'll always be my MVPs.

Bibliography

Books

Altman, Richard and Kaufman, Mervyn. *The Making of a Musical.* Crown, 1971.

Bell, Marty. *Broadway Stories*. Limelight, 1993

Bianculli, David: *Dangerously Funny*. Touchstone, 2009.

Bogar, Thomas A. *American Presidents Attend the Theatre*. McFarland, 2006.

Burrows, Abe. *Honest Abe*. Atlantic–Little Brown, 1980.

Chapin, Ted. *Everything Was Possible*. Knopf, 2003.

Fredrik, Nathalie, and Ariel Douglas. *History of the Academy Award Winners*. Ace, 1974.

Gilvey, John Anthony. *Before the Parade Passes By*. St. Martin's, 2005.

Goldman, William. *The Season*. Harcourt Brace, 1969.

Hanan, Stephen. *A Cat's Diary: How the Broadway Production of Cats Was Born*. Smith and Kraus, 2001.

Holmes, Rupert. *The Mystery of Edwin Drood*. Nelson Doubleday, 1986.

Howard, Ken, and Edward Tivnan. *Act Natural: How to Speak to Any Audience*. Random House, 2003.

Kander, John, Fred Ebb, and Greg Lawrence. *Colored Lights*. Faber and Faber, 2003.

King, Larry L. *The Whorehouse Papers*. Viking, 1982.

Kirkwood, James. *Diary of a Mad Playwright*. E. P. Dutton, 1989.

Kissel, Howard. *The Abominable Showman*. Applause, 1993.

Lehman, Ernest. *Sweet Smell of Success*. Signet, 1957.

Leonard, William Torbert. *Broadway Bound*. Scarecrow, 1983.

Mandelbaum, Ken. *"A Chorus Line" and the Musicals of Michael Bennett*. St. Martin's, 1989.

Mandelbaum, Ken. *Not Since "Carrie."* St. Martin's, 1991.

McKechnie, Donna. *Time Steps*. Simon and Schuster, 2006.

Miletich, Leo N. *Broadway's Prize-Winning Musicals*. Haworth, 1993.

Miller, Scott. *Let the Sunshine In*. Heinemann, 2003.

Mordden, Ethan. *Coming Up Roses*. Oxford University Press, 1998.

Mordden, Ethan. *The Happiest Corpse I've Ever Seen*. Palgrave Macmillan, 2004.

Mordden, Ethan. *One More Kiss*. Palgrave Macmillan, 2003.
Mordden, Ethan. *Open a New Window*. Palgrave, 2001.
Napoleon, Davi. *Chelsea on the Edge*. Iowa State University Press, 1991.
Norton, Elliott. *Broadway Down East*. Boston Public Library Books, 1977.
Ostrow, Stuart. *Present at the Creation, Leaping in the Dark, and Going against the Grain*. Applause, 2005.
Plummer, Christopher. *In Spite of Myself*. Knopf, 2008.
Poole, Wakefield. *Dirty Poole*. Alyson, 2000.
Prince, Harold. *Contradictions*. Dodd, Mead, 1974.
Reynolds, Regina Benedict. *Paper Mill Playhouse: The Life of a Theatre*. David M. Baldwin, 1999.
Rich, Frank. *Hot Seat*. Random House, 1998.
Rose, Philip. *You Can't Do That on Broadway*. Limelight, 2004.
Sabinson, Harvey: *Darling, You Were Wonderful*. H. Regnery, 1977.
Seff, Richard. *Supporting Player*. Xlibris, 2007.
Stevens, Gary, and Alan George. *The Longest Line*. Applause, 2000.
Suskin, Steven. *More Opening Nights on Broadway*. Schirmer, 1997.
Suskin, Steven. *Opening Nights on Broadway*. Schirmer, 1990.
Suskin, Steven. *Second Act Trouble*. Applause, 2006.
Swayne, Steve. *How Sondheim Found His Sound*. University of Michigan, 2005.
Taymor, Julie. *The Lion King: Pride Rock on Broadway*. Hyperion, 1997.
Taylor, Theodore. *Jule: The Story of Composer Jule Styne*. Random House, 1979.
Turan, Kenneth, and Joseph Papp. *Free for All*. Doubleday, 2009.
Viagas, Robert. *The Alchemy of Theatre*. Playbill/Applause, 2006.
Wasserman, Dale. *The Impossible Musical*. Applause, 2003.
Whitburn, Joel. *The Billboard Book of Top 40 Albums*. Billboard, 1987
Zadan, Craig. *Sondheim & Co*. Macmillan, 1974.

Articles and Notes

Brodsky, Jack. Liner notes of *Funny Girl* soundtrack album. Columbia, 1968.
Hoffan, Wayne. "Jeanine Tesori Modernizes 'Millie.'" *Billboard*, April 6, 2002
Meers, Erik. "Passion Play." *The Advocate*, April 30, 2002.

Olson, John. "The Long and Winding Road to Road Show." *The Sondheim Review*, Winter 2008.
Wrore, Simon, and Andrew Johnson. "Bart Paid Off the Real Author of Oliver Musical?" *The Independent*, April 19, 2009.

Websites

Bacharachonline.com
Ibdb.com
Imdb.com
Iobdb.com
MasterworksBroadway.com
Sondheim.com
Sondheimguide.com

Interviews

Loni Ackerman
Lynn Ahrens
Jason Alexander
George Lee Andrews
Kaye Ballard
Kelly Bishop
Larry Blank
Jerry Bock
John Bowab
Joe Bravaco
Mel Brooks
Wayne Bryan
Gene Castle
Richard Chamberlain
Carol Channing
Theodore S. Chapin
Martin Charnin
Alexander H. Cohen
Cy Coleman
Marilyn Cooper
Joan Copeland
Betty L. Corwin
Angelo Del Rossi
Joe DiPietro
Ervin Drake
Brian Drutman
Sandy Duncan
Christine Ebersole
Lada Edmund Jr.
Joshua Ellis
Larry Fineberg
Richard Frankel
Rita Gardner
Larry Gelbart
Sara Gettelfinger
William Goldman
Howard Gradet
Ellen Greene

Michael Greif
Carol Hall
Marvin Hamlisch
Stephen Hanan
John Harrison
Sheldon Harnick
Jerry Herman
Rupert Holmes
David Jones
Robert Kamlot
Kenneth Kantor
Judy Kaye
Skip Koenig
Arthur Kopit
Michael Korie
Nathan Lane
Bonnie Langford
Arthur Laurents
Linda Lavin
Baayork Lee
Margo Lion
Galt MacDermot
Richard Maltby Jr.
Jane Milmore
Karen Morrow
Natalie Mosco
Donna McKechnie
Walter Newkirk
Elaine Paige
Mandy Patinkin
Kurt Peterson
Lonny Price
Gerome Ragni
John Raitt
Anthony Rapp
Claibe Richardson
Milton Rosenstock
Michael Rupert
Stephen Schwartz
Richard Seff
Bert Silverberg
Sheila Smith
Stephen Sondheim
Peter Stone
Susan Stroman
Charles Strouse
Pat Tolson
Jane Sell Trese
Tommy Tune
Gwen Verdon
Bruce Vilanch
Walter Willison
Scott Wise
Maury Yeston

Index